Advanced Joomla!

Dan Rahmel

Apress·

Advanced Joomla!

ISBN-13 (pbk): 978-1-4302-1628-5

ISBN-13 (electronic): 978-1-4302-1629-2

President and Publisher: Paul Manning
Lead Editor: Ben Renow-Clarke
Technical Reviewer: Chad Windnagle
Editorial Board: Steve Anglin, Mark Beckner, Ewan Buckingham, Gary Cornell, Louise Corrigan, Morgan Ertel, Jonathan Gennick, Jonathan Hassell, Robert Hutchinson, Michelle Lowman, James Markham, Matthew Moodie, Jeff Olson, Jeffrey Pepper, Douglas Pundick, Ben Renow-Clarke, Dominic Shakeshaft, Gwenan Spearing, Matt Wade, Tom Welsh
Coordinating Editor: Anamika Panchoo
Copy Editors: Ralph Moore, Nancy Sixsmith
Compositor: SPi Global
Indexer: SPi Global
Artist: SPi Global
Cover Designer: Anna Ishchenko

Distributed to the book trade worldwide by Springer Science+Business Media New York, 233 Spring Street, 6th Floor, New York, NY 10013. Phone 1-800-SPRINGER, fax (201) 348-4505, e-mail orders-ny@springer-sbm.com, or visit www.springeronline.com. Apress Media, LLC is a California LLC and the sole member (owner) is Springer Science + Business Media Finance Inc (SSBM Finance Inc). SSBM Finance Inc is a Delaware corporation.

For information on translations, please e-mail rights@apress.com, or visit www.apress.com.

Apress and friends of ED books may be purchased in bulk for academic, corporate, or promotional use. eBook versions and licenses are also available for most titles. For more information, reference our Special Bulk Sales–eBook Licensing web page at www.apress.com/bulk-sales.

Any source code or other supplementary materials referenced by the author in this text is available to readers at www.apress.com. For detailed information about how to locate your book's source code, go to www.apress.com/source-code.

To Elizabeth, Alexandra, and Josephine who have supported me through it all.
I couldn't possibly love you more.

Contents at a Glance

Contents

About the Author

Dan Rahmel has been writing about Joomla! for more than a decade. He is the author of almost two dozen books, including *Beginning Joomla!, Nuts and Bolts Filmmaking,* and *Building Web Database Applications with Visual Studio.* His books have been translated into numerous languages including Chinese, Japanese, Spanish, French, and Portuguese. When not focusing on Joomla!, Dan specializes in high-scalability web technology and machine learning applications. He is currently Lead PHP Engineer on eHow.com, a web site with more than 90 million unique visitors each month. Dan has developed several iOS and Android apps and authored the Sonic Flashcards application that placed in the top 25 percent of the Google Android mobile application contest.

About the Technical Reviewer

Chad Windnagle graduated with a bachelor's degree in Business and IT management in 2013 from SUNY Delhi University in Upstate New York, and received the Web Design Student of Note award from TC3 in 2010. He is a significant contributor to the Joomla! project and actively contributes to the community in various efforts, such as Joomla! Framework developers; as well as leading community efforts like the Joomla! Google Summer of Code Program. Chad is currently lead developer, and has been employed by CohesiveWebsites.com since 2006.

Photo Credit: Dianne Henning

Acknowledgments

This book would not have been possible without the patience, persistence, and backing of Ben Renow-Clarke. His care and frequent suggestions have improved the book's quality a thousandfold. Also to Dominic Shakeshaft, who has been with the project from the very beginning and believed in the book during the darkest days when it felt like it might never be completed. I can't thank both of you enough.

The superior Apress staff often made the difficult seem easy. I'd like to thank the people with whom I worked directly (Anamika Panchoo, Chad Windnagle, Ralph Moore, Nancy Sixsmith, and all the others who had to work tirelessly in production and editing to produce this book).

I'd like to thank my wife Elizabeth who has supported me working on this book longer than anyone should ever have to endure. How many weekends did she hear the dreaded words "I have to work on the book" and graciously taken care of the kids? For her many sacrifices, there are no adequate words to express my thanks. Also, thanks to my friends (Don Murphy, Greg Mickey, John Taylor, Juan Leonffu, Ed Gildred, David Rahmel, and Weld O'Connor) for their unconditional support.

Most of all, I'd like to thank the readers. By buying this book, you make it possible for all of us in the book industry to labor to produce good work. When pulling the long hours to complete a book, knowing that every little improvement will help the Joomla! community is what really makes the difference. Thanks.

Introduction

If you've opened this book, I imagine you already appreciate how easy Joomla! makes it for you to run your web site or blog. Like me, you may be astonished that the excellent Joomla! developers have created such a solid, professional content management system and then made it free for all the world to use. Similar to its open-source cousin WordPress, Joomla! has grown from being used on a few hundred rudimentary web sites to literally having millions of advanced site deployments.

Joomla! has evolved to become such a comprehensive system that you can literally do anything on a Joomla! site that is possible on an expensive, custom web site. And most of the time, there is a free extension available that augments the Joomla! core to do exactly what you want—with your only investment being the time it takes to install and configure.

If you've read my other book, *Beginning Joomla!*, you have already seen the possibilities available to you if you go beyond the basic features of Joomla!. This book will take you up to the next levels. Whether you've created a small Joomla! site that you want to polish into a gem or you run a huge site that is straining to make that next growth step, this book will show you how to push Joomla! to its limits and beyond.

I have written the book so you can add tremendous capabilities to your Joomla! site whether you have any development training or not. It will cover everything from advanced server deployment to using sophisticated extensions to creating world-class templates. If you have a development background, the information and source code presented here will provide you with an advanced understanding of how the Joomla! system operates from a foundation level all the way up to using some of its cooler bells and whistles. If you've never written a line of code, as long as you can use a text editor as simple as Notepad, you can take advantage of most of the technology presented in this book.

I included all the source code in the text of the book because I find my learning experience frustrated if I have to leave the text to go look for some repository to examine the actual code. I like the code to be right where I can see it in context. That said, I wouldn't want you to have to tediously enter the numerous lines of source to get the various projects working. All the source code is available on the Apress web site and I have also created a project on Github at `https://github.com/drahmel/Advanced-Joomla`. I would love for you to fork the code and make enhancements.

Joomla! has flourished because of the number of people that have made significant contributions to the project from code to templates to tutorials. The real strength of Joomla! is the community. I hope you'll be one of us!

CHAPTER 1

■ ■ ■

Streamlining the Authoring Process

If you have been using Joomla to create and manage a web site, you've probably been amazed by the power and flexibility that it gives you. You've created an attractive and robust web site in the time it would have taken you to manually create a simple page. Now you're ready to turbo-charge your site with advanced configuration and custom extensions. You want to add new content quickly and skirt some of the potholes on the road to Joomla mastery. For this expertise, you've come to the right place.

The new features available in the Joomla line have made it possible to run a professional, high-traffic web site without forcing you to learn to program. You get literally tens of thousands of man-hours of development—all for free download. Even better, Joomla was written by programmers who have a keen understanding of the best ways to allow developers to extend the existing system without compromising the fundamentals and the security of the core framework. So you can do as much or as little customization to your site as you want.

This may be preaching to the choir, but here are some of the awesome Joomla features that we will build upon in this book:

- *Templating system that is both robust and easy to use*: The template system is in some sense the core of Joomla in that the wide variety of fantastic templates (both free and commercial) have allowed any web master to simply install Joomla and add a template to make a completely professional and elegant site. The templating system has been augmented in many ways to allow a Joomla site to have all of the variety and flexibility of a custom developed site (more of this will be covered in Chapter 3).

- *Content management*: Joomla has some superior ways of managing content, including the ability to move hundreds of articles at a time or set the URL for one specific article. You can share content editing responsibilities by setting up an authorization system. Joomla also includes the more basic capabilities such as rich text editing, metadata entry, pagination, and more (advanced content administration will be covered in Chapter 8).

- *Extension system that allows all manner of customization*: Joomla has one of the most robust and well-developed extension systems allowing modules, components, and plug-ins to extend the functionality of the web site. You may already know how to create your own simple extensions, but in this book, I'll take you to the next level where you can create almost any functionality that you might need to add to your site (and for the non-programmer, you'll learn how to use third-party widgets in the next chapter).

- *Complete GUI Administrator interface*: The Administrator interface is attractive and powerful. With each new Joomla version comes many refinements and revisions, and the management user interface has become consistent among the various Managers (Extension Manager, Content Manager, and so forth).

- *Search Engine Optimization (SEO) features*: The developers of Joomla have spent a great deal of effort to "bake-in" job SEO features so a Joomla web master receives optimizations that companies usually have to pay an expert to detail for them. Most of the common problems that plague custom-built sites are never an issue for sites built on Joomla. Joomla makes sure every page has a title, that the URLs are search-engine friendly (if the option is switched on), includes 301 redirect support to manage page rank, and a slew of other features (you'll learn how to configure these features in Chapter 7).

Although Joomla is a fantastic product, there is rarely any formal training to configure and use Joomla. That means that some of the most powerful features go unused or are used improperly. For many Joomla content creators, sometimes creating and adjusting the presentation of that content can be a challenging process.

In this chapter, I'll help you resolve some of these common problems and make the life of a Joomla site administrator much easier and more satisfying. More productivity with the system will increase both the quality and quantity of the site content because time won't be consumed dealing with these obstacles.

Once you gain a fundamental understanding of the basic technology underlying the Joomla system—knowledge that is difficult to obtain without routine examination of the actual Joomla code—you will go a long way toward mastering Joomla. Taking advantage of new Joomla features and adopting auxiliary technology (such as the Search-Engine-Friendly technology or installing an alternate third-party WYSIWYG editor) can mean the difference between effective content maintenance and daily frustration.

This chapter will describe the causes of some of these problems and various remedies or workarounds. Most often solutions come from rethinking how a desired outcome needs to be accomplished. Joomla was designed to be used in specific ways and sometimes forcing it into an unsuitable process of operation can be counterproductive.

Setting the Editor Style Sheets

Have you noticed that often the appearance of an article in the editor doesn't match the one shown on the final page? Fonts change, sizes get bigger and smaller, and sometimes despite exacting formats set in the editor, the appearance is completely different. This situation can be frustrating for a Joomla web master, but it serves as a useful case to learn how to track down and correct a problem using the Joomla Administrator interface. Let's take a look at an example.

In Figure 1-1, you'll see a side-by-side display of an article in the TinyMCE Editor and another on the display of the main page. The font in the case of the editor is a sans-serif font (such as Arial or Helvetica) but the page shows a serif font (such as Times New Roman). The sizes look completely different, too. When the editor and the final display differ so greatly, it is hard for any site author to have confidence in the display of his or her work.

Figure 1-1. *This side-by-side display of the editor view of an article (on the left) and the site display of the same article (on the right) shows how different they can be*

How can we resolve this issue? The first place to try and resolve the problem is the configuration settings of the editor plug-in. In this case, you can easily access the TinyMCE editor settings under the Extensions ➤ Plug-in Manager menu. Once the plug-ins are displayed, you'll find TinyMCE listed under Editor - TinyMCE. Click on the link provided by the title.

In the Basic Options pane, you'll see two options relevant to the display of the editor. The first, Template CSS classes, is set to Yes. The second, Custom CSS Classes, is left blank. We could go ahead and set the style sheet to a custom one, but first let's take a look at why, in many cases, the first option does not work automatically.

Because the default setting of the Template CSS is set to Yes, it stands to reason that the editor display should already match the one shown on the main page. However, the problem lies not with the TinyMCE editor, but most templates—including some of the default templates that ship with the Joomla system.

The TinyMCE editor looks specifically for a CSS file with the name `editor.css` in the `/SELECTEDTEMPLATE/css` directory. Many template creators don't include this file in the `/css` directory. That means that the editor reverts to default styles for display. To see how this works in action, select the Beez template as the default display template for your Joomla installation. Then create an `editor.css` file in the CSS directory of the template. On my local Windows machine, the path of the new file was:

```
C:\Apache22\htdocs\joomla\templates\beez_20\css\editor.css
```

To make the demonstration somewhat outrageous, let's make the main paragraph font 300% larger than the default and set it to italics. To do this, add the following definition to the editor.css file:

```
p {
        font-size:500%;
        font-style: italic;
}
```

After you save the file, open any document in the editor in the Joomla Administrator interface. As shown in Figure 1-2, all of the paragraph text in your editor should now be very large and italic. The `editor.css` file gives you the power to include exactly the template styles that you want in the editor, while excluding those that would simply clutter the interface.

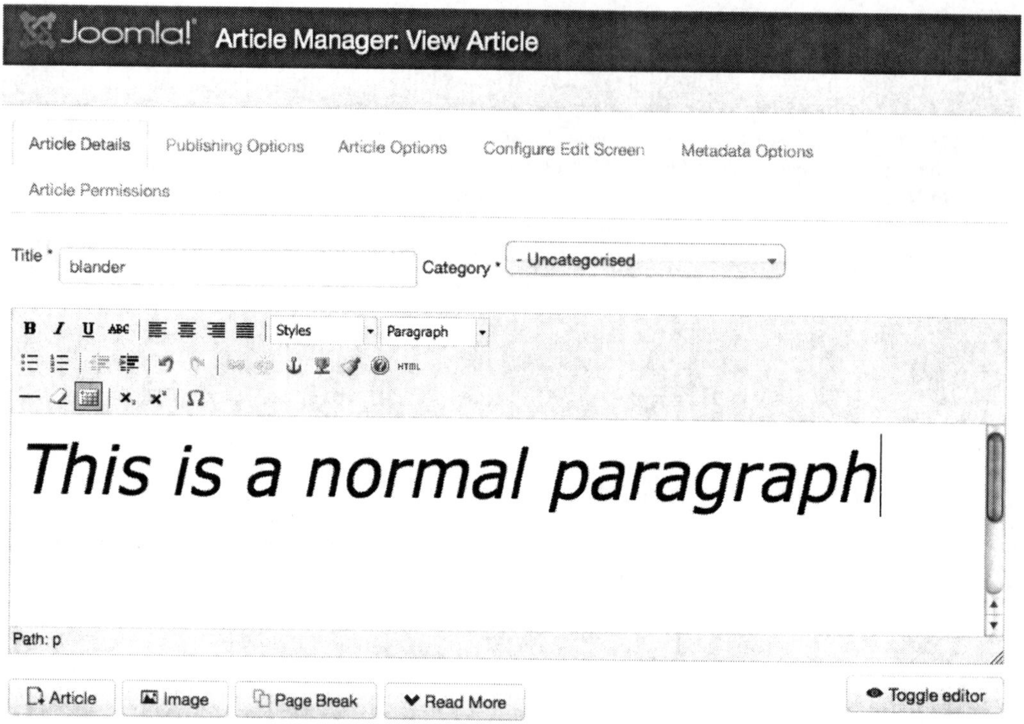

Figure 1-2. *The oversized appearance of the paragraph text should show that* `editor.css` *is working*

If you don't want to explicitly set the editor styles, you could use the Custom CSS Classes setting to specify the main `template.css` of the selected template. On the Administrator interface, select the Plug-in Manager from the Extensions menu. Click on the Editor - TinyMCE plug-in, which will display the options for TinyMCE. In the Custom CSS Classes text box, enter the name of the file in the template's css folder you want to use for the editor and TinyMCE will load those styles.

This places all of the styles that are available to the template in the Styles menu, as you can see in Figure 1-3. The presentation of the editor also instantly adopts the style that will be used for the general display of content on your site.

Figure 1-3. *The styles from the* `template.css` *will be displayed in the drop-down menu of the editor*

I prefer to duplicate the main CSS of the template and rename it `editor.css`. That way I can control exactly the styles that are available to my contributors. By creating the editor style sheet file, you also don't have to use custom settings if you are managing multiple sites. Simply installing a template with the `editor.css` will activate the appropriate styles in the editor.

Whatever your preference for configuration, the TinyMCE editor can now display the content in exactly the same manner as will be posted to the site. With final styling available directly in the editor, the display will actually become What-You-See-Is-What-You-Get.

■ **Tip**   In the past, getting this feature working has frustrated many Joomla administrators. While I am not certain of the source of the difficulty, many of the admins finally resolved the problem by making sure Joomla was looking in the right place for the `editor.css` file. If you know a little PHP, you can open the Joomla file that initializes the TinyMCE (located at `/plugins/editors/tinymce/tinymce.php`). In this file, you'll find a line something like `if (!file_exists($templates_path . '/' . $template . '/css/editor.css'))` and you can simply add a PHP echo like `echo $templates_path . '/' . $template . '/css/editor.css';` on the line before it. When you refresh the editor page and perform a View Source in your browser, you should see the exact path where Joomla is looking for the template CSS file.

Setting Up an Article "Staging" Category

On most live sites (commonly referred to as "production sites"), you won't want in-progress edits to appear on the site. Because Joomla doesn't distinguish between versions of an article as some other CMSs do, you will need a workaround to make sure that content that is not ready for world publication is not seen prematurely. The easiest method of solving this problem is the creation of a "staging" category.

In professional development, web sites often create a "staging area" or "staging server" that either exists on the production server or exactly replicates the server environment. In this staging area, items that are nearly ready for production can be tested for quality assurance before they actually go live. Creating a staging category on your production server offers the same test-on-production-before-go-live environment.

In addition to holding new content, a staging category can contain articles that are meant to replace other articles. If the article is new content, simply setting the publication date in the future may be good enough to keep the article unavailable, so placing it in the staging category is not necessary. However, with editing existing content, you probably don't want to unpublish the article while it is being revised and you also don't want the public seeing an in-process editing job. You will need to make a copy of the existing article and place it somewhere where it won't be confused with the existing version.

For example, if you open the article in the Article Manager, clicking the Save as Copy button will create a copy in the same category where the original resides. However, the difference between the two is not very obvious, as shown in Figure 1-4.

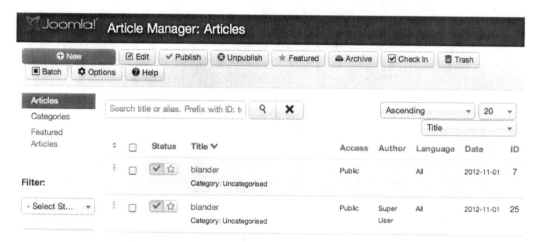

Figure 1-4. *The only difference between the currently published article and the in-process update is the article ID*

While you can check the right column for the higher article ID (the new article will always have a higher number), there is a substantial possibility that the wrong article will get updated. A much better method is creating a category where updated articles can be copied from—the staging category. There should never be any confusion because the category will clearly declare that the article is not in a category that will be displayed on the site. Set up your staging category like this:

1. Select the Content ➤ Category Manager ➤ Add New Category option to display the manager.

2. Set the title of the new category to Staging Category.

3. Set the *Status* to Unpublished.

4. Set the permissions as desired. Generally, you will reserve the Delete and Edit Own properties for Editors, Publishers, and Administrators.

5. Click the Save & Close button to create the new category.

6. Select the Content ➤ Article Manager to show all current articles.

7. Open a live articles that need to be edited by clicking on the title.

8. In the Category drop-down menu, select the Staging Category.

9. Click on the Save as Copy button to create the duplicate in the staging area.

You can now edit the copy in the Staging Category without any danger to the original article or an in-progress document being exposed to the public. When you're ready to publish the revised version, take the current version offline by opening the original article, changing the alias to include a suffix such as "-old" (two documents can't have the same alias in the same category), and then changing the state to Unpublished. For the new article, set the state to Published and set the category to the location of the original article and the new version will be live.

If you want to make your staging environment even closer to production, you can set up a menu item that references this category and makes it available only to those behind the scenes (such as editors and administrators). This technique will allow you to see the articles in a published setting such as a Category Blog layout for tuning of "read more" links and other aspects of the article display.

Such a system also provides a convenient place for site editors to go to see all article updates that are being worked on. Creating a category named "staging" in all of the major sections of your site can greatly simplify the management process for updates.

■ **Note**   In professional software development, the term "staging" refers to a server (for example, "push the code to the staging server") or designation where code or data is kept right before it is pushed to production. It comes from the building trade where it refers to a temporary structure used in the building process such as the horizontal platforms that allow workers to stand on the scaffolding. For software development, it is a holding area or special server where things can be modified and tested in a near-production environment.

Anatomy of the Article Display Process

After using Joomla for any length of time, you've probably experienced some confusing results when you try to get articles to display in a certain way. There are dozens of problems that may have you shaking your head in frustration.

A font, size, and style choice may have exactly the right appearance in the editor, yet when rendered by the site it looks completely different (as you saw in the previous section). Perhaps a setting that you've used dozens of times may not work the way you expect. For example, you may turn off the *Show Title* option for an article, only to find the title display persists. Other times, changes to global preferences seem to have no effect at all. You may waste hours trying to track down the source of the problem.

Rarely are these types of configuration puzzles caused by an actual bug in Joomla. Because Joomla is designed for maximum control, it has many interwoven and interlocking settings that can affect when, where, and how the items of an article are displayed. This means that a display setting in one place may be ignored in another. Unfortunately, when several of the settings come into play for a single article, it is sometimes difficult to determine which setting in the chain is the dominant one that is used.

The number of locations for various settings can even confound an experienced user. The next section will help you untangle the relations of the various settings and provide a map so you can quickly achieve the presentation you desire. Learning *where and how* to configure various pieces of metadata used by the presentation system will let you achieve the look you desire on your site. It will also streamline your efforts to provide your site with a consistent persona and give your site visitors a coherent brand experience.

We'll progress through each of these areas and demonstrate the various situations where a setting that seems like it should directly affect the display does not. Then the setting that actually will make the change is demonstrated.

Configuring Article Display

It's important to remember that in the Joomla model, an article—by itself—is not displayed directly. Unlike a standalone HTML web page, which is a text-based file stored on the server, a Joomla article is stored as data in a database that is rendered by PHP code for presentation. The article data is recast by the component or module used to render it.

When an article is displayed by a system component (whether it is com_content or another extension), there is a great deal of metadata (or information about information) related to the article. Metadata determines how the Joomla code will render the article and its various pieces (such as title, header, and so on). Because an extension manages most aspects of the actual presentation of the article, the extension needs to reference the metadata to choose what may be used or ignored.

■ **Note**   In computer terminology, the term "metadata" means information about information. I'm properly (but broadly) using that term here to indicate information such as settings, properties, or parameters that provide information and have an effect on the presentation of the article content. In the Joomla Article Manager, the Metadata Options panel contains metadata narrowly specific to SEO properties about a particular article. Therefore, when you read the term metadata in this chapter, please think of it in the broader sense.

Article Settings

Let's take a look at an example of some of the article metadata settings. You have surely used each of these configuration settings independently before. However, it is the process through which they interact and override each other that can sometimes make a setting's lack of immediate effect baffling. The progression of settings is shown in Figure 1-5.

Figure 1-5. *Article settings start at the top and progress from the global settings down to the local article settings*

In this example, you'll create a new article and modify settings related to it. Starting with the parameter settings on the article itself, you'll progress to the menu settings, and finally to the global settings in the Parameters pane.

Start by creating a new article:

1.   From the select the Content ➤ Article Manager option and click the New button to create a new article.

2.   Add an article title and fill the body edit box with some dummy content. I created an article called Article Anatomy 1 and entered some general text.

3.   Set the *Status* setting to Published.

4.   Set the *Featured* setting to Yes.

5.   Set the *Category* (I selected a category called *Advanced Joomla!* that I'd created earlier).

6.   Click on the *Article Options* tab and set:

   • *Show Title* to Use Global

   • *Show Category* to Show

   • Show *Voting* to Show

   • *Show Author* to Hide

   • *Show Create Date* to Use Global

7.   Click the Save & Close button.

Once the article is saved, you have an item that uses several of the available settings (Show, Hide, and Use Global). This will allow you to see how other settings in different places affect the article display. Open the home page of your web site in a browser and you should see an article like the one in Figure 1-6.

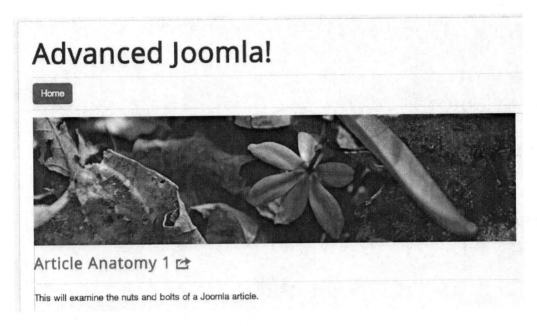

Figure 1-6. *The article as it is displayed on the home page of the web site*

You will notice that some of the settings worked as expected, while others didn't. At the top of the column there is no category title (in my case, Advanced Joomla) that was set on the article to Show. The *Article Voting* was set to Show, but it doesn't appear on the page, either. The Show *Author* was set to hide and it hasn't been displayed, so that setting worked. *Show Title* was set to Use Global and because the article title is shown, it appears that the global setting was set to show it.

Global Settings

Let's return to the Admin interface and see if we can do better. From the Content menu, select the Article Manager again. You'll see an icon labeled Options on the toolbar. Click on the icon and you'll see the global options for articles as shown in Figure 1-7.

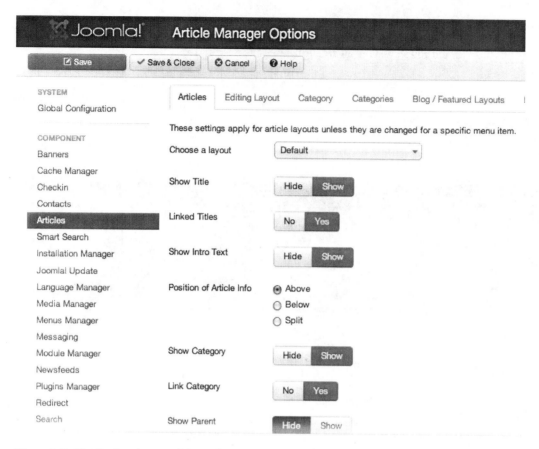

Figure 1-7. *The Options button of the Article Manager displays the Global options*

Surprisingly, the *Show Category* shows Show, yet the category title didn't appear. Choose the following Global options:

- Set *Show Title* to Hide
- Set Show *Category* to Show
- Set Show *Author* to Show
- Set Show *Create Date* to Hide
- Set Show *Modify Date* to Hide
- Set *Article Voting* to Show

Click the Save & Close button to store these settings and refresh the home page. As you can see in Figure 1-8, the `Advanced Joomla!` category text is still missing! Also, the article title is still there. The author name, although set to Show, does not appear. It shouldn't because the article was set to hide the author and the global setting should not override the individual article settings. The create date doesn't appear. However, the *Article Voting* now shows correctly.

Advanced Joomla!

Home

Article Anatomy 1 ↪

★★★★★
○○○○◉ Rate

This will examine the nuts and bolts of a Joomla article.

Figure 1-8. After saving the new global settings, the article display has changed slightly

You've now covered the two primary settings levels, but haven't resolved the extra unwanted title and the missing category. After the article and global settings, the next level up in the display process is the menu that renders the display. In this case, it is the menu that displays the "featured" or *Home* menu.

Menu Settings

Even if you've dramatically changed your Joomla configuration, you can find the Home menu like this:

1. Select the Menus menu in the Administrator interface.

2. In the drop-down menu, look for the item with the gold star following the menu title.

3. Select that item to display the Menu Item Manager.

4. One of the items should have a gold star in the Default column (likely it is named *Home*). Once again, the gold star next to one of the entries indicates the home page. Click on the title of that menu item.

Once you have the Home menu open, you can make selections that determine how content displayed by that menu will be handled. To make a few more demands on our simple article, select these options:

5. Click on the Advanced Options tab and you should see the traditional options again.

6. Set the *Show Title* to Hide.

7. Set the Show Category menu to Use Global.

8. Click the Save & Close button.

When you refresh the home page, the *category title* will be displayed.

9.   Click the New button to create a new menu.

10. For the Menu Item Type, select Articles and then the Article ➤ Single Article option.

11. Set the Menu Title to Setting Tester.

12. Select Menu Item Root in the Parent Item list that will make it easy for you to find the article.

13. In the Required Settings pane, click on the Select button to select the article you just created.

14. Click the Save & Close button.

Once again refresh your browser window. Again some things change, but some stay the same. Now it's time to re-evaluate our assumptions about where the article is being displayed and what is being presented.

In this case, my category title happens to match the name of the site: Advanced Joomla!. What I had thought was a category title was in fact the page title inserted by the component. How did I figure this out? When I did a View Source in the browser window and performed a Find for my target text, I saw that the HTML code to display the text read like this:

```
<div class="componentheading">Advanced Joomla!</div>
```

That made me realize that the component considered this text the matching title of the component. Because this component was displaying home page content, it seemed possible that this page was displaying the title of that page. I went to the Page Display Options pane of the article's menu and checked for the page title. It was actually blank!

However, when I went to the Global Configuration of the site, it was indeed set to Advanced Joomla!. When I made a slight modification to the site title and performed a refresh, I was rewarded with the text shown in Figure 1-9.

This will examine the nuts and bolts of a Joomla article.

Figure 1-9. *Changes to the site name were displayed in the title at the top of the column*

Now I had a problem. I didn't want to clear the name of my site, yet I didn't want any text to display at the top of the column. However, I also realized that the home page was handled uniquely by the system. Perhaps a setting doesn't work the same as it might on other places in the site.

Title of the Home Page

A problem that frustrates many Joomla users is determining the place where the title is set for the main index page. Setting this title properly is critical to optimizing your web page for the search engines. Because it is the lead page to your site, it will weigh most heavily in the search engine spider's attempt to categorize your site. By default, Joomla sets the title of this page to the name of your site.

Because the entire structure of a Joomla site is determined by the menus configuration, each menu provides a place to explicitly override the page title so it won't just contain the title of the site. If the Browser Page Title parameter for the Home menu items is set, this title will *override* the default site name setting for the home page. So to set the name of the home page, you only need to modify the home menu.

In the Administrator interface, drop-down the Menus menu and look for the item with the gold star as you did earlier. As shown in Figure 1-10, the star is a visual marker that tells you the menu that contains the default home page.

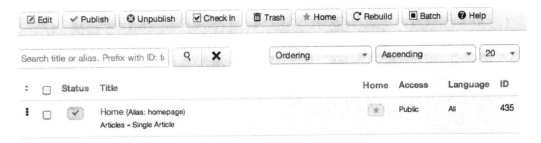

Figure 1-10. *The star shows which menu contains the 'home' page menu*

Select the menu that holds the star. A list of menu items will be displayed for that menu. Click on the title of that menu. On a default installation of sample data, this menu will be titled 'Home'. When the menu is displayed, select the Advanced Options tab and the page title will be located in the same place as other menu items—in the Page Display Options pane. If you expand the pane, you'll see a text box labeled Browser Page Title, as shown in Figure 1-11.

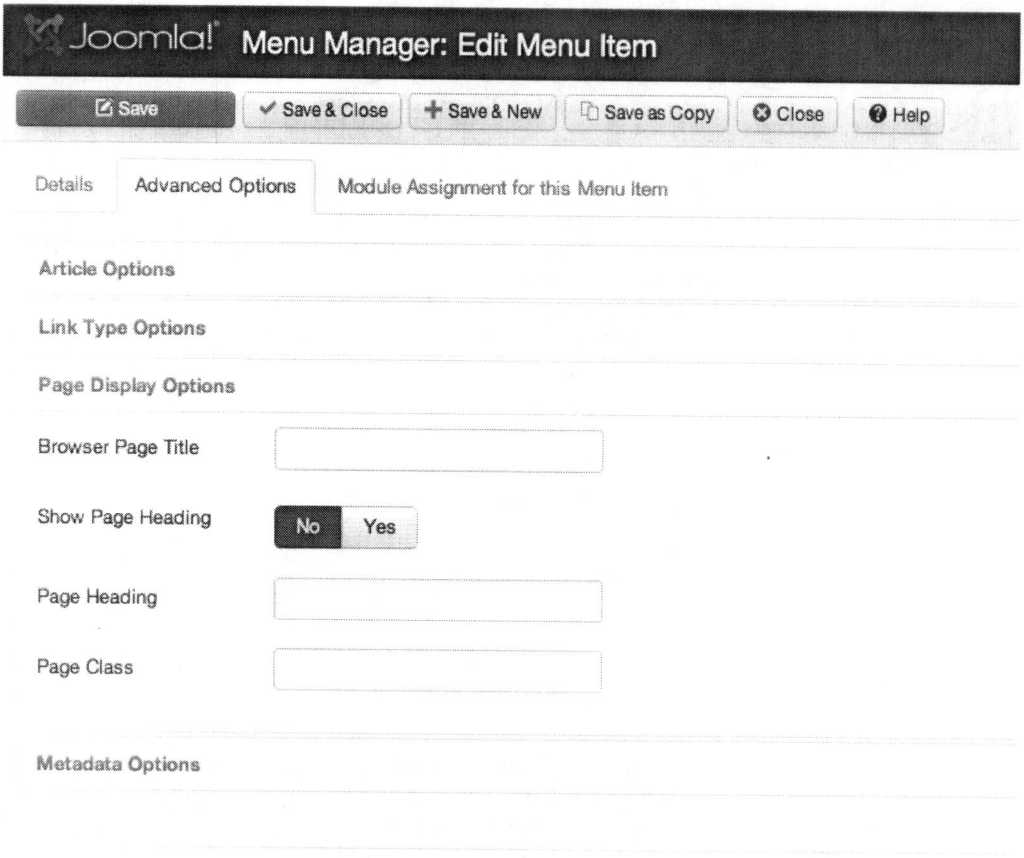

Figure 1-11. *Expanding the Page Display Options pane for the menu item with the star will display the title of the home page*

Change the page title to something that will help maximize your search engine ranking. Remember that a page title that matches the content of the page will greatly increase your chances of being properly categorized. For example, a site title of 'Tall Ships' that has a menu titled 'Tall Ships of the Atlantic' is likely to be recognized as a site focusing on this topic.

Article Voting

The final piece of the puzzle is the missing article voting. First restore the global setting of Yes to the Show Title option that you changed in the previous exercise in the Article Options of the Home menu and in the global Options of the Article Manager. Let's make the article title a link to the article, click on it, and see the article when it isn't displayed on the home page. When troubleshooting a Joomla problem, it is often a good idea to move the targeted item off the home page because specialized settings might be involved, as you have just seen.

First create a menu that is a landing page for the article. Once you have the landing page set up, click on the article so it is displayed in the window. Set a voting display by selecting one of the radio buttons and clicking the Rate button to create at least a single rating on the article. When you check the home page, you should now see the voting, as shown in Figure 1-12.

Advanced Joomla!

Figure 1-12. *The current rating for your test article should now show on the home page display*

The article rating doesn't appear until a user has clicked on the rating and applied one. Once it has been rated once, the voting will appear even on the front page.

Summary of Article Presentation

Understanding when each setting will actually affect the article display will help you properly configure your web site. Let's begin the process by creating an article and leaving the default settings and watching where settings NOT on the article will change.

The three main locations of article settings in order of precedence are:

1. Settings on the article itself

2. Settings on the menu that displays the article

3. Settings in the global settings of the Options for the site

Now that the menu for the home page is displayed in the title, notice anything? Well, if in the case of the home page, the menu title were displayed as the page title. What would happen if you turned off the page title? In the Parameters (System) pane, set the *Show Page Title* to No and refresh the home page in your browser. Jackpot! The Advanced Joomla! text is finally missing.

In this process, sometimes figuring out proper Joomla settings is a bit like detective work. It can take some time to track down these things, but very often there is a configurable solution to your problem. Now let's take a look at some other configurations that are not obvious and learning to use them can dramatically increase your control over the look and feel of your site.

URLs and Their Challenges

When you activate the Search-Engine-Friendly (SEF) URLs on a Joomla site, understanding how they are created can be puzzling given the context. Is the alias of the article used or the menu alias? How are articles referenced within categories? Can multiple URLs lead to the same page? Answering these questions can help you understand how Joomla approaches site organization. It can also help you to optimize your site so the search engine spiders can more effectively understand your content and surface it to visitors.

In this section, I'll try to dispel some of the mysteries surrounding the system of routing that Joomla uses to generate the URLs that are presented to the user. You'll also see how you can manually display content by article ID, which can be useful when you're testing particular articles with extensions that you are developing.

Puzzling Out a URL

The best place to start looking at the Joomla URLs is a standard, non-SEF URL that is generated for a Joomla menu. In the Administrator interface, select the Site ➤ Global Configuration menu item. In the SEO Settings pane, change the Search Engine Friendly URLs setting to No. Then use your browser to go to the site home page (or refresh the page if you are already there). If you hover over menus, you can see the actual structure of each link now.

From the Administrator interface, you can always examine the URL to any menu by checking the Link field for a menu, as shown in Figure 1-13.

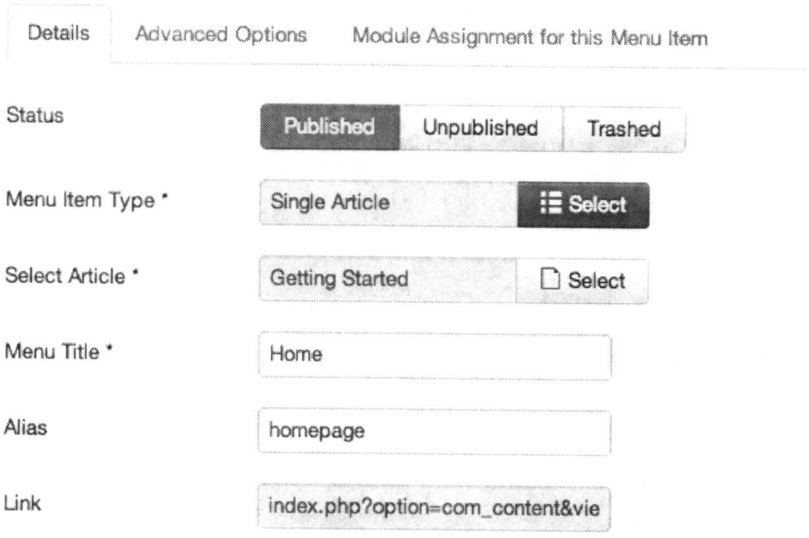

Details	Advanced Options	Module Assignment for this Menu Item

Status	[Published] [Unpublished] [Trashed]
Menu Item Type *	Single Article [≔ Select]
Select Article *	Getting Started [☐ Select]
Menu Title *	Home
Alias	homepage
Link	index.php?option=com_content&vie

Figure 1-13. The link for any menu is displayed in the Link text box of the menu editor

For a single article layout menu, the displayed link will be something like this:

```
index.php?option=com_content&view=article&id=1
```

This link, however, is incomplete. If you move to the browser and click on this menu link, you'll see that the URL actually has an additional parameter:

```
index.php?option=com_content&view=article&id=1&Itemid=3
```

The Itemid parameter is very important in controlling an advanced Joomla site, because it determines the *menu* and thereby the menu settings to be displayed for this article. By customizing this parameter, you can make an article display in almost any manner you want. Most often, you will want to use this feature to create custom links to content that uses one template or another. In other words, by creating a custom link in an article or on a page, you can have the same piece of content displayed *in more than one way*.

For example, perhaps there is a single article that you want to be shared between the customer side of the site and the developer side of the site. However, depending on the location of the link, you need it to display with the proper template or different left side menus.

If an article was left to the default template, such as `Atomic`, the article would display using that template. However, another menu might be set to use the `Beez` template. You can select templates for individual menus by opening the template entry in the Extensions ➤ Template Manager and then using the Menu Assignment pane and selecting individual menus, as shown in Figure 1-14.

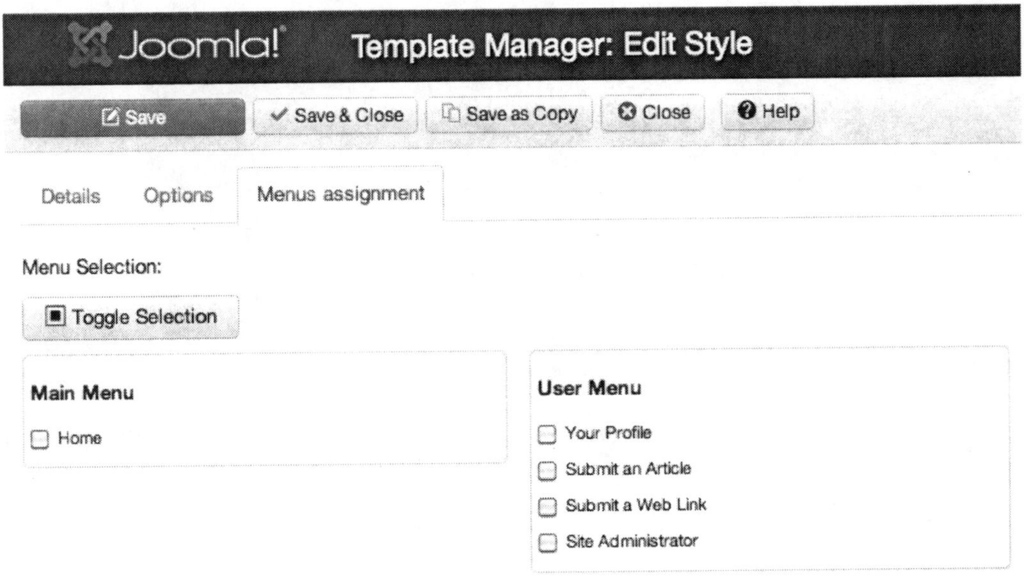

Figure 1-14. *You can assign a template to display on specific menus*

If you attempt to select multiple templates for the same menu item, when the template entry is saved, Joomla will simply de-select it from the previous template. For this example, however, I'm going to set up a menu called Developer Section and set it to use the Beez template using the Extensions ➤ Template Manager. Once I have the menu set up, I'll open the Menu Item Manager and look at the far right column labeled ItemID of the menu item list. I'll make a note of that menu ID to use in my URL. Now I can set up a custom link that reads like this:

```
index.php?option=com_content&view=article&id=1&Itemid=4
```

When a browser window is opened to this address, you'll see that the same article is displayed using the different template, as shown in Figure 1-15. This method provides the freedom to control exactly how an article will be displayed depending on the parameters of the link.

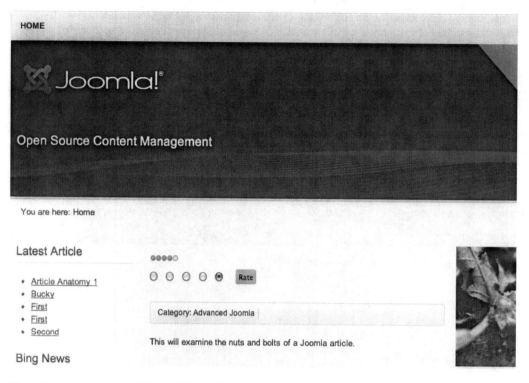

Figure 1-15. *Article when displayed through the Beez template*

Even if your site uses SEF URLs, the basic URL is a good place to start when trying to diagnose routing problems. This is especially true as the SEF routing follows essentially the same patterns with regard to article IDs.

Examining the SEF URL

Once the SEF options in Joomla are activated, it can become difficult to know exactly how a URL will be routed. If the SEF option (non-mod rewrite) is activated on the example URL used earlier (`index.php?option=com_content&view=article&id=1`), when the menu URL is examined, it appears like this:

`index.php/component/content/article/3`

The router breaks down the original link string into the following parts:

- host: The base url, such as `www.example.com`, but it will also include the subdirectory if the host is not at the root (`www.example.com/myjoomla`).

- port: If the port is 80 (the standard web port), this variable on the server side is empty.

- path: The path of the page requested that is in the form of SEF setup, so it may appear in one of those forms (for example, `/index.php`, `/index.php/mymenu`, or `/mymenu`).

- query: The options of the request. For a site with no SEF mapping activated, this field would contain a value like `option=com_content&view=article&id=173`.

The path itself is the most important variable when trying to determine your URL. It is parsed by the system to determine the SEF URL. The path will always be based upon the menu that is used to reach it.

▪ **Tip** If you're interested in examining the code Joomla uses to encode and decode URLs, you can look at the `router.php` file in the `/libraries/joomla/application/` directory of your Joomla installation. In the file, the `build()` function is called to create the URLs for the menus and other items in the presentation of the page and the `parse()` function receives the URL (such as a SEF URL) and converts it to an internal URL. Note that the actual SEF parsing is performed by the `_parseSefRoute()` in the `router.php` file in the `/includes/` directory.

For example, if you have a hierarchical menu like the one shown in Figure 1-16, the URL will include the menu alias of each level. If the Page Heading parameter of the menu is empty, the article title is used. Otherwise, the Page Heading becomes the title of the window.

- Your Profile
- Submit an Article
- Submit a Web Link

- Getting Started
- Using Joomla!
  - Using Extensions
    - Components

Figure 1-16. Hierarchical menus create the different levels of the URL

In the example shown in the figure, the hierarchy of the titles means that the final menu will have a URL like this:

`/using-joomla/using_extensions/components`

If the final menu is a component such as the Category Blog layout, then the individual IDs of the articles will be the final number in the URL. That means that an article in a blog would have a URL like this:

`/mytopmenu/mysubmenu/81-article-anatomy`

In later chapters, you'll see how you may want to create a master menu for you site with all of the required hierarchical organization so the SEF URLs will be exactly as you need them. Then you will create various menu aliases to reference the master menu to put the necessary menus where you want them in the template display.

Configuring the Search Results Page

The search functionality in Joomla is divided into two separate pieces: the search module and the search component that displays the search results. The search module that displays a text box of the page where a user can enter a search phrase and initiate a search is as easy to control and style as any other module. If you've ever tried configuring the look of the search results page that is rendered by the search component, you may have become very frustrated. Because the results are generated and displayed by the Search component, there isn't a menu to which you can directly attach a specific template. That means that you can't configure which menus appear or don't appear on a search results page.

For example, perhaps the site you are building features two different visitor types: customers and developers. The menus that are displayed for a customer are not the same as those displayed for a developer and vice versa. Perhaps you want the search functionality only available to the developers because the search is customized for the technical notes stored in your article database.

When you set up your site, you can use the module configuration list box like the one shown in Figure 1-17 to specify where modules are displayed. In this case, you only want the search module displayed on the developer pages. Next, you can use the Template Manager to specify which menus will use which templates for presentation. In our example, a developer template (with small fonts and a minimalist style) is on the developer pages. On the customer pages, a much warmer and user-friendly accessibility-oriented template is desired.

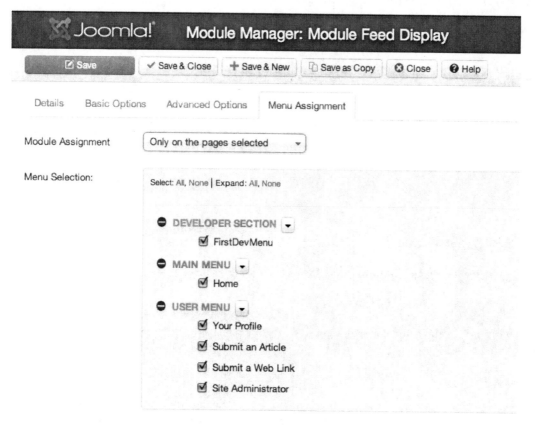

Figure 1-17. *The listbox is used to specify where a module will be displayed*

This system of custom module and menu display works perfectly until you reach the search results page. On that page, the template reverts to the default (customer template) and the menus that are displayed are only those available on all pages. This will appear unprofessional to your developers and ruins the consistency of the design of your site. Despite searching, you can't find any setting that allows you to determine the display of the search results page. To solve this problem, you will need to create a new menu specifically for search results. Following a process to figure out what the search results page currently displays can help you debug some of your own problems with Joomla, so that's what we'll do in this section.

Because the search results display some modules, that would be the place to start to determine how to customize the display. The main menu is displayed on the search results page, so let's start by shutting off this module and see if it has any effect on the search results display.

Under the Extensions ➤ Module Manager option of the Administrator interface, you'll see a list of module items. There will be one module for each menu of the system. The module renders the actual display of the menu. You should see one row with a module name titled *Main Menu* and the type column should hold the text Menu. This is the menu you want to test.

Click on the *Main Menu* item and you should see the display of the various menu parameters. In the Menu Assignment pane, the default setting should be set to *On all pages* so the menu appears on all pages.

Click on the *No pages* setting and click the Save button to save the change. Go back to the Search Results page and refresh it in your browser. The Main Menu should now be gone from the page (as well as all the others). Excellent! You've established that the Menu Assignment settings do have an effect on the search results just like other pages.

Return to the Menu Assignments pane and this time you'll do a custom select of all the individual menus that are available. Click on the Select All button to add the menu to all of the pages. Click Save to save the changes.

When you refresh the search results, you'll see something odd. The Main Menu DOES NOT appear on the search results page. However, if you navigate to any other page in the site, the Main Menu module does appear as expected. Therefore, there is an invisible page that Joomla must keep for the search results that is handled by the *On all pages* menu selection, but is not shown in the menu list.

For these types of menus, you need to create a placeholder menu for the component (see Figure 1-18). You can configure this placeholder to display as you want it to and will be used by the system as the touchstone for the particular component. You can hide the page under any other menu. As long as it exists, the system will pick it up and use the configured settings.

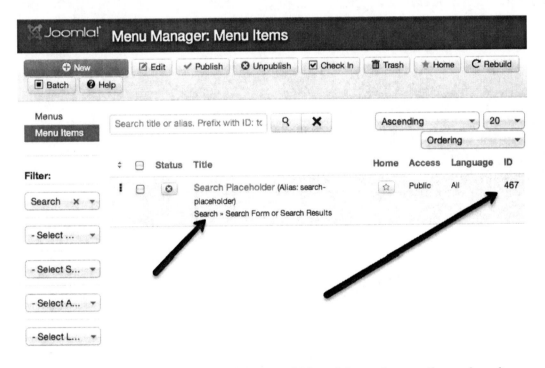

Figure 1-18. *Create a placeholder menu to determine which modules are shown on the search results page*

In order to set what does and doesn't appear on the search page, you must first create a search placeholder menu:

- Create a new menu called *Search Placeholder* in the Menu Manager.

- Unpublish the menu. The system will still recognize the menu, but it won't be displayed anywhere.

- Create a new menu item on the Search Placeholder menu and set the type to Search Form or Search Results.

- Note the ItemID of the menu (in Figure 1-18, it's 467) because you'll need it in a moment.

- Go to the Module Manager and click on the Search module.

- Select the Basic Options tab and put the ItemID of your placeholder menu item in the *Set ItemID* text box, as show in Figure 1-19. This setting will make Joomla use the specified menu item for module display settings and template selection.

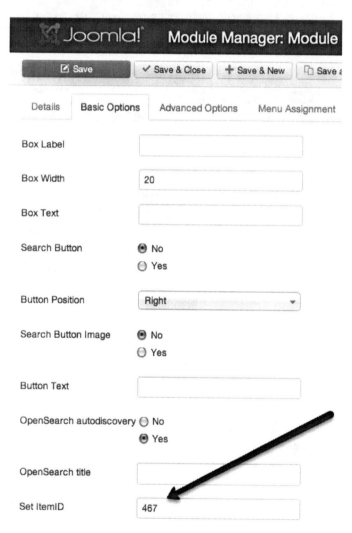

Figure 1-19. *Set the ItemID to match the menu id of the Search Placeholder menu item*

- In the Module Manager, enable the Footer module in the list of modules.

- Click on the Footer module and on the Menu Assignment tab, set it to only appear on the Search Placeholder menu from the list box that specifies where the module will appear.

The Footer should be configured to only appear on the Search Results page. Go to the browser window and execute a search and the search results are now displayed with the footer module.

Conclusion

In this chapter, you learned a few techniques for customizing the presentation and usability of your Joomla site to match your needs. Whenever you work through tough problems in Joomla, put on your detective's hat and test your assumptions. You'll find that taking problems step-by-step and doing things such as putting in marker text will lead you to the source of the setting that you need to change.

You can configure each piece of information displayed for a Joomla article in several different places. Configuring the article title, authorship display, and other items can occur in the settings of the article itself, the Global Configuration, the menu settings that access it, or the extension that is used for the actual display. Be sure to set each of these to levels to configure the display to meet your needs. The next chapter will demonstrate an easy and quick way to substantially increase the functionality of your Joomla web site using third-party widgets. You won't have to wait for someone to write an extension or even install anything to add maps, calendars, translators, and more.

CHAPTER 2

■ ■ ■

Customizing Joomla with Widgets

Joomla is famous for its extensibility—everything from custom templates to the broad array of available third-party extensions. Beyond that, the built-in Custom HTML module provides a blank canvas through which Joomla can host a variety of web services, widgets, and APIs without the need for custom programming or extension installation. In this chapter, you'll see how to use this module to augment your Joomla web site with no additional installation. Widgets can provide everything from chat to event calendars to maps to online virtual storefronts. You will see examples of all of these widgets in this chapter and learn how you can add them to your site.

There are many advantages to using widget code on your site. The most important include:

- *No additional server resources needed*: Some of these widgets use large databases or advanced serving technology to provide their functionality. Because the code for the widgets is executing on a remote server, your web server doesn't need to provide any of the resources to enable the features they provide.

- *No slowdown in page load speed*: Most of these widgets display in an iFrame or use asynchronous JavaScript calls, which means they don't prevent your page from loading while they are being retrieved. The widget loads in parallel with the rest of your page content, so your visitors can see the rest of your page in their browser and the widgets will populate as they become available. This is supported in all modern browsers.

- *Code for the widgets is stored in the Joomla database*: The HTML or JavaScript code in the Custom HTML module, unlike Joomla extensions (which are a mixture of code files and database entries), is stored in the Joomla database. That means every database backup will also archive all the widgets on the site. It also means that transferring them to other sites or other servers is much easier than relocating installed extensions.

- *Upgrades are automatic*: Since the actual widget is stored on the servers of the vendor that is making them available, when they upgrade their code, the upgraded version of the widget automatically appears on your site without requiring you to do any change or installation. Of course this can be a disadvantage if you don't like the new features or changes in advertisement policy, but this auto-upgrade is generally a benefit.

This chapter will take you through the implementation of the following widgets to your Joomla site:

- Google Calendar
- Google Map
- Google Translate
- Live Chat box
- Survey

- Related Content Module
- Virtual Storefront
- Google Maps

To use the widgets, you will need to include iFrame or JavaScript code within the pages where you want the widget to display. This code could be added to the template that is being used for the site, but that requires custom modification of the site template—whether you've constructed the template yourself or purchased from a third-party template vendor.

Modifying the template also makes using the widget less flexible and more difficult to manage through the Joomla Administrator interface. In contrast, Joomla supplies a wrapper module called the Custom HTML module that can be used just like any other module. It essentially allows any HTML- or JavaScript-based widget to be embedded in the module code and it will appear on any page and position specified for that module.

Creating a Custom HTML Module

Using the Custom HTML module allows you to customize a Joomla site quickly and painlessly. The module enables you to encapsulate custom HTML, CSS, and JavaScript code into a module with all of the functionality afforded normal modules including menu-selectable display, security features, administrative positioning of the module within the template, and control over the user level who can see the module.

Creating a Custom HTML module is extremely simple—let's take a look at the process now. Before we start, we need to configure the editor settings because the default editor settings will corrupt or delete any widget code pasted into the HTML field of the module. The Custom HTML module was created to enable users to add HTML code to a page—not the JavaScript needed by most widgets. For general security reasons, WYSIWYG text editors have built-in functionality to either delete JavaScript code outright or process the JavaScript code in an attempt to protect the site from a malicious scripting attack. To allow you to paste un-corrupted custom HTML or JavaScript code into the module, you need to select the "No editor" option in Joomla for your user so the code added to the HTML module is saved as-is.

Unfortunately, the Toggle Editor button at the bottom of the editor window, which lets you paste HTML code directly into the window, still processes the code in the text field through the editor (deleting or corrupting the widget code). Since I want to make sure that my widget code stays intact, I create a second administrator account called *widgetadmin* that has the simple text editor (or no editor) selected as the user's default editor. I then use that account to add or edit any of my widget modules. To create the *widgetadmin*, follow these steps:

1. From the Administrator interface, select the Users ➤ User Manager menu option.

2. Click the New button to create a new user account.

3. Set the username as *widgetadmin* and set the password to the same password as your admin account.

4. Select the Editor - None option in the Basic Settings pane.

5. Set the account type to Administrator or Super Users so you can easily edit any module from this account.

6. Click the Save and Close button to save the account.

Log in as the *widgetadmin* and create an example module by following these steps:

1. From the Administrator interface, select the Extensions ➤ Module Manager menu option.

2. Click on the New button.

3. Click on the Custom HTML link.

4. Enter "Hello Joomla World" as the module title.

5. Enter the following text in the body: `<script>document.write("Hello Joomla World!")</script>`

6. Set the position to the Footer position (depending on your selected template, this will vary). I selected "position-14" that is the last footer position in the Beez templates.

7. Click the Save and Close button.

When you view your site with a browser, you should see the module in the footer as shown in Figure 2-1.

Figure 2-1. *The hello message should appear on the web page in whatever position was selected for the module*

This demonstration used simple JavaScript to write text into the document, although you could have made it a little more advanced and used HTML tags such as `<b>` or `<h1>`. For widgets, you will use a combination of iFrames, JavaScript, or HTML code to inject the custom module code into the Joomla page.

Adding Custom Widgets to Your Site

Using the Joomla Custom HTML module, you can often add a great widget to your site in less than five minutes. Although the widgets demonstrated in this chapter are only a very small sampling of the large number available on the Internet, you can download most widgets that are available and activate them using the same steps as you will follow here.

One of the most widely helpful widgets is the addition of a calendar to a web site. A calendar is useful if your Joomla site represents an organization, a user group, or a special interest group (such as gardening, chess, bicycling, and so forth). If you have a personal landing page, you can share personal events with your visitors. There are a number of available calendar widgets, but we'll use the Google Calendar because of its easy availability and popularity.

Implementing the Google Calendar

There are numerous excellent Joomla extensions that offer event calendars, but most are only local to your site. The Google Calendar widget, in contrast, can feed all types of events directly onto your site calendar and allows your events to be published into a networked calendar. Since the calendar can both publish events to the broader world as well as import other events into it, it is often the perfect solution for a public-facing event calendar.

To set up a calendar, go to the Google Calendar page (www.google.com/calendar), log into your Google account, and click the *Create* button. Fill in the details of your calendar and set the privacy to Make this calendar public, as shown in Figure 2-2. Clicking the Save button will generate the calendar and create an accessible URL.

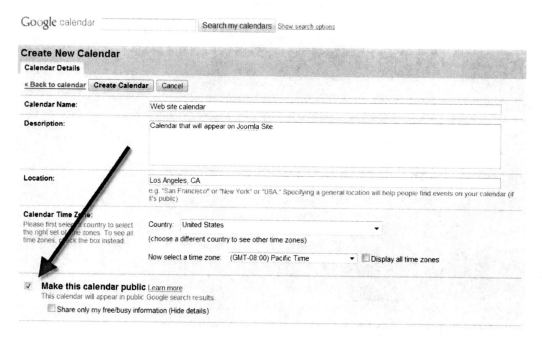

Figure 2-2. *Select Make this calendar public to share entries on the calendar with the Web*

Create a few events on the calendar by clicking on a day or time slot depending on the display mode that you are using. The calendar even lets you create recurring events that can be especially useful for relevant holidays that fall on the same day every year.

Once you have several events on your calendar, select the actions arrow for the calendar in the left rail and click on the Calendar settings option as shown in Figure 2-3. This screen will display most of the settings that you selected when you initially created the calendar. You can modify any of those now if you want the Joomla calendar on the site to vary from the original settings.

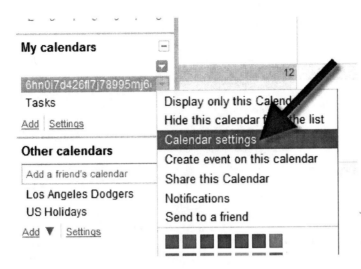

Figure 2-3. *Open the Calendar settings to access the iFrame code for the calendar*

Click on the Calendars tab and then click on the link for the Calendar you just created. If you scroll down in the window, you'll find the section titled *Embed This Calendar* that has a text box with HTML code in it as shown in Figure 2-4. If you want the default viewing options, you can select and copy this code now. To make modifications in the display, click on the *Customize the color, size, and other options* link and you'll be presented with a screen that allows you to customize the display of: the title, the date, the Print icon, the tabs, the calendar list, the time zone, display type (week, month, or agenda), size (width and height), day starting the week, language (select among 40 languages), colors, and the inclusion of other calendars.

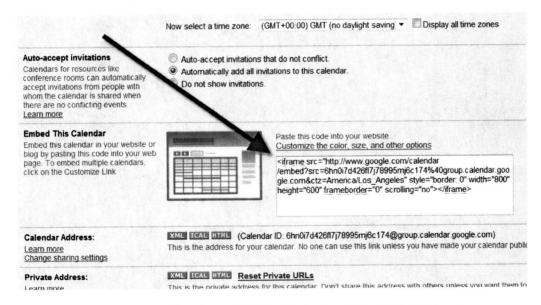

Figure 2-4. *The necessary iFrame code to embed the calendar is contained in the text box*

If you make some of the customizations to the various aspects of the calendar, you will get iFrame code that resembles something like this:

```
<iframe src="https://www.google.com/calendar/embed
  ?showTitle=0&amp;height=600&amp;wkst=1&amp;
  bgcolor=%23FFFFFF&amp;
  src=6hn0i7d426fl7j78995mj6c174%40group.calendar.google.com
  &amp;color=%23856508&amp;
  src=en.usa%23holiday%40group.v.calendar.google.com&amp;
  color=%23182C57&amp;ctz=America%2FLos_Angeles"
  style=" border-width:0 " width="800" height="600"
  frameborder="0" scrolling="no">
</iframe>
```

You can now paste this code into a Custom HTML module and put the calendar at an appropriate location on your Joomla site. Follow the instructions from the earlier section and paste the custom iFrame code into the HTML text area instead of the JavaScript "hello world" code used earlier. In Figure 2-5, I've placed the calendar at the bottom of my front page.

Figure 2-5. *Put the code into a Custom HTML module in Joomla and then select an appropriate position to display the module and it will appear on your Joomla page*

You can have different calendars for different pages or combine the calendars in the Google Calendar admin to all appear on a single calendar. Events may have reminders applied to them and you can even a link a geographic location to the entry. The calendar is one of the simplest of many widgets available for free from Google. One example of a powerful web widget is the Google Map widget that lets you embed a custom map directly into your Joomla site.

Adding a Google Map to Your Joomla Site

Google has a whole set of widgets, including Google checkout, custom search, groups, news, translate, cloud print, presentations, YouTube news, and, of course Google Maps. Maps are extremely easy and convenient to add to your web site and they can provide a lot of visual interest. If you have information that can be represented geographically, such as store locations, convention locations, special historical sites, the locations of relevant bargains, or even the geolocations of some of your users, you should consider adding a Google Map to your Joomla site.

▓ **Note** Google changes the URLs of Google Maps APIs and wizard frustratingly often—usually without redirection to the new location. Therefore, if you go to a URL specified in this chapter and it doesn't show the item mentioned here, please perform a Google search for the relevant feature and you should be able to locate the specified resource.

To add a map to your site, start by registering for an API key here:

```
https://code.google.com/apis/console
```

Then follow these steps:

1. Click on the Services link in the left column.

2. Find the "Google Maps API v3" entry and switch it on.

3. Click on the "API Access" link in the left column

4. Copy the API key in the Simple API Access pane to the clipboard

Once you have the API key, you're almost ready to get started. To map anything, you need coordinates. The Google Map interface expects the coordinates in longitude and latitude values. You can use the Google Geocoding API to obtain coordinates from a street address. For example, to find the location of Apple's headquarters, you can use a query like this (either from the browser address bar or a CURL request):

```
http://maps.googleapis.com/maps/api/geocode/json
    ?address=1+Infinite+Loop,+Cupertino,+CA&sensor=false
```

The request will return the data in JSON format. There will be a results field that will contain entries in the geometry section that should appear like the one shown in Figure 2-6.

```
              ,
          ],
          formatted_address: "1 Infinite Loop, Cupertino, CA 95014, USA",
        - geometry: {
            - location: {
                  lat: 37.3317055,
                  lng: -122.0305982
              },
              location_type: "ROOFTOP",
            - viewport: {
                - northeast: {
                      lat: 37.3330544802915,
                      lng: -122.0292492197085
                  },
                - southwest: {
                      lat: 37.3303565197085,
                      lng: -122.0319471802915
                  }
              }
          },
        - types: [
              "street_address"
          ]
      }
```

Figure 2-6. *Find the longitude and latitude of a location that you would like to map using the Geocoding API*

Create a new Custom HTML module as you have in the last sections and enter the following code in the text field:

```html
<meta name="viewport" content="initial-scale=1.0, user-scalable=no" />
    <style type="text/css">
      html { height: 100% }
      body { height: 100%; margin: 0; padding: 0 }
      #map_canvas { height: 100% }
    </style>
    <script type="text/javascript">
function init () {
  var mapOptions = {
    zoom: 15,
    center: new google.maps.LatLng(37.3308525, -122.0296837),
    mapTypeId: google.maps.MapTypeId.ROADMAP
  }
  var map = new google.maps.Map(document.getElementById("map_canvas"), mapOptions);
}

function load_map() {
  var script = document.createElement("script");
  script.type = "text/javascript";
  script.src = "http://maps.googleapis.com/maps/api/js?key=APIKEY&sensor=false&callback=initialize";
  document.body.appendChild(script);
}

window.onload = load_map;
    </script>
  </head>
    <div id="map_canvas" style="border:2px solid red;min-height:300px;width:100%;
height:100%"></div>
```

In the load_map() function, replace the text that reads APIKEY with the key you generated earlier. If you have selected a different location for the center of the map, alter the coordinates specified in the init() function.

Pasting this code into a Custom HTML editing window will let you display the Google map on your site. It is very common to add multiple maps to a single site to show various points of interest. You can easily use the map control to show specific locations that you want to highlight (such as store locations), regions of interest (places for good biking routes, scenic campgrounds), visitor locations to show a geographic user map, and many other points of geographic information.

You can find more information about the map API here:

```
http://code.google.com/apis/maps/documentation/javascript/
```

Maps can provide information and a nice visual element to your site. However, perhaps more compelling is the ability to extend the global reach of your site through the Google Translate web element that can dynamically translate the entire contents of a page into the language selected by the site visitor.

Adding a Google Translate Web Element

Joomla provides fantastic language services with site translations into dozens of languages. The international pedigree of Joomla makes it *the CMS* for world communication. Despite the fact that the user interface itself is available in many native languages, the articles on a site are generally written in a single language—that of the primary site author(s). This can restrict the international reach of the site. Additionally, all languages that the site wants to support must be individually downloaded and installed into the Joomla system—and this can be a long and tedious process.

Google, however, provides a widget that can help overcome these limitations. The Google Translate web element will dynamically translate the text of a site page from any language available from the translator to any other language. While the translation is performed by a machine and therefore far from perfect, it can allow a visitor to read an article and gain a general understanding of the information it communicates, even if that visitor doesn't read a single word of the language in which it was written.

■ **Note**   While the Google Translate web element or widget is free, the more powerful Google Translate API that allows a REST query to actually obtain a translation of specified text has become a paid service. Although extremely affordable, it requires billing information to be set up for all accounts before you can use it.

To obtain the code for the translate module, go to this page:

```
https://translate.google.com/manager/
```

The translation wizard lets you select options such as whether to translate the whole page or specific sections (specified using a CSS class), translation background color, whether to allow translations to all languages or specific targeted languages, display mode for the translation selector, and whether you want to track the translations in Google Analytics. Once you've made your selections, you'll be presented with JavaScript code like this that you can add to a Custom HTML module:

```
<!-- Google Translate Element -->
<meta name="google-translate-customization"
content="88b41a78d39d638a-ZZZZ"></meta>
<div id="google_translate_element"></div>
<script type="text/javascript">
```

```
function googleTranslateElementInit() {
  new google.translate.TranslateElement({pageLanguage: 'en',
    layout: google.translate.TranslateElement.InlineLayout.SIMPLE},
  'google_translate_element');
}
</script><script type="text/javascript"
    src="//translate.google.com/translate_a/element.js
    ?cb=googleTranslateElementInit">
</script>
```

This simple code will put a drop-down menu on the page like the one shown in Figure 2-7. If the visitor selects a different language from the menu, the entire page will be translated and re-rendered in the selected language. Navigating to other pages that contain the widget will retain the selected translation setting and render those pages in that language.

Figure 2-7. *The Google Translate widget allows the user to select a different language than the native one on the site and the entire page will be translated*

The Translate widget makes worldwide communication possible since your site can now be read by almost anyone without requiring them to speak the source language of the site. While this is powerful for English language sites, it can be potentially even more powerful for non-English sites. Considering the widespread adoption of English as a second language, a site can be authored in a native language and the Google Translate module can make it accessible to millions of English speakers.

Sites always broaden their reach when they facilitate communication. The Translate web element can increase the audience for a site in almost any language. By adding widgets to increase interaction, such as a live chat widget, a Joomla site can become the nexus for live communication as well.

Adding Chat to Your Site with Chatango

Many sites would like to offer chat services, but the overhead of hosting it yourself can make this prohibitive. Further, the administrator tools included with many of the free extensions are not very robust or easy to use. However, there are a number of online chat widgets that you can easily incorporate into a Joomla site.

In this section, you'll use the Chatango widget (www.chatango.com) to provide chat functionality on your Joomla site. Before you begin, you need to go to the Chatango web site and register a new group. All you need is a group name and e-mail address to get started. You can pick a color scheme and introductory message that will be displayed as users log into the system.

When you complete the registration process, you will be given a snippet of HTML code like this:

```
<object width="250" height="360" id="obj_1292120911398">
<param name="movie"
  value="http://joomlajumpstart.chatango.com/group"/>
<param name="wmode" value="transparent"/>
<param name="AllowScriptAccess" VALUE="always"/>
<param name="AllowNetworking" VALUE="all"/>
<param name="AllowFullScreen" VALUE="true"/>
<param name="flashvars"    value="cid=11&b=60&s=1"/>
<embed id="emb_1292120911398"
  src="http://joomlajumpstart.chatango.com/group"
  width="250" height="360" wmode="transparent"
  allowScriptAccess="always" allowNetworking="all"
  type="application/x-shockwave-flash" allowFullScreen="true"
  flashvars="cid=11&b=60&f=50&l=999999&q=999999&r=100&s=1">
</embed>
</object>
```

Add this code to your site using the Custom HTML module as described earlier. You should be able to paste the code supplied by the Chatango web site directly into the body of the new Custom HTML module for use on your site. Make sure you locate the module in a module position that has enough room to properly show a chat conversation or users will likely not use an abbreviated display.

■ **Note** The Chatango chat client does require your users to have Flash installed in their browser. The Adobe Flash plug-in has an extremely high installed base, so this will generally not be a problem. If you don't like Flash or want to provide chat capabilities to mobile browsers that don't support Flash (at the time of this writing, the iPhone browser still lacked Flash capabilities), there are several other widget services that are purely Ajax-based and don't require Flash. Some of the most popular include MeeboMe (www.meebome.com), Plugoo (www.plugoo.com), and Mabber (www.mabber.com).

When you reload the Joomla site page, you should see a chat box like the one shown in Figure 2-8. Since the chat window displays in an iFrame, the rest of your page should load properly even if Chatango is slow to load. Also if Chatango would ever go offline, it won't prevent your page from loading normally. That's all you need to do.

Figure 2-8. *The Chatango chat box will appear within the module frame and allow live chat on your Joomla site*

Visitors to your site need only register an email account with Chatango and they can chat with one another. There is also a full moderator interface where you can manage the chat clients and review past chat sessions. Chatango provides a number of online tools that you can use to manage your chat group. You can also allow other moderators of the discussions if you have volunteers that can take on that extra work.

A live chat system can really increase the interaction with your site. However, many site owners don't want to provide unfettered communication between individuals in the wake of cyber stalking incidents and other problems. Some organizations only allow chat during specific working hours or during special events so it can be effectively moderated. Joomla's ability to easily publish and unpublish modules makes this convenient. If chat isn't the right fit for your site, another method of interaction that is extremely controlled and yet offers active feedback is the use of surveys. Survey Monkey provides a very easy-to-implement widget that you can add to your site in minutes.

Adding the Survey Monkey Widget to Your Site

Survey Monkey lets anyone quickly and easily create web surveys or forms and stores the data generated from these forms in a management interface that allows the host of the form to see statistics of the responses. You can display the survey on your site using a variety of methods: as a JavaScript widget, as a link that the visitor clicks to go to the Survey Monkey site where they can fill out the survey, or as a shared survey on Facebook.

To create a new survey, go to the Survey Monkey web site (www.surveymonkey.com) and register for an account. All you need is an email address and then you can immediately start creating surveys. As shown in Figure 2-9, you can easily add multiple-choice questions, essay questions, rating scales, and a variety of other selections. You can have many questions per page, but generally three questions per page is a good average.

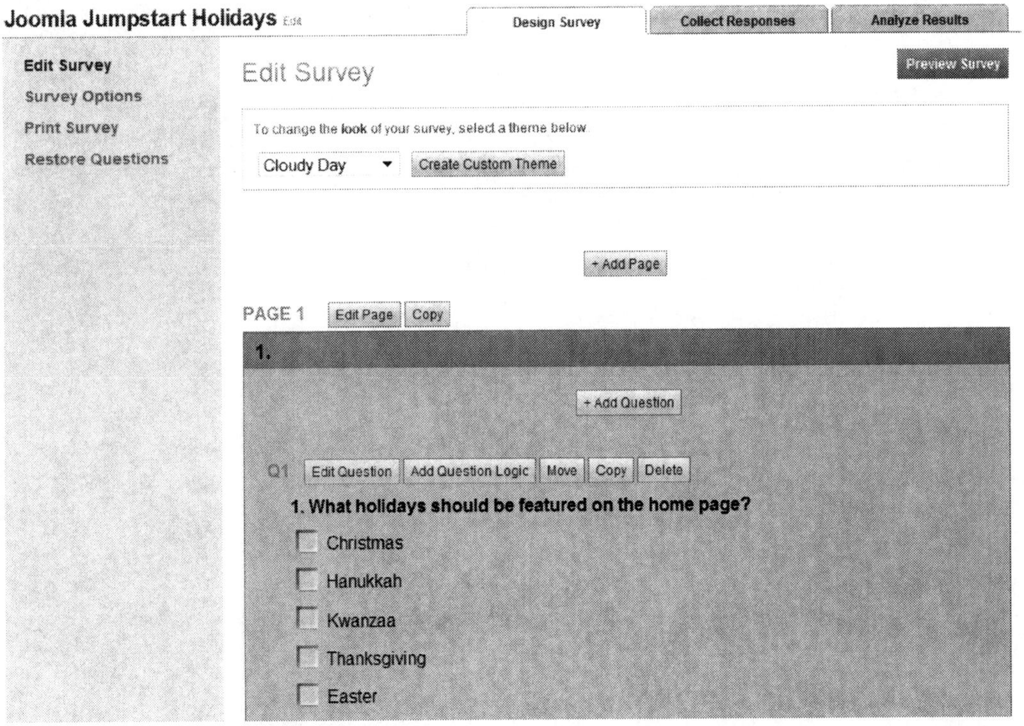

Figure 2-9. *Create a survey with various types of questions, ranging from full text entry to multiple choice to rating scales*

Let's create an example survey by following these steps:

- Select the Create a new survey option.

- Enter a survey name.

- Select a category such as Market Research and click the Continue button.

- Select a survey theme or create a custom theme that matches your site.

- Click the Add Question button.

- Add some question text and select the type of question (such as multiple choice, ranking, etc.).

- Click the Send Survey button when you've selected all of the options that you'd like.

Once you've completed your survey construction, you can add it to your Joomla site as a link that takes the visitor to the Survey Monkey site. To allow the survey to appear on your site instead, simply add a Custom HTML module and the JavaScript code for the survey on the Survey Monkey site. The code should appear something like this:

```
<div id="surveyMonkeyInfo">
<div>
<script src="http://www.surveymonkey.com/jsEmbed.aspx?sm=JKAJD">
</script>
</div>Create your
    <a href="http://www.surveymonkey.com/">free online surveys</a>
    with SurveyMonkey, the world's leading questionnaire tool.
</div>
```

When the JavaScript embeds the survey on your site, it will appear like the survey shown in Figure 2-10.

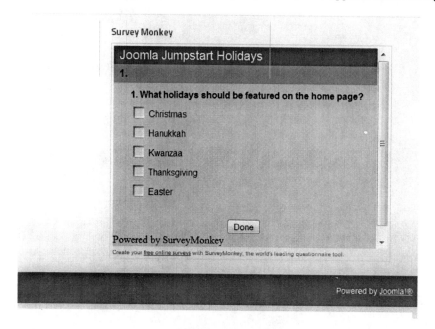

Figure 2-10. A Survey Monkey survey as it appears placed in the Joomla footer with a Custom HTML module

■ **Note** The Survey Monkey code is JavaScript, so unlike the previous widgets that primarily used iFrames or asynchronous JavaScript, loading this JavaScript code blocks the rest of your page load. Because Survey Monkey is a large company, this probably won't cause any issues for your web site. However, you may consider putting the module on its own page on your site so if the Survey Monkey servers were to go down, only that page on your site would be taken offline. If you want it to appear as a module on your page, try locating it in the right column so even if the survey is slow to load, all of the content in the header, left, and center columns will not be blocked from loading.

Creating effective surveys is as much of an art as a science. Here are a few guidelines to help make your surveys more effective and increase your response rate:

- Ask questions where the user can understand the relevance. Asking for the birthplace of a user taking a survey on shoe fashion will seem out of place and intrusive. This will make many of your visitors abandon the survey. Try to make all questions on a survey directly relevant to each other and the topic of the survey.

- Don't include too many pages or too many options per page. It will hurt your survey results if your visitors suffer from survey fatigue and don't complete the form. It's nearly always better to have fully completed forms so the data is not skewed to the first few pages of the survey before the user has quit and left the page. Stating up front the number of questions that the survey will ask helps make the survey more palatable.

- Be sure to include some of the results of the survey on your site after the conclusion of survey time period. There is seldom any benefit to the user for filling out these types of forms except that their voices are heard. Displaying summaries of the results of the survey on your site, they can see that their feedback was received and appreciated.

Surveys can be one of the most useful feedback tools for improving a web site if they are well constructed and short. By using the Survey Monkey widget, you can add surveys to your Joomla site easily and obtain a variety of insights into how your user base looks at your site.

Adding a Related Content Module to Your Site

When a visitor comes to your site from a search engine, they will likely land on a specific page more often than the home page. That means they've already shown interest in the particular subject of document and it is likely they might also want to read other documents on your site that have related content.

To have a related content module on your web site requires a special search engine server that can match internal content in much the same way that the Google search engine could suggest similar articles if you pasted the title of an article into the search box. Installing and maintaining this type of search engine would be difficult and complex for most webmasters.

For this reason, I created a free widget called RcModule (`www.rcmodule.com`) that I use on my Joomla sites (and you can use it on yours). Simply go to the web site, enter your site URL, select the options you want, and click on the "Generate Code" button (see Figure 2-11). This will output a small piece of JavaScript code and your site will be queued for indexing.

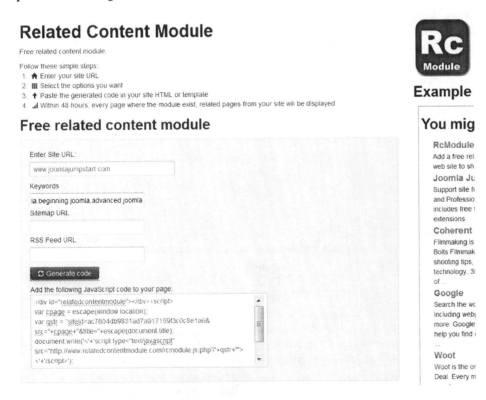

Figure 2-11. *To set up an RcModule, just enter your site address, keywords, and click the Generate Code button to render the JavaScript for the widget*

It takes about 48 hours to spider your entire web site. Create a Custom HTML module, add the code, and display the module on any page where you want a related content module. When this widget is displayed in a visitor's browser, it calls `rcmodule.com` and requests related articles to the currently displayed page.

For example, on the site shown in Figure 2-12, I have some articles on upgrading Joomla and Joomla for beginners. You can see that the RcModule has surfaced other articles about upgrading and beginning Joomla that appear on the site.

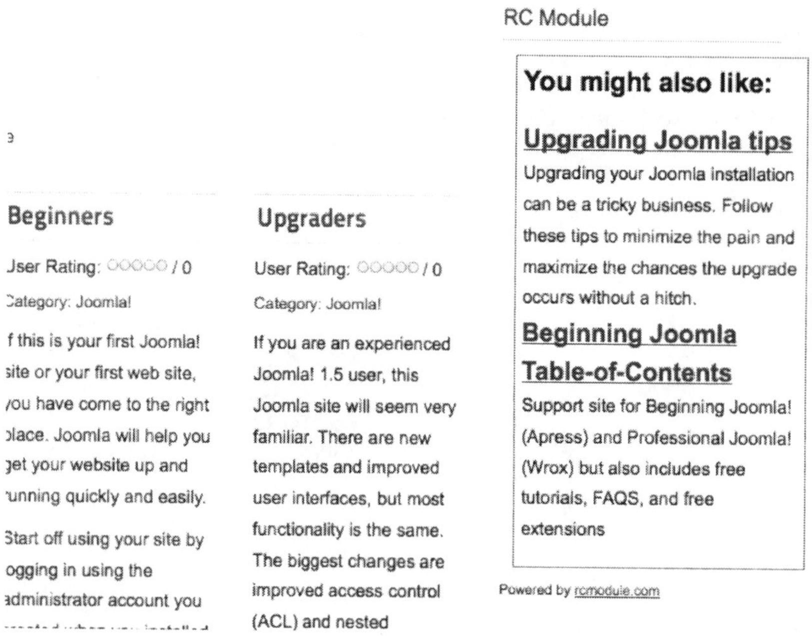

Figure 2-12. *Once the widget is placed on the page, it will display articles that are similar to the one being read*

An RcModule is a very effective way of increasing the number of page views from each visitor. It also makes it more likely that a visitor will find all the information they need on your site. In many ways, adding a site search isn't as effective as a related content module because search requires that the user knows exactly what they are looking for, while related content often supplements that material located by a specific search.

Using the PayPal Storefront

One popular use of Joomla is to create an e-commerce site where people can sell products or services with all the benefits that online shopping affords. Because Joomla is so extensible, several full-featured shopping cart solutions have been made available, with VirtueMart being the most popular e-commerce extension on the Joomla platform.

However, even with the shopping cart extensions available to install and configure easily, there are many obstacles to easily setting up an online storefront. Some of these include selecting a payment processor, securing the private financial information the site is collecting from hacker penetration, timely processing of the transaction, ensuring reliability of the payment transaction connection, and so forth. To use payment processing, you must choose from a myriad of vendors offering different rates, contracts, commitments, and more.

If you don't have the need to create a complete e-commerce site or you simply want to start selling products or services very quickly, you can set up a mini-storefront with the PayPal widget. Setup is as easy as working through the PayPal wizard and selecting options for under a dozen screens. You can add as many products as you want in the Products tab of the wizard (see Figure 2-13).

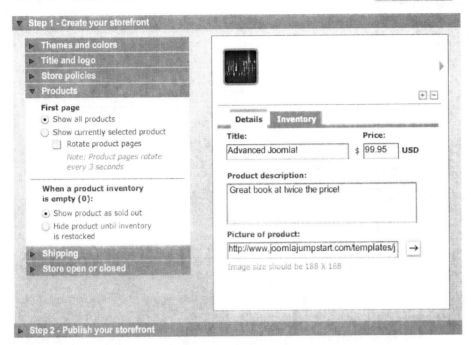

Figure 2-13. *Create a new PayPal storefront using the wizard to set up your products*

To create your store, log in to PayPal and then open the wizard in a browser (`https://storefront.paypallabs.com/`).

■ **Warning**   At the time of this writing, the PayPal virtual store was still a beta product. Beta products are generally not recommended for production sites because the terms, conditions, and implementation details can change quickly and possibly produce breakage on the hosting site. Be sure to read the terms and conditions of any beta program so you realize the ramifications of the program before implementing it on your site.

You can choose themes and colors, select your title and logo, set up store policy, add one or more products, set up shipping, and open the store or take it temporarily offline. Once you've completed the wizard, you will be presented with HTML code that you can add to a Custom HTML module like this:

```
<object classid="clsid:D27CDB6E-444553540000"
  codebase= "http://macromedia.com/flash/swflash.cab"
  width="215" height="355"><param name="movie"
  value="http://storefront.paypallabs.com/portablestore.swf?
  store_id=865851101a08012e006b000d60d4b7b8"/><param name="quality"
  value="high" /><param name="FlashVars"
  value="store_id=865851101a08012e006b000d60d4b7b8"><param
  name="allowScriptAccess" value="always" /><param
  name="allowNetworking" value="all" /><embed
```

41

```
allowScriptAccess="always" allowNetworking="all"
src="http://storefront.paypallabs.com/ps.swf?store_id=4b7b8"
quality="high"
pluginspage="http://www.macromedia.com/ getflashplayer"
type="application/x-shockwave-flash" width="215" height="355">
</embed></object>
```

As shown in Figure 2-14, embedding the code in a Custom HTML module will display the self-contained storefront module on your Joomla site. The PayPal servers handle all of the transactions for the store so you can focus on selling your products.

Figure 2-14. The PayPal store will appear on your Joomla site at the module position you select

The PayPal widget is even more compelling because of the trust the PayPal Corporation has generated in their brand. While a visitor may be hesitant to enter a credit card number into a site they have never previously visited because of fears of identity theft and fraud, a purchase through PayPal is restricted to that transaction, making it more likely first-time visitors will trust a purchase with this method. The fact that it is a widget makes it a natural for e-commerce functionality to be added to a Joomla site.

Summary

Joomla provides the foundation around which you can create nearly any type of web site. With the easy-to-use Custom HTML module, you can add third-party widgets and web services directly to your web site without any installation, coding, or modification to your site. You've learned how to use widgets to add calendars, maps, translation modules, and other features to your site.

The widgets shown in this chapter should be just the beginning of your journey to customize Joomla with widgets. There are literally hundreds of free widgets available on the Web. Google itself hosts many of these widgets in the Google Gadgets portion of its web site (`www.google.com/ig/directory?synd=open`) including games, finance modules, sports, news, and many other categories.

Although these types of modifications can make a Joomla site more robust, the customization that really sets one Joomla site apart from others is the use of a custom template. In the next chapter, you'll learn how to create a fully dynamic template that can provide the foundation for any type of template you might want to create in the future.

CHAPTER 3

■ ■ ■

Constructing a Dynamic Template

Creating an excellent Joomla template is something of an art. If you've read Chapter 6 of Beginning Joomla!, you already know the general structure and design of a very simple template. The template created in that chapter was a barebones example that included none of the advanced functionality that has become standard in popular Joomla templates. Further, the simple template didn't leverage the substantial features and flexibility available through the Joomla system. In this chapter you'll learn how to make a far most robust template that is infinitely configurable and dynamically changes based on the presentation requirements.

This chapter will lead you through the complete construction of a dynamic template, including:

- Designing the template

    - *Setting goals for the template*: How much flexibility do you want in a single template? What should be included in the template and what functionality should be added through modules instead?

    - *Using a spreadsheet to create the initial wireframe of your templates*: Use a spreadsheet as a tool to create your initial design wireframe of the site template.

- Implementing the template

    - *Creating the template skeleton*: Adding the basic HTML code, selecting the right Doctype, using the Joomla includes for proper position of module elements, setting up a single or multiple column layout.

    - *Using Twitter bootstrap for template styling*: The Twitter bootstrap CSS will give you advanced, compatible styling.

    - *Adding template parameters*: Using template parameters so the site administrator can reconfigure the template without modifying the template code or styles.

- Refining the template

    - *Joomla template specifics*: Using multiple CSS files in a template, sharing resources in a multi-template system.

    - *Advanced template design techniques*: Stylesheet tips, planning for CDN, versioning for resource files.

    - *Being mobile friendly*: Adding responsive design to a template to optimize your site for mobile devices.

Crafting a good dynamic template requires some forethought and planning. When you create a template, you're taking on the roles of graphic artist, user interface designer, and creative director all at once. The material in this chapter should help ease the decisions you have to make. You'll also be provided with a complete, working foundation template that you can adjust and modify to your own needs so you don't have to start from scratch.

Designing the Template

Some of the worst templates on the commercial market suffer from lack of fundamental layout expertise. They may have a fantastic appearance, but are so rigid that they are nearly useless when you deploy them on a real site. For example, most templates have a front page banner graphic like the one shown in Figure 3-1. There are many poorly designed templates that fail to include the option to turn off this banner graphic, so each and every page on the site must have a large graphic that takes up a great deal of the screen acreage. Advanced templates should always have a method to configure the layout to adapt to different types of pages.

Figure 3-1. *Well-designed templates can be used to display many page types, not just the home page with a large top banner*

One of the challenges faced by all template developers is the abstract nature of the task. Until the template is rendered as a web page by the Joomla system (which embeds the requested components, modules, headers, and so forth), the template itself is difficult to envision because it consists mostly of placeholder elements. This is much different from the design of static HTML pages or pages designed with a templating system such as Smarty (www.smarty.net) that have all the essential elements appear directly in the HTML code.

Advanced template development requires that the creator of the template foresee how the template will be used on a site and how it might appear with the myriad of extensions that a site deployer might deploy within its display area. Therefore, providing the most dynamic template with substantial user configuration options is of paramount importance for a template that will be used in the long term.

To this end, we'll decide on the needs of the template that will define what the template must accomplish before we begin actual template construction. Then we'll use a spreadsheet as a quick and dirty layout tool to wireframe how the various pages of the template will be displayed.

Setting Goals for the Template

Templates have a tendency to grow in number and complexity rather quickly. Sometimes it can be difficult to plan ahead and know exactly what templates you or your clients will need to complete the site properly. As with most aspects of Joomla site construction, however, a little planning can save a great deal of later work. To make the planning effective, you need to approach the task by setting goals in terms of the primary areas of web page design such as graphic layout, search engine optimization, and multi-purpose flexibility.

If you're hiring a graphic designer to make everything look good in the template, there will be a tendency to focus on the most graphically beautiful pages such as the homepage. However, in this age of the search engine, visitors are actually more likely to land on the content pages than the home page.

Before you begin creating your template, keep these things in mind:

- *Begin by drawing pencil/pen sketches of the page layouts*: This will help you determine the basic layout of the page. You might consider purchasing the book *Graphic Design Cookbook: Mix & Match Recipes for Faster, Better Layouts* by Leonard Koren and R. Wippo Meckler (Chronicle Books, 2001), which has a broad range of samples of basic layouts. The book presents the layout options in almost iconic fashion, so you'll find yourself using it effectively today and for years to come. It can be very helpful at the early stages of envisioning the site presentation.

- *Create a gallery of similar web sites you like*: You can bookmark pages, print them to paper, save PDFs of the layout, or whatever you find most convenient. Making a basic survey of other sites will be critical to making your site contemporary and will help you decide what areas of your Joomla site will require extra focus.

- *Define the needs of the client (even if it is you)*: The template should reflect the needs of the site including style (fun, professional, professionally fun) or market if the template is to be sold on a template market site.

- *Make search engine optimization decisions*: Sites that structure their pages in a particular way (semantic html coding, strategic heading choices, and so forth) can maximize their page rank in the search engines. These decisions are primarily implemented at the template level, so make choices in this area before beginning template construction.

- *Design with a two year lifetime in mind*: After the initial launch, most templates remain essentially static on a site for a long time with changes coming from new content, extensions, or minor display tweaks. If you make your template up-to-the-minute, when that minute passes, your site may appear out of fashion. Therefore, you should design enough features into the template (such as varying color schemes) that you can easily alter the site from the Administrator interface without significant new development. This type of flexible template allows the site to change even when there is no time or budget available for more fundamental changes or updates.

- *Determine if a single dynamic template can fulfill all requirements*: Most sites can use a single dynamic template if it can be adjusted through parameters and stylesheets to fit many of the presentation necessities of a site (homepage, navigation page, content pages, and so forth). Having a single template is usually preferable because it only requires maintaining a single PHP/HTML file, but depending on the demands of the site, it is not always possible. Some pages require special technology (such as video players, Flash, or HTML5), non-standard layout (such as some sitemaps), or use mashup technology (such as web APIs that bring information from other sources onto a page).

Once you have made decisions on these fundamentals, you're ready to start laying down the structure of the template. Creating the structure should always precede the beginning design of the template. It is easy to add good graphics atop a solid foundation structure, but a bad structure will require your design to fight, patch, and work around a poorly designed system to get the results you want.

Page Types Displayed by a Template

The structure of the template is determined by the basic menu structure that you will create (or already have created) in Joomla. Most Joomla sites need a template to accommodate at least three page types that will be used throughout the site:

- *Home page*: A home page will often have a large header graphic, various links to navigate to the primary content, feed icons (such as RSS and Atom feeds), and perhaps a latest news module of some type.

- *Subhome page*: A subhome page displays the section or category and the articles within it. The design of the subhome mirrors the basic layout of the home page but generally has a smaller version of the main banner (or masthead). Most sites need more than one subhome page type. On a Joomla ecommerce site, for example, one subhome page might show the list of how-to articles available on the site, while another subhome page may be a landing page to navigate the online catalog.

- *Article page*: The most fundamental content piece of a Joomla site is always an article. An article page usually features less navigation (because the user is already on the desired content) with a small top banner graphic. For most sites, this page will be the most important because visitors are likely to arrive directly at an article page through a search engine.

To create a good dynamic template, you will need to create the HTML so that it is flexible enough to accommodate all of these different page types. For example, the goal of the home page is to entice the visitor into the site, which may be best served by having a single column layout with impressive graphics or animation. In contrast, the goal of an article page is to convey information, so it may favor a standard three-column layout.

The template should adjust itself to the needs of the different page display types. Expanding and collapsing columns, including places for JavaScript embedded content, and providing header injection areas are a few of the needs a template should accommodate. After you've collected a gallery of similar web sites and created simple sketches of page designs you might like, you can formalize your page design using your favorite spreadsheet.

Drafting the Template with a Spreadsheet

Most people don't think of a spreadsheet as a design tool, but using Microsoft Excel, Google Docs spreadsheet, or Open Office spreadsheet can enable you to quickly draft various layouts that can help you make the hard decisions of site design. These layouts are not meant to be the type of compositions that graphic artists render for a client. Instead, they are a simple visualization tool to imagine where the components and modules might be. Further, you can test various color schemes that you might be considering for the site so you can set up the basic palette of the site before the graphics and CSS are created. Coordinating the color, layout, and graphics will help give the site visual coherence.

Start by creating three worksheets (or more if you have selected a more varied or ambitious goal for your template) called Home, Subhome, and Article. Using the border and fill properties available in your spreadsheet, create the layout of your templates. In Figure 3-2, you can see the basic layout that might be used for the home page. I generally use specific colors to represent the major areas of the template (left column, center column, header, and so forth) so I can see these same areas on the different worksheets even if they alter in size and shape.

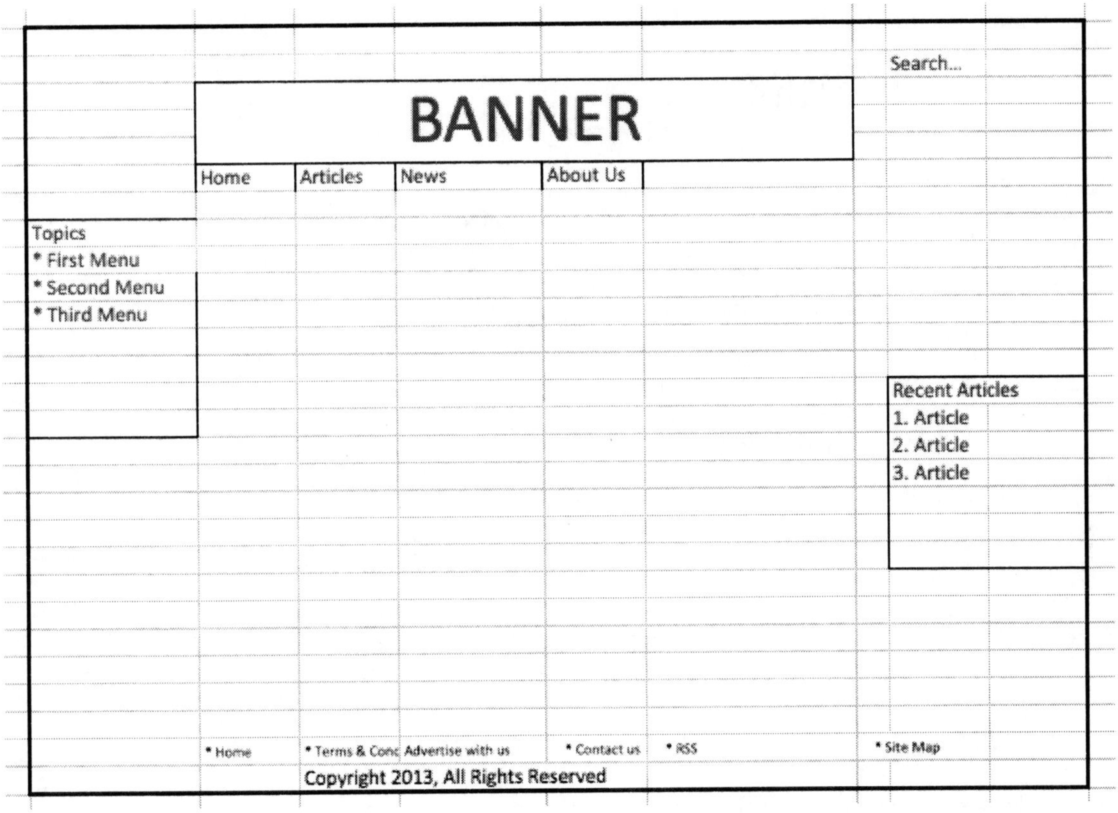

Figure 3-2. *A basic home page layout using a spreadsheet for layout and design*

You can see an example of a subhome page template in Figure 3-3. The subhome is missing the central big banner that is present on the home page to provide additional information space. There are generally a number of modules on the subhome page type that show the most recent articles or highlighted articles that can be found in this site area. In many site layouts that include tabs or pill menus across the top of the header, the subhome will be the destination if the user clicks on one of those tabs.

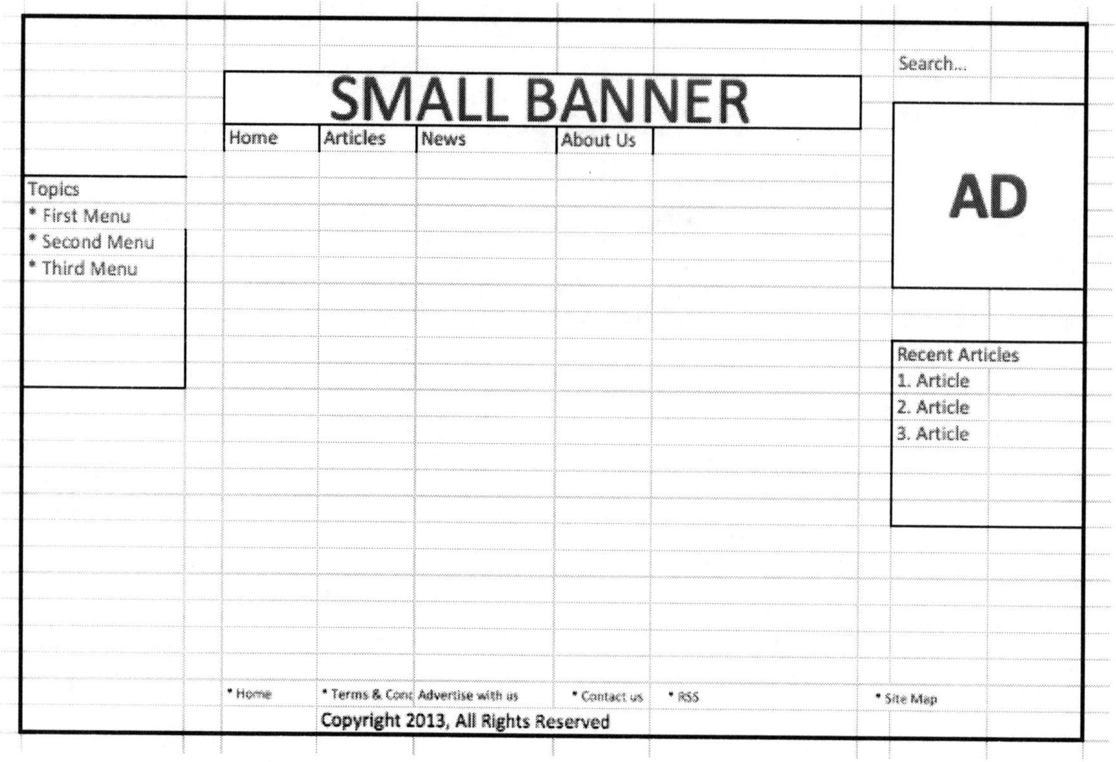

Figure 3-3. *The subhome template is primarily for navigation*

The Article page template is perhaps the most important template (see Figure 3-4) because it's likely the majority of your page views will occur there. Many visitors will land on your article pages, so it is important to entice them to other parts of the site from here as well. The two sometimes conflicting goals of the article page are to present the material of the page in a clear and unobstructed way and at the same time offer enough related content from other parts of the site to encourage multiple page views. Effective template layout must attempt to balance these two goals to ensure the success of the site.

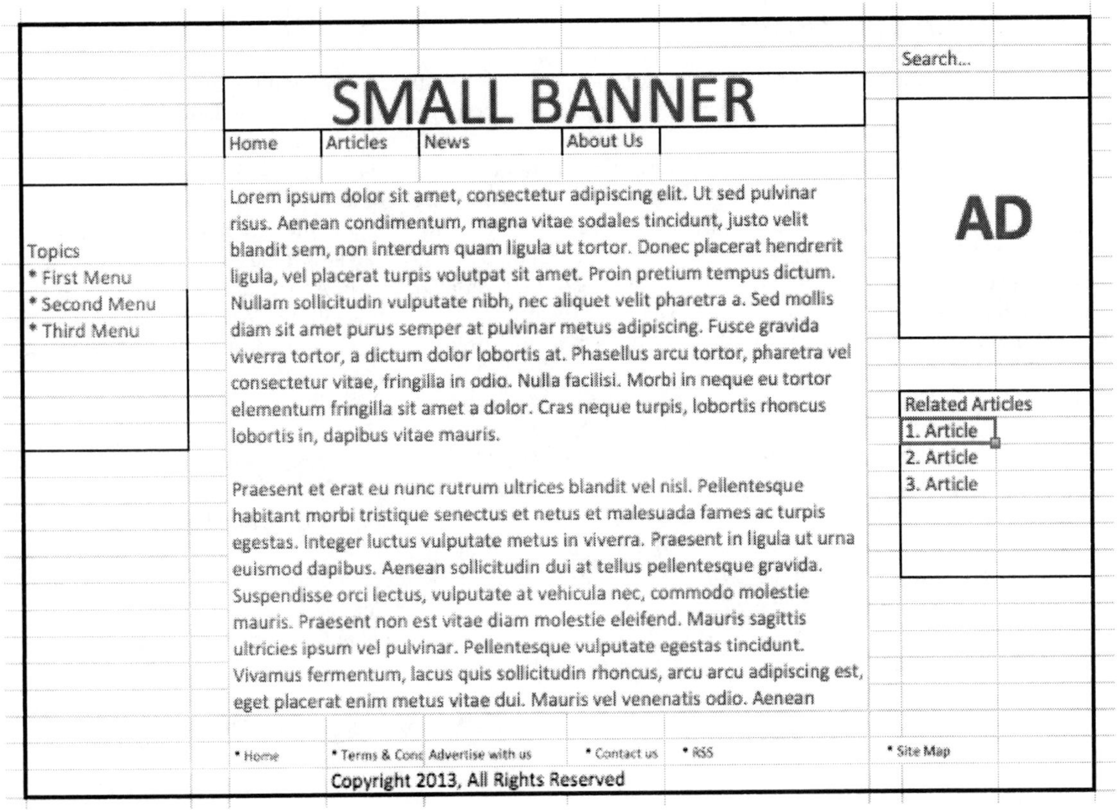

Figure 3-4. *The article page is extremely important because search engines links will land many visitors there*

■ **Tip** When creating the initial layout, it is often a good idea to look at the available module types in the Joomla Module Manager. That will help you to avoid forgetting some module type you may want to use in your template. Likewise, you can go to the Joomla Extension Library (`http://extensions.joomla.org`) and look for some non-default extensions that your site might use (such as drop-down menus) that would affect the final layout of the template.

Once you have one initial sheet drafted, you can copy this layout to the other sheets and make modifications for the specialized display. This process should be quick and dirty. The point of the exercise is to determine the basic layouts that the dynamic template will need to accommodate and provide a reference that you can re-examine when you're in the difficult and sometimes disorienting process of converting your template vision to HTML, CSS, and JavaScript code. With your page types designed, let's begin implementing the pages you've designed.

Implementing the Template

With the basic groundwork of the template laid, it's time to get into the actual implementation. Constructing a template from scratch can be daunting because there are so many choices to make. The good news is that you don't have to make these choices all at once. Even though this chapter presents the wide range of possibilities, you can begin by only implementing the ones that you see are immediately relevant to your situation. Then in subsequent versions you can progressively refine the template as your site or deployment comes into sharper focus.

Start your new template by creating a folder to contain all the necessary files and the subfolders that will contain the styles, images, and scripts that the template will use. This folder can be located anywhere on your hard drive as it will become the installation source that the Joomla Administrator interface will access to install on the system.

Most Joomla templates have standardized on a basic organization that makes editing the template easier. Create a main folder to hold the template that matches the name of your template so it is easy to find and reference, such as:

```
aj_dynamic/
```

Make the name of the main folder unique and distinctive—not "mytemplate" or "template1" or something else that is generic. It is very common for beginning template developers to name their first templates template1, template2, and so on, and then later become confused as to which template is which (for example, which template was the one for the home page and which was the one for the online catalog).

Also avoid using the name of the site in the template. Almost invariably a person who creates one site will later create others. A template "supersite" then gets renamed "kindasupersite" to match the new site even though it is the same template. Picking a name that doesn't match the site (such as "atomic") makes template re-use cleaner.

Now create the following subfolders inside that directory:

- aj_dynamic/css/
- aj_dynamic/images/
- aj_dynamic/js/
- aj_dynamic/html/

■ **Tip** While it is highly recommended to look at the templates created by quality template vendors, keep in mind that template vendors often take shortcuts that may not be easy to understand or advisable to copy. Always use one of the templates included with the Joomla system as the basic reference template as these templates are created as the Rosetta Stones of template design. The Joomla team plans for changes to the Joomla system well into the future, so the templates actually included with Joomla are the best guide to creating a template that will be compatible with current and future systems. You can find the sample templates that ship with each version of Joomla in the templates/ folder of your Joomla installation.

Once you have the folder structure in place, you're ready to start adding the core files. There are only two files that are required by all templates the index.php file and the templateDetails.xml file, so that's where we'll begin.

Create the Index and Template Details Files

For most templates, all of the HTML and PHP code that generates the page display is held in a single file named index.php. Because that single file contains many different parts, we'll break up the construction of the file into several sections. This chapter is about building a dynamic template – not just downloading and installing it.

For that reason, let's get a very primitive template created and installed to your Joomla installation. Then we'll edit the template while it's active and in-place on the site (just like professional template designers do) so you can immediately see changes made to the template on the actual Joomla site.

Start by creating a new file at the root directory of your template, name the file index.php, and add the following code:

```php
<?php
// no direct access
defined( '_JEXEC' ) or die( 'Restricted access' );

// Template setup code
$user =& JFactory::getUser();
?>
<!DOCTYPE html PUBLIC "-//W3C//DTD XHTML 1.0 Transitional//EN"
    "http://www.w3.org/TR/xhtml1/DTD/xhtml1-transitional.dtd">
<html xmlns="http://www.w3.org/1999/xhtml"
        xml:lang="<?php echo $this->language; ?>"
        lang="<?php echo $this->language; ?>">
<head>
</head>
<body>
<h1>Advanced Joomla! Template</h1>
</body>
</html>
```

We'll examine this file closely in the next section, but let's move on to create the template details file so we can get the template installed and see it in action.

Create another file at the root directory called templateDetails.xml and add the following code:

```xml
<?xml version="1.0" encoding="utf-8"?>
<!DOCTYPE install PUBLIC "-//Joomla! 2.5//DTD template 1.0//EN"
  "http://www.joomla.org/xml/dtd/1.6/template-install.dtd">
<extension version="2.5" type="template" client="site">
    <name>aj_dynamic</name>
    <creationDate>25 September 2012</creationDate>
    272103_1_EnDan Rahmel</author>
    <authorEmail>drahmel@joomlajumpstart.com</authorEmail>
    <authorUrl>http://www.joomlajumpstart.com</authorUrl>
    <copyright>Copyright (c)2012-2013 Dan Rahmel. </copyright>
    <license>GNU GPL</license>
    <version>2.5.0</version>
    <description>Responsive template created in the book
  Advanced Joomla!</description>

    <files>
        <filename>index.php</filename>
        <filename>templateDetails.xml</filename>
    </files>

    <positions>
        <position>debug</position>
        <position>position-0</position>
    </positions>
```

```
    <config>
        <fields name="params">
        </fields>
    </config>
</extension>
```

Once you've create these files, install the template to your Joomla system. If you have Joomla installed on your local machine (preferred for development), you can use the Extension Manager to point Joomla directly at the template directory, and it will install from there. If you need to install on a remote server such as a directory on your ISP ftp site, you should zip all of the directories and use the upload functionality of the Extension Manager to upload it.

Once installed, use the Template Manager to select the template as the default template by clicking on the gold star in the column marked *Default*. Go to your Joomla site in your browser and you should see the template headline. Congratulations! You've created the template installation that you'll use as a foundation to develop the template. To edit the template on the remote server, you can use the excellent open source text editor *jEdit*.

Editing the Template on a Remote Server with jEdit

Although it is preferable to perform development on a local server, that isn't always possible. If you already have an editing solution you're comfortable using, please use that. If not, I would like to recommend the free, open source, Java-based editor named *jEdit*. It is a fantastic editor that features syntax highlighting, cross-platform (Windows, MacOS, and Linux) support, robust plug-in architecture, advanced macro language, and more. Most importantly, it allows you to directly edit files on a remote server either through the FTP protocol or using SSH/SFTP. The jEdit application performs remote editing transparently to the user so it appears as if editing is happening on a local hard drive.

I'll quickly take you through the steps of setup for remote editing with jEdit so you can get started right away. First, you'll need to install Java if it isn't already on your system. If you type the command `java` at the command prompt of your system and it prints the usage information, you already have it installed. If not, you can download it from the Sun web site (`www.java.com/getjava/`).

Once Java is installed, download one of the jEdit installers from the web site (`http://www.jedit.org/index.php?page=download`). If you want to compile it from the source code, you can get the code at the project home page (`http://sourceforge.net/projects/jedit/`). The installer will create the desktop icons and other standard options.

Execute the jEdit application and select the Plugins ➤ Plugin Manager option to display the currently installed plugins. At the top of the window, you will see three selection buttons: Manage, Update, and Install. Click the Install button and you should see a variety of available plugins. In the filter text box, type FTP and you should see the FTP plugin listed with a check box in the far left column. Click on the check box and then click the Install button that is below the plugin info text box.

The FTP plugin will be installed and you may or may not have to quit and restart jEdit before it is available. If it's active, you should be able to click on the Plugins menu and the FTP menu should be available in the list. From the FTP sub-menu, select the *Open from FTP Server* option if you will be editing from an FTP server or *Open from Secure FTP Server* if you will be editing through an SSH session.

A dialog box will appear that has text boxes for remote host, username, and password. If you're accessing your files through an FTP server, you will simply enter your host address like this:

```
ftp.example.com:21
```

Enter your username and password that you use to log into your FTP server and then click the OK button. That's it! You should be presented with a standard file open dialog box that lets you browse through the files on the server as if they were on your local drive, as shown in Figure 3-5. Selecting a file opens it in the text editor. If you want to open another file on the server, selecting the File ➤ Open menu option will display the files in the location of the currently displayed file. If you're editing a file on the remote server, the file dialog will show other files there. Saving changes works just as expected—the File ➤ Save option will save the changes to the remote server.

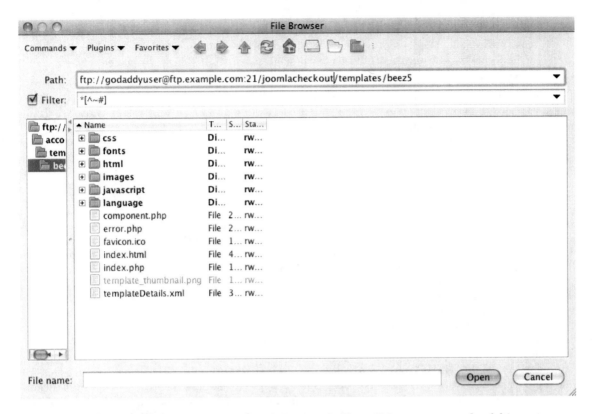

Figure 3-5. *The jEdit file dialog lets you browse and open remote files as if they were on your local drive*

If you continue to use jEdit, I would recommend installing these plug-ins as well:

- *Beauty*: Provides code beautifiers for code reformatting, including PHP.

- *CSS Editor*: Allows you to select a CSS block in your code or CSS file and then provides all of the common CSS options as drop-down menus for easy editing. It also provides a great GUI interface for common CSS directives.

- *JDiff Plugin*: Provides color differencing between two files—even if the files are located on different servers. Very useful in comparing a local file to a remote file and determining the differences.

- *JSLint*: JavaScript code source checker and validator based on the popular tool created by Douglas Crockford (`www.jslint.com`).

- *MacroManager*: Provides access to hundreds of macros through a simple GUI interface similar to the Plugin Manager. I would recommend installing the Sort Lines macro and the WikiWord macro.

- *PHPParser Plugin*: Parses PHP code for errors and highlights the code problems in the scrollbar. This code check provides an excellent way of checking your Joomla extension code for errors before uploading a new version.

- *SideKick*: Provides a dockable window for other plugins.

- *XML*: Parses XML, HTML, JavaScript, and CSS files and provides an expandable tree display of the document. Also provides a function that properly indents XML, which can be used very effectively with strict HTML code to see where matching brackets are missing.

I've used jEdit for years on both MacOS and Windows to edit my Joomla files on all my remote hosts. It is a fantastic tool for an unbelievable price (free). This editor is particularly useful for making on-server tweaks to a Joomla module, or in our case, a new template.

Examining the Template Foundation

With the template installed on the server, open the index.php file in your favorite editor and let's take a look at the code. Most of the header code that appears at the top of the template will be the same as most templates you create.

For a traditional static HTML page, the DOCTYPE block is the first thing that appears in the file (I will discuss this block in the next section). A Joomla template file usually differs in that the DOCTYPE is preceded by a small block of PHP code that does the basic setup for the page, determines if the visitor needs to be redirected to another page before rendering begins, and kills the executing process if the template is accessed outside the Joomla framework.

In the template example, you can see the defined or die() logic that ensures the template is loaded by the Joomla system. To take advantage of the Joomla system settings, the <html> tag has been modified to include a namespace reference and a language reference using the lang attribute. Because Joomla is international, adding this tag allows the Joomla template to tell the visitor's browser the default language selected for the site that was chosen through the Site ➤ Global Configuration menu in the Administrator interface. This can aid the browser in automatically selecting the proper character set for page display.

Presumably you're already familiar with this basic HTML document structure, but it is useful to review particulars of each section. Remember that when you're constructing a template file, you're not just making a single page where small design errors will have a small effect. If you have an error in your template, it will affect most of the site. Selecting the incorrect Doctype is generally the first mistake made by beginning template designers. For this reason, we should examine it closely.

Understanding the Effects of Doctype Settings

The very first element of an HTML document (or the first output element of a template) is the DOCTYPE. The tag (that differs in structure from a traditional HTML tag) instructs the browser on the format of the HTML information to follow. Selecting a Doctype of one kind and then formatting your template with another style can lead to a great deal of frustration when dealing with browser presentation and site HTML validation. A standard DOCTYPE tag looks like this:

```
<!DOCTYPE html PUBLIC "-//W3C//DTD XHTML 1.0 Transitional//EN"
    "http://www.w3.org/TR/xhtml1/DTD/xhtml1-transitional.dtd">
```

The DOCTYPE for an HTML5 document is much simpler:

```
<!DOCTYPE html>
```

There have been several DOCTYPE specifications since HTML was first released (and many specialty standards) that have different expectations in how the browser will render the page. Some examples include HTML 4, XHTML 1, XHTML 1.1, HTML 5, MathML, SVG, HTML 2, and HTML 3.2.

■ **Tip**   It is extremely important to make sure you include a DOCTYPE tag in your template. Without it, the browser needs to guess how to properly interpret the HTML tags of your site pages. If the browser guesses incorrectly (and each browser seems to have a different default), the presentation of your site will vary greatly. The easier you make it for browsers to understand how you want your page displayed, the more likely visitors will see the page exactly as you intended.

For the last several years, the Joomla team has been moving toward making all of the available templates use the strict definitions for page tags often known as XHTML. At the very heart of XHTML is the idea that HTML can conform to the XML standard (which is a data exchange standard). XML has some strict rules such as the requirements that all opening tags must have a closing tag and that all tags must be lowercase (with a few exceptions described in the standard). The most useful aspects of XHTML have been incorporated into the HTML5 standard, which seems destined to become the standard for the web.

To understand the difference between XHTML and one of the older standards, it may be easiest to see a few examples. In traditional HTML, you might have a line that looked like this:

```
John is running.<BR>Then John stopped.<p>
```

This code violates the two rules mentioned—it has two tags with no closing tags and there is an uppercase tag. To rewrite in XHTML, that same line of page code might look like this:

```
John is running.<br/><p>Then John stopped.</p>
```

This code uses the "short" version of a closed tag (for example, `<br/>`), which serves the same function as an empty open and close tag (such as `<br></br>`). Also, the paragraph tag is used as a wrapper to delineate the paragraph. The XHTML standard contains all of the elements of the HTML4 standard, but they comply with the XML structure standards.

Choosing the Proper Doctype

Choosing a standard (and a DOCTYPE that specifies it) is not always easy. Although you can set your template to use a DOCTYPE that enforces strict XHTML, there are many conventions that conflict with the strict definitions (such as the unclosed line break like `<br>`), so HTML document validation checkers will generate many errors that are not relevant to your actual template formatting. A DOCTYPE that specifies a "transitional" type is fairly forgiving, so errors reported by an HTML checker will more likely lead you to real problems instead of "crying wolf" at many unimportant minor violations.

The tag for the transitional Doctype looks like this:

```
<!DOCTYPE html PUBLIC "-//W3C//DTD XHTML 1.0 Transitional//EN"
    "http://www.w3.org/TR/xhtml1/DTD/xhtml1-transitional.dtd">
```

If you wish to create your template in strict XHTML, you can use this Doctype at the head of your template:

```
<!DOCTYPE html PUBLIC "-//W3C//DTD XHTML 1.0 Strict//EN"
"http://www.w3.org/TR/xhtml1/DTD/xhtml1-strict.dtd">
```

You can always change the type if you find "strict" type is too nit-picky or if you subsequently modify the template to conform to all the XHTML rules. You can see a complete list of valid DOCTYPEs on the W3 site (www.w3.org/QA/2002/04/valid-dtd-list.html).

If you'd like to use the newer simplified Doctype, you can use this simple line:

```
<!DOCTYPE html>
```

This type is the one supported by HTML5 and will be the adopted standard of the future. If most of your visitors use a modern browser, this tag is the one to choose.

■ **Tip**   Use the items reported by various HTML checkers (such as the popular Unicorn validator at http://validator.w3.org/unicorn) as a guideline reference rather than an absolute rule. In the real world, correcting some of the violations actually creates errors in browser renderings because many browsers do not correctly support the DOCTYPE standards. Further, large vendors regularly violate these rules so that accessing a popular web site (for example, www.msn.com) will generate a flood of errors. The best policy is to comply with the standards as much as possible, but make exceptions when it is causing problems for your page rendering.

Although the Doctype is a simple single line definition, it can have far-reaching effects on the document display. A page can literally implode when the incorrect Doctype is used (or the tag is omitted altogether). When there is no Doctype tag, the browser is left to its own devices to guess the formatting of the document information. Sadly, most browsers guess incorrectly most of the time, so leaving the Doctype tag out of the template definition is a disservice to your template.

Augmenting the Basic Template

With the working template skeleton installed, we can start building the core functionality of the dynamic template. For the template styling, we'll be using Twitter Bootstrap (http://twitter.github.com/bootstrap/), which is an excellent, free, front-end toolkit created by Twitter and made available for public use. It provides an extremely flexible CSS grid and styling system for page layout, forms, icons, and more. With a single file include (or two if you want the responsive CSS capabilities for mobile display), you can add a lot of styling to your template that will automatically make it likely your template will look good.

Starting from version 3, the Joomla developers have adopted Twitter Bootstrap and included it in the Joomla system. Bootstrap is used to layout and format the Administrator interface. Because we want our template to be compatible with Joomla versions before V3, this example template will include the necessary Bootstrap files to install with the template.

Styling for a template should be placed in the head section of the HTML document so the page appears correctly as soon as it is displayed. Let's start by expanding this portion of the index file you've created.

Creating the Head Section

The head section for a template refers specifically to the material that appears between the <head> tags. Anything that appears between these tags does not display in the browser window. Instead, it contains all of the information that the browser needs to properly display the rest of the page. This generally means:

- *Title of the document*: The title displayed in the title bar of the browser window and perhaps the single most important item a search engine reads. Because the title in a Joomla system is determined by the menu selection, in a template this item simply echoes a passed variable that contains the title for that menu item.

- *Metadata*: Data (such as the page description and keywords) about the document that is not directly displayed in the page, but is used by search engines and other technology (such as JavaScript page view trackers) to properly index and collate the page.

- *Style sheets*: The linked style sheets and `<style>` tags that determine the display of the page.

- *Core JavaScript and libraries*: All of the main JavaScript files for a document, including framework libraries such as jQuery, MooTools, or YUI as well as common JavaScript function files should appear in the head section.

Items in the head section essentially set the stage for the rest of the page rendering. In a Joomla template, much of the head is dynamically generated depending on the page being displayed. For example, the HTML metadata for a page (description, keywords, and so forth) is rendered by the Joomla system with a single line. In a Joomla template, the first line in the head section should look like this:

```
<jdoc:include type="head" />
```

This single line, when rendered for the page, will appear like this:

```
<base href="http://www.joomlajumpstart.com/" />
<meta http-equiv="content-type" content="text/html; charset=utf-8" />
<meta name="generator" content="Joomla! - Open Source Content Management" />
<title>Advanced Joomla home page</title>
<link href="/index.php?format=feed&amp;type=rss" rel="alternate"
    type="application/rss+xml" title="RSS 2.0" />
<link href="/index.php?format=feed&amp;type=atom" rel="alternate"
    type="application/atom+xml" title="Atom 1.0" />

<link href="http://www.joomlajumpstart.com
    /index.php/component/search/?format=opensearch"
    rel="search" title="Search Advanced Joomla!"
    type="application/opensearchdescription+xml" />
<script src="/media/system/js/mootools-core.js"
    type="text/javascript"></script>
<script src="/media/system/js/core.js" type="text/javascript"></script>
<script src="/media/system/js/caption.js" type="text/javascript"></script>
<script type="text/javascript">
    window.addEvent('load', function() {});
</script>
```

You can see that Joomla injects metadata, script includes, and more. Components, modules, and plugins can all inject content into the header and that content is rendered with this `include`. The template designer doesn't have much control over the data that is rendered in this section. For that reason, it is included at the top of the head section so that even if styles are injected in this area, the template style sheets that follow can override styles defined by the modules. However, you should always examine the content rendered by this `include` on your production site to make sure there isn't something rendered by a particular component that may cause problems.

Let's edit the `index.php` file and change the head section so it appears like this:

```
<head>
    <jdoc:include type="head" />
    <meta http-equiv="Content-Style-Type" content="text/css" />
    <!-- Viewport definition for responsive style sheets -->
    <meta name="viewport" content="width=device-width, initial-scale=1.0" />

    <!-- Favicons for browser tabs, Google TV bookmark, and iPhone/iPad-->
    <link rel="icon" href="/ui/template/" type="image/png" />
```

```
<!-- iPhone standard bookmark icon (57x57px) home screen -->
<link rel="apple-touch-icon" href="/ui/template/" />
<!-- iPhone Retina display icon (114x114px) home screen -->
<link rel="apple-touch-icon" href="/ui/template/" sizes="114x114" />

<!-- Load minimized Twitter Bootstrap styles -->
<link rel="stylesheet" href="<?php echo $template_path;
    ?>/css/bootstrap.min.css" type="text/css" />
<link rel="stylesheet" href="<?php echo $template_path;
    ?>/css/bootstrap-responsive.min.css" type="text/css" />

<!-- Load custom font from Google fonts -->
<link href="http://fonts.googleapis.com/css?family=Cabin+Condensed:700"
    rel="stylesheet" type="text/css" />

<!-- Load other template-specific CSS -->
<link rel="stylesheet" href="<?php echo $template_path;
    ?>/css/template.css" type="text/css" />
<link rel="stylesheet" href="<?php echo $template_path;
    ?>/css/position.css" type="text/css" />

<!--[if lte IE 6]>
<link href="<?php echo $template_path; ?>/css/ieonly.css"
    rel="stylesheet" type="text/css" />
<style>
    #content{height:100%;overflow:hidden}
</style>
<![endif]-->

<script type="text/javascript" src="<?php echo $template_path;
    ?>/js/jquery.js"></script>
<script type="text/javascript" src="<?php echo $template_path;
    ?>/js/common.js"></script>
</head>
```

You will notice that the Joomla include begins the head section so all of the system code is rendered first. After the Joomla include, we've added the following items:

- *Content style*: Defines the default style sheet language for the page. Not absolutely necessary, but good practice to include.

- *Viewport definition*: For the page to render properly on tablets and mobile browsers (when responsive layout is used), this tag tells the browser that the template will control the scaling so the auto zooming functionality doesn't treat the page like a generic non-mobile page.

- *Favicon definitions*: Until recently, a single favicon definition was good enough for most browsers. The explosion of mobile devices, high-resolution screens, and home screen icons has made it necessary to supply multiple icons so they will display properly at the various rendering locations.

- *Twitter bootstrap files*: The two Twitter bootstrap files are loaded here. In the next section, we'll download them and add them to your template.

- *Custom font*: Designers have always been constrained by the poor selection of web browser fonts. Now, all major browsers support the ability to download a vector-based font for use during page rendering so pages can appear refined and distinctive. Google hosts a number of these fonts for free use and this template uses the Cabin Condensed font.

- *Template-specific CSS files*: Styles specific to the template.

- *Internet Explorer 6 CSS*: Any CSS that needs to be used to allow the page to be rendered properly on IE6. As IE6 becomes less common, this style include may disappear from modern templates.

- *JavaScript files*: Any additional JavaScript files required by the template.

The head portion of the HTML should contain only the elements that can't be loaded later. If, for example, you only need the functionality from a JavaScript library when the user clicks on an item, it's best to add the script tag that loads it as late in the HTML as possible. Pushing non-essential file loads outside the head section means that page rendering can begin more quickly in the user's browser.

■ **Note**   The `<style>` or `<script>` tags located in the header load external files, such as a JavaScript library or a CSS file. These tags are known as "blocking" because page rendering does not start until the files they reference are loaded. When located in the head section, that means the browser will display a blank page until the files load. In practice, this generally isn't very important because most of the page content is loaded from the same web server. However, if you load a CSS or a JavaScript file from another site, if that site goes offline or is blocked by a corporate firewall, your page won't render until the visitor's browser times-out trying to retrieve that content. That generally means that if the external server is offline, the browser displays a blank page for 30 seconds. For more information and workarounds, see the "Asynchronous Loading" section of Chapter 9.

If you refreshed the page after making these changes to the head section, the page would show a number of page not found errors as it tried to load files that we haven't put in place yet. To start, create empty files at the following locations in your template so you can add code to them later:

- `aj_dynamic/css/template.css`
- `aj_dynamic/css/position.css`
- `aj_dynamic/css/ieonly.css`
- `aj_dynamic/js/common.js`

Downloading Twitter Bootstrap and jQuery

For Twitter bootstrap, you have several options. You can download the basic versions of Bootstrap here:

`http://twitter.github.com/bootstrap/`

You can also customize exactly which components of Twitter Bootstrap you want for your template and download a custom minimized version of the framework here:

`http://twitter.github.com/bootstrap/customize.html`

Alternately, you could allow the Bootstrap files to be served directly from NetDNA's CDN (www.bootstrapcdn.com/) by replacing the two Twitter style includes with the following link:

```
<link href="//netdna.bootstrapcdn.com/
twitter-bootstrap/2.1.1/css/bootstrap-combined.min.css" rel="stylesheet">
```

Finally, you could copy the version of Twitter Bootstrap included with the Joomla installation from the following path:

```
/media/jui/css/bootstrap.min.css
```

Which choice you make depends on a number of factors. I like to host my own libraries because that means if the site is up, the styles are being properly served. If another host were to go out of business or their servers were overwhelmed with requests, you site would suffer—and often you wouldn't know it. However, if the host is operating properly, your page benefits with a faster page load for your visitors because the browser limits the number of concurrent requests by host. That means placing files on a different host means it will load more files in parallel.

Note   It may seem counter-intuitive to have a separate copy of Bootstrap in your template when it is already included natively with Joomla. Bootstrap is still fairly young and each revision seems to bring a substantial number of changes that break existing deployments. If you use the version included with Joomla and the Joomla team upgrades that version in the future, your template may break. Not to mention the number of different versions of Joomla that site administrators who use your template may have installed. By including Bootstrap yourself, you are in control of any Bootstrap upgrades and you can update your template accordingly.

For jQuery, you have similar options. You can download the current version of jQuery from the jQuery web site (http://jquery.com/download/) or use one of the many CDN hosts. To use the Google CDN, replace the jQuery script tag with:

```
<script src=
  "//ajax.googleapis.com/ajax/libs/jquery/1.8.1/jquery.min.js">
</script>
```

Using jQuery from the Google CDN is one of the most popular methods of loading jQuery around the web. This popularity provides the added advantage that if the browser has recently visited a site that uses the Google CDN for jQuery, when the user visits your Joomla site, the browser will automatically use the locally cached version of jQuery and your page load time will be minimized.

Checking the Template Load

Once you have set up the directories and uploaded the proper files to your template directory, you should be able to refresh the Joomla site and all the files (except the favicon files, which we'll create later) should load properly. If you have other JavaScript libraries (such as jQuery UI) that you want to use for the template, you can add them to the proper directory and modify the template accordingly.

You can duplicate the head section of a template verbatim for most templates as there are not many variations of the head section since it defines the foundation elements of the document. The body section of the document that we will construct next will display the content of the page and will vary much more sharply from template to template.

Create the Body Section

The majority of time spent on template development occurs in fashioning the `<body>` section so it correctly presents the CMS content. In this section, you'll learn how to construct a multi-column body section that will dynamically change based on the modules available for each module section. Before we begin, it will be useful to examine the considerations of using semantic HTML or XHTML, which you learned a little bit about in the earlier section on DOCTYPE.

Semantic HTML or XHTML

Web developers and graphic designers who focus on the proper rules for using HTML tags often pay close attention to what are known as "semantic design principles." While the XHTML standard sets the technical rules of tag use, the semantic HTML design philosophy chooses the best way to use the tags `http://alistapart.com/article/ semanticsinhtml5`. A semantic HTML or XHTML designer seeks to use tags in specific ways to make a page more machine-readable for search engine indexing, accessibility, and text-only browsing. In other words, make it easy for a machine to understand and access the content of a page.

For example, a traditional designer who needs some white space to visually separate the first paragraph from the second paragraph might simply add a number of sequential paragraph tags (for example, `<p></p><p></p><p></p>`). While this conforms to the XHTML standard, for a semantic designer, this would be poor form. A search engine spider analyzing the page would try and understand the role of the three empty paragraphs in the context of the page—for which there is no semantic sense. The empty elements would add more "noise" to the page that a spider needs to overcome while processing. Instead of adding multiple empty elements, by adding spacing to a CSS style for a single element, you would achieve the same effect while keeping the page semantically "clean."

The intention of semantic design is to separate style from content. By doing so, a spider/page analyzer/page processor has a much higher chance of understanding the clear information on the page. Keeping the styling in the CSS also makes the page easier to edit, maintain, and refine because all of the presentation information is held in one place—the style sheet. This also makes most page files smaller, allowing them to load into the browser (or spider) marginally quicker. Additionally, changes to the presentation don't affect the content of the document itself.

The intentions and advantages to semantic design should be clear to any experienced Joomla user. One of the reasons Joomla has gained so much popularity over the years is the ability to change the presentation of the entire site by simply installing a new template or adjusting an existing one. This mirrors the objectives of semantic designers—to separate presentation from content. The more closely a template follows the semantic design guidelines, the more flexible it is to be customized and extended.

The template body that you'll now construct will seek to follow the ideas of semantic HTML by placing as much layout and spacing information as possible in the template style sheets and keeping the actual HTML as minimal as possible to contain the most meaningful organizational tagging possible. One of the tremendous advantages of using an existing CSS framework such as Twitter Bootstrap is that most of the core styles have already been designed for us.

Creating a Multi-Column Body

The body of the template generally contains the various `<div>` tags that specify the columns, including the placeholders for module locations and the component rendering. In the past, templates were made up of tables that defined the boundaries of columns and other positions. These are rarely seen now as designers have traded the inflexibility of table layout for the use of `<div>` tags, `<span>` tags, and CSS rules to achieve much greater control over the final page display.

For these rules, Bootstrap sets up a grid system for easy, attractive layout. Grids have long been used for print layout (see `http://en.wikipedia.org/wiki/Grid_(page_layout)`) to make attractive pages very quickly. Predefined column sizes, built-in margins, and exact positioning all made using a grid system the standard for layout in print for everything from advertising to newspaper pages. When CSS had evolved enough to support a web-based version of the grid system, CSS frameworks began to appear, such as the popular 960 Grid System (`http://960.gs/`).

Subsequently, Twitter open sourced Bootstrap, which provided not only a fixed and fluid grid, but also included many styling refinements that made something as simple as a button appear stylish and colorful by adding only a simple class or two to existing HTML. It makes template creation and design a pleasure.

The most basic decision you need to make (and you can easily change your mind) is choosing whether your template layout will be fixed or fluid. A fixed grid means that the grid is a specific width (in Bootstrap, this width is 940px by default) and the 12 columns that make up the grid split up that space. That means that each column will always be exactly 70 pixels in width (with the remainder of the space used by margins and gutters). With a fluid grid, the columns are a percentage of the total browser window width, so if a browser window is 2000 pixels wide, the column will be much wider than a column where the browser window is 800 pixels wide.

There are advantages and drawbacks to fixed and fluid layouts. The fixed layout is generally easier to design because the columns are always the same size and graphics can be specifically scaled to match the exact column width. However, on the increasingly large displays, a fixed layout only uses a finite amount of the screen space with the rest occupied by large gutters. Fluid layouts, while challenging for graphic elements, will use all the space available and work very well for sites like Joomla in which the text content can reflow to use the extra space. In this template, we'll use the fluid layout (but you can change it by simply removing the -fluid suffix from the element classes).

Let's modify our body element to see how a simple grid looks. Insert the following code between the <body> tags:

```
<style>
.color {
    background-color: gray;
    text-align: center;
    color:white;
}
</style>
<div class="container-fluid">
    <div class="row-fluid">
        <div class="span1 color">1</div>
        <div class="span1 color">2</div>
        <div class="span1 color">3</div>
        <div class="span1 color">4</div>
        <div class="span1 color">5</div>
        <div class="span1 color">6</div>
        <div class="span1 color">7</div>
        <div class="span1 color">8</div>
        <div class="span1 color">9</div>
        <div class="span1 color">10</div>
        <div class="span1 color">11</div>
        <div class="span1 color">12</div>
    </div>
</div>
```

When you refresh the page, you should see a page that looks like the one shown in Figure 3-6. The white space on the left and the right sides of the columns is called the gutter. There are automatically margins between the columns. Each column shows a number from 1 to 12. In this case, we have 12 columns, but in a normal template layout, you can define one <div> to span multiple columns.

Figure 3-6. *The template display shows all 12 columns on a page with gutters on the left and right sides and margins between each column*

A traditional three column layout would have CSS code that looked more like this:

```
<div class="row-fluid">
        <div class="span3 color">left</div>
        <div class="span6 color">center</div>
        <div class="span3 color">right</div>
</div>
```

Each div now spans multiple columns, so the left <div> uses the span3 class to use 3 of the 12 grid columns. The center uses 6 of the 12 grid columns, and the right uses 3. If you added this code to the template and refreshed the page, you would see a page like the one shown in Figure 3-7. If you wanted a larger center column, you could simply change the center to use the span8 class and make the left and right use span2. This simple example should show you how powerful and flexible the Bootstrap framework can be and how much it can simplify complex design tasks.

Figure 3-7. *The template displays the three columns as they span the 12 grid columns*

Now that you understand the basics of the grid system, creating an effective Joomla template is easy. Simply wrap the various module include tags within specific grids and the layout will flow properly. Note that we also have to add the Joomla-specific styling classes, otherwise modules and module overrides will not appear correctly.

Insert the following code between the <body> tags:

```
<div id="bodydiv" class="container-fluid">
    <div class="row-fluid">
        <?php if($this->countModules('atomic-search') ||
            $this->countModules('position-0')) : ?>
        <div class="span9">
        </div>
        <div class="joomla-search span3 last">
            <jdoc:include type="modules" name="position-0" style="none" />
        </div>
        <?php endif; ?>
    </div>
    <?php if($this->countModules('atomic-topmenu') ||
        $this->countModules('position-2') ) : ?>
    <div class="row-fluid">
        <div class="span12">
            <jdoc:include type="modules" name="atomic-topmenu" style="container" class="nav" />
            <jdoc:include type="modules" name="position-1"
    style="container" />
        </div>
    </div>
    <?php endif; ?>
    <div class="row-fluid">
        <div id="leftslab" class="span2">
            <div id="breadcrumbs">
                <jdoc:include type="modules" name="position-2" />
            </div>
```

```
            <jdoc:include type="modules" name="atomic-sidebar"
                style="sidebar" />
            <jdoc:include type="modules" name="position-7"
                style="beezDivision" headerLevel="3" />
        <jdoc:include type="modules" name="position-4" style="sidebar" />
        <jdoc:include type="modules" name="position-5" style="sidebar" />
        <jdoc:include type="modules" name="position-6" style="sidebar" />
        <jdoc:include type="modules" name="position-8" style="sidebar" />
        <jdoc:include type="modules" name="position-3" style="sidebar" />
            <jdoc:include type="modules" name="login" />
    </div>
    <div id="centerslab" class="span9">
        <div id="headerholder">

            <?php
                if(!empty($user->name)) {
                    echo " <div style='text-align:center;'>Welcome, ".
                    $user->name.'</div>';
                }
                ?>

        </div><!--end headerholder-->


        <div id="contentholder">
            <div id="contentarea">
                <div id="textcontent">
                    <jdoc:include type="component" />
                </div><!--end textcontent-->

            </div><!--end contentarea-->
        </div>
    </div><!--end centerslab-->
    <div id="rightslab" class="span1">
        RIGHT
    </div>
</div>
</div><!--end bodydiv-->
<div id="footerholder">
    <div class="row-fluid"  id="footermenu">
        <div class="span4 box box1">
            <jdoc:include type="modules" name="position-9" style="beezDivision" headerlevel="3" />
        </div>
        <div class="span4 box box2">
            <jdoc:include type="modules" name="position-10" style="beezDivision" headerlevel="3" />
        </div>
```

```
        <div class="span4 box box3">
            <jdoc:include type="modules" name="position-11" style="beezDivision" headerlevel="3" />
        </div>
    </div>
    <div class="row-fluid"  id="footermenu">
        <div>
            <jdoc:include type="modules" name="footer" />
        </div>
        <?php if($this->countModules('syndicate')) : ?>
        <div id="syndicate">
            <jdoc:include type="modules" name="syndicate" />
        </div>
        <?php endif; ?>
    </div>

</div><!-- end footerholder-->

<div id="debug">
    <jdoc:include type="modules" name="debug" />
</div>
<div id="dev">
    <jdoc:include type="modules" name="dev" />
</div>
<div id="preload">
    <jdoc:include type="modules" name="preloadimages" />
</div>
<div id="shared">
    <jdoc:include type="modules" name="shared" />
</div>
```

If you look through this code, you should see that most of it is simply various <div> tags holding Joomla include blocks. This layout is an expanded version of the simple three column layout that you saw earlier. If you refresh the page now (and you've installed the Joomla example data), you should see a template that looks like Figure 3-8. Pretty cool, eh? You now have the complete foundation for almost any template design that you want.

Figure 3-8. *The working dynamic template with the example Joomla data*

You may notice at the very end of the template a number of include tags lie outside the main content <div> tag. The first include can show debugging information if activated in the Global Configuration. When debugging mode is activated through the Administrator interface, the output of event timings, SQL query strings, and other information is included in this area. This debugging information is excellent for profiling when you're either debugging your site or first deploying it to production, so you can optimize the performance of the site.

You now have the core skeleton of a good template that you can use for many basic layouts. However, if we add a few more features to the template, it can be much more useful for a broader range of display possibilities. One way to give the template more power is allow configuration of the presentation to occur through template parameters that the administrator can set.

Using Template Parameters

Template parameters are one of the most useful aspects of template creation in allowing the site administrator to control the display of the site. With template parameters, an administrator configures a template to match the presentation and features of the site without the need to know how to modify HTML tags, adjust CSS configuration, or write custom PHP code. Best of all, Joomla makes template parameters easy to implement and use.

Before you begin creating your own templates parameters, let's see how the Joomla template "Beez2 - Default" uses them to allow for fundamental color changes.

1. Open the Template Manager using the Extensions menu.

2. Click on the Beez2 - Default entry to edit the settings of that template.

3. Click on the Options tab and the template parameters will be displayed, as shown in Figure 3-9.

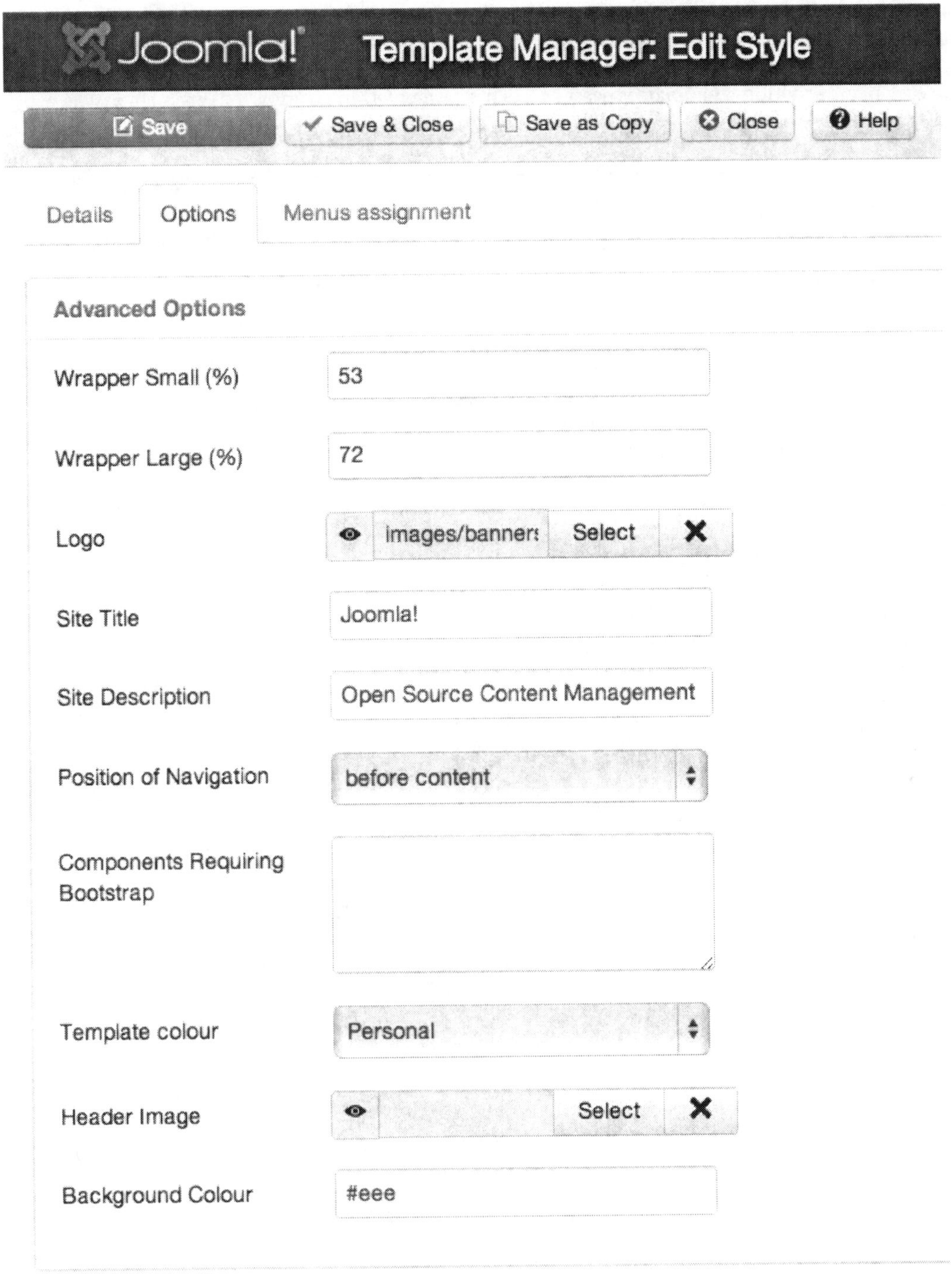

Figure 3-9. *The Beez template has a number template parameters that can modify the template display without changing the template code*

Adding template parameters to be displayed in the Joomla Administrator interface is as easy as including the fields in the template's details XML file. When the template is installed, Joomla automatically adds the default settings to the template entry in the database. When the site administrator modifies the settings, the parameters are stored in the database. With each page rendering, a template is passed all of the parameters in an array, making them easy to use for template customization.

■ **Note** If you've created templates for older versions of Joomla or you're converting a template to the new version of Joomla, note that the name of the parameter tags in the XML details file have changed. Parameters were previously included between `<param>` tags. Now, parameters are held in `<field>` tags. You only need to change the name of the tag to have the parameters work.

Let's add a few parameters to the aj_dynamic template we just created. Open the `templateDetails.xml` file in your favorite editor. Near the bottom, you should already see the `<config>` tag, which contains the `<fields>` tag. Inside the `<fields>` tag, you can add any parameters that you want. Between the `<fields>` tags, add the following code:

```
<fieldset name="advanced">
    <field name="include_jquery" type="radio"
            default="1" label="Include jQuery"
            description="Inject jQuery library reference into head section">
        <option value="1">Yes</option>
        <option value="0">No</option>
    </field>

    <field name="background_color"  type="text" default="white"
        label="Background color"
        description="Set the background color of the body tag"
        filter="string" />
</fieldset>
```

After you save the file, if you open the template in the Template Manager, you will immediately see the parameters, as shown in Figure 3-10. The radio type parameters that allow you to turn off the jQuery include is presented by Joomla as a radio button selection, while the color selection is a text field so either CSS colors or explicit hex values can be entered. Changing the settings on these options will be stored in the database so they can be referenced on the page.

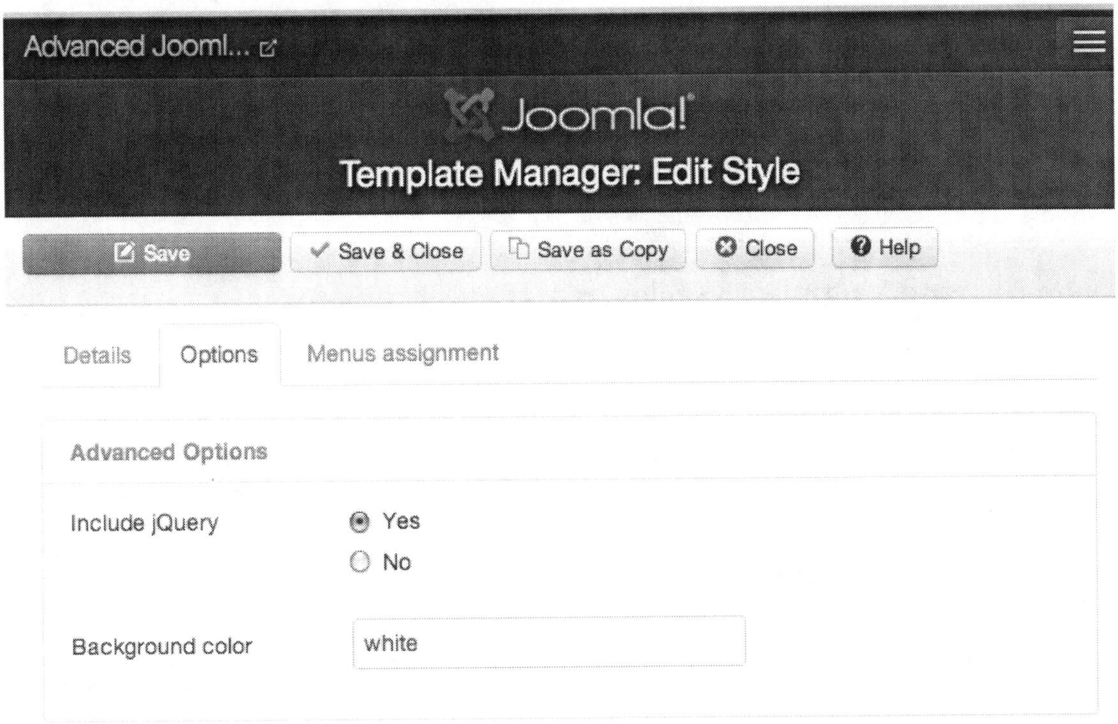

Figure 3-10. *The template parameters you've added to the template should be immediately available*

Now we need to add the code to use these parameters into the template itself. For the `include_jquery` parameter, let's add an `if` code block to determine if the template should output the `include` reference depending on the setting. Wrap the jQuery JavaScript tag so the code matches this:

```php
<?php if($this->params->get('include_jquery')): ?>
    <script type="text/javascript"
        src="<?php echo $template_path; ?>/js/jquery.js"></script>
<?php endif; ?>
```

If you change the setting from the Template Manager to false, the jQuery reference will disappear from the code. Likewise, add the following code to the body tag to implement the background color parameter:

```php
<body style="<?php
    $bg = $this->params->get('background_color');
    if(!empty($bg)) {
        echo "background-color:".$bg.';';
    }
?>">
```

Changing the color parameter will now be reflected in the template display. Template parameters can be very useful to allow the user to modify how the template works.

Template parameters are one way a user can configure the template. For a truly advanced template, though, it should dynamically change to suit the conditions under which it is rendering. For example, what if when sending to a mobile browser, the template automatically sends smaller images? Or if the template makes server-side adjustments on whether the browser supports it, such as using HTML5/CSS3 or the <canvas> tag? Or if the type of Joomla page displayed (article, category, home page) could determine which CSS files would be included in the rendering? Having different CSS sent depending on the page type would make Joomla much more like a custom-designed web site in which selective CSS is standard practice.

Selecting Among Multiple CSS Files in a Single Template

What if you could isolate the styles for a login page so that it doesn't load the styles for a category list page and vice versa? That would make loading of pages faster than if all the styles for the page were packed into a single monolithic file. It reduces complexity since styles don't interfere with each other and also increases organization since the styles that apply to a particular type can be found in the CSS file for that page type.

Adding this type of functionality is relatively easy. If you get the menu type (which determines what is rendered on the page), then you simply need to add a few extra if blocks to the code. To determine the menu type, add the following line of code to the top of the template (after the $app variable is defined):

```
$menu_view = $app->getMenu()->getActive()->query['view'];
```

Once that is defined, you need only change whether the menu is a category list (category) or a featured page (featured) or any other specific menu type. For example, to include a specific CSS file for a category listing page, you could add a code block like this:

```
<?php if($menu_view=='category'): ?>
    <link rel="stylesheet" href="<?php echo $template_path;
        ?>/css/category.css" type="text/css" />
<?php endif; ?>
```

Because your template has access to the full back-end parameters of the Joomla system, it can customize the display depending on the document contents, selected menu, browser information, cookies, or any of a variety of other factors. If you make your template dynamic in this way, your Joomla site can be far more sophisticated than a traditional Joomla installation.

Tip Be sure not to split style sheets across too many files because each file must be retrieved from the web server using a separate request. This can slow down the loading of a page and degrade the user experience. As a general rule of thumb, between three and five CSS files per page is usually about right. Fewer files and your template may be trying to pack too many styles into a single file. Styles are generally organized as good programming code files are organized—by grouping the various definitions into logical groups. Styles used by the entire system, for example, may reside in template.css or system.css, while styles specific to a particular menu type are generally found in a file named appropriately, such as category.css.

If the template uses too many files, the page will load much more slowly. You can manually combine your CSS definitions into fewer files or use a program known as a "minifier" that will not only combine separate files, but will also strip out white space and unnecessary definitions to decrease the overall file size and therefore download time necessary to retrieve the page.

■ **Tip**   At the time of this writing, the two most popular minifiers are Yahoo's YUI Compressor (`http://developer.yahoo.com/yui/compressor`) and the online CSS Compressor (`www.csscompressor.com`). There are also numerous language-specific CSS compressors such as Minify (`http://code.google.com/p/minify`), a PHP-based utility that can minify CSS and JavaScript files. There are similar minifiers written for most languages including Python, C#, C++, and even JavaScript.

Optimizing the Dynamic Template for Mobile, Tablet, and Other Viewing Platforms

Increasingly, accommodating a browsing audience that is visiting your site with a variety of devices is becoming more the rule than the exception. With the explosion of new devices from smart phones to tablets (iPad, Google Nexus, Kindle, and so forth) to alternate platforms like web television browsers, there is now a huge spectrum of display sizes and capabilities. Although this expansion provides the opportunity for a larger potential audience, it also creates many new challenges for template designers. A Joomla site template should be flexible enough to accommodate visitors who use these different viewing platforms.

Creating a template for varying devices is as much art as science. The template may simply remove elements of the template that are too large for the smaller screens of the devices (which we'll do using responsive design using Bootstrap). More dramatically, the template may contain specific functionality such as the ability to change the layout of the screen depending on whether the page is viewed in landscape or portrait mode as the device is rotated.

Even when the alternate device provides an excellent rendering of standard web pages, there are a number of factors that can make a self-customizing template compelling:

- *Small screen size*: A page that adapts to the smaller screen size means that the user doesn't have to frequently zoom in and out to effectively read or use the web site.

- *Orientation adjustments*: Most smart phones now provide the option of tilting the phone for automatic adjustment between portrait and landscape modes. Through CSS, a template can adapt to the best presentation for the viewing orientation.

- *Buttons for large fingers*: You may want to enlarge buttons and links to make them more easily clickable by the touch of a finger.

- *Column layout*: The standard 3-column layout of many Joomla templates is typically less than ideal for a mobile browser screen. Hiding one of the columns may be good enough or you might make them appear at the end of the document.

- *Optimized page load*: When phones connect to data networks, the transfer speeds may vary substantially. Optimizing the template to load more compact versions of files such as images can improve the browsing experience.

Some sites use a special template only for mobile browsers and redirect a browser that visits the normal URL of a web site to the mobile site. For example, if you visit `www.cnn.com` from a mobile browser, you'll be automatically redirected to `http://m.cnn.com`, which uses a template optimized to the small screens of most mobile browsers.

Most large sites adopt this strategy because it provides the most control of the site presentation. They use a database library of known mobile user agents such as Device Atlas (`http://deviceatlas.com`) to detect the capabilities of the specific user browser and then adapt the template to match. The same page may have a targeted template for every major browser from iPhone to Android to Windows Phone to Blackberry.

While this method is probably the best one to use if there are large budgets available for design customization and quality assurance, most Joomla template designers lack the substantial resources necessary to take advantage of the most useful features of this strategy. Instead, it is possible to add particular stylesheet rules and JavaScript that will address a majority of the mobile browser issues without requiring custom programming or the creation of separate mobile templates.

In this section, we'll modify the Dynamic Template you created earlier with three overlapping techniques to address alternate browser layout challenges:

1. Use the built-in responsive design in Twitter Bootstrap to change template presentation.

2. Set up special CSS rules that the browser can activate to change the display.

3. Implement JavaScript that can sense changes in layout and device orientation and modify the page to accommodate those changes.

You will probably want to use some of these techniques together to cover the widest set of visitor variants. To begin, using the functionality already included with Bootstrap will let you address many of the browsing cases with only the most minimal effort.

■ **Note**   At the dawn of handheld or mobile browsing, standards such as Wireless Access Protocol (WAP) and Wireless Markup Language (WML) were created to allow for web browsing on the very limited data networks then available. As generations of data networks have increased the capacity for data transfer, adoption of these minimal rendering standards has waned in popularity as the promise of using traditional web browsing standards on a mobile platform has become a reality. Although these standards are still useful for particular specialized applications, they are not especially relevant to a Joomla webmaster.

Using Responsive Design for Mobile Browsers

Twitter Bootstrap has numerous features that make rapid template design possible and one of the most exciting is the built-in responsive presentation capabilities. Responsive design works very simply—you add CSS classes to particular elements of your template and these specific classes will trigger whether page elements will be shown or hidden depending on the browser window size.

Bootstrap includes three basic target presentation sizes:

- *desktop*: For elements that are best viewed in a full screen desktop browser with horizontal resolution of 1200 pixels or more

- *tablet*: Elements that are still useful on a limited screen with a screen size of 768 pixels or more

- *phone*: Defines a screen that is 480 pixels or less in width

For each of these targets, there are two prefixes (`visible-` and `hidden-`) that define whether elements are or are not hidden on a particular platform. For example, if you add the class `visible-phone` to an HTML element, it will only be visible when displayed in a phone browser—it will not be visible when viewing the page on tablet or desktop size browsers. Using the `hidden-phone` class will hide the element if a phone browser is used for the display—but it will be visible on the other two size targets. Let's try adding this functionality to our template.

Open the dynamic template `index.php` file and edit the class of the left `<div>` so it includes the following:

```
<div id="leftslab" class="span2 hidden-phone">
```

That will hide the left column when a phone browser is used. For a tablet, which is wider than a phone, but not as wide as a desktop, we can hide the right column (so the right column is hidden on the phone and tablet and only visible on the desktop) by adding the visible-desktop class:

```
<div id="rightslab" class="span1 visible-desktop">
```

That's it! If you make these changes to your template and either look at your site in a mobile browser or shrink the width of your browser window to match that of a tablet or phone, you will see the elements progressively appear and disappear.

There are six classes available in Bootstrap:

- *visible-phone*: visible only on a phone

- *visible-tablet*: visible only on a tablet

- *visible-desktop*: visibly only on a desktop

- *hidden-phone*: visible on a tablet and a desktop

- *hidden-tablet*: visible on a phone and a desktop

- *hidden-desktop*: visible on a phone and a tablet

This example hides particular columns based on the target width, but you can also display other <div> elements to provide information styled specifically for the mobile experience (such as larger buttons or vertical layout). For example, on a phone display, you may hide the left column that holds a vertical menu for site navigation at the same time you make visible a horizontal menu with the same options at the top of the page so no navigation links are lost.

Adding responsive design functionality to your template is a big win for your mobile visitors. They'll be able to much more easily read specific content on your Joomla site without constantly zooming in and out of the page. However, make sure that you do provide alternates of hidden items for the mobile experience or visitors may become frustrated with a version of the site that is difficult to navigate.

General Guidelines for Handheld Templates

Bootstrap's responsive design lets you modify your template quickly and easily to address some of the alternate viewing platforms. Before we continue with more advanced strategies, it is a good idea to examine a few guidelines that can help make an alternate browsing experience more robust.

Whether you decide to adopt a database-driven solution for mobile browser detection or something simple, here are some general guidelines that apply to creating templates for most mobile platforms:

- *Try to eliminate horizontal scrolling*: Though the finger swipe gesture, up/down movement is a standard part of most browsing experiences, horizontal movement—especially with a zoomed screen—can be tedious. By focusing your layout on a more vertical design, you can minimize this browsing irritant.

- *Eliminate unnecessary columns*: Columns are not very useful in a narrow viewing perspective. They force zooming and horizontal scrolling, which generally slows the user experience. By using a single column display, the user of most devices can easily perform vertical scrolling.

- *In a multi-column display, put the center column first*: If you want a multi-column display even for mobile browsing, place the most important column (usually the center column) first or leftmost in order. A narrower screen will usually knock columns downward so a three-column display on a very narrow screen will show the three columns stacked one atop another. That means in a normal three-column display, the center column will appear far down the scrolling region. Instead, order the center column first and then re-arrange the presentation in CSS.

- *Minimize images and image sizes*: The bandwidth constraints on most mobile connections makes it a time-consuming and frustrating experience to view a site that is heavy with images. Use smaller, lower resolution images and thumbnails wherever possible to optimize the visitor's experience.

- *Avoid CSS absolute positioning and tricky floats*: When a page is displayed in a non-standard size, most absolute positioning won't work at all, and floats may not work very well unless carefully controlled. This can make the page a jumbled mess on the small browser screen. When absolute positioning is available, it can place an element off the visible page and make the content unavailable to the mobile browser visitor.

- *Make sure all images have alt text*: Even if the image displays properly, mobile browsers are typically on slower transfer connections, so an image-rich page will look empty on a mobile browser for much longer than a standard desktop view. The `alt` attributes of image tags can provide the user a sense of what will be displayed.

- *Avoid mouse-driven user interface elements*: Drop-down menus, hover-over popups, and other user interface enhancements can be difficult or impossible to navigate in a mobile browser and are best avoided for a mobile browser experience. If browser-detection is used, convert hover-over popups to click-based events for display.

If you follow these general guidelines in your template, your site will be a lot more likely to display properly on a mobile platform. Major web sites are reporting that the percentage of mobile browsers visiting their site is eclipsing that of obsolete desktop browsers such as Internet Explorer 6. Many are moving the design and QA budgets that were previously spent on old browser compatibility to mobile browser compatibility. Template designers would be wise to follow suit.

■ **Tip** There are some search engines that specialize in finding mobile versions of web sites. At the time of this writing, `http://tiltview.com` offers a free service to find the URL of a mobile version of a web site. Once you've set up the mobile version, it is a good idea to use a site like this to test and make sure mobile devices can recognize your mobile version.

You can go much farther than simply using the Bootstrap classes to target the mobile platform. You can actually specify a custom CSS file to be used by mobile devices. Unlike, say, the `print.css` stylesheet, the `handheld.css` file for styling your mobile site will likely not be based upon your original page CSS. Rather, you will probably want to create it from scratch and radically simplify the rules you use for display on your normal web site.

Creating a `Handheld.css` to Optimize Mobile Browsing

The primary method of making a template mobile-friendly lies in either using responsive CSS as demonstrated earlier with Bootstrap or creating a separate CSS file that specifies layout for mobile access of a site. Generally, the CSS file to make this possible is named `handheld.css` and is specified in the header of the template with a reference like this:

```
<link rel="stylesheet" href="handheld.css"
    type="text/css" media="handheld">
```

For inline styles, the open tag would look like this:

```
<style type="text/css" media="handheld">
```

Your normal style sheets should have the addition of the screen media type, like this:

```
<link rel="stylesheet" href="handheld.css"
    type="text/css" media="Screen">
```

On the mobile platform, if the handheld style sheet is available, it will supersede the standard `template.css` and all of the styles it contains. That means that even if your `handheld.css` is empty, it may improve mobile browser display because all your styles will be eliminated, allowing the mobile browser to render you page with its default settings. The default settings are likely best calibrated to the best font size, margins, and colors for that particular platform. We can do better than simply eliminating all of the desktop styles.

■ **Note** You may have noticed that the "Screen" media type is capitalized. Older Windows Mobile browsers would use the screen CSS even if a handheld CSS was available and specified. Giving the media type a capital letter made these browsers ignore the stylesheet and use the handheld style sheet instead.

For the Joomla template, we will want to replace the header and hide the left and right columns to provide the maximum screen space for the site content. The Joomla template that you created earlier in the chapter would have a handheld style sheet like this:

```
@media handheld {
    html, body {
        color: #000000;
        background: #FFFFFF;
        padding: 3px;
        margin: 0;
    }
    h1, h2, h3, h4, h5, h6 {
        font-weight: normal;
    }
    img {
        max-width: 250px;
    }
    .rightcol {
        display: none;
    }
}
```

The iPhone doesn't recognize the handheld CSS because Apple wanted to make the mobile Safari browser display the same web page a desktop web browser would show. While the iPhone rendering engine (based on Webkit) was able to handle rendering an actual web page, the screen size is still a hindrance to a good browsing experience. Therefore, to target the browsers that may have the features but not the screen size to properly display a web site, you can use the specification to select a CSS file based on the maximum screen width, like this:

```
<link rel="stylesheet" href="webkit.css"
media="only screen and (max-device width:480px)"/>
```

This CSS directive will make the `webkit.css` file selected for those browsers that want the screen media type, but have a viewing area of 480 pixels or less. Unlike the minimal styles in `handheld.css`, the styles in this style sheet would mimic those present in your normal `template.css` since the browser can effectively display them. The adjustments in the `webkit.css` will be directly related to the narrow viewing area and small screen size.

Style types that would best be adjusted for Webkit-type browsers on the mobile platform include:

- *Larger font sizes*: Small font sizes can be terrible on a mobile browser because most mobile screens have a higher pixel density than a desktop screen. Desktop screens often have a dots-per-inch (DPI) around 100, while mobile devices like the iPhone may have a DPI in the 300 range. That means the same font without zoom would appear around a third the size on the mobile device as the same font on the desktop.

- *Padding and margins*: These setting are usually scaled back on a handheld style sheet because the limited screen area means some sacrifice in white space may result in more viewable information.

- *Float and display*: These are often used for multi-column layout. While they are perfect for making layout flexible for use with a mobile screen, they must be closely controlled so they don't create additional horizontal scrolling.

- *Background images*: These images tend to be much larger than necessary for mobile screens. They may also create visual clutter when the size of the screen is reduced to smaller sizes.

Making these adjustments for powerful mobile browsers will make your site much more browser-friendly. As the mobile and tablet markets grow, the better experience your site can provide, the more visitors will return with any device. Although screen sizes can even vary on desktop browsers, the dynamic switching between portrait and landscape viewing modes are particular to handheld devices. A site that can automatically adapt to these changes will be welcome to users.

■ **Tip** The Web Developer toolbar add-on for Firefox demonstrated an earlier section is excellent for handheld debugging. Under the CSS menu, the Display Styles by Media Type ➤ Handheld will display the site with the handheld styles within the Firefox browser. The option lets you quickly and easily get an idea of what your site will look like on a mobile browser even if you don't have one handy for testing.

Handling Mobile Switches from Portrait to Landscape Mode

One feature that makes web browsing more pleasant on a small phone or PDA screen is the ability to turn the device so it displays a page in either portrait or landscape mode. If you've constructed your screen CSS properly, the site should automatically adjust to the device orientation. However, there are times when your site would benefit from a completely different layout when the orientation changes. For example:

- A tall header graphic that looks reasonable in portrait mode may take up a majority of the screen space in landscape mode.

- A right column showing the latest articles may be narrow enough to fit on the screen in landscape mode, but in portrait mode it may crush the left and center columns.

- A horizontal menu or toolbar that is useful in portrait mode may be more convenient as a vertical menu or bulleted list in landscape mode.

You can adjust CSS elements using the orientationchange JavaScript event. You can add the following code and then add the necessary extra classes to the portrait and landscape items that should be hidden or made visible by the orientation changes:

```
<script type="text/javascript">
function orientationChange() {
    switch(window.orientation) {
        // Portrait
        case 0:
        case 180:
            $('.portrait').each(function(element, i) {
                element.setStyle('display','');
            });
            $('.landscape').each(function(element, i) {
                element.setStyle('display','none');
            });
            break;

        // Landscape
        case undefined:
        case 90:
        case -90:
            $('.portrait').each(function(element, i) {
                element.setStyle('display','none');
            });
            $('.landscape').each(function(element, i) {
                element.setStyle('display','');
            });
            break;
    }
}
$(document).ready(function(){
        window.onorientationchange=orientationChange;
        orientationChange();
});
</script>
</head>
<body>
<div id="items">
        <div class="portrait">Portrait banner</div>
        <div class="landscape">Landscape banner</div>
</div>
```

Adding this small amount of JavaScript to your template can allow you to control the display when the orientation of the viewer changes.

Making the Template Effective for Text Browsers

There are also numerous text browsers that are used to access the Web including the popular Lynx (http://lynx.isc.org/) browser that is available for most platforms. Other text browsers are available for those with special needs, such as users with motor skills or visual impairments. For many sites, this may seem like too small of a user base to consider. However, Joomla is known for the diversity of its applications and target audiences so you might want to customize the site to cater to an audience with special needs.

If you wish to make a text-based template, you might first check what your site looks like when rendered to only text. The w3accessibility web site (www.w3accessibility.com) features the ability to enter any URL and view the site as a text-only browser would. This view alone may be valuable in designing your template so the most important features of the site appear early in the rendering.

Google also features the ability to look at the text-only version of a site (so you can see a site as the Google spider does). If you do a search on Google and find a site, it may have a link titled "Cached" to the right of the URL in the Google results list. Clicking on the link will show the version of the site that has been cached. In the top-right corner of the cached display, you should see a link titled "Text-only version." Clicking on that link will display the page with only text and links.

To create a proper template for text-only browsing, you need to follow essentially the same rules that are needed to design your site for accessibility. In this section, you'll learn how to make sure that your site contains all of the additional tags and attributes necessary to make your site navigable to browsers with accessibility features. If your template complies with these recommendations, you will find that your template is completely usable in a text-only browser as well.

When creating a template that can be used in a text-only module, follow these guidelines:

- *Make sure all images have alt text*: Text browsers obviously won't render images, so each image should have an alt attribute. Many web page images are also links and without an alternative text, the visitor won't know what clicking on the link represents.

- *Present alternatives to mouse-driven user interface elements*: Drop-down menus, hover-over popups, and other user interface enhancements will not be available in a text-only experience. Therefore, make sure that every mouse-driven navigation item has an equivalent within a <noscript> tag.

- *Place important links near the top of the page*: Like a mobile browser experience, you will want to place the more important links and information early in the text stream. This will make it so the user doesn't have to move past large amounts of formatting and place-holding text.

- *Use semantic HTML for your template*: Semantic HTML seeks to contain all page formatting within the style sheets to minimize the number of newlines and other formatting code. This makes text-only browsing a much cleaner experience since formatting that isn't effectively rendered anyway is ignored altogether because text browsers don't read CSS.

You should be able to accommodate all of these requirements within a standard template without requiring a separate template for the text browser.

Refining the Dynamic Template

The dynamic template included in this chapter provides an excellent foundation for nearly any type of Joomla template you would want to create. There are more specific enhancements you can make to the template depending on your target audience and the amount of time you have to put into the project. In this section, we'll look at ways to refine the table for specific situations and needs.

We'll cover:

- Avoiding common template pitfalls

- Making a shared template shell for sharing of resources between templates

- Adopting style sheet best practices

- Planning for caches, proxies, and content delivery networks (CDNs)

- Creating CSS sprites

- Using template testing tools

These sections do not need to be covered in order. They can help you solve specific problems that you may need to address as you are refining your template.

Avoiding Common Template Pitfalls

The following sections examine some common pitfalls of creating a new template and some possible solutions. These problems are common to any web site construction when you're creating a user interface or front-end to a web site. When creating a Joomla template, attention to detail is typically more important than when you're building a custom web site because a template is often re-used or sold for use across multiple web sites. Problems with a template are then multiplied across deployments.

When you create a template, it is very important that you understand how the page will appear to your web visitors. Beginning template designers commonly make this mistake—overestimating how closely the way the template appears on their development platform will appear to other users. Here are a few of the ways this perceived universality can be a problem.

Assuring Font and Anti-Alias Support

Macintosh users see fonts more attractively than browsers on other platforms because of the advanced anti-alias support within the Macintosh version of the Safari browser. Designers sometimes test only on the Macintosh and pretend that other platforms don't exist—even if the majority of their site visitors will be on another platform.

This distinction is very important when it comes to small fonts. Smaller fonts are often much more readable with anti-alias support than without. So you may believe your site is far more legible than it is for many of your users.

Font support, likewise, is a difficult subject. Windows, MacOS, and Linux all support a different subset of fonts. Triangulating the proper font that fits with your design and also supports a majority of your visitors can be difficult. There are less than a dozen fonts that will render on all major platforms (Windows, Macintosh, and Linux). Selecting fonts with proper fail-down choices is central to making a template appear nearly the same on all platforms.

The first and best protection against these problems is testing on multiple platforms. Almost every Macintosh user has access to a Windows machine (through a friend, local public library, and so forth) and the extra effort should be applied to make sure your template has the broadest possible reach.

In addition to that, many font problems can be mitigated by providing effective font family fail-down options. There is a web site called CSS Font Stack (http://cssfontstack.com/) that provides a list of the most common fonts, each font's availability on the different platform (in percentage of users), and an effective CSS font family list for graceful failure on the missing platform. Using the font-family attribute in CSS, whether the list comes from this web site or another, is something you should address in your template.

Considering Screen Sizes

Another very common problem is the assumption that the screen size you favor will match that of your visitors. There are so many monitor sizes and types in use that it can sometimes seem like mission impossible to accommodate them all. However, if you avoid these two mistakes, you'll have much more success with your template:

- *Large screens*: Some template designers look for the most common screen size even if a majority of their visitors have large screens. That makes all the site content appear like a small island of text in an ocean of screen space.

- *Small screens*: Some templates, particularly those with three columns, fail miserably on a smaller screen. If even 20% of your visitors have small screens, you should be sure to test the template on a smaller screen to make sure that it resizes gracefully for the small screen visitor.

One of the best ways to avoid the problem is to test with your existing traffic. If you have Google Analytics on your site, Google is already recording the screen size of every visitor. On the Analytics dashboard, under the Content panel, you'll find an option called In-Page Analytics that will show an interactive window of a current page from your site. It provides a slider at the top with a percentage that allows you to see the screen size that different numbers of your visitors can see.

The In-Page Analytics will even provide a click-map that shows you which areas of the page are clicked on most often and where the vertical areas that result in more or fewer clicks are located, as shown in Figure 3-11. This information is extremely useful to template developers who can refine the template organization to optimize for real-world use.

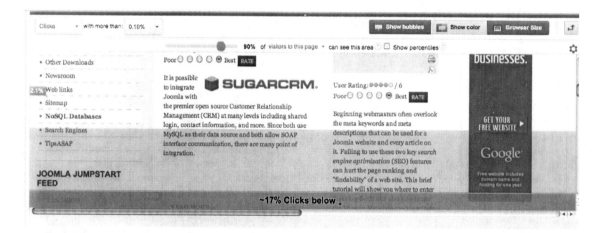

Figure 3-11. *Google In-Page Analytics lets you see the most common user browser window sizes and where you get your clicks*

Most of these problems can be mitigated by using a little common sense. The tools available to the Joomla site owner grow every day. Google Analytics itself often adds more free tools to the service and I recommend that you make a habit of reading the related blog (http://analytics.blogspot.com/) where new features are announced.

Creating a Shared Template Shell to Share Resources in a Multi-Template Site

Some sites absolutely require multiple templates to accomplish the site objectives. There are limits to the changes you can make within a single template layout. The computer proverb of Keep It Super Simple (KISS) can affect template design in two ways. If a single template is forced to make labyrinthine adjustments to allow for a variety of presentations, it is probably best to use more than one template rather than making one template stretch to fit every presentation need. If it is less complex to use several templates instead of a single over-taxed template, then creating multiple templates for a single web site can present its own set of obstacles.

Multiple templates can create special challenges in areas of shared code, style sheets, and components. For a multi-template system, it is important to minimize the amount of replication of code and styles. Whenever styles and code need to be replicated, the chances for bugs and errors occurring are increased.

One of the most useful techniques is to create a template that is not a template or, more specifically, a template that is never used by any actual pages. This template shell can contain many of the shared resources, including images, style sheets, and JavaScript files.

When I need to create such a template, I name it differently depending on the target deployment. For myself, I name the template simply "common" for easy typing and access. If other users will be configuring the server, I usually name it something such as `common_DO_NOT_USE` or `common_DO_NOT_SELECT_THIS_TEMPLATE`. This may seem a little over the top, but I have had the common template selected inadvertently by administrators who didn't understand the purpose of the template.

If you find yourself using more than one template, it is a good idea to create a shared template that acts as a repository for your most common resources. These might include:

- *JavaScript library files*: Libraries like jQuery and Backbone should be placed in the shared template so their version is standardized.

- *Standardized JavaScript functions*: It is usually a good idea to keep code close to the place of execution, so JavaScript specific to particular templates should be kept with the templates.

- *CSS library files*: Libraries like Bootstrap and jQuery UI should be stored in the common library.

- *Main style sheet files*: You can store common CSS files (such as *reset.css*) in this template.

- *Shared image files*: Universal images such as toolbar icons, banner graphics, and background images are perfect for storage in the common template. Not only does this cut down on file duplication across templates, it also maximizes the browser cache on a user's machine since the images have the same path regardless of the template that is using them.

- *Reference files*: Most applications have one or more reference files (such as URL routing maps or ZIP code directories) that contain data that is faster to reference by file than request from the database. These can be most effectively used when located at a common location.

- *Shared non-Joomla components*: There are many modules, plug-ins, and extensions that are used on a Joomla site that are simply wrapped in a Joomla extension for use. Examples include a Flash video streaming component, sIFR (which allows the use of custom fonts on a web page with the use of JavaScript and the Flash player), audio players, and widgets from other sites. These can be usefully placed inside the common template folder for shared access.

Keep in mind that like all shared resources, modification of an element can affect more than a single file, so it should be done with discretion.

Creating such a template is as simple as creating a new template structure as introduced at the beginning of the chapter and populating it with the appropriate resources. The template itself will likely never be used directly—it will simply hold the common resources of the site. Centralizing these resources in a single place is the best guarantee you have that you won't upgrade some resource in one part of the site and forget to do it somewhere else.

Adopting Basic Style Sheet Best Practices

The style sheets that you create in CSS can be among the most challenging aspects of template design. Often getting something right in one browser will result in a problem in another. Creating good CSS is more of an art than a science. One of the reasons for the popularity of Twitter Bootstrap is the excellent cross-browser support, which takes a great deal of the uncertainty out of creating a design for a web site and having confidence it will work regardless of the browser choice.

However, even when using Bootstrap as a foundation, you will invariably need to create custom CSS if for no other reason than to make sure every template you create doesn't look like the vanilla Bootstrap styling. Here are some basic CSS tips to make sure your CSS is maintainable:

- *Avoid placing styles in style attributes*: It is a common shortcut to use the style attribute available on most tags to add temporary styles. All too often, these remain in the final template. Instead, use a `<style>` block in the body of the HTML during the development phase—even though this violates HTML guidelines. It is much easier to move these into your CSS file at the final step than breaking out inline style attributes. Also, these blocks will throw errors during your HTML validation to remind you to move them, while inline style attributes will not.

- *Adopt a common naming convention for style names*: Styles are case-sensitive, so a style named .myStyle isn't the same as .MyStyle. Therefore, always use the same naming conventions for the style names. Alternatively, some designers use capital styles for global styles (e.g. .GlobalBody) while they use lower-case for styles that are unique to a particular page or module (e.g. .moduleBody). That way, they can tell the general location of the style at a glance.

- *Use percentages for font sizes*: Many designers hate using font percentages because then they can't control the exact look of the layout. In this world of varied browsers, including mobile browsers, using percentages for the font size is perhaps the only stable way to make sure your text remains properly sized in comparison to other text.

▨ **Tip**   Creating an effective template sometimes requires you to let go of learned ideas of commonality. Many, many hours are spent by template designers who attempt to get a page to look identical in multiple browsers (IE, Firefox, Safari, and so forth). You should decide if matching elements exactly is worth the expenditure of your time to achieve. Why does a site need to look the same in all browsers when it can look good in all browsers? If the font Trebuchet MS looks good on a Windows machine, but the MacOS font Calibri looks equally good when viewing from Safari, could you use it? Within a certain range, a site should look the same regardless of browser in order to ensure proper branding of the site. Beyond that, using two different styles on two different browsers may be the appropriate choice. The pages may not look identical, but if they look generally the same and the chosen styles are the best choices for each browser, consider if parity is a necessary goal.

Planning for Caches, Proxies, and CDNs

There are many layers between the content on the web server and the viewer's experience. The browser makes a request for the page through an ISP or corporate local area network. That request may not in fact ever reach your web server. If a proxy server with caching features exists in line between the user's machine and your web server, and the page has been previously accessed and the cache has not expired, the page may be served from the proxy server.

Even if it does make the request from the server, the browser itself will cache as much information as possible so it doesn't have to reload files it already has stored locally. For example, your style sheets located in `template.css` may be held on the local machine and, rather than downloading anew for each page, they are instead retrieved from the local cache. Changes made to the style sheets on your server may not be reloaded because the browser may not recognize that the file has changed.

One problem web developers have struggled with is the problem of stale cached files. Whether the file is cached by the local browser, on a proxy server, or on a CDN, nearly any web designer has had the problem of viewing a site and seeing old content that hasn't refreshed properly. Caches often fail to recognize file changes, so they don't refresh the file from the source server. To avoid this problem, you can alter the URL in a way that is ignored by the source server, but appears to the caching mechanism as if the file is new.

■ **Note** Another layer of caching that should be considered is a content delivery network or content distribution network (CDN). A CDN is a network of caches that are used by sites to provide distributed caching and transmission of content. Perhaps most easily understood with an example; imagine a site with a large amount of worldwide traffic. This site, with a URL of `www.example.com`, wants to give a user the fastest response to web requests and also minimize the amount of static requests (retrieval of style sheets, images, and so forth) so resources on the main web server can be dedicated to dynamic rendering. After subscribing to a CDN service, an extra reference is added to the URL of static files (such as `cdn.www.example.com/template.css`). When the browser requests the file, the request goes to the CDN server instead of the main web server. The CDN checks if the requested file is located in the CDN cache and, if not, retrieves it from the main web server. Thereafter, the file is served from the CDN server and there is no load on the main web server. CDN servers are located worldwide, so a request from a browser in India will cache the file on a server in India, allowing the response time for people in India requesting that content to be much faster. Also, because of economies of scale, CDNs offer rates on serving that data far cheaper than the costs for bandwidth and server resources if the site paid for this itself. Many CDN providers require contracts but Amazon CloudFront (`http://aws.amazon.com/cloudfront/`) has a very convenient pay-as-you-go model.

You can control which version of a resource is cached by adding a request string parameter to the URLs of your images and style sheets. The request string parameters are ignored by the file types themselves, but they are interpreted by proxies, CDNs, and even the browser's cache as being different from the cached files. So instead of a standard CSS reference like this:

```
<link rel="stylesheet" type="text/css" href="template/mystyle.css">
```

You would add a parameter to the end, like this:

```
<link rel="stylesheet" type="text/css"
    href="template/mystyle.css?v=1018">
```

When you have made changes to your style sheet files, you can ensure that old cache files are not used by incrementing this parameter:

```
<link rel="stylesheet" type="text/css"
    href="template/mystyle.css?v=1019">
```

To a cache, this is a different file name than the one that preceded it. In this case, the caching system won't find an existing file cached by the new name and will draw the file fresh from the source web server. Then that cached file (with the new request increment number) will be used until the cache expires or the number changes again. This strategy puts control back in your hands rather than relying on caches to recognize file changes or flush stale files.

Except in very special circumstances, you don't want to make this number change all the time. After all, caching benefits a web site (less unnecessary hits to the web server for the same file), a visitor (caches are much faster than retrieving things again and again), and the web itself, which doesn't need to waste a great deal of bandwidth sending identical files time after time.

■ **Tip** This technique is especially useful when managing Adobe Flash SWF files. Flash caching is notoriously bad at detecting a changed or upgraded SWF file. Additionally, Flash has its own internal cache that makes the problem even more intractable. Using this technique on the references to SWF files can save both you and your regular site visitors a great deal of confusion and frustration.

Adding this capability is easy in a Joomla template using a template parameter. By simply setting a parameter for the template that holds the cache flushing value, you can increment it from the Administrator interface without having to change any template code. Add the following to the `templateDetails.xml` to include the parameter:

```
<field name="mediaVersion"  type="text" default="white"
    label="Version number for media files"
    description="Change this value to flush caches of CSS and JS files"
    filter="string" />
```

Add the retrieval of the parameter once at the top of your template like this:

```
$mediaVersion = $this->params->get('mediaVersion');
```

Then all desired file references simply add this parameter after the filename like this:

```
<script type="text/javascript" src="media/system/js/mootools-more.js?v=<?php echo $mediaVersion; ?>"></script>
```

When you view the source for the page in a web browser, you should see this line output like this:

```
<script type="text/javascript" src="media/system/js/mootools-more.js?v=1"></script>
```

Now a simple change of the number in the Template Manager will make the files with this reference appear as a different name to the various caches. Whenever you make a change to any of these files, I would suggest incrementing this number to make sure all the visitors to your site see the most current version.

It's up to you whether you want to create separate values for the various types of media you use within a template. In this example, I've used a single value that, when changed, flushes all CSS, JavaScript, and other file resources. There are many sites that only change their CSS files regularly or update only their JavaScript often. For these types of sites, it makes sense breaking the cache flushing variable into separate variables so files of a single type (such as the JavaScript) can be flushed while leaving the other caches intact.

Using Page Class Suffix for Custom Styles

For designers who need to customize individual pages, there is a powerful feature in Joomla called the *page class suffix*. When a page is rendered, if a suffix is entered in the Joomla configuration for a particular menu item, that suffix is added to all of the key styles of that page. This allows you to set up custom CSS that will affect only pages that have the suffix configured in the Joomla menu system.

For a quick example, here is the HTML code for displaying a menu for a standard Joomla page:

```
<ul class="menu">
        <li><a href="/gsdashboard">Home</a></li>
        <li><a href="/gsproject/scaffer">Projects</a></li>
        <li><a href="/gsstories/scaffer">Stories</a></li>
        <li><a href="/gsproject/scaffer">Calendar</a></li>
        <li><a href="/gsrewards/scaffer">Rewards</a></li>
        <li><a href="/gswiki/scaffer">Wiki</a></li>
        <li><a href="/graphs">Graphs</a></li>
</ul>
```

Now, if the page class suffix is set to _customstyle, that same page is now rendered like this:

```
<ul class="menu_customstyle">
```

Because the name is different, you can create a custom style in your CSS code with the name menu_customstyle and only the pages that use this suffix will display the custom style.

This feature isn't limited to a single style name, either. You can place a space in front of the page class suffix to allow it to use a separate class. For example, if the suffix of myclass was added, but preceded by a space in the configuration, the HTML would be rendered like this:

```
<ul class="menu_customstyle myclass">
```

Now all of the items on the page would fall under the style defined with myclass entries. This feature can be really useful if you want every element of a particular page to have a special style such as a larger font size.

Using CSS Sprites

If a Joomla template is rich in images, it can take some time to load into the user's browser because each image requires a separate CSS request. A template should be designed such that it minimizes the amount of loading overhead it will add to the content of the page. One common problem in many poorly designed templates is the use of many small images for items such as icons and hover-over highlights. The solution to this problem is to combine multiple images into a single image file and then use CSS to position and crop the large image to show only the desired piece of the image. This technique is called *CSS sprites*.

Generally a CSS sprite is constructed as a grid with each image a consistent distance from other images (see Figure 3-12). This design makes it easy to design and eliminates the need to use a tool like the Photoshop slice tool to create a number of smaller image files from a single larger image.

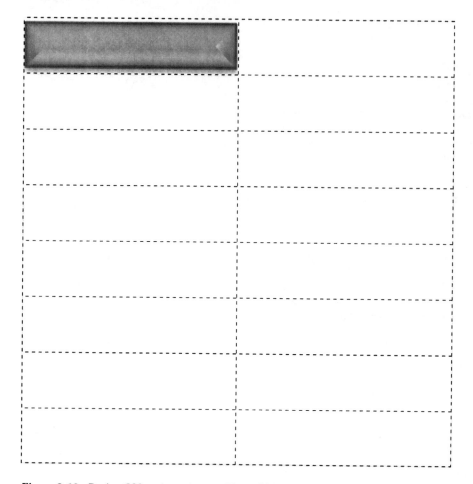

Figure 3-12. *Design CSS sprites using a grid so adding new images is simplified*

To see how this works, let's create a few example buttons with rollovers using the free, open source painting tool GIMP (available for download at www.gimp.org). These same instructions can be easily adapted to Adobe Photoshop or another image editing tool.

1. Begin by opening a new document with a size of 512 x 512, which will let us create buttons of 256 x 64 pixels with two across and eight down.

2. To make organizing them easy, define a grid or guide to help you draw in the proper places. In GIMP, show the grid using the View ➤ Show Grid menu option.

3. Use the Image ➤ Configure Grid option to show the Grid Options dialog.

4. Click on the link icon to break the link between width and height, set the width to 256 and the height to 64, and set the line style to *Double dashed* to make the grid easy to see. When you click the OK button, you should see the grid properly formatted to make sprite creation easy.

5. To create a number of buttons that can be used with rollovers, select the View ➤ Snap to Grid option.

6. From the toolbox, select the Rectangular Select tool.

7. In the options for this tool, select the Rounded Corners option and set the Radius to 20.0.

8. Now draw a selection from top-left to bottom-right of one of the grid squares. You should see the outline of what will become one of our sprite buttons.

9. To make the button really simple, you can select one of the Fill options from the Edit menu (such as Fill with Foreground color, Fill with Pattern, and so forth). For this example, I used the Blend Tool to create a simple gradient inside the selected area.

10. To create the button edge, I selected the Select ➤ Shrink option, set the size to 3, and clicked OK. I again used the Blend Tool, but this time I dragged it in the opposite direction.

11. Using the Text Tool I entered some text (in this case, "Open") on top of the button, selected the proper font (in this case, Franklin Gothic Heavy), size (42px), and centered the text within the grid area.

I repeated the exact same process (you can alternately copy and paste and then change the hue) in the grid rectangle on the right, with the exception that I selected a blue foreground color so the gradient would be colored (for the rollover). When the button was complete, the image looks like the one shown in Figure 3-13. I also made the font on the right italic to give it a slight change with the rollover.

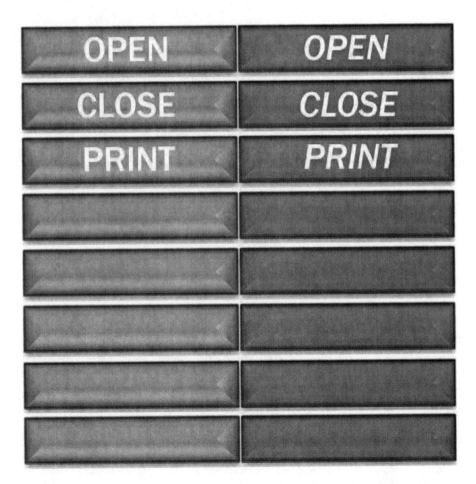

Figure 3-13. *Create a button with a different color for the rollover in the right rectangle*

Now that you have a single file with multiple sprites, save it into your template directory structure. I saved my template images as button_sprite.png in the /template/images folder. Remember that in CSS, file names are case-sensitive (ButtonSprite.png and buttonsprite.png are treated differently) so make sure that the capitalization of your file name is the same when you reference it in the CSS file later.

■ **Tip**   You probably want to save an XCF file (GIMP's native file format) as well as a PNG that will be used in the template. The XCF will retain the layers, type, and other information if you want to edit the sprite later.

Next, add the following CSS to your template.css file:

```
#toolbar {
        width: 256px;
        height: 64px;
        background: url(../images/button_sprite.png);
        margin: 10px auto;
        padding: 0;
        position: relative;
}
#toolbar li {
        margin: 0; padding: 0; list-style: none;
        position: absolute; top: 0;
}
#toolbar li, #toolbar a {
        height: 64px; display: block;
}
#btnOpen {left: 0; width: 256px;}
#btnClose {left: 256px; width: 256px;}

#btnOpen a:hover {
        background: transparent url(button_sprite.png)
                -256px 0 no-repeat;
}
#btnClose a:hover {
        background: transparent url(button_sprite.png)
                -96px -200px no-repeat;
}
```

Now add this HTML at the top of the index.php of your template:

```
<ul id="toolbar">
        <li id="btnOpen"><a href="#"></a></li>
        <li id="btnClose"><a href="#"></a></li>
</ul>
```

When you refresh the template, you should see the buttons as shown in Figure 3-14.

Figure 3-14. *The buttons in the CSS sprite appear separately and change when the mouse hovers over them*

To use this in a template, you will probably want to create one or more sprites that contain all of your key icons. Bootstrap includes a CSS sprite that has dozens of commonly used icons. You can use these yourself or examine how Bootstrap uses a single image file to provide all of these icons.

Using Template Testing Tools

Being a Joomla template developer can sometimes seem overwhelming with the number of disciplines that you need master. In addition to making a site attractive, you will need to effectively debug problems that are visual (caused by CSS or browser compatibility) and programmatic (JavaScript or PHP). One of the most important steps in addressing problems effectively is finding the right tools to diagnose and solve your problems.

Having the appropriate tools is usually the difference between an amateur and an expert—whether in the field of auto mechanics, astronomy, or template development. Assembling a toolbox of effective working tools can take a great deal of time seeing as there are so many tools available and it is difficult to tell on the surface which tools are useful and which tools are too limited or buggy to be of much use.

Here are some of the tools used most commonly by professional user interface specialists. Amazingly, all of these high-quality tools are free and available for quick download. If you use them effectively, you'll find your productivity skyrocketing.

■ **Note** Firebug (http://getfirebug.com/) is not given a section here because if you're reading this book, you're probably already using it effectively. If you aren't using it already, it's worth downloading and installing the Firefox browser just to use the Firebug tool. At the time of this writing, other knock-offs of Firebug such as Chrome Developer Tools still have a long way to go before they include all of the ease of use and functional features available from Firebug. Not to mention the large number of Firebug extensions that are available.

Using the Web Developer Toolbar in Firefox

One of the best add-ons for addressing browser problems is the Web Developer Toolbar plug-in (https://addons.mozilla.org/en-us/firefox/addon/web-developer). The Web Developer Toolbar has dozens of features, with some of the most useful to a Joomla template developer being:

- Instantly disable and re-enable JavaScript

- Clear and modify cookies

- Validate HTML, CSS, and DTD

- Display form details

- Measure sizing and color layouts on the screen

- Show hidden elements

You can see the Web Developer Toolbar in Figure 3-15. After Firebug (http://getfirebug.com/), the Web Developer Toolbar is likely the most important browser-based tool for template development.

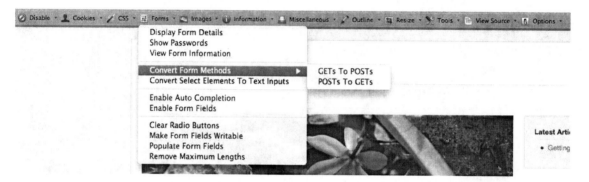

Figure 3-15. *After Firebug, the Web Developer Toolbar is likely the most important browser-based tool for template development*

Some of these functions are particularly useful when creating Joomla templates because they provide a way of looking into the page after it is rendered.

Disabling JavaScript

Too often, web developers become accustomed to their own machines and ignore the experience of their users. One of the best ways to judge the lowest common denominator of visitors to your site is to simply disable JavaScript. Many libraries will be deactivated, including such JavaScript injections as Google AdSense. Viewing the site in JavaScript-disabled mode will give you some conception of how the search engine spiders, accessibility browsers, and text-based browsers will see the site.

Through the Web Developer extension, on the toolbar select the Disable ➤ JavaScript ➤ All JavaScript option to deactivate the browser processing of JavaScript code. If you disable JavaScript and surf to most of the major sites, you will notice while the site experience changes, most of the functionality remains intact. You can still navigate the site and see most of the major items.

This should be your objective when testing a Joomla template. Most of the advanced JavaScript features that you include on your site should have good fail-down functionality so even if the JavaScript is not functioning properly, the site is still usable.

Examining CSS

For most needs, the Firebug add-on for the Firefox browser provides all the necessary capabilities to examine and even modify live site CSS. It will automatically expand minified CSS to make it easier to see structures and locate problems. The Web Developer Toolbar allows you to quickly test global CSS changes by allowing you to disable entire CSS files or examine and edit style information.

Under the CSS menu on the Developer Toolbar, you can select the Disable Styles submenu and find a variety of options, including the ability to deactivate inline styles (great for finding styles that should be moved into your CSS files), embedded styles, print styles, and more. Select the Individual Style Sheet option to choose an individual file to disable.

Examining and Altering Cookies

Cookie problems can be one of the most difficult to debug and troubleshoot when you're doing custom Joomla development. Cookies are used for everything from user login registration to A/B Testing (see Chapter 9) to storing local preferences to user session tracking. The ability to easily examine and modify cookie values can take a great deal of pain out of resolving cookie issues.

The Web Developer Toolbar introduced earlier includes some powerful functionality to examine, analyze, modify, and delete cookies. Using the Cookies ➤ View Cookie Information option, you can get a list of all of the cookies stored in the browser that are relevant to the site that is currently being displayed. In Figure 3-16, you can see the formatted list generated by selecting this option.

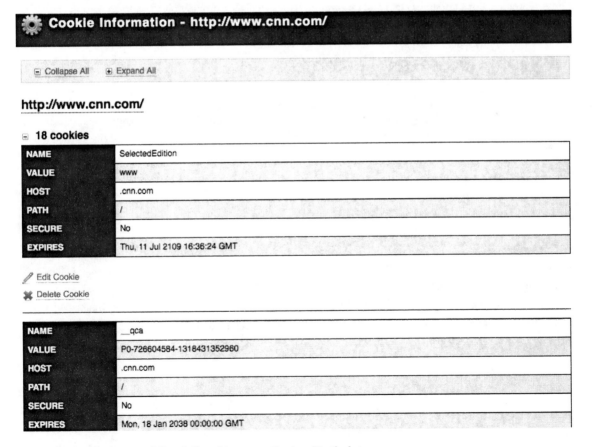

Figure 3-16. The formatted list of all cookies currently stored in the browser

The Toolbar also lets you delete cookies related to a specific context. This can be very useful to the template developer when trying to test or debug particular template problems. For example:

- *Delete Domain Cookies*: This can be useful if your site alters its presentation based on the session length and other parameters. If your template displays a banner on the first user visit (determine by checking for a site cookie), deleting this cookie will allow a refresh to show a fresh visit perspective of the site.

- *Delete Path Cookies*: Sites often set information about the current browsing progress via a cookie or web session (where a cookie is used to track the session). Clearing cookies registered at a particular path will eliminate the information that is recorded for the visit.

If you're using IE8 or above, hitting the F12 key will display the Developer Tools window, which provides many of the same options. The Cache menu has the following options:

- Disable Cookies

- Clear Session Cookies

- Clear Cookies for a Domain

- View Cookie Information

These can aid you in debugging cookie issues in Internet Explorer. Most cookie problems will be the same regardless of browser, but sometimes login and registration issues will vary among browsers and cookies are helpful when debugging these sorts of problems.

Using IE Tester to Assure Internet Explorer Compatibility

Although many web developers prefer Firefox or Google Chrome, Internet Explorer will be used by 40% or more of the visiting users for most web sites. Because of developer preference for non-IE browsing, even at large companies, designers and testers often overlook problems with their page rendering in the IE browser. Imagine the impact if half of your users can't view or use your site properly. Testing your Joomla template in Internet Explorer is critical if you want to maximize your audience.

Given the significant percentage of IE users in the world, it is important to ensure that your Joomla site operates properly when accessed by this browser. However, the wide variation of features and operation of the different versions of the Internet Explorer browser (IE6 renders much differently than IE7, which renders differently than IE8, and so on) makes it difficult for even a conscientious developer to have confidence the template works well across the IE product family.

■ **Warning**   The IE problem is not a hypothetical one. On a web site I worked on, designers made a change to the CSS that corrupted the display on IE and made the page unreadable. After the problem was detected and corrected, post-mortem analysis revealed that the unreadable layout had appeared for over 9 million page views. Although your Joomla site likely won't have this volume of visitors, it is even more important that you make every page view count.

To ease the burden of testing, there is an excellent free tool named IE Tester (`www.my-debugbar.com/wiki/IETester/HomePage`) that allows you to test your site as it would appear in all of the different variations of Internet Explorer. IE Tester simulates the rendering of all the major versions of the Internet Explorer browser. After installing IE Tester on your machine, you can enter a URL and select the browser versions you want to test and the application will render the selected page with all of the specified variations. Make sure you try this tool when you're approaching the launch of a new template. You may be surprised at the different results.

■ **Tip** There are many tools that will show you a web site using the rendering of various browsers. Adobe Browserlab (`https://browserlab.adobe.com/en-us/index.html`), for example, provides a free online version of browser testing. Whichever tool you choose, be sure to look at all of your Joomla page types and especially test the JavaScript functionality. A site may render properly in a particular browser but key features may be inoperable because of JavaScript compatibility issues.

Conclusion

In this chapter, you've learned how to create an advanced template that will provide some of the greatest flexibility to a Joomla site. This template can accommodate a variety of page types, including home, subhome, and article pages and can automatically select appropriate options (such as different CSS files) given the page that is displayed. Creating a single template to handle most of the page types your site will require decreases the time spent maintaining the site because you can make changes in one place and propagate to all the pages on the site. Creating a good foundation template can make all the difference in allowing a site to expand properly.

Following the best practices of layout and CSS creation will help make your template more accessible, search-engine friendly, and crawlable. You can also use techniques such as CSS sprites to optimize the download and tools to profile your page to make sure it can load in a reasonable time. In the next chapter, you'll learn how to add overrides to your template so you can customize the look and feel of existing Joomla extensions, such as the login module, to match the functionality of your template.

CHAPTER 4

■ ■ ■

Using Template Overrides

The dynamic template you created in the last chapter gives you a great deal of control over the presentation of your site without requiring you to use multiple templates. The styles included in Twitter Bootstrap can be used as-is or overridden for custom presentation. However, the custom styling is often limited to the template itself leaving modules and components that retain the look and feel of the default Joomla experience. Joomla, however, provides a feature known as template overrides that let you customize all of the modules and components included with Joomla (and many third-party extensions) to match your template exactly.

Template overrides allow you to make small tweaks to existing modules and components instead of having to recreate the entire functionality. For example:

- You might want to use the current login system, but you need the presentation to match the rest of your template in styling or semantic layout (and CSS changes won't do)

- You need to swap out the main menu module to have an integrated breadcrumb, but you want the rest of the system to use it without resetting all of the menus to the new module

- You want to add a better search engine component, but you want to leave the main search module in place so it feeds directly to your new search engine

Traditionally, a CMS would require you to modify the foundation system to accomplish these sorts of things—and changing core system components is never a good idea. Further, to install your new features on another site (or to sell your template), the system would require the modifications on every site where it was installed. If you used one or more extensions to add the features, it would require packs of new extensions that you must install individually—particularly if they replace an extension that's already in place. Template overrides solve all of these problems.

What a Template Override Can Do

There are generally five areas where a template override is needed:

1. *Module override*: The display of a module needs to be overridden to provide custom HTML layout, extra JavaScript code, or an alternate destination for the submission destination of a form.

2. *Module chrome change*: When you want to change certain display or "chrome" aspects of the module without completely replacing the view, you can use module chrome code that will inject particular aspects into the module code.

3. *Creating a component override*: All Joomla components are organized in the Model-View-Controller (MVC) structure, so all of the presentation logic for a component is stored in the views/ folder of the component. You can therefore override any of the presentation logic of any component.

4. *Overriding a third-party component or module*: You can override any third-party component or module that complies with the Joomla MVC structure of building extensions with the standard Joomla system. That means you can alter the display of popular components without modifying the extension's code.

5. *Special page overrides*: There are special pages in the Joomla system, including the 404 page and the Offline page, that you can override with a template override.

With template overrides, you can store replacement views in the template directory and, if that template is selected for a page, the items will override the display of that extension. That means you can create a custom login box without rewriting or uninstalling the default module. Alternatively, you can include a new search component form or a custom mod_mainmenu without having to touch the original files.

Even better, all the template overrides are installed with your template, so you can use a single extension installation to place all these items on a site. You can essentially package an entire site presentation structure within a single file!

Before you actually create a template override, it is useful to have an overview of the location of overrides within a template directory structure and how Joomla determines which override replaces which interface presentation. You can also see how these overrides are included in your template descriptor file.

■ **Note** For the sake of brevity, I will use the term *extension* in this chapter to indicate a module or a component—not a plug-in or language pack. While extensions in a general context include plug-ins and language packs, they cannot be overridden by template overrides so are not relevant for this chapter.

Including a Custom Module in a Template Package

All template overrides must be located in the html/ directory of the template directory (with the exception of page overrides, which are located in the template root). Inside the html/ directory, you will need to add folders that match the name of the module or component that you want to override. For example, to add a new view file, your directory structure would look like this:

```
html/TARGET_EXTENSION/VIEW_FOLDER/VIEW_FILE.php
```

To change a view of the login module, you would start with the path to the original file that you want to override. In this case, the path for that file (from the Joomla installation root) would be:

```
/modules/mod_login/tmpl/default.php
```

So the path to the override inside a template directory would look like this:

```
html/mod_login/tmpl/default.php
```

The complete path to the override from the Joomla root might be:

```
/templates/MYTEMPLATE/html/mod_login/default.php
```

If a template with an override is active, the template directory will be checked first for an available view and, if found, the template override file will be used instead of the main file. Although you've overridden the view, the rest of the module functionality executes as normal, so you don't need to rewrite anything.

That's about as simple as it can be. Overrides only need to be placed in the appropriate directory path; there is no registration necessary. You can override any display view—even the component view that displays articles. In that case, the original component display is located here:

```
/components/com_content/views/article/default.php
```

So you could create the same override in your template:

```
/MYTEMPLATE/html/com_content/views/article/default.php
```

Note that the location of the overrides for a component is slightly different from the path structure of a module. Modules do not generally have a full MVC structure that a component does. A module looks for the view override in the root directory of the module override folder—even if the original module uses a subfolder. For example, for the login module, the view file is located at the following path:

```
/modules/mod_login/tmpl/default.php
```

However, for the template override to work, it can't be located inside the `tmpl/` folder in the template (it should be located at the root folder of the override):

```
/templates/aj_dynamic/html/mod_login/default.php
```

This can be slightly confusing sometimes. Once you have a prototype template that uses overrides in the proper place, you can use that as a foundation for other templates so it will be apparent where the files are located. Now that you understand the basic structure, let's create a custom login module that has a presentation that differs from the original.

■ **Note**　If you're interested in seeing exactly how the module override code operates, you can examine the `getLayoutPath()` method in the `/libraries/joomla/application/module/helper.php` file where the view that will be displayed is loaded. You can see the module chrome loader in the `renderModule()` method in the same file.

Creating a Custom Login Module

Very often, templates need to add custom modules to properly adapt to the layout of the main template pages. Nowhere is this need more common than the customization of a login and registration module. Some common reasons to include a custom login module include:

- *Hidden form display*: Many templates require the login to be a hidden form so that it can either be exposed when the user clicks a link or it can pop up in a floating dialog box. Making the login form only appear when the user wants it prevents the form from cluttering the interface—especially if the login needs to be placed near the top of the layout.

- *Extra form fields*: Some logins require custom fields that you can easily add if custom HTML form code is needed.

- *Client-side validation*: If client-side validation is needed to confirm a valid user name or prevent illegal character entry (such as bars or ampersands), you can easily add the JavaScript code into the template override.

In this example, you'll create a custom login display that is displayed or hidden based on the user clicking a link. When the form is initially displayed, it will appear as shown in Figure 4-1. By having the form initially collapsed, you can place it much more prominently in a template layout and yet it is less intrusive.

Example Pages
Modules Cat
Login Form
Show Login

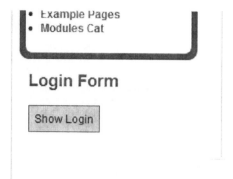

Figure 4-1. *When the login form appears with the module view override, it appears as a single Show Login link*

Clicking on the Show Login link will display the complete form as shown in Figure 4-2. In a real template, clicking the link would display a floating/pop-up window that would hover over the area of the page.

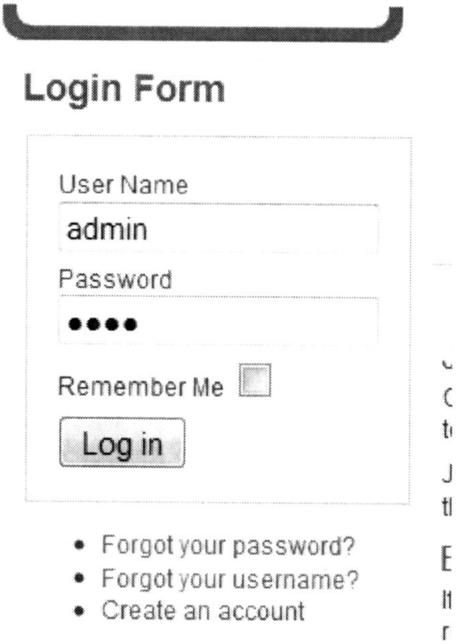

Login Form
User Name
admin
Password
●●●●
Remember Me
Log in
Forgot your password?
Forgot your username?
Create an account

Figure 4-2. *After the user clicks on the link, the hidden form will be displayed*

To begin, we should add the html/ folder to the templateDetails.xml file so it will install with the template. Because of the number of possible files and depth of folders, you should add the entire directory tree of the folder. In the <files> section, add the bolded entry:

```
<files>
        <folder>html</folder>
</files>
```

For the actual code, first create a folder to hold the template so you have a path like this:

aj_dynamic/html/mod_login

Normally, you should copy the existing file and from that base, create any modifications you need. Here, you'll use the code to make a new file. Create the default.php file for the custom login and enter the following code:

```php
<?php
// no direct access
defined('_JEXEC') or die;
JHtml::_('behavior.keepalive');
?>
<script type="text/javascript">
function showLogin() {
    var btnLogin = document.getElementById("show_loginlogout");
    var frmLogin = document.getElementById("loginlogout");
    btnLogin.style.display = "none";
    frmLogin.style.display = "";
}
</script>
<div id="show_loginlogout">
<br/>
<a href="#" onclick="showLogin();"
    style="padding:6px;background-color:lightblue;
        border:1px solid blue;">
    Show Login</a>
</div>
<div id="loginlogout" style="display:none;">
<?php if ($type == 'logout') : ?>
<form action="index.php" method="post" name="form-login"
    id="login-form">
<?php if ($params-> get('greeting')) : ?>
    <div class="login-greeting">
    <?php if($params->get('name') == 0) : {
        echo JText::sprintf('MOD_LOGIN_HINAME', $user->get('name'));
    } else : {
        echo JText::sprintf('MOD_LOGIN_HINAME',
            $user->get('username'));
    } endif; ?>
    </div>
<?php endif; ?>
    <div class="logout-button">
        <input type="submit" name="Submit" class="button"
            value="<?php echo JText::_('JLOGOUT'); ?>" />
    </div>
```

```
        <input type="hidden" name="option" value="com_users" />
        <input type="hidden" name="task" value="user.logout" />
        <input type="hidden" name="return" value="<?php echo $return; ?>" />
</form>
<?php else : ?>
<form action="<?php echo JRoute::_('index.php', true,
    $params->get('usesecure')); ?>" method="post" name="form-login"
    id="login-form" >
    <div class="pretext">
    <?php echo $params->get('pretext'); ?>
    </div>
    <fieldset class="userdata">
    <p id="form-login-username">
        <label for="modlgn-username"><?php
            echo JText::_('MOD_LOGIN_VALUE_USERNAME') ?></label>
        <input id="modlgn-username" type="text" name="username"
        class="inputbox"  size="18" />
    </p>
    <p id="form-login-password">
        <label for="modlgn-passwd"><?php
            echo JText::_('JGLOBAL_PASSWORD') ?></label>
        <input id="modlgn-passwd" type="password" name="password"
        class="inputbox" size="18"  />
    </p>
    <?php if (JPluginHelper::isEnabled('system', 'remember')) : ?>
    <p id="form-login-remember">
        <label for="modlgn-remember"><?php
        echo JText::_('MOD_LOGIN_REMEMBER_ME') ?></label>
        <input id="modlgn-remember" type="checkbox" name="remember"
        class="inputbox" value="yes"/>
    </p>
    <?php endif; ?>
    <input type="submit" name="Submit" class="button" value="<?php
        echo JText::_('JLOGIN') ?>" />
    <input type="hidden" name="option" value="com_users" />
    <input type="hidden" name="task" value="user.login" />
    <input type="hidden" name="return"
        value="<?php echo $return; ?>" />
    <?php echo JHtml::_('form.token'); ?>
    </fieldset>
    <ul>
        <li>
            <a href="<?php echo
              JRoute::('index.php?option=com_users&view=reset'); ?>">
            <?php
              echo JText::_('MOD_LOGIN_FORGOT_YOUR_PASSWORD'); ?></a>
        </li>
        <li>
            <a href="<?php echo
              JRoute::('index.php?option=com_users&view=remind'); ?>">
```

```
            <?php echo
            JText::_('MOD_LOGIN_FORGOT_YOUR_USERNAME'); ?></a>
    </li>
    <?php
    $usersConfig = JComponentHelper::getParams('com_users');
    if ($usersConfig->get('allowUserRegistration')) : ?>
    <li>
        <a href="<?php echo JRoute::_
            ('index.php?option=com_users&view=registration'); ?>">
                <?php echo JText::_('MOD_LOGIN_REGISTER'); ?></a>
    </li>
    <?php endif; ?>
</ul>
<div class="posttext">
<?php echo $params->get('posttext'); ?>
</div>
</form>
<?php endif; ?>
</div>
```

After you've added this file to your template, reload the home page in your browser (with the login module activated). You will see your new styling, and clicking on the button will show the JavaScript pop-up. This example provides a simple foundation that you can use to override any module. However, modules aren't the only things that you can override. You can customize any component that follows the MVC structure in the same manner.

■ **Tip** Debugging a template (especially written by someone else) can be difficult if you forget to check the overrides section. I've seen developers who don't know about template overrides and give up in frustration when they can't locate the display logic for a piece of the interface. As always, doing a file search or "grep" in Linux based on some text you find in the View Source window of the browser is the best method of tracking down the exact code that is rendering the item you need to modify.

Including a Custom Component in a Template Package

Creating a component override can be more complicated than a module since the component generally has more code and the directory structure can be several levels deep (compared with the path structure of most modules). The process of creating a custom component generally follows the following steps:

1. Locate the component view file that you want to override.

2. Create the appropriate folder path that matches the original.

3. Copy the file into the template folder.

4. Modify the copy of the original file.

In this section, we'll perform one commonly needed task: overriding the com_content component for semantically correct HTML layout. Semantic HTML is HTML that has been optimized for machine reading (a complete example was presented in Chapter 3) so that the search engine bots can process and properly understand the content of a web page.

The default com_content component has historically done a poor job of creating semantic HTML output of articles. By overriding the component display in the template, any site that uses that template will automatically gain semantically proper HTML code.

To begin the creation of the component override, copy the com_content view code from the default extension. You'll find it here:

```
/components/com_content/views/article/tmpl/default.php
```

Copy the code file here:

```
/templates/MYTEMPLATE/html/com_content/article/default.php
```

In this example, we'll make a simple change that adds an icon to allow the currently viewed article to be in a separate window. In reality, you would want to modify the content component for things such as moving the location of the pagination arrows to the top of the article or adding missing CSS IDs to items such as the author display so you can easily access the element using a CSS selector.

Simply add the bolded line into the article code:

```
<?php if ($params->get('link_titles') &&
    !empty($this->item->readmore_link)) : ?>
<a href="<?php echo $this->item->readmore_link; ?>">
    <?php echo $this->escape($this->item->title); ?></a>
<a href="<?php echo $this->item->readmore_link; ?>"
    target="_readmore" title="Open article in new window">
    <i class="icon-share-alt"></i>
</a>

<?php else : ?>
    <?php echo $this->escape($this->item->title); ?>
<?php endif; ?>
```

When you look at an article page, you should now see the open link beside every article, as shown in Figure 4-3.

Figure 4-3. Using a component override allows you to add customizations such as this tab opening icon to all items rendered by the component

You can make all sorts of modifications to the component views to match the visual presentation of your template. Most common targets for template overrides are the content component, banners component (where lightbox display can be added), search component, and newsfeeds component. You're not limited to modifying the core Joomla components, either. If a third-party component follows the Joomla MVC structure, you can apply overrides to it within a template.

Modifying the Offline page

If a site is set to Offline status in the Global Configuration, it displays a basic offline page with a login form such as the one shown in Figure 4-4. The page is meant to provide a basic offline message and it succeeds at that. However, you probably would like to have something more informative—especially if you want new visitors to return when your site returns.

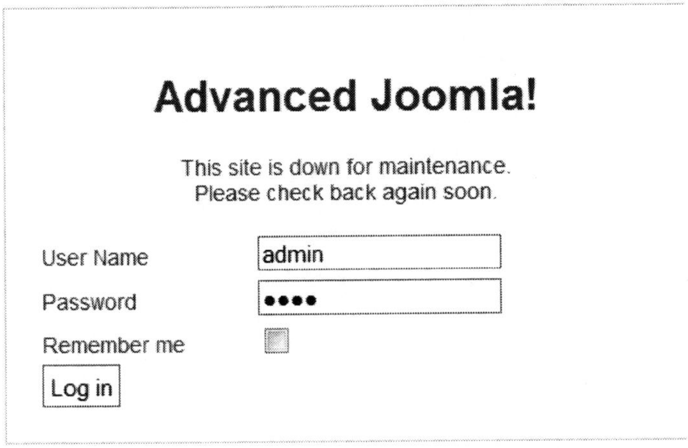

Advanced Joomla!

This site is down for maintenance.
Please check back again soon.

User Name admin
Password   ●●●●
Remember me ☐
Log in

Figure 4-4. *The basic offline page is not very informative or compelling and the login form can be confusing*

When a visitor arrives at the offline page, we can show the remaining time before the site comes back online in an entertaining way. If we show progress bars until the return time is reached, a visitor is more likely to feel that the offline message is temporary (see Figure 4-5).

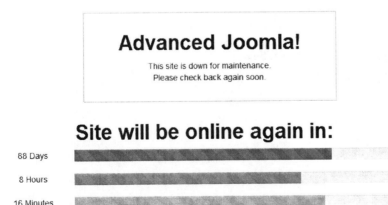

Advanced Joomla!

This site is down for maintenance.
Please check back again soon.

Site will be online again in:

88 Days
8 Hours
16 Minutes

Figure 4-5. *A more interesting offline message includes a countdown until the site returns*

The Twitter Bootstrap CSS framework that we used in Chapter 3 includes a simple progress bar that is extremely easy to use. All we need to do is check the current time and provide the information and the status bars that reflect the current time.

Additionally, let's hide the login form. For visitors unfamiliar with the Joomla offline status, the form will not allow you to login if you are not a super user or administrator. The login simply fails, even if you are a registered user, and that can be confusing. If we hide the form, it will be a little less puzzling to our users. Because the standard registered user is blocked from logging into the system anyway, hiding the login form is a better user interface. We can make it display when the user clicks on the "online again" message (an unlikely user action except by those who know to do it), so the functionality will remain available to those who need it.

First copy the existing offline page (/templates/system/offline.php) to the path of your template:

/templates/MYTEMPLATE/offline.php

Now modify the offline page until it looks like this:

```php
<?php
defined('_JEXEC') or die;
$app=JFactory::getApplication();
?>
<!DOCTYPE html PUBLIC "-//W3C//DTD XHTML 1.0 Transitional//EN"
"http://www.w3.org/TR/xhtml1/DTD/xhtml1-transitional.dtd">
<html xmlns="http://www.w3.org/1999/xhtml"
    xml:lang="<?php echo $this->language; ?>"
    lang="<?php echo $this->language; ?>"
    dir="<?php echo $this->direction; ?>">
<head>
    <jdoc:include type="head" />
    <link rel="stylesheet"
      href="<?php echo
      $this->baseurl ?>/templates/system/css/offline.css"
      type="text/css" />
    <?php if ($this->direction == 'rtl') : ?>
    <link rel="stylesheet" href="<?php echo
        $this->baseurl
        ?>/templates/system/css/offline_rtl.css" type="text/css" />
    <?php endif; ?>
    <link rel="stylesheet" href="<?php echo
        $this->baseurl ?>/templates/system/css/general.css"
        type="text/css" />
    <link href="//netdna.bootstrapcdn.com/twitter-bootstrap
        /2.1.1/css/bootstrap-combined.min.css" rel="stylesheet" />
</head>
<body>
<jdoc:include type="message" />
    <div id="frame" class="outline">
        <?php if ($app->getCfg('offline_image')) : ?>
        <img src="<?php echo $app->getCfg('offline_image'); ?>"
            alt="<?php echo htmlspecialchars(
            $app->getCfg('sitename')); ?>" />
        <?php endif; ?>
        <h1>
            <?php echo htmlspecialchars($app->getCfg('sitename')); ?>
        </h1>
```

```php
<?php if ($app->getCfg('display_offline_message', 1) == 1 &&
        str_replace(' ', '', $app->getCfg('offline_message'))
        != ''): ?>
    <p>
        <?php echo $app->getCfg('offline_message'); ?>
    </p>
<?php elseif ($app->getCfg('display_offline_message', 1) == 2 &&
    str_replace(' ', '', JText::_('JOFFLINE_MESSAGE')) != ''): ?>
    <p>
        <?php echo JText::_('JOFFLINE_MESSAGE'); ?>
    </p>
<?php  endif; ?>
<form action="<?php echo JRoute::_('index.php', true); ?>"
    method="post" id="form-login"  style="display:none;"
    onclick="document.getElementById('form-login').">
<fieldset class="input">
    <p id="form-login-username">
        <label for="username"><?php echo
          JText::_('JGLOBAL_USERNAME') ?></label>
        <input name="username" id="username" type="text"
           class="inputbox" alt="<?php echo
           JText::_('JGLOBAL_USERNAME') ?>" size="18" />
    </p>
    <p id="form-login-password">
        <label for="passwd"><?php echo
          JText::_('JGLOBAL_PASSWORD') ?></label>
        <input type="password" name="password" class="inputbox"
            size="18" alt="<?php echo
            JText::_('JGLOBAL_PASSWORD') ?>" id="passwd" />
    </p>
    <p id="form-login-remember">
        <label for="remember"><?php echo
           JText::_('JGLOBAL_REMEMBER_ME') ?></label>
        <input type="checkbox" name="remember" class="inputbox"
          value="yes" alt="<?php echo
          JText::_('JGLOBAL_REMEMBER_ME') ?>" id="remember" />
    </p>
    <input type="submit" name="Submit" class="button" value="<?php
        echo JText::_('JLOGIN') ?>" />
    <input type="hidden" name="option" value="com_users" />
    <input type="hidden" name="task" value="user.login" />
    <input type="hidden" name="return" value="<?php echo
        base64_encode(JURI::base()) ?>" />
    <?php echo JHtml::_('form.token'); ?>
</fieldset>
</form>

</div>
```

```php
<?php
$online_ts = strtotime("2012-12-24 23:59:59");
$ts = time();
// If the return time has already passed, make it next Friday
if($ts>$online_ts) {
    $online_ts = strtotime("next Friday");
}
define('ONEDAY',60*60*24);
$delta = $online_ts-$ts;
$days = floor(($delta)/ONEDAY);
$days_in_secs = $days*ONEDAY;
$hours = floor(($delta-$days_in_secs)/60/60);
$hours_in_secs = $hours*60*60;
$minutes = floor(($delta-$days_in_secs-$hours_in_secs)/60);
// Calculated percentages for progress bars
$days_perc = floor(((365-$days)/365)*100);
$hours_perc = floor(((24-$hours)/24)*100);
$minutes_perc = floor(((60-$minutes)/60)*100);
?>

        <div class="container">
            <div class="row">
                <h1 onclick='document.getElementById
                    ("form-login").style.display=""'
                 >Site will be online again in:</h1>
                <div class="span2">
                    <p>
                        <?php echo $days; ?>Days</p>
                </div>
                <div class="span10">
                    <div class="progress progress-striped  active">
                        <div class="bar" style="width:
                            <?php echo $days_perc; ?>%;"></div>
                    </div>
                </div>
            </div>
            <div class="row">
                <div class="span2">
                    <?php echo $hours; ?> Hours
                        </div>
                <div class="span10">
                    <div class="progress progress-striped
                        progress-success active">
                        <div class="bar" style="width: <?php
                            echo $hours_perc; ?>%;"></div>
                    </div>
                </div>
            </div>
            <div class="row">
                <div class="span2">
                    <?php echo $minutes; ?> Minutes
                        </div>
```

```
        <div class="span10">
            <div class="progress progress-striped
                progress-warning active">
                <div class="bar" style="width: <?php
                    echo $minutes_perc; ?>%;"></div>
            </div>
        </div>
    </div>
</div>

</body>
</html>
```

Our new offline form is much more attractive and user-friendly than the standard offline page. Not only does it inform the user when the page will be available again, it does so in a professional and elegant manner. The more attention you pay to small details of a site, the more likely that users will recognize that your site is something special.

You can enhance the offline page even more by adding the native styling and logo of your site. Site offline messages shouldn't be left up for any length of time, but it is possible that Google will spider and cache your offline message, so it is best to provide something representative of your site.

Adding a Custom 404 Page

Like the offline page, you can use a template override to handle site errors. Unlike the offline page that can still use much of the Joomla framework's functionality, the error page is somewhat separate from the Joomla system. It can't use any plugins in the system and cannot include modules or use other <jdoc:include> tags. In other words, the error page needs to be much more self-contained.

Most often, site administrators would like to create a custom 404 page to at least display the site skin so the visitor knows they've landed on your site. The standard Joomla 404 page looks like the one shown in Figure 4-6.

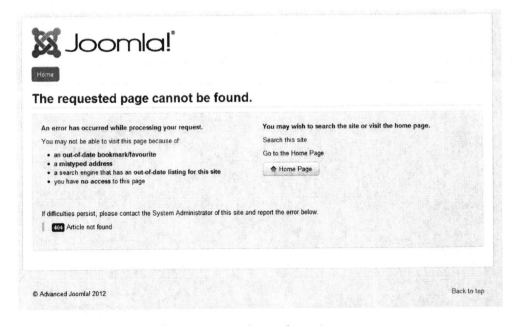

Figure 4-6. *The standard Joomla 404 page is plain and generic*

Let's make a custom error page so you can see how it works. Copy the basic error page from the system templates directory (/templates/system/error.php) to the root of your template directory and then open the copy in your favorite text editor.

You can add custom logic to handle any of the error codes like this:

```php
<?php if (($this->error->getCode()) == '404') {
    echo "My Custom 404 page";
    exit;
}
?>
```

Within the if statement block, you can render a custom page. You can use the PHP function include() to inject another file to render the custom error page. I prefer this method because I can include all the custom styles and even add an automatic search box to help the user find the article that they've been looking to access.

■ **Note** For Joomla versions older than 2.5, use this code check instead:

```php
<?php if ($this->error->code == '404') { ?>
```

You can simply redirect to an article in the Joomla system if you want to create the custom error page there. For example, adding the code header('Location: /mycustom404'); exit; would redirect to a Joomla menu defined for that URL. The problem is that this page would return an HTTP response code of 200 instead of the proper error code (such as 404). For example, you can return a 404 code like this:

```php
<?php if (($this->error->getCode()) == '404') {
    header("HTTP/1.0 404 Not Found");
    echo "My Custom 404 page";
    exit;
}
```

Taking the time to customize the error reporting page or the offline message can seem to be of minor importance. However, you will never see a major web site that does not have an error page that reflects the styling of the main site. Emulating this practice of paying attention to small template details is what distinguishes good professional templates from simple, amateur templates.

Conclusion

Overrides can provide a convenient way to include specific extensions with your template. The most popular overrides are the ones that override the views to provide a custom interface for templates such as the login form. The flexibility of the Joomla system lets a template override just a piece of a component (such as a view) and leave the other parts of the MVC intact. This makes template solutions far less prone to incompatibilities when components upgrade because they are only overriding one element of the whole component.

Even more useful, template overrides provide a method of packaged installation of multiple extensions. Rather than installing a template and then installing two or three other pieces, overrides let you override multiple components in a single installation.

This chapter showed an effective way you can change the front-end display of existing modules without modifying the core code in the Joomla system. In the next chapter, we'll spend time building back-end functionality by enhancing Joomla to access web services. We'll also see how to build Joomla extensions that can use web services to enhance your site. With web services, you can add content to your site such as Twitter postings or Flickr images by having your site call an API.

## CHAPTER 5

Using JavaScript and Ajax to Dynamically Load Page Elements

Web applications are adopting advanced user interface features traditionally found in desktop applications. Drop-down menus, dynamic list boxes, pop-up windows, expanding and collapsing display panes, and live data updates were once available only on platform-specific applications or code-heavy Java apps. Now these features can be found on quick-loading web sites that use technology built into almost every web browser to provide much more immediate and dynamic site interaction.

At the center of this push for a rich user experience on web pages is a set of technologies collectively known as *Ajax*. The name Ajax, originally shorthand for Asynchronous JavaScript and XML, denoted the three original technologies used in dynamic solutions. Ajax has outgrown the original initials, as most sites now use the JSON data format for data communication rather than XML, and CSS has become nearly as important in Ajax solutions as JavaScript. Ajax has been repurposed as a general term to indicate asynchronous technology that is used to dynamically update a web page without requiring a new page load—typically with new information obtained through background interaction with a server-side interface. For example, the Joomla Administrator interface could be set up so that clicking on the publish or unpublish icon could update the article without refreshing the page.

In this chapter, you'll build some Ajax solutions in Joomla:

- *Dynamic JavaScript loader*: A simple function that allows you to dynamically load or lazy load JavaScript files so your main page load is never blocked by an unavailable resource.

- *Article Injector*: Allows creation of Joomla articles without a page refresh.

- *Image lazy loader*: If your Joomla site has a lot of images to display, a lazy loader can make the page display much more quickly.

By constructing these solutions, you can understand how to optimize your Joomla user experience with dynamic elements. You will also see how you can use Joomla as a platform for the most up-to-date user interface features.

How Ajax Changes Web Interaction

In web applications without Ajax, interaction between the user and the web page usually happens in distinct steps, such as:

1. A user makes entries or selections (such as entering a search term).

2. The user clicks a button to submit the selections and a spinning clock is displayed while the user waits for the server to complete the requested operation. The browser must wait for the server response—a process known as synchronous communication, where the user cannot begin another operation until the currently executing one is complete.

3. When the server begins sending the response data, the browser screen clears briefly and then fills with the new page, which has the resulting data.

The next generation of data-driven web pages have a different interactive process. When the user clicks a button or makes a selection, JavaScript sends a request to the server in the background (an asynchronous process) and the user continues interacting with the page in the browser (see Figure 5-1). After the server operation is complete, the resulting data is used to make updates directly on the current page rather than loading a new one.

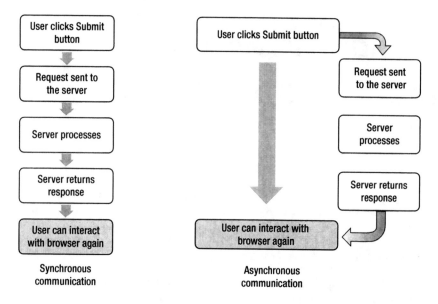

Figure 5-1. *With asynchronous communication, the user can continue to interact with the page immediately after triggering a process*

Some common examples of Ajax functionality include:

- *Live data writing*: You've probably seen the add-to-list functionality, where a text field at the bottom of a list lets you add another entry (a movie to a movie queue, groceries to a shopping list, tasks to a project list, and so forth) and clicking the submit button adds the item to the list on the server without requiring a complete page reload.

- *Autocomplete fields*: When entering text into a search box, a small drop-down menu shows popular searches that might match what is being typed. The menu of possibilities is generally populated by a background Ajax call to the server and then the returned items are inserted into the menu.

- *Lazy loading*: Lazy loading (also called content-on-demand) means loading content after the page has been sent to the browser. Natively, most browsers perform lazy loading for images by first displaying the web page in the browser and subsequently retrieving and displaying images as they are available. Ajax makes this process possible for JavaScript files, image processing, and even data results.

- *Filtering and data ordering*: A row and column data table that shows sales data can allow the user to click on a column head and have the data resorted by that column. Or the user might select a filter to show only sales by quarter that, through Ajax, can re-query the database and update the display table to contain the new information.

- *Manipulating grid data*: The ability to sort grid data based on column headings, collapse and expand data subheads, hide or unhide columns, or perform actual data editing within the cells of a table (called in-place editing) are all common Ajax implementations.

- *Display options in a carousel, slider, or infinite scroll*: Using the dynamic interactive capabilities allowed by JavaScript, you can create new user interface controls that allow changes on the page such as a carousel display or slider control. Infinite scroll is a new user interface paradigm made possible by Ajax, where the user can scroll to the bottom of a page and new content is added dynamically from the server. A fantastic example of infinite scroll is the geo-photo site Trover (www.trover.com).

- *Pop-up information windows*: Allows mouseover events to trigger the retrieval of additional information from the server and display it in a pop-up window. The Netflix movie web site has an excellent example of this functionality where a mouseover of a movie cover activates a pop-up that contains a short description of the movie, running time, rating, and other relevant information. While this feature first appeared prominently on Netflix, it is now used by many large web sites, including Amazon and Wal-Mart.

These are just a few examples of uses for which you can apply Ajax. The asynchronous part of the Ajax acronym represents the decoupling of requests and returned information. In synchronous communication, one request must follow another until the sequence is complete. By switching interaction to asynchronous processes, the site can supply information as it is ready or when it is requested, giving a web application the ability to replicate the more responsive and fluid interaction possibilities of a desktop application.

Joomla sites can benefit from implementing Ajax technology to give users more flexibility and making a Joomla site more contemporary. Let's start with learning how to implement lazy loading to dynamically load JavaScript files and Ajax request calls to update information on the Joomla servers. You can use both of these examples as an effective foundation from which you can create more complete extensions.

■ **Note**   Even though the X in Ajax stands for XML, web sites are increasingly using the JSON (JavaScript Object Notation) data interchange format for communications between the client and server. JSON is smaller and lighter-weight than XML, making is faster to transfer over the web. In this chapter, all of the Ajax implementations will exchange data using JSON data structures.

Dynamic Loading or Lazy Loading of Content

One very useful aspect of Ajax implementation is the ability to load content dynamically, a process commonly referred to as *lazy loading*. Dynamically loading content can improve the user experience by letting the page display before all of the pieces have been retrieved from the server. Implementing dynamic loading in a Joomla site lets you load content only when and where it is needed. Most major web sites practice lazy loading because the site owners understand that the sooner the core content is displayed, the more responsive the site will feel to the visitor.

Although implementing dynamic loading can make the design and implementation of a site more complicated, it has the following advantages:

- *Allows initial content to be displayed more quickly*: The page displays much more quickly because the browser receives a "page ready" signal after the bare-bones version of the page is complete, so the page begins rendering in the browser window. The remaining content is added to the page as it is needed or becomes available.

- *Eliminates blocking or stop content*: When content is accessed from another site, whether it is a JavaScript file or a call to a web API, the page load may wait for the communication to complete before the page displays. This can be a huge problem if the remote hosting site goes offline or is blocked by the user's corporate firewall. If the reference to the remote content occurs in the <head> section of your web page, the display of your page will be delayed until a timeout occurs—usually 30 seconds or more.

- *Prevents loading unnecessary items*: Rather than load all content for all users, you can load only the libraries or files that are needed for that user. If a web page contains 100 images, the dynamic loading routine can download an image only when the user scrolls it into the window view. If your site supports Facebook Connect, the JavaScript library that provides that functionality could be loaded only after the user has requested a Facebook service with a link or button click.

- *Present a friendly display for items with long query times*: Sometimes a database query can take more time to complete than you want to force your visitor to stare at a blank screen. By accessing it asynchronously, the page will display and the data will be displayed as it becomes available. While the page is waiting for the content, you can display an animated "Data Loading" or progress bar.

You've probably seen dynamic loading on many sites you access regularly, although you may not have recognized the technology that was used until now. Given the compelling advantages of lazy loading content detailed in the list above, it seems like you would want to dynamically load much of the content displayed on your Joomla site. However, before you begin converting all your components and modules to use Ajax technology, you need to consider the drawbacks, and make decisions accordingly.

Here are some of the drawbacks of dynamically loading content:

- *Works best on the latest browsers*: Dynamic loading generally works much better with more up-to-date browsers, so very old browsers (such as Internet Explorer 5) won't be able to use a page that includes this type of dynamic content.

- Content is invisible to search engine spiders: Since JavaScript execution is required to populate the content, search engine spiders that retrieve and index raw HTML content will not execute the JavaScript that retrieves the Ajax-based content. An aggressive Ajax-loading page can appear virtually empty to a search engine and is therefore unlikely to be found by users. This "invisible content" problem can have a significant impact on the page's search engine ranking if you're using lazy loading text or data that might be relevant to the content of the page.

- *Can be processor-intensive*: With multiple operations executing at the same time, dynamic loading can slow down the user's browser. This is generally not a problem on desktop machines if it isn't used excessively, but can cause poor performance on mobile browsers and tablets.

- *JavaScript is required*: If JavaScript isn't enabled or is unavailable, then the content is never loaded. This can be a problem particularly with text-based browsers.

- *Unpleasant pop-up content experience*: Some sites that populate content as it is loaded have layouts that seem to skitter and shake as the lazy loaded content is displayed and existing page elements need to make room for the new items. It can be particularly annoying if, just as the user is about to click on a piece of content, a new piece of content pops into the display, shifts the existing content, and the user clicks on an item other than the intended one.

- *Potential accessibility problems*: Some "accessible" browsers for those with handicaps can have problems with the dynamic content, although this is becoming less of a problem as all browsers become more advanced.

A good rule of thumb to judge what content to dynamically load is to ask yourself: if the loaded content was invisible to a search engine, would that matter for the site? If your site has a forum and you want to display a list of the top ten people posting messages, this information would be largely ignored by the search engines anyway. The long query times to tabulate this data may make it an ideal candidate for dynamic loading. In contrast, the content of written articles directly related to the rest of the page would be a poor choice for this technology because you would want it indexed by the search engines to give the page context.

Joomla's module-based display system lends itself extraordinarily well to dynamic loading of content. You can create specific modules that send a JavaScript asynchronous request to a Joomla component that performs the operations (such as database queries) and returns the information for display. Likewise, you can adapt templates to use dynamic loading methods.

■ **Note** Although dynamic loading is covered in this chapter, advanced JavaScript-based client-side dynamic binding is beyond the scope of this chapter. If you have needs of this type of heavy data interaction, I suggest examining one of the JavaScript frameworks that provide a complete client-side MVC model. Some of the most popular frameworks include AngularJS (http://angularjs.org, maintained by Google), the Knockout framework (http://knockoutjs.com/), Backbone.JS (http://backbonejs.org), Ember (http://emberjs.com), or Agility.JS (http://agilityjs.com).

In this chapter, you'll see how to adapt Joomla templates and extensions to use dynamic loading features such as loading JavaScript code and injecting it into the document. You can use dynamic JavaScript loading to prevent slow responses from remote servers stalling page load or failed requests and stopping your page load. You can also use this technique to provide on-demand loading so the JavaScript is retrieved only when it is needed. To implement this technique, you'll use the jQuery JavaScript library that is built into Joomla to provide the events system needed to best handle the dynamic loading.

Injecting JavaScript Libraries into a Page

Many modern web pages are bristling with JavaScript to provide features such as analytics tracking, connecting with external APIs (such as Facebook or Twitter), custom advertisement display, and dynamic Ajax interaction. With so many JavaScript files to read, page load times can suffer.

Further, if the files that are loaded in the page's head section are external to your web server and the firewall restricts access to the third-party hosting site (as some organizations are blocking access to Facebook URLs), your page display in the visitor's browser will be prevented until the request for the file times out (sometimes more than 30 seconds). Until the timeout, your user will stare at a blank browser window.

By allowing the JavaScript that is not absolutely necessary to the page display to be added as it is available or only when needed, the page can load, display, and then retrieve the extra information after the visitor can already interact with the page.

You can see how necessary adding lazy loading can be by profiling the load of a web page. One of the features of the Firebug add-on for Firefox will profile a page showing the individual load times of each file on your page. If you haven't already installed Firebug (http://getfirebug.com/), you should install it now to check the loading of your page.

Display the Firebug window by clicking on the Firebug icon or hitting the F12 key and then select the Net tab. The Net tab profiling is disabled by default, so if you haven't enabled it already, click on the menu arrow of the tab and select the Enabled option. Once the Net tab is displayed and enabled, refresh the page you want to profile and you will see a graphic display of the load time for various files of your web page, as shown in Figure 5-2. This profile of a popular web site shows how many files are loaded with each page view. On a slow connection, this can mean a very poor load time for the page.

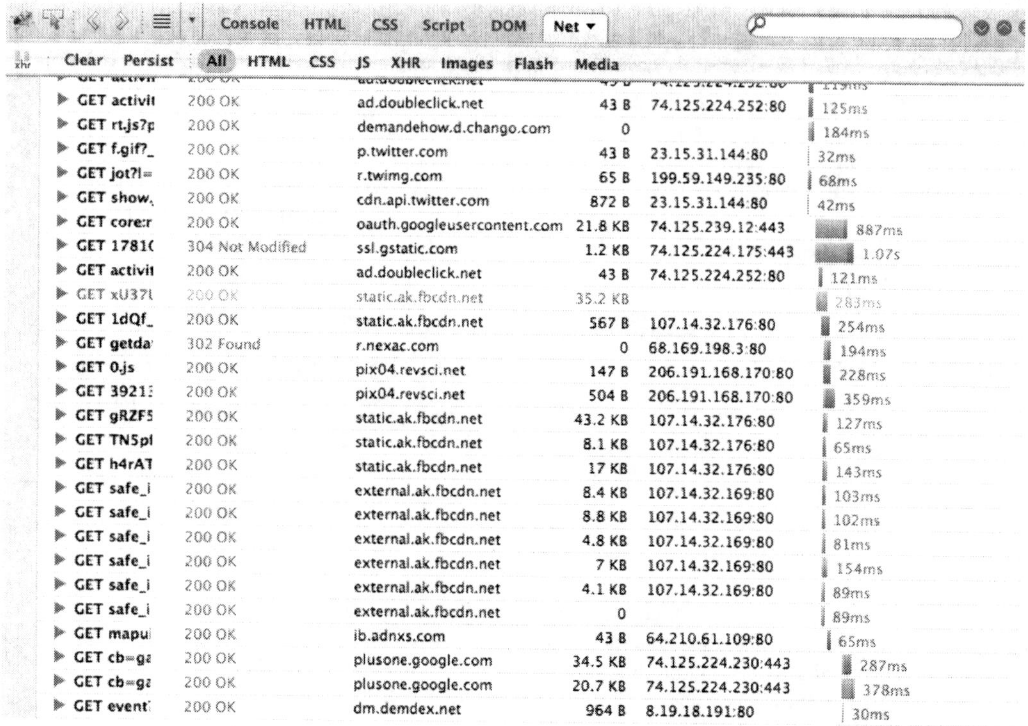

▶ GET activit	200 OK	ad.doubleclick.net	43 B	74.125.224.252:80	125ms
▶ GET rt.js?p	200 OK	demandehow.d.chango.com	0		184ms
▶ GET f.gif?_	200 OK	p.twitter.com	43 B	23.15.31.144:80	32ms
▶ GET jot?l=	200 OK	r.twimg.com	65 B	199.59.149.235:80	68ms
▶ GET show,	200 OK	cdn.api.twitter.com	872 B	23.15.31.144:80	42ms
▶ GET core:r	200 OK	oauth.googleusercontent.com	21.8 KB	74.125.239.12:443	887ms
▶ GET 1781(	304 Not Modified	ssl.gstatic.com	1.2 KB	74.125.224.175:443	1.07s
▶ GET activit	200 OK	ad.doubleclick.net	43 B	74.125.224.252:80	121ms
▶ GET xU37(	200 OK	static.ak.fbcdn.net	35.2 KB		283ms
▶ GET 1dQf_	200 OK	static.ak.fbcdn.net	567 B	107.14.32.176:80	254ms
▶ GET getda	302 Found	r.nexac.com	0	68.169.198.3:80	194ms
▶ GET 0.js	200 OK	pix04.revsci.net	147 B	206.191.168.170:80	228ms
▶ GET 3921:	200 OK	pix04.revsci.net	504 B	206.191.168.170:80	359ms
▶ GET gRZF5	200 OK	static.ak.fbcdn.net	43.2 KB	107.14.32.176:80	127ms
▶ GET TN5pl	200 OK	static.ak.fbcdn.net	8.1 KB	107.14.32.176:80	65ms
▶ GET h4rAT	200 OK	static.ak.fbcdn.net	17 KB	107.14.32.176:80	143ms
▶ GET safe_i	200 OK	external.ak.fbcdn.net	8.4 KB	107.14.32.169:80	103ms
▶ GET safe_i	200 OK	external.ak.fbcdn.net	8.8 KB	107.14.32.169:80	102ms
▶ GET safe_i	200 OK	external.ak.fbcdn.net	4.8 KB	107.14.32.169:80	81ms
▶ GET safe_i	200 OK	external.ak.fbcdn.net	7 KB	107.14.32.169:80	154ms
▶ GET safe_i	200 OK	external.ak.fbcdn.net	4.1 KB	107.14.32.169:80	89ms
▶ GET safe_i	200 OK	external.ak.fbcdn.net	0		89ms
▶ GET mapu	200 OK	ib.adnxs.com	43 B	64.210.61.109:80	65ms
▶ GET cb=ga	200 OK	plusone.google.com	34.5 KB	74.125.224.230:443	287ms
▶ GET cb=ga	200 OK	plusone.google.com	20.7 KB	74.125.224.230:443	378ms
▶ GET event:	200 OK	dm.demdex.net	964 B	8.19.18.191:80	30ms

Figure 5-2. *Firebug allows you to profile the loading of individual pages to see which net requests took the longest time to complete*

The profile can help you see which files are slow to load and you can consider how necessary these files are for initial page load. Then consider the likelihood of the file being unavailable. If the file is not necessary for initial page load and may block your site, that file is a definite candidate for dynamic loading.

Implementing Dynamic JavaScript Loading

Creating a system to dynamically load JavaScript can be complicated because the files that need to be loaded can be spread across many locations (in the template, in a component, in a module, and so forth). Additionally, when the loading occurs, it must happen in generally the order that is specified by the sequence, otherwise code block B that needs code block A to execute will fail if that code block still hasn't loaded.

A system that queues dynamic loading of files can best be created by designing a function that can be called by other pieces of code to queue files for later loading. The function can follow the order that it is passed load requests to handle the load order and you can place it in a common file that contains your site JavaScript that is already included in your Joomla template. For example, most templates load a JavaScript file called `template.js` that has all of the core JavaScript functions used by the page. This file is the perfect location to place your dynamic loading function.

Look at the `index.php` file of the template you're using and you should see a reference like this that loads a common JavaScript file:

```
<script type="text/javascript"
  src="<?php echo $this->baseurl ?>/templates/<?php
  echo $this->template ?>/javascript/template.js"></script>
```

Adding the dynamic loader function to a common JavaScript file such as template.js not only allows it to be called by other JavaScript functions used by the template, but it can also be accessed by any custom Joomla extensions that you build for the site.

Fortunately, adding this function with jQuery is a very simple process. The jQuery framework includes the getScript() function that you can use to dynamically load JavaScript. If, for example, your template needed to use a Facebook library for certain aspects of the user experience, but Facebook wasn't critical to use the page, dynamically loading the library is ideal. This simple example of the Facebook JavaScript file would look like this:

```
$.getScript('
    http://static.ak.connect.facebook.com/js/api_
    lib/v0.4/FeatureLoader.js.php')
```

Creating a function to manage the lazy loading of multiple files is just slightly more complex because we want to make sure a JavaScript library is loaded only once and also provide a callback function to execute additional JavaScript once the script load is complete in case the sequence is important. Open the template.js of your current template (or create it if need be) and add the following dynamic loading function:

```
function dynaLoadJS(url,callback) {
  if(url==undefined) {
    return false;
  }
  if(document.scripts==undefined) {
    document.scripts = {};
  }
  if(document.scripts[url]!=undefined) {
    return true;
  }
  if(callback != undefined) {
    $.getScript(url, callback);
  } else {
    $.getScript(url);
  }
}}
```

You can use this function to dynamically load a JavaScript file and then execute a function. For example, if we wanted to modify the Beez template to load the md_stylechanger.js file dynamically, we could add the following line (which must appear after the template.js is loaded):

```
<?php $path = $this->baseurl . '/templates/' .
        $this->template . '/javascript/md_stylechanger.js'; ?>
<script>
dynaLoadJS('<?php echo $path; ?>',function(o){alert('loaded:'+o);});
</script>
```

When the template is loaded, the JavaScript for the style changer will be dynamically loaded and, once complete, an alert box will display a loaded message. This demonstrates one simple use of Ajax to change the load dynamics of a page. In the next section, you'll create a small, but complete, Ajax application that can quickly and conveniently add articles to a Joomla site. The Ajax application is built as a self-contained Joomla component.

■ **Note**   Whether the browser is dynamically loading files or using a more traditional method, note that browsers only allow a maximum of five simultaneous connections to a single web domain. That means if you try to show 100 images from the same domain (for example, `www.example.com`), only 5 will be loaded in parallel. To circumvent this limitation, you can look into a CDN or use multiple domains or subdomains to store your content (`myjs.example.com` and `www.example.com` are treated as two different sites and can each have 5 simultaneous connections).

Creating the Article Injector Component

Creating new articles in Joomla can be a tedious process when you want to enter small and fast "happening now"-type update articles for a blog or create the drafts of many articles quickly. You typically don't need the power of the complete TinyMCE editor or access to the full gamut of article properties for these types of tasks. What you need is a quick front-end interface to create articles. Enter the Article Injector.

With a simple interface (see Figure 5-3), you can enter the introtext, title of an article, category, and published flag for each article—all on a single line. This type of interface is perfect for blogging a live event or quickly brainstorming articles that you might write later by entering the basic premise of the article that may be expanded upon later. As you insert each new article, that article is added to the row above the current line so you can see the articles that are already entered successfully.

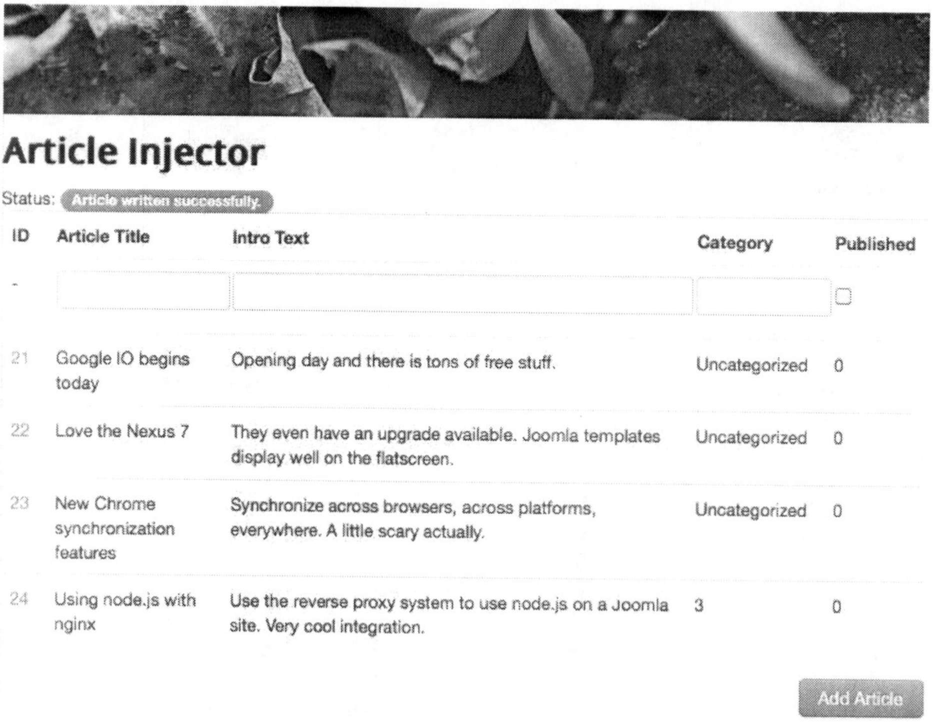

Figure 5-3. *The Article Injector lets you quickly enter the summaries of articles for later editing and writing*

This type of component can be useful by itself, depending on your needs, but its real power comes as a useful learning tool that shows how you can construct a Joomla Ajax component. Let's start by setting up the basic Joomla infrastructure for installing the component.

Creating the Directory Structure and the Installation file

To create the Article Injector, start by making a folder named com_articleinjector/ and a JavaScript folder inside it with the path com_articleinjector/js. This directory structure will hold the basic component. In your favorite text editor, create a file called articleinjector.xml in the root of the component folder.

Add the following text to the XML file:

```xml
<?xml version="1.0" encoding="utf-8"?>
<extension type="component" version="2.5.0">
    <name>COM_ARTICLEINJECTOR</name>
    <creationDate>November 2012</creationDate>
    <author>Dan Rahmel</author>
    <authorUrl>http://www.joomlajumpstart.com</authorUrl>
    <version>0.1.0</version>
    <description>Component that allows fast article creation
    for blog entries and article placeholders.
    You can access it on your site at the URL:
 /index.php?option=com_articleinjector&view=categories
    </description>

    <files>
        <filename>articleinjector.php</filename>
        <filename>articleinjector_view.php</filename>
        <filename>index.html</filename>
        <folder>js</folder>
    </files>
    <administration>
    <!-- Administration Menu Section -->
        <menu>Article Injector</menu>
        <files>
            <filename>index.html</filename>
        </files>
    </administration>
    <media destination="com_articleinjector" folder="media">
        <filename>index.html</filename>
    </media>
</extension>
```

This XML metadata file simply tells the Joomla installer the component to be created and the files that will be needed for it. The installation script is very simple and doesn't include structures that you would normally include for a component, such as menu icons and an administrator interface. The tagged <administration> section is included for the sole reason that the Joomla installer throws an error during installation if this section is missing.

In the root of the directory, create an empty text file named index.html. This file is a placeholder to prevent directory browsing if the web server hosting the site is set up incorrectly. Once you have those basic files in place, you can begin constructing the component.

Constructing the Component View

The front-end interface for the Article Injector is actually a fairly simple HTML structure. It consists of an HTML form with the fields to accept the text field input and the JavaScript call to add each new article instance. With Ajax-centric applications, there is generally much less server-side code because the client JavaScript is handling the heavy lifting.

The Article Injector component assumes that two files will already be loaded by the site template within which it will be displayed—the jQuery JavaScript framework and the Twitter Bootstrap CSS framework. If either of these is missing, be sure to either add them to your template.

You can use a third-party CDN to load each of these libraries. Using external CDNs will usually speed page load for a variety of reasons, including the geographic proximity of the edge server. If you would like to load jQuery from the Google CDN, you can add the following line to your template:

```
<script src=
"//ajax.googleapis.com/ajax/libs/jquery/1.9.1/jquery.min.js">
</script>
```

For Twitter Bootstrap, you can use the NetDNA CDN by adding the following to your Joomla template:

```
<link rel="stylesheet" href=
"//netdna.bootstrapcdn.com/twitter-bootstrap/2.3.0/css/bootstrap-combined.min.css" />
```

If you would prefer not to use CDNs and want to load both jQuery and Bootstrap from your Joomla server install, add the following lines to your template instead:

```
<script src="/media/jui/js/jquery.min.js"></script>
<link rel="stylesheet" href="/media/jui/css/bootstrap.min.css" />
```

Now that we have those two dependencies covered, let's start creating the core component. In the root of your component folder, create a new file named articleinjector_view.php and enter the following code:

```
<script type="text/javascript" src="<?php
    echo JURI::base(true);
    ?>/components/com_articleinjector/js/articleinjector.js"></script>
<div>
    Status: <span id="txtStatus" class="badge"></span>
</div>
<table class="table">
    <tbody id="entry_table">
        <tr>
            <th style="width:5%;">ID</th>
            <th style="width:20%;">
                <?php echo JText::_( "Article Title"); ?></th>
            <th style="width:60%;">
                <?php echo JText::_( "Intro Text"); ?> </th>
            <th style="width:20%;">
                <?php echo JText::_( "Category"); ?> </th>
            <th style="width:5%;">
                <?php echo JText::_( "Published"); ?> </th>
        </tr>
        <tr id="proto_row" style="display:none;">
            <td class="ai_id"></td>
            <td class="ai_title"></td>
```

```
            <td class="ai_text"></td>
            <td class="ai_category"></td>
            <td class="ai_published"></td>
        </tr>
        <tr id="entry_row">
            <td>-</td>
            <td>
                <input style="width:100%;" type="text"
                    name="article_title" id="article_title" />
            </td>
            <td>
                <input style="width:100%;" type="text"
                    name="intro_text" id="intro_text" />
            </td>
            <td>
                <input style="width:100%;" type="text"
                    name="category" id="category" />
            </td>
            <td>
                <input type="checkbox" id="chkPublish"
                    name="chkPublish" value="" />
            </td>
        </tr>
    </tbody>
</table>
<div style="text-align:right;">
    <button class="btn btn-success" type="button"
        onclick="ajaxInsert();return false;">
            <?php echo JText::_( "Add Article"); ?> </button>
</div>
```

The design of this component is simple. It displays an entry table that allows you to enter the article title, article name, category (optional), and check whether the article is published when it is created.

You might notice that the second row of the table is hidden. It contains a prototype of the table row that will be displayed with each new article insert. When a new row needs to be added, the JavaScript clones the prototype row and then populates it with data returned from the successful article insertion.

■ **Note** Many JavaScript libraries insert a great deal of HTML through JavaScript, but using JavaScript for HTML generation moves the presentation (or view) of the content into JavaScript code. Having presentation layout in code will limit the ability of graphic designers to make structural changes to the layout and eliminates the opportunity to use graphic design tools. By including a prototype element that is hidden, as shown in this code, you can use design tools such as Dreamweaver to customize the presentation by simply making the element visible during the editing phase. The code then clones the prototype element for additional entries. This allows the best of both worlds where the code can dynamically augment content and yet you can create the design of the dynamic items using standard user interface tools.

As you can see, the Article Injector view does very little processing. The real activity of the component takes place between the back-end component code and the JavaScript that executes the Ajax processing.

Coding the Ajax JavaScript

After the user enters the basic information into the form, the JavaScript handles sending this information to the component for back-end processing (inserting the article into the Joomla database). When the back-end processing is complete, the success or failure of the insertion is returned along with additional information such as a link to the new article. With the jQuery ajax() function, handling a dynamic post (that doesn't require a page reload) becomes a very simple process.

Create a new file called articleinjector.js in the js/ folder of the component and enter the following code:

```javascript
// This function will add the item to the display table after it
// receives confirmation from the Ajax request
function addTableItem(response) {
    if(response.success==0) {
        jQuery("#txtStatus").html("Article write failed: "+response.msg);
        return;
    } else {
        jQuery("#txtStatus").html("Article written successfully.");
    }
    if(document.clonenum==undefined) {
        document.clonenum = 0;
    }
    document.clonenum++;
    // Get the container of the entry form and
    // make a copy of the prototype row and inject it before the entry row
    var my_clone = jQuery('#proto_row').clone().appendTo('#entry_table');
    // Set the ID of the new row so it's different from the prototype
    my_clone.attr("id","cloneid"+document.clonenum);
    // Set the text fields with values from the Ajax return
    jQuery(my_clone)
        .find(".ai_id").html('<a target="_blank" href="'+response.url+'">'+
            response.id+'</a>').end()
        .find(".ai_title").html(response.title).end()
        .find(".ai_text").html(response.text).end()
        .find(".ai_category").html(response.category).end()
        .find(".ai_published").html(response.published).end()
        ;
    // Clear the style that hides the protorow so this one will be visible
    my_clone.show();
    // Clear the text fields for the next entry
    jQuery('#article_title').val('');
    jQuery('#intro_text').val('');
    jQuery('#category').val('');
}

function ajaxInsert() {
    jQuery("#txtStatus").html("Posting new article...");
    jQuery.ajax({
        type: 'POST',
        url: '/index.php?option=com_articleinjector'+
            '&task=insert&format=raw',
```

```
    data: {
        'title' : jQuery('#article_title').val(),
        'text' : jQuery('#intro_text').val(),
        'category' : jQuery('#category').val(),
        'publish' : jQuery("#chkPublish").is(':checked')
    },
    success: function(response) {
        addTableItem(response);
    }
});
}
```

Let's start by examining the JavaScript code that performs the POST of the form information. If you are a beginning jQuery user, you might be puzzled by the code's use of the jQuery() object instead of the simpler $() object, which performs the same function. Joomla has historically used the MooTools JavaScript framework and included it with all of the versions of Joomla prior to version 3. Although Joomla has transitioned itself to jQuery, many templates still use MooTools and even load it on the same page as jQuery.

MooTools itself defines a $() operator and this tends to dominate the jQuery definition. There are several ways to work around these sorts of conflicts. For simplicity, I just replaced the $() operator with jQuery(), which will work in all contexts. You can also use the jQuery.noConflict() function, but simply getting in the practice of the jQuery() call on a shared library page will help you if you're using the browser console to execute jQuery commands.

When the user clicks the "Add Article" button on the interface, the ajaxInsert() function actually performs the Ajax post. The call to the jQuery routine includes four parameters:

- *type* property: Determines the type of Ajax request, which in this case is 'POST', but might be a 'GET' request for other applications.

- *url* property: Reference URL for the com_articleinjector component that you'll build in the next section.

- *data* property: Holds the data to be sent to the server during the post. In normal post operations (such as a standard HTML <form>), the browser automatically populates the post request with data from the form. Because this code is using a JavaScript Ajax request, the data property holds an associative array of the values we want to send. Here again the jQuery() selector function is used and the value property of each item (title, text, category, and publish) is retrieved and included in the array. Alternately, you can use jQuery's serialize() function to collect all the form values.

- *success* property: Code to be executed when a successful Ajax call has been completed. You can see that this success function calls the addTableItem() function to display the new addition in the article list.

The addTableItem() function is called to process the response from the Ajax post. The first executing line of the function checks for the success of the call. If unsuccessful, the status message displays the failure reason to the user and returns from the function.

If the post was successful, the status is updated appropriately and the clonenum (used for the CSS id value of the new row) is incremented by one. The line that follows makes a clone of the prototype row and appends it to the current table. The remainder of the function code simply populates the rows with the text of the inserted entry and clears the entry boxes of the inserted data.

The code that dynamically populates the text of the prototype row in the table is one of the more powerful and useful utilities available from jQuery. Very often, a JavaScript developer will want to locate one element on the page and then access and modify the children of that item. Using a new selector to find each item can be expensive because the entire DOM must be traversed with each call. Instead, this code will find the parent element once and then all other operations are performed on children of that element:

```
jQuery("#myParentElement")
    .find(".ai_text").html(response.text).end()
    .find(".ai_category").html(response.category).end()
    .find(".ai_published").html(response.published).end()
    ;
```

Each find() method call will traverse only the children of a specified target and any processing of the children nodes can be followed by a call to end(). The end() call will close the process of the current find and then allow further find operations. With this technique, you can chain find() selectors and modification scripts. You can see that the addTableItem() function uses five of these chained find() methods to quickly and efficiently populate the table row with the data returned by the article insert.

I suspect you can already see how this simple Ajax implementation can provide a much more elegant and user-friendly interface than a traditional full page post operation. Using a small amount of JavaScript code in your web applications can make a dramatic difference in how your Joomla site is perceived.

If this same functionality were to be handled as a traditional form post and full page refresh to show a single small added entry, it would seem a little clunky and non-responsive. In contrast, this update is quick, dynamic, and increasingly the user interface experience that is expected from advanced web applications. To complete the Article Injector functionality, you need to build the article insertion portion of the component that is called by the Ajax post.

Building the Controller

Now that all of the client-side logic is complete, we need to create the back-end Ajax logic that handles the posting of the article to the Joomla content engine.

Create a new file in the component folder called articleinjector.php and enter the following code:

```php
<?php
// no direct access
defined('_JEXEC') or die;

jimport('joomla.application.component.controller');
$app = JFactory::getApplication();
$task = $app->input->get('task');
$document = JFactory::getDocument();

switch($task) {
    case 'insert':
        $db = JFactory::getDbo();
        $user = JFactory::getUser();
        $app = JFactory::getApplication();

        // Create a user access object for the user
        $access                 = new stdClass();
        $access->canEdit        = 1;
        //$user->authorize('com_content', 'edit', 'content', 'all');
        $access->canEditOwn     = 1;
```

```
//$user->authorize('com_content', 'edit', 'content', 'own');
$access->canPublish       = 1;
//$user->authorize('com_content', 'publish', 'content', 'all');

// load the category
$catID = 2;
$cat = JTable::getInstance('category');
$cat->load($catID);

// Include the content plugins for the onSave events.
JPluginHelper::importPlugin('content');

$title = $app->input->get('title');
$text = $app->input->get('text');
$category = $app->input->get('category');
$category = is_numeric($category) && intval($category)>1
    ?  intval($category)    :   2;
$category_name = $category==2
    ?  'Uncategorized' :    $category;
$publish = $app->input->get('publish')=='false'
    ?  0   :   1;

// Get an empty article object
$article = JTable::getInstance('content');
$value = 0;
if ($value) {
    $article->load($value);
}
$article->title     = $title;
$article->alias     = strtolower(str_replace(' ','-',$title));
$article->introtext = $text;
$article->fulltext      = '';

$article->catid     = $catID;
// At the time of this writing, these had no default values,
// so need to be set and sent through
$article->images = '';
$article->urls = '';
$article->attribs = '';
$article->metakey = '';
$article->metadesc = '';
$article->metadata = '';
$article->language = '';
$article->xreference = '';

$date = JFactory::getDate();

$article->created       = $date->toSQL();
$article->created_by    = $user->get('id');
```

```php
        $article->publish_up    = $date->toSQL();
        $article->publish_down   = $db->getNullDate();
        $published = ($publish && $access->canPublish) ? 1 : 0;
        $article->state     = $published;
        $article->version++;

        $success=1;
        $msg = '';
        if (!$article->check()) {
            $msg = JText::_('Bad data');
            $success=0;
        } else {
            $result = $article->store();
            if (!$article->id) {
                $msg = JText::_('Duplicate article alias');
                $success=0;
            }
        }
        // At the time of this writing, JRoute isn't working properly
        //$articleURL = JRoute::_('index.php?option=com_content&id='.$article->id);
        $articleURL = '/index.php?option=com_content&view=article&Itemid=1&id='
            .$article->id;

        // create a new content item
        header('Content-Type: application/json');
        echo json_encode(array(
            'success'=>$success,
            'msg'=>$msg,
            'id'=>$article->id,
            'title'=>$title,
            'text'=>$text,
            'category'=>$category_name,
            'published'=>$published,
            'url'=>$articleURL)
        );
        exit;
    default:
        $a=1;
}

$title = "Advanced Joomla Article Injector";
echo '<h1>Article Injector</h1>';
$app = JFactory::getApplication();
$document = JFactory::getDocument();

$document->setTitle($title);
$link = '';
$attribs = array();
include("articleinjector_view.php");
?>
```

The controller code begins by determining the task to be performed. This controller only handles two task types: view and insert. The view simply displays the `articleinjector_view.php` file for entry of new articles. The insert task performs the creation of a new article from the data sent by the Ajax call.

The code instantiates various Joomla objects it can use for page creation. This includes the user access object that checks the permissions of the logged in user to ensure that the user has the necessary privileges to post an article to the site. You don't want anyone who obtains the URL to be able to post to your site.

Next, the category is loaded by the category ID. If the category ID specified by the user is invalid, then the uncategorized "category" with an ID of 2 is used.

The `input->get()` method is used to obtain variables posted by the form. You should use this method for all of the data that is sent from the outside world because it cleans the data on entry and helps prevent various types of hacking attacks.

With the data loaded into variables, it's time to create the article. The `getInstance()` method is used to generate a new 'content' document object that is used for articles. That object is then populated with the data sent from the Ajax call. Note that the alias is cleaned of non-alphanumeric characters and set to lowercase in compliance with Joomla's general alias standards.

The `check()` method is called once all of the article data is added to make sure it conforms to article type standards. If it does, the `store()` method is called to add the article to the Joomla database. The results of the store are then returned to the Ajax call as a JSON object that the receiving JavaScript can process and act upon.

Once you've created this file, you are ready to install the component. In a test setup, you can simply use the Install from Directory option in the Extension Manager. If not, zip the files and install the component to your remote server. Now you're ready to start adding articles. Note that the creation of the article uses all of the standard Joomla article creation objects, so articles created through this interface should function seamlessly for later Joomla upgrades.

This implementation demonstrated a new component that benefited in usability and user experience by using Ajax instead of traditional page reload methods. However, you don't need to create something completely new to take advantage of Ajax. You can add enhancements such as lazy loading of images to existing extensions and templates.

Adding Lazy Loading of Images

Many Joomla sites include some form of gallery. Others sites have pages that contain dozens of images—whether these images are included in content articles or displayed by various extensions. With a little extra work, you can create articles and extensions that load images as they are displayed by the browser. You can also modify existing extensions to provide these capabilities.

You can create your own image lazy loader, but there are a great number of special cases for browser compatibility glitches and special features (such as dynamic below-the-fold loading) that can make creating a loader a large task. For that reason, this section will describe the basic concepts used by a lazy loader and then show you how to use an excellent jQuery loader that has all of the bells and whistles.

A lazy loader works by populating image elements with a placeholder image (such as a transparent single pixel) and then setting the `src` attribute as needed. For example, before loading, an image element might appear like this:

```
<img src="transparentpixel.png" data-src="/images/mymainimage.png" />
```

The real image path, `/images/mymainimage.png`, is stored in the `data-src` attribute which is ignored by the browser renderer. Under whatever conditions are desired, such as the user scrolling the image into view, the `src` attribute is populated with the path in the `data-src` attribute. In jQuery, you can perform this replacement with code like this:

```
$("#belowthefold").find("img[data-src]").each(
        function() {
                $(this).attr('src',$(this).attr('data-src'))
                        .removeAttr('data-src');
        }
);
```

You can use this type of code to load almost any resource. Adding this type of on-demand image loading is easiest if the core code is added at the template level. There is a very good jQuery plug-in that provides excellent lazy loading capabilities written by Mika Tuupola and available here for download:

https://github.com/tuupola/jquery_lazyload

Download the minified version and place it in the /media/jui/js/ folder of your Joomla installation. Next, add a reference to the file in your template following the script loading of jQuery like this:

```
<script src="/media/jui/js/jquery.min.js"
    type="text/javascript"></script>
<script src="/media/jui/js/jquery.lazyload.js"
 type="text/javascript"></script>
```

Now you only need to change your <img> tags to use a placeholder image (one is included with the lazy loader plug-in). The tag would look like this:

```
<img class="joomlazy" src="img/grey.gif"
    data-original="img/example.jpg"  width="640" heigh="480">
```

At the bottom of your template (or within a DOM ready structure), add an activation call:

```
$("img.lazy").lazyload();
```

You can modify any image tag in any article or modify the image tag generators of any extensions to use the lazy loading.

Ajax Implementation Particulars

Building a Joomla site around Ajax functionality means that you have to make certain the features work across multiple browsers. Before Ajax, a failure of a web page in a browser typically meant that the page displayed poorly or looked a little funky. If the JavaScript fails in a particular browser, that could mean that functional portions of the web site could be lost to users of an incompatible browser. Therefore, it is important for even small sites to test across a variety of browsers. Generally testing on the three major browsers (Microsoft Internet Explorer, Mozilla Firefox, and Google Chrome) provides enough evidence that the site will satisfy most users.

You can minimize the number of adjustments to your Ajax code by understanding some of the most common differences between the browsers. Whenever a JavaScript implementation is required, there are nearly always special factors that must be taken into account to ensure compatibility. Even setting text to a particular value exposes differences in browser implementations.

InnerText and TextContent

Many Ajax solutions inject text into the displayed HTML page document to do everything from updating a progress bar to populating a data table. As in many areas of browser incompatibility, the addition of text to a document through the Document Object Model (DOM) requires special handling particular to specific sets of browsers. A common example is a list of items (such as a message list) where clicking a button to the left of the item performs an action (such as update or delete) and a message appears at the top of the page when the action is complete.

Internet Explorer and most other browsers implement the innerText property to get and set text contained by an element (such as a cell of a table). Firefox, however, uses the textContent property for the same functionality. For cross-browser compatibility, a JavaScript program normally would have to determine the browser type before inserting text with an if statement such as this:

```
if(typeof document.getElementById('myid').innerText
    != "undefined") {
    document.getElementById('myid').innerText = "mytext"
} else {
    document.getElementById('myid').textContent = "mytext"
}
```

Fortunately, jQuery provides methods for getting and setting text that automatically selects the correct property, so you don't need to include browser tests in many parts of your code. The same cross-browser functionality outlined above could be handled by a single jQuery statement:

```
$('#myid ').html('text');
```

For adjusting the contents of a document, therefore, try to use the jQuery methods that exist for these functions to ensure the broadest compatibility. What may work in testing on one browser may not work on others."

Compatibility Between JavaScript Libraries

The jQuery framework is just one of many JavaScript libraries that are available. Unfortunately, many of them conflict when used on a single web page, making it necessary to choose a single library. Most commonly, the $ operator has been adopted as a standard by most libraries to access individual items in the DOM. That means when you load a library like the Prototype framework (http://prototypejs.org) after jQuery loads, it will take over the $ operator, thereby breaking jQuery code that executes after the load.

The jQuery library, very popular on professional sites, provides a special parameter called noConflict that turns off the $ operator so jQuery can co-exist with other libraries. Using this switch can allow you to load jQuery onto a page that uses another library and simply use the jQuery operator, which provides the same functionality. This would make it seem that jQuery could easily be used in conjunction with an additional library.

For example, to wrap code that uses jQuery's $(), but leaves the $() operator from another library intact to be used by the rest of the page, you could add code like this:

```
jQuery.noConflict()(function(){
    // jQuery selector
    $("#myid").show();
});
// Code that follows can use the MooTools libraries operator
$("myid").set("display","none");
```

The problem comes when you want to use one or more of jQuery's vast and popular library of plug-in functions. At the time of this writing, many of them (including the widely used UI library) use the $ operator in their own code. Therefore, if you deactivate jQuery's $ operator and another library such as MooTools uses it, the plug-in code calls to the operator will access the non-jQuery library and often fail.

If you are using Yahoo's YUI, there should be no problem with running it within a Joomla site. Yahoo uses the prefix object YAHOO before any function calls to create a namespace that will not conflict with any other methods or objects. This wise strategy requires a bit more typing, but allows you to use the JavaScript library of your choice and then use some of the built-in Yahoo framework functionality (such as autocompletion, rich text editing, and charting) without worrying about any conflicts.

Therefore, when coding for a web site, I suggest selecting only one JavaScript library and sticking with it. Although this chapter focuses on jQuery because it is included with a standard Joomla installation, few parts of the front-end Joomla system rely on jQuery. So if you're designing your own templates or not using Joomla Extensions that rely on jQuery, you are free to pick nearly any library to use with your Joomla site.

Creating the Entries Returned from the Ajax Request

As you saw in the Article Injector component, Joomla provides an excellent mechanism for encapsulating Ajax functionality within a single extension. Normally, pages requested from the Joomla system (even components or modules) include the headers and other HTML-specific surrounding text that would break any standard JSON processor. Joomla includes a mode parameter that allows the request string to specify the type of output to be returned. Many extensions use this mode to allow the specification of specific types of HTML such as standard HTML or XHTML. For Ajax calls, the raw mode returns only the output of the component itself without the surrounding page HTML.

For example, the Article Injector post used the following URL with the format parameter set to raw:

```
url: '/index.php?option=com_articleinjector'+
    '&task=insert&format=raw',
```

This output mode allows an extension to use all of the functionality of the Joomla system (including abstracted database access, user account information, and interface security) without rendering the entire Joomla web page. The raw mode is perfect for Ajax calls where a response can include information output in JSON or XML format. The raw output format avoids rendering all of the other components, modules, and plug-ins of a normal page access.

Conclusion

This chapter covered some of the implementation basics of using Ajax for a Joomla web site. The information should provide a solid foundation of the ways you can use JavaScript with Joomla so that you can effectively use JavaScript and Ajax technology within the context of a Joomla system.

The applications presented here are literally the tip of the iceberg of possibilities for a Joomla/Ajax solution. You can adapt the search box for auto-completion, dynamically reload banners, use graphic effects to make the presentation more dynamic, and many other possibilities.

In the next chapter, you'll learn how Joomla can interact with other systems through a variety of web services. This functionality can extend the power of your web site beyond the borders of your own server.

CHAPTER 6

■ ■ ■

Joomla and Web Services

Almost daily, the number of available web services that a site can use for free is increasing. You can post photos, keep a journal, access e-mail, create presentations, post messages, author a blog, and use numerous other offerings. Although you cannot integrate all of these web services into your own web site, the breadth and reach of those you can use is impressive.

For a Joomla site owner, there are a number of back-end web services that can be added to a web site, such as:

- Using Google or Flickr to search for and display images based on the page being visited

- Playing video on your site through YouTube

- Adding relevant news postings via the Bing search API

- Displaying current tweets specific to a topic using the Twitter search API

- Incorporating a map with the appropriate markers via Google Maps directly into your Joomla page

- Supplying financial news about particular subjects through the Yahoo Finance API

These are just a handful of the numerous available services. In this chapter, we'll examine some of the APIs available for some of these services as well as create several custom extensions that interface to the services that add content to your Joomla site.

As the old saying goes, there's no such thing as a free lunch. Most of these services require very explicit licensing. Some widgets display advertisements on your site—ads you may or may not think are in keeping with the editorial direction of your site. APIs usually place strict restricts on the use of the content and have specific attribution requirements. None of these costs are very high for the average site owner, so adopting these technologies can be compelling.

Web Services Overview

Web services come in many forms. Most web services require signing up for a free account with the web service provider and setting the desired parameters. Implementation generally takes one of two forms: access to the supplied data via an API or embedding a widget within your web page that provides the desired functionality (that was demonstrated in Chapter 2).

The more sophisticated services allow requests to be sent to an application programming interface (API) to perform a specific action, such as searching for Flickr photos. Calls to an API are accomplished in a Joomla extension by making an HTTP request from the web server to the destination API. When the request returns the desired information (often in XML or JavaScript Object Notation (JSON) format), the Joomla extension processes the data and then formats it for display on the site.

In contrast, using a widget involves embedding an image tag or small piece of JavaScript code into your web page. The service itself injects the code to display the widget—possibly including a basic user interface. Widgets are very popular because of the ease by which they can be added to a web site. However, what you gain in set up ease, you lose in controlling what and how information is displayed.

There can be a great deal of overlap between these divisions (API or widget), but understanding the essential differences between these two types of technologies can be helpful when evaluating a web service. Seldom does a single web service provider offer both types for the same service, although many providers offer the same service with different features and implementations. Deciding which type of service you want to use on your Joomla site will play a part in determining which service you choose.

Using a Web Service with an API

To access a web service with an API, a program will generally send parameters via a query string or post the variables via a form and then process and display the returned information to present it in a custom format. If the parameters are sent via a query string, the URL will look something like this:

```
http://search.twitter.com/search.json?q=joomla
```

If you enter this URL into a browser that isn't Internet Explorer and perform a View Source on the returned data, you will see that Twitter was searched and returned JSON-formatted data of all of the tweets that have been tagged with the "joomla" keyword. If you're using Internet Explorer, the browser will prompt you to save the returned information, which you can then open in your favorite text editor.

For example, formatted data returned by the Twitter search will look something like this:

```
{
    results: [
            {
        profile_image_url:
                http://a1.twimg.com/images/648202564/me08_normal.jpg
                created_at: "Mon, 19 Apr 2010 21:45:12 +0000"
                from_user: "jolanda_hains",
                metadata: {
                    # result_type: "recent"
                }
                to_user_id: null
                text: "But we made another step tonight!
                    #Joomla Good night everybody!"
                id: 12477545315
                from_user_id: 6032897
                geo: null
                iso_language_code: "en"
                source: "&lt;a href=&quot;http://www.tweetdeck.com&quot;
                    rel=&quot;nofollow&quot;&gt;TweetDeck&lt;/a&gt;"
        }
    ]
    max_id: 12477551601,
    since_id: 0,
    refresh_url: "?since_id=12477551601&q=Joomla",
    next_page: "?page=2&max_id=12477551601&q=Joomla",
    results_per_page: 15,
```

```
    page: 1,
    completed_in: 0.025757,
    query: "Joomla"
}
```

The data returned by the results include fields such as the profile image URL (`profile_image_url`), the name of the tweeting user (`from_user`), the actual tweet (`text`), and other fields.

If your Joomla server were to perform this request and parse the returned data, it could display the individual tweet results on the page via a module in any format desired. The example Twitter data could be displayed as a list of tweets with each entry featuring the profile photos included in the `profile_image_url` field. Such a module could continually display topical and relevant information on your web page with no extra effort after the initial installation.

In Figure 6-1, you can see how I've used a Twitter search on `www.joomlajumpstart.com` to show tweets in a simple module. Tweets relevant to a particular article (these tweets appear on an article about MongoDB) are formatted with the styling of my template.

Figure 6-1. *Data from the Twitter API can be formatted and displayed on your site*

The advantages of using an API include:

- *Power and features*: Most APIs have far more features and capabilities than widgets. That means you can do more with an API and the number of possible applications is not limited to a single purpose.

- *Control of the display*: Aside from the legal restrictions specified in the license for using the service, the information from the API comes to your site as data, which means you can mash it with other data, display it in specific areas of your web site, or use it to add value to other pieces of content.

- *Data processing*: Because the results from each API call are data, you can do your own filtering for display. If the Flickr search returns large and small images, your code can categorize this data between the two sizes and only display the large images to registered users. Or you might do a general blog search for sports but have your code put any results returned about badminton at the top of the results.

- *Server resource control*: Processing is handled on your server so you can perform caching, add extra processing power, do background retrievals, and other optimizations.

The drawbacks of using an API include:

- *Requires medium to advanced programming*: Beginning programmers may feel overwhelmed when trying to understand how an API works. Because it can be a complicated interaction, a decent level of development knowledge is required. Web APIs are nearly always more complicated to implement than widgets. Therefore, a great level of development expertise is required to effectively use an API.

- *Danger of cut-off*: Site owners have to read the legal agreements and attribution requirements of the API. You may not know you're in violation of the agreement until the web service host decides to cut off the feed. This rarely happens with widgets because the web service provider controls the content and display, but it happens more frequently to those using API feed information in violation of the license agreements. These violations can include making too many API calls, placing content on pages that contain unsavory or adult content, or not including proper citation or attribution on displayed content.

- *Server technology required*: A server must be configured to perform back-end calls to the API. Generally this means that support of the CURL library and PHP plug-in must be enabled. Not all service providers allow CURL calls from code that executes on their server. Some even limit the ports that a CURL request can access. For example, GoDaddy only allows a CURL request to access a remote server on ports 80 and 443. Also, the cost associated with the processing, storing API data in the server database, and memory resources should be considered.

- *Blocking while loading*: Because the API queries generally (although not always) occur on the server, typically the visitor's browser will be kept waiting until the API has responded to the request. Only after the API request has completed can the server send the page to the user. If the API service is slow or the servers that host it are down, the API can block your Joomla page from loading.

Access to an API requires adding functionality on the server side, generally with various Joomla extensions. This requires PHP programming and a certain amount of skill at implementing server-side solutions. Widgets generally offer a lighter-weight alternative.

■ **Tip** When you create a Joomla extension to pull data from an API feed, the extension shouldn't hit that feed every time the user accesses a page. This wastes a great deal of processor resources both on your server and the server providing the feed. For most needs, you will want to cache the feed once it's been drawn. Then as each subsequent user accesses the page, the extension will be populated with the cached version and no API call will be required. This will make your site more responsive to the user and also protect you from wearing out your welcome with the feed provider (and possibly getting blacklisted for API access to the service).

Some Available Free API Services

As mentioned previously, there are literally dozens and dozens of web services you can use for either free or a very small fee. Some examples of these include:

- *Yahoo Finance API*: Available from search giant Yahoo, the Yahoo Finance API lets you pull current news stories using specified search terms. For example, if your Joomla site specialized in Iowa grain farming, a call placed to the Finance API could request all of the financial stories that relate to that topic. We'll demonstrate the API in this chapter or you can find more information on the Yahoo site (`http://www.yqlblog.net/blog/2009/06/02/getting-stock-information-with-yql-and-open-data-tables/`).

- *YouTube Video API*: You can include topic-specific YouTube videos on your web site by querying the Video API (`https://developers.google.com/youtube/2.0/developers_guide_protocol`).

- *Wolfram API* (`http://products.wolframalpha.com/api/`): The Wolfram search engine is a special type of search that can actually solve problems put to it by checking huge volumes of reference material. For example, Wolfram could be queried to tell the number of calories in 1.76212 cups of milk and it would find the calorie information for milk and perform the calculation. You can have your site send these types of queries to Wolfram and obtain the results for display.

- *Search Monkey*: Yahoo has created a platform that allows you to provide additional custom information in your search results. For example, if you have a site that features restaurants, you can include store hours, Zagat ratings, information from Yelp, and other information in the search results entry that appears on Yahoo instead of the standard text description.

- *Flickr image search*: The Flickr API allows searching by keywords, creator, tags, and other fields and returns an XML-based feed with the information to access the images on Flickr's CDN. Calls to Flickr can also be filtered by license type so you can limit returned photos to a particular license such as the Creative Commons License.

- *Twitter tweet search*: The Twitter search will return tweets based on search terms or topics.

- *Weatherbug*: Through the Weatherbug API (`http://weather.weatherbug.com/desktop-weather/api.html`), your site can access live weather conditions, weather alerts, daily weather forecasts, images from weather cameras, and international weather forecasts.

In the remainder of this chapter, we'll focus on embedding a few of these services on a Joomla site. Use of most APIs is implemented in essentially the same manner, so these prototypes should provide you with enough experience and understanding that you can use them as a foundation for adapting any web service that you want for your site.

Using Yahoo Finance with Joomla

The Yahoo Finance API allows you to add stock tracking to your web site. You can query the API without a key for stock information such as stock price, trading volume, dividends per share, and many other financial statistics. Because it is so easy to use and returns data in comma-separated value (CSV) format, it is easy to parse the data and display it attractively.

You can see in Figure 6-2 a formatted table of some of the information returned. In the request string of the URL, you can specify the financial information that you want returned. The limit for unauthenticated calls into Yahoo API is 1000 calls per day, so first we'll create a caching system so that if your page gets more than 1000 page views, the limit isn't exceeded.

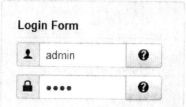

Figure 6-2. *After you retrieve information from the Yahoo API, it can be formatted and displayed in a Joomla module*

Creating a Simple File Cache

When accessing a web API, your server will generally be making a call to a remote server. Every call to an external server will slow your page load speed. Additionally, if you make too many calls to the API, the provider of the web service may block future requests if you exceed your usage limit. A method of avoiding page load slowing and excessive API calls is to use a caching layer that saves the data from a query for hours or days. When a new page request is issued, if the cached data isn't too old (and expired), it can be used on the page.

Joomla has a caching class that it uses for storing rendered modules and data. However, it is customized to exactly the types of data Joomla uses, so it isn't flexible enough for general data caching needs. You can create a very simple file caching class called SimpleCache that can easily handle any range of caching needs.

Create a new file called SimpleCache.php in the libraries/ and enter the following code:

```php
<?php
class SimpleCache {
    static public $basePath = 'cache/';

    static function getCache($key,$expireHours=24,$forceUpdate=false) {
        $key = strtolower($key);
        $cacheName = self::$basePath.$key.'.dat';
        $outInfo = false;
        if(is_file($cacheName)) {
            $dateDiff = time() - filemtime($cacheName);
            $deltaHours = $dateDiff/(60*60);
            if($deltaHours<$expireHours) {
                if(!$forceUpdate) {
                    $data = file_get_contents($cacheName);
                    $outInfo = unserialize($data);
                }
            }
        }
        return $outInfo;
    }
    static function setCache($key,$data) {
        $key = strtolower($key);
        $cacheName = self::$basePath.$key.'.dat';
        file_put_contents($cacheName,serialize($data));
    }
}
?>
```

This class only has two methods: getCache() and setCache(). For those unfamiliar with caching, PHP code that uses a cache follows a simple pattern of requesting cached data using a unique "key" or text string that identifies the data for the SimpleCache class. Generally this key is a concatenated string of the type of data (for example, "flickr_images_") followed by the id or search term that makes the cache key unique (such as "national parks"). For example, a key for user information might by "user_john_doe_1234" while a key to Twitter search results data for parks might be "twitter_parks" or other identifier.

If the data is available in the cache (and isn't expired), it's returned to the calling function. If it isn't available, the data gathering operation such as a database call or web API request is performed. Once the data is retrieved, it is then cached under the particular key name so the next cache request will return the data without accessing an API or database.

For example, code that uses this cache class might look like this:

```php
$key = 'tweet_'.$searchTerm;
$data = SimpleCache::getCache($key,1);
if($data===false) {
        // In actual use, this data would be the results of an API call
    $data = array('text'=>"This is my test");
    SimpleCache::setCache($key,$data);
}
```

The rest of the code implementations in this chapter will use this SimpleCache class to cache the results of API calls.

Creating the Yahoo Finance Module

Yahoo provides a number of excellent APIs that allow you to access everything from financial information to maps services to communicating with Yahoo Answers. The Finance API is one of their most popular because you can get slightly delayed (non-realtime) information on stocks. Additionally, they allow unauthenticated access to their APIs (although authenticated access provides less rate limiting).

You can see the Finance API by entering the following into a browser window:

```
http://finance.yahoo.com/d/quotes.csv?s=dmd&f=price
```

That call to the API will return a CSV that you can easily open in Microsoft Excel that will contain the current price of the stock and a few other numeric factors.

Let's create a module for a Joomla site that can display some of the financial information from the API. This module can then display exactly the information that is desired with the styling to match the template.

Create a mod_yahoofinance/ folder and use your favorite text editor to create the mod_yahoofinance.php file inside the folder with the following code:

```php
<?php
$params = 'l1c1va2xj1b4j4dyekjm3m4rr5p5p6s7';

<?php
/**
* @version $Id: mod_yahoofinance.php 5203 2012-08-22 02:31:14Z DanR $
* This module will displays data from the Yahoo Finance API
*/

// no direct access
defined('_JEXEC') or die('Restricted access');

jimport('SimpleCache');

// Get the module parameters set in the Module Manager
$cacheExpire = $params->get('cache_expire', 4);
$ticker = $params->get('ticker_symbol','DMD');

// Make sure caching is On to prevent site from hitting Yahoo excessively
if(!$cacheExpire) {
    echo 'No entries available<br/>';
    return;
}

$document = JFactory::getDocument();

// In case multiple modules used on the same page, avoid redefining
if(!function_exists('getYahooFinance')) {
    function getYahooFinance($ticker,$expire,$forceUpdate=true) {
            $params = 'l1c1va2xj1b4j4dyekjm3m4rr5p5p6s7';
        $url = "http://finance.yahoo.com/d/quotes.csv?s={$ticker}&f={$params}";
```

```php
        $keyName = 'yahoofinance_key_'.md5($url);
        $data = false;
        if(!$forceUpdate) {
            $data = SimpleCache::getCache($keyName,$expire);
        }
        if($data===false) {
        $csv = file_get_contents($url);
        $csv = trim($csv);
        $values = explode(',',$csv);
                $data['price'] = $values[0];
                $data['change'] = $values[1];
                $data['volume'] = $values[2];
                $data['avg_daily_volume'] = $values[3];
                $data['stock_exchange'] = $values[4];
                $data['market_cap'] = $values[5];
                $data['book_value'] = $values[6];
                $data['ebitda'] = $values[7];
                $data['dividend_per_share'] = $values[8];
                $data['dividend_yield'] = $values[9];
                $data['earnings_per_share'] = $values[10];
                $data['52_week_high'] = $values[11];
                $data['52_week_low'] = $values[12];
                $data['50day_moving_avg'] = $values[13];
                $data['200day_moving_avg'] = $values[14];
                $data['price_earnings_ratio'] = $values[15];
                $data['price_earnings_growth_ratio'] = $values[16];
                $data['price_sales_ratio'] = $values[17];
                $data['price_book_ratio'] = $values[18];
                $data['short_ratio'] = $values[19];
                $json = json_encode($data);
            SimpleCache::setCache($keyName,$json);
        } else {
                $data = json_decode($data,true);
        }
        return $data;
    }
}

$data = getYahooFinance($ticker,$cacheExpire);

$display_fields = array('price', 'book_value', 'price_earnings_ratio',
    'earnings_per_share');

?>
<table class="table table-striped table-bordered table-hover
    table-condensed">
        <tr>
                <th>Ticker</th><th><?php echo $ticker; ?></th>
        </tr>
```

```php
        <?php foreach($display_fields as $display_field): ?>
        <tr>
                <td><?php echo ucwords(str_replace('_',' ',$display_field)); ?></td>
                <td><?php echo $data[$display_field]; ?></td>
        </tr>
        <?php endforeach; ?>
</table>
```

The Yahoo API takes a number of parameters in the request string and returns the data for those parameters as a CSV string. This module requests all of the information provided by the Yahoo API (price, price_sales_ratio, price_book_ratio, and so forth), caches the results, and then displays all of the fields enumerated in the `$displayed_fields` array.

This module displays all of the key aspects of using an API to add information to your Joomla site. It queries the API using parameters specified in the module configuration screen. It caches the results so the API is not accessed excessively. It uses custom display HTML and styling to match the presentation of the information to the Joomla template.

We can use nearly the same basic functionality to add more specific information such as posts to the Twitter feed to provide dynamic content to your site.

Adding Tweets to Your Site

Whether you're running a small Joomla site or a large Joomla portal, the key problem is usually the same: how to add new, relevant content inexpensively enough to support the site. Small sites are often born from a passion to communicate and share information. Unfortunately, over time the operators of the site can become fatigued because of the amount of work needed to add new content to the site to prevent it from becoming stale. Large sites struggle with the expense of hiring content writers or cultivating user-generated content (such as forums or posts) to provide a decent baseline quality.

While there are no magic bullets to solve these problems, one method of obtaining very of-the-moment content is to incorporate Twitter feed content into your site, see Figure 6-3 for an example. For no cost, your site can query the Twitter feed with topics and keywords relevant to a page that is being displayed and include tweets that match this criteria. With the number of Twitter users growing daily, there is almost certainly content being written into the feed that matches the content direction of your site.

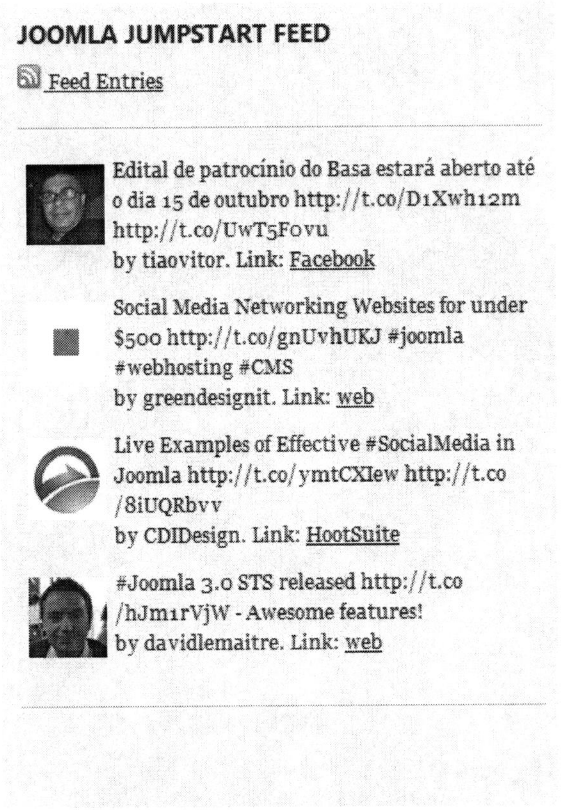

JOOMLA JUMPSTART FEED

📶 Feed Entries

Edital de patrocínio do Basa estará aberto até
o dia 15 de outubro http://t.co/D1Xwh12m
http://t.co/UwT5Fovu
by tiaovitor. Link: Facebook

Social Media Networking Websites for under
$500 http://t.co/gnUvhUKJ #joomla
#webhosting #CMS
by greendesignit. Link: web

Live Examples of Effective #SocialMedia in
Joomla http://t.co/ymtCXIew http://t.co
/8iUQRbvv
by CDIDesign. Link: HootSuite

#Joomla 3.0 STS released http://t.co
/hJm1rVjW - Awesome features!
by davidlemaitre. Link: web

Figure 6-3. *The Twitter feeds can add relevant information to your page*

Accessing the Twitter API

Let's see how easy it is to access the Twitter API. Open a browser window and put the following in the address bar:

```
http://search.twitter.com/search.json?q=advanced%20joomla
```

You should see a number of results returned in JSON data format as you saw earlier in the chapter. A great deal of information is contained in each tweet entry including the user id, the user name, the text of the tweet, the language of the tweet, the geo location (if available), the source URL, and more information. When your program retrieves this information, it can process it and use only the data necessary for the best presentation.

■ **Note** Originally, most web APIs returned data as an XML data set. Much more common now is the JSON data format that is smaller, cleaner, and easier to process by both JavaScript and most other languages. PHP includes the functions json_encode() and json_decode() that can be used to encode and decode JSON data, respectively.

You can use the individual data items in the tweet to even make an interactive Joomla module such as one that uses the iso_language_code field to sort by language type. That would make it possible on a Spanish-language site, for example, to display the tweets in Spanish before those in another language.

This sorting-by-language example shows one of the possibilities available to a developer addressing an API that is often not available when widgets are used. Because the API returns information as data (instead of a display template), it can be sorted, parsed, filtered, or combined—limited only by the skills of the developer and the limitations of the API license.

Retrieving the Information

To make the call to the Twitter API, you need to have your hosting web server make an HTTP request to another server. This request can be generated by using the PHP function that makes calls to the CURL library. For simple implementations, however, PHP has a very useful function called `file_get_contents()` that, in addition to being able to read the contents of a file, can make an HTTP request and retrieve the contents (whether that is an HTML page, XML feed, or JSON string). In the Twitter module, we'll use this function to query the API and obtain relevant tweets that match the search terms of a page.

Once the Twitter feed has been retrieved using a `file_get_contents()` call, it is very easy to process because the feed is returned in JSON format. A simple call to the PHP `json_decode()` function will return the data as either an object or an array.

You may also want to filter the body posting for offensive words. Because the content of the Twitter postings will come directly through the feed to be posted on your site, you won't be able to effectively monitor all of the posts that are displayed. Filtering for offensive words can help prevent some embarrassing content from appearing on your site.

■ **Note**   Although the example code in this chapter uses the `file_get_contents()` function to obtain the data from the API, in most medium-to-high volume cases, you would want to use a library known as CURL to access the API. CURL is a fast and feature-rich library installed in most PHP-based sites that can perform a variety of HTTP access functions including secure connections through SSH, asynchronous querying, multi-threaded calls for multiple simultaneous accesses, and more. It is also quite a bit faster for each call than the `file_get_contents()` function. However, because not all PHP configurations include CURL and because it makes the code slightly more complex, the simple function was used here. Additionally, the `file_get_contents()` function does not support many common HTTP options such as cookies, custom request headers, and browser agent settings. For these types of advanced HTTP interactions, you need to use the CURL library. Use the `phpinfo()` function and search for the CURL module to check if your web installation has the CURL library available.

For a module of this type, adding a module parameter would let an administrator specify what the parameters of the feed might be. In many cases, a parameter would allow you to specify the register API key for the web service. Such module parameters might also allow you to specify keywords that will aid in making the feed more specific (and relevant) for the pages that it, is being displayed upon. You can create and target different module instances (see Beginning Joomla! Chapter 3) for specific pages. For this module, however, we're going to use a pre-existing field already available in a Joomla document to customize the Twitter feed.

Formatting the Tweets Within a Module

At the time of this writing, the Twitter search API limits the number of searches from a single IP to 150 requests per hour. Therefore, you want to make sure your site can cache searches so it doesn't go over this limit.

■ **Tip** Some sites, even with caching, need to perform searches in excess of this rate limit because of the level of site traffic. There are a number of methods for checking your current rate usage and working around search problems detailed in the Rate Limiting FAQ (`https://dev.twitter.com/docs/rate-limiting-faq`) on the Twitter site.

The Twitter module code includes examples of several items you can use in a variety of other extensions:

- *Access to the document object*: The module accesses the JDocument object of the page currently being displayed to obtain the keyword metatags for the page. Accessing the document object can be very useful for modules when you're trying to contextualize the functionality to the page where it is being displayed.

- *file_get_contents() for web access*: This code uses the file_get_contents() function to access a web URL and retrieve the output. Although not the best implementation option for heavy traffic sites, it does provide a very quick and simple method of calling to a web service and reading information.

- *Handling JSON data*: The Twitter information is returned in JSON data format. JSON is a text-based data format that PHP can easily convert into either an object or an array. Most web APIs use JSON to communicate, so the information provided here can be used to decode data from other services.

Let's create a Twitter module like the one shown earlier. This module will output the tweets related to the keywords it finds in the article's meta keywords field. It is almost universally agreed that the search engines ignore the specified keywords because of spammer abuse of this field in the early days of the web. Because the ability to add keywords is built into the Joomla editor interface, why not take advantage of it? This module reads a comma-delimited list of keywords from the meta keywords field and uses those keywords to search Twitter.

Create a folder called mod_twitter. Then enter the following code into your favorite program editor and save the file in the folder as mod_twitter.php.

```php
<?php
/**
* @version $Id: mod_twitter.php 5203 2013-01-27 01:45:14Z DanR $
* This module will displays a Twitter widget
*/

// no direct access
defined('_JEXEC') or die('Restricted access');

jimport('SimpleCache');

// Get the module parameters set in the Module Manager
$cacheExpire = $params->get('cache_expire', 4);
// Not used now, but can be used for more advanced Twitter operations
$apiKey = $params->get('twitter_api_key');
$numItems = $params->get('num_items',3);
$shuffle = $params->get('shuffle',0);
$expire = $params->get('expire',4);
```

```php
// Make sure caching is On to prevent site from hitting Twitter excessively
if(!$cacheExpire) {
    echo 'No entries available<br/>';
    return;
}


$document = JFactory::getDocument();

$metaTags = trim($document->_metaTags['standard']['keywords']);
$keywords = explode(',',$metaTags);
$keywordArray = array();
// Filter for any empty keywords and eliminate duplicates
for($i=0;$i<count($keywords);$i++) {
    $keyword = strtolower(trim($keywords[$i]));
    if(!empty($keyword)) {
        $keywordArray[$keyword] = true;
    }
}
$searchStr = implode('%20',array_keys($keywordArray));
$searchStr = !empty($searchStr) ?   $searchStr  :   'joomla';
if(empty($searchStr)) {
    echo 'No entries available<br/>';
    exit;
}


// In case multiple modules used on the same page, avoid redefining
if(!function_exists('getTwitter')) {
    function getTwitter($searchStr,$expire,$forceUpdate=false) {
        $searchStr = urlencode($searchStr);
        $keyName = 'twitter_key_'.md5($searchStr);
        $tweets = false;
        if(!$forceUpdate) {
            $tweets = SimpleCache::getCache($keyName,$expire);
        }
        if($tweets===false) {
            $url = 'http://search.twitter.com/search.json?q='.$searchStr;
            $tweets = file_get_contents($url);
            SimpleCache::setCache($keyName,$tweets);
        }
        $tweetData = json_decode($tweets,true);
        return $tweetData;
    }
}


// Output all tweets but hide beyond a certain point
$tweetData = getTwitter($searchStr,$expire);

$i=0;
if($shuffle) {
        shuffle($tweetData['results']);
}
```

```php
foreach($tweetData['results'] as $tweet) {
    $extraStyle = '';
    if($i>=$numItems) {
        $extraStyle = 'display:none;';
    }
?>
<div class="tweet" style='margin-bottom:10px;<?php echo $extraStyle; ?>'>
<img src="<?php echo $tweet['profile_image_url']; ?>" align="left" width="48" height="48"
    style="margin:5px;"
    alt="<?php echo $tweet['from_user']; ?>" />
<?php echo $tweet['text']; ?><br/>by <?php echo $tweet['from_user']; ?>. Link:
<?php echo html_entity_decode($tweet['source']); ?>
</div>
<div style="clear:both;"></div>
<?php
    $i++;
}
?>
```

The code is well-commented, so you should be able to follow the definition. It begins by importing the SimpleCache class that you created earlier in the chapter in order to cache the responses from the Twitter API. The next section loads several parameters that you can set for the module, including the cache expiration (the number of hours to keep the cache before refreshing it), the Twitter API key (not used by this module, but if you enhance the module for sophisticated features it is available), number of tweets to display, and whether to shuffle the results or not.

There follows a check to make sure there is some cache expiration set so that the results are cached. If you want to shut off the query of the Twitter API, you can set the cache expire to 0.

The JDocument object is then retrieved so the meta keywords for the current page can be retrieved. Through the Joomla Administrator interface, you can set a list of meta keywords for any menu or article. If you add a comma-delimited list of keywords to the meta keywords, this list will be used as Twitter search keywords.

Next, the getTwitter() function is defined. Note that before it is defined, the code checks to make sure it hasn't already been defined by a previous module on the page. This is important because if you include a function definition in the page and the function is already defined, the web server will throw an error. The getTwitter() function checks the cache and, if empty or expired, it queries the Twitter API, caches the results, then returns the tweets it found.

The rest of the module simply calls the getTwitter() function to obtain tweets based on the keywords and then formats and outputs the tweets that it finds. That's it! The structure of this module matches most modules that you'll create to query an API and process and output the results.

Once you've saved the module, you will need to package it for installation on your system.

▓ **Tip** In this example module, the code pulls data from the feed and sends it out during the page rendering. Many sites build the module as an Ajax widget instead. After the page is rendered, Ajax code requests the latest feed information and displays it in some form of carousel. This provides a better user experience, although it does it at the expense of search engine spidering of the content. You can easily adapt this module to just that sort of local widget. If you move the API call into a component, you can have this module simply call into that Joomla component to perform the actual API query.

To allow the Joomla installer to use the module, you need to create the mod_twitter.xml descriptor file and save it to the same folder:

```xml
<?xml version="1.0" encoding="utf-8"?>
<extension
        type="module"
        version="3.0"
        client="site"
        method="upgrade">
   <name>Twitter</name>
   <version>1.0.0</version>
   <description>This module will performs a Twitter search and displays the results</description>
      <!-- This section is for Joomla 1.5 compatibility -->
   <params>
      <param name="twitter_api_key" type="text" default="" label="Twitter API ID"
         description="Register on the Twitter API site and enter the API key here." />
      <param name="cache_expire" type="int" default="4" label="Cache expire (hours)"
         description="Number of hours to cache results." />
      <param name="num_items" type="int" default="3" label="# of items"
         description="Number of news items to display" />
      <param name="shuffle" type="int" default="1" label="Shuffle"
         description="Shuffle item results" />
   </params>
      <!-- This section is for Joomla 1.6 compatibility -->
   <config>
      <fields name="params">
         <fieldset name="basic">
            <field
               name="twitter_api_key"
               type="text"
               default=""
               label="Twitter API ID"
               description="Register on the Twitter API site and enter the API key here." />
            <field
               name="cache_expire"
               type="int"
               default="4"
               label="Cache expire (hours)"
               description="Number of hours to cache results" />
            <field
               name="num_items"
               type="int"
               default="3"
               label="# of items"
               description="Number of news items to display" />
            <field
               name="shuffle"
               type="int"
               default="1"
               label="Shuffle"
               description="Shuffle item results" />
```

```
            </fieldset>
        </fields>
    </config>
    <files>
            <filename module="mod_twitter">mod_twitter.php</filename>
    </files>
</extension>
```

Now simply zip and install the module to your Joomla system. Using this Joomla module on your site provides a number of advantages:

- *Supplies new content to your site*: The very nature of Twitter is to publish the moment-by-moment messages that users publish into the world. Even if you update your site infrequently, it will have new items of likely interest to your visitors that relate to the specific topic shown on the page.

- *Provides visual interest*: The avatars of Twitter users can be attractive and colorful, adding some visual interest to the page without too much clutter.

- *Offers possible SEO value*: Although it is an often argued topic among professionals what types of items optimize a page best for search engine visibility, it is likely valuable to have more content and links relating to the page content for the search engine spiders to index.

Given the simple nature of implementing the Twitter module, it is difficult to find a reason NOT to add tweets to your site. If you find it too intrusive or many of the tweets in your topic area are spammy, you can add the module to specific articles or menu items instead of activating it site-wide.

■ **Note** Twitter has a limit (at the time of this writing) of 150 searches per hour. After that number, the Twitter feed returns a simple error code. That is one important reason that the module caches the results of the search so it doesn't use up the available searches with multiple searches on the same page. If you have a compelling reason for performing more than the limit each hour, you can apply for a white listing of particular IP addresses. For more information, read the explanation at `https://dev.twitter.com/docs/rate-limiting-faq`, which includes a link to the white listing application form.

Bing News API

Although tweets are instant and often very relevant, you might want your site to have content that is more professionally written or news-worthy rather than moment-worthy. Bing provides API access to numerous services including maps, spelling, translation, and news. In this section, you'll create a module that will harvest news from the Bing API and display topical articles relevant to your search term.

To begin, you will need to obtain an API key from the Bing site. Use your browser to go to the developer center and register for a free key here:

`http://www.bing.com/developers`

The API supplies access to the web, images, InstantAnswer, phonebook, related searches, news, and other services. The results of searches can be returned in JSON or XML format. Bing even provides a SOAP-based interface if you want to interact with the system using the SOAP protocol.

The Bing news module (see Figure 6-4) follows the same process as the other modules in its request and cache cycle. When a request is made and the cache time has expired (24 hours is a good cache time for this sort of thing), a new feed is read and the cache is overwritten with the new data. By using this method, the amount of traffic on the source provider is minimized, your site is more responsive (the response from a feed request can vary anywhere from a second to several minutes), and the information stays available to the visitor for the duration of the expiration.

Figure 6-4. *Bing news can provide timely professionally researched content to a Joomla page*

Create a new folder called mod_bingnews and add the following Bing news source code to the mod_bingnews.php file:

```php
<?php
<?php
/**
* @version $Id: mod_bingnews.php 5203 2012-07-27 01:45:14Z DanR $
* This module will displays a news entries from the Bing search API
*/
```

```
// no direct access
defined('_JEXEC') or die('Restricted access');

jimport('SimpleCache');

// Get the module parameters set in the Module Manager
$cacheExpire = $params->get('cache_expire', 4);
$apiKey = $params->get('bing_api_key');
$numItems = $params->get('num_items',3);
$shuffle = $params->get('shuffle',0);

// Make sure caching is turned on to prevent site from hitting Bing excessively
if(!$cacheExpire) {
    echo 'No entries available<br/>';
    return;
}
if(false && empty($apiKey)) {
    echo "Empty API key parameter. Use the Module Manager to set API key<br/>";
    return;
}

$document = JFactory::getDocument();

$metaTags = trim($document->_metaTags['standard']['keywords']);
$keywords = explode(',',$metaTags);

// Filter for any empty keywords and eliminate duplicates
$keywordArray = array();
for($i=0;$i<count($keywords);$i++) {
    $keyword = strtolower(trim($keywords[$i]));
    if(!empty($keyword)) {
        $keywordArray[$keyword] = true;
    }
}
$searchStr = implode('%20',array_keys($keywordArray));
$searchStr = !empty($searchStr) ?  $searchStr  :  'joomla';

// In case multiple modules used on the same page, avoid redefining
if(!function_exists('getBingNews')) {
    function getBingNews($searchStr,$apiKey,$cacheExpire=4,$forceUpdate=true) {
        $searchStr = urlencode($searchStr);
        $keyName = 'news_key_'.md5($searchStr);
        // Set a default value of false in case of force update
        $data = false;
        if(!$forceUpdate) {
            $data = SimpleCache::getCache($keyName,$cacheExpire);
        }
        if($data===false) {

                $ServiceRootURL =  'https://api.datamarket.azure.com/Bing/Search/';

                $WebSearchURL = $ServiceRootURL . 'Image?$format=json&Query=';
```

```php
                $context = stream_context_create(array(
                'http' => array(
                'request_fulluri' => true,
                'header' => "Authorization: Basic " . base64_encode($apiKey. ":" . $ apiKey)
                )
                ));
                $request = $WebSearchURL . urlencode( '\'' . $searchStr . '\'');

                $response = file_get_contents($request, 0, $context);

            // Decode JSON to an array
            $data = json_decode($response,true);
        }
        return $data;
    }
}


// Output number of news items specified in parameters
$newsData = getBingNews($searchStr,$apiKey);
if($shuffle) {
    shuffle($newsData);
}
$newsData = $newsData[0]['results'];
$totalItems = count($newsData);
// If there are fewer items then the # requested, only display available
$numItems = $totalItems < $numItems ?   $totalItems :   $numItems;

for($i=0;$i<$numItems;$i++) {
    $newsItem = $newsData[$i];
    ?>
    <div>
        <div class="title">
        <a href="<?php echo $newsItem['SourceUrl']; ?>">
            <?php echo $newsItem['Title']; ?>
        </a>
        <div><?php echo '<img src="'.$newsItem['MediaUrl'].'" />'; ?></div>
    </div>
        <?php
}

?>
```

Create the mod_bingnews.xml descriptor file with the following code:

```xml
<?xml version="1.0" encoding="utf-8"?>
<extension type="module" version="1.5.0">
    <name>Bing News</name>
    <version>1.0.0</version>
    <description>This module will performs a Bing News search and displays the results</description>
        <!-- This section is for Joomla 1.5 compatibility -->
```

```xml
    <params>
        <param name="bing_api_key" type="text"
            default="" label="Bing API ID"
            description="Register on the Bing API site and enter the API key here." />
        <param name="cache_expire" type="int"
            default="4" label="Cache expire (hours)"
            description="Number of hours to cache results." />
        <param name="num_items" type="int"
            default="3" label="# of items"
            description="Number of news items to display" />
        <param name="shuffle" type="int"
            default="1" label="Shuffle"
            description="Shuffle item results" />
    </params>
        <!-- This section is for Joomla 1.6 compatibility -->
    <config>
        <fields name="params">
            <fieldset name="basic">
                <field
                    name="bing_api_key"
                    type="text"
                    default=""
                    label="Bing API ID"
                    description=
                    "Register on the Bing API site and enter the API key here."
                />
                <field
                    name="cache_expire"
                    type="int"
                    default="4"
                    label="Cache expire (hours)"
                    description="Number of hours to cache results.
                        Set to 0 to disable module." />
                <field
                    name="num_items"
                    type="int"
                    default="3"
                    label="# of items"
                    description="Number of news items to display" />
                <field
                    name="shuffle"
                    type="int"
                    default="1"
                    label="Shuffle"
                    description="Shuffle item results" />
            </fieldset>
        </fields>
    </config>
    <files>
        <filename module="mod_bingnews">mod_bingnews.php</filename>
    </files>
</extension>
```

By default, Joomla uses a file cache for its caching operations. If you have a high-volume site, you will likely want to use server memory caching such as APC (`http://php.net/manual/en/book.apc.php`) or Memcache (`http://memcached.org/`, see Chapter 8). For a low-volume web site, it is convenient to keep the cached information in the database because you can easily manage and back it up with the standard database backup extensions or phpMyAdmin admin procedures that are used for the rest of the Joomla site.

Alternately, you can use the JCache class to take advantage of whatever the caching mechanism is that is configured for the site-wide caching. Search the Joomla source code for examples of how JCache is already used for the site. Using the site-wide cache has disadvantages detailed earlier, but does provide some advantages such as the use of Memcache if it is configured and available.

Adding a Flickr Mashup

Flickr is one of the most popular photographic web sites. It allows you to easily upload and share images and, more importantly to a Joomla site operator, they provide an API that allows you to search and locate pictures that you can use on your own site. You can use the API to add images to articles, categories, or nearly any other location in the site that could use more visuals.

Like many of the other web services, you will need to first register for a Flickr API key. You can register for the key here:

```
http://www.flickr.com/services/api/misc.api_keys.html
```

Once you have the key, you can call into the Flickr API. There are a number of available options that allow you to specify exactly the types of images that you want, including:

- *Text*: Search the text or caption of the images to match the requested search terms.

- *Tags*: Search tags of the images to match the requested search terms. Note that many images are not tagged, so this will limit the number of results available.

- *License*: There are many different licenses attached to photos provides through the Flickr API. You can filter the results to include only photos with particular licenses. You can use the API itself to retrieve a list of licenses (see `http://www.flickr.com/services/api/flickr.photos.licenses.getInfo.html`).

- *Sort*: Determines the order in which the results are returned. The sort defaults to date posted in descending order that returns the newest first, but I've found sorting by relevance produces much better results.

- *Format*: The default format is XML, but in PHP selecting the JSON format makes the results much easier to process.

- *Extras*: Allows you to specify extra fields that you want returned that are not included by default in the results. Examples include owner_name, license, and path_alias.

To create the Flickr module, use your text editor to create a module called `mod_flickr.php` and enter the following source code:

```php
<?php
/**
* @version $Id: mod_flickr.php 5203 2010-07-27 01:45:14Z DanR $
* This module will displays a a Flickr image depending on the search
*/
```

```
// no direct access
defined('_JEXEC') or die('Restricted access');

jimport('SimpleCache');

// Get the module parameters set in the Module Manager
$cacheExpire = $params->get('cache_expire', 24);
$apiKey = $params->get('flickr_api_key');
$numItems = $params->get('num_items',2);
$shuffle = $params->get('shuffle',1);
$width = $params->get('width',400);
$height = $params->get('height',300);
$border = $params->get('border',4);

// Make sure caching is turned on to prevent site from hitting the Flickr API excessively
if(!$cacheExpire) {
    echo 'No entries available<br/>';
    return;
}
if(empty($apiKey)) {
    echo "Empty API key parameter. Use the Module Manager to set API key<br/>";
    return;
}

$document = &JFactory::getDocument();

$metaTags = trim($document->_metaTags['standard']['keywords']);
$keywords = explode(',',$metaTags);
$keywordArray = array();
// Filter for any empty keywords and eliminate duplicates
for($i=0;$i<count($keywords);$i++) {
    $keyword = strtolower(trim($keywords[$i]));
    if(!empty($keyword)) {
        $keywordArray[$keyword] = true;
    }
}
$searchStr = implode('%20',array_keys($keywordArray));
$searchStr = !empty($searchStr) ?   $searchStr  :  'joomla';


if(!function_exists('getFlickr')) {
    function getFlickr($searchStr,$apiKey,$forceUpdate=false) {
        $searchStr = urlencode($searchStr);
        $keyName = 'flickr_key_'.md5($searchStr);
        $data = false;
        if(!$forceUpdate) {
            $data = SimpleCache::getCache($keyName,$cacheExpire);
        }
        if($data===false) {
            $callMethod = 'flickr.photos.search';
            $url = "http://api.flickr.com/services/rest/?&api_key=$apiKey&method=$callMethod";
            $url .= "&extras=owner_name,license,path_alias";
```

```php
            $url .= "&sort=relevance";
            $url .= "&text=$searchStr";
            // Request no JavaScript wrapper function
            $url .= "&format=json&nojsoncallback=1";
            $json = file_get_contents($url);
            $data = json_decode($json,true);
            if(isset($data['photos']['photo'])) {
                foreach($data['photos']['photo'] as &$photo) {
                    $id = $photo['id'];
                    $farm = $photo['farm'];
                    $server = $photo['server'];
                    $secret = $photo['secret'];
                    $photo['url'] = "http://farm{$farm}.static.flickr.com/{$server}/{$id}_{$secret}.jpg";
                }
            } else {
                $data = array();
            }
            SimpleCache::setCache($keyName,$data);
        }
        return $data;
    }
}


$flickrData = getFlickr($searchStr,$apiKey);
if($shuffle) {
    shuffle($flickrData['photos']['photo']);
}
$borderStyle = "";
if($border) {
    $borderStyle = "border:{$border}px solid gray;";
}
$totalItems = count($flickrData['photos']['photo']);
// If there are fewer available items then the # requested, only display available
$numItems = $totalItems < $numItems ?   $totalItems :   $numItems;
for($i=0;$i<$numItems;$i++) {
    $photo = $flickrData['photos']['photo'][$i];
    $baseURL = $photo['url'];

?>
    <div class="image"
    style="<?php echo $borderStyle; ?>overflow:hidden;padding:2px;
        text-align:center;">
        <div style='width:<?php echo $width; ?>px;
            height:<?php echo $height; ?>px;
            background-position:center;
            background-repeat: no-repeat;
            background-image:url(<?php echo $baseURL; ?>)'>
```

```
                </div>
                <div><?php echo $photo['title'].' from '.$photo['ownername']; ?></div>
        </div>
        <?php
}

?>
```

Once installed, the Flickr module can be used to add images to articles, category pages, and just about anywhere on your Joomla site.

Create the XML file descriptor file and name it mod_flickr.xml:

```xml
<?xml version="1.0" encoding="utf-8"?>
<install type="module" version="1.5.0">
    <name>Flickr</name>
    <version>1.0.0</version>
    <description>This module will performs a Flickr search and displays one or more images</description>
        <!-- This section is for Joomla 1.5 compatibility -->
    <params>
        <param name="flickr_api_key" type="text"
            default="" label="Flickr API key"
            description=
            "The API key that allows Flickr searches."
        />
        <param name="cache_expire" type="int"
            default="4" label="Cache expire (hours)"
            description="Number of hours to cache results."
        />
        <param name="num_items" type="int"
            default="3" label="# of items"
            description="Number of news items to display"
        />
        <param name="shuffle" type="int"
            default="1" label="Shuffle"
            description="Shuffle item results"
        />
        <param name="width" type="int"
            default="400" label="Width"
            description="Width of containing DIV"
        />
        <param name="height" type="int"
            default="300" label="Height"
            description="Height of containing DIV"
        />
        <param name="border" type="int"
            default="1" label="Border pixels"
            description="Number of pixels for gray border"
        />
    </params>
        <!-- This section is for Joomla 1.6 compatibility -->
    <config>
        <fields name="params">
```

```xml
            <fieldset name="basic">
                <field
                    name="flickr_api_key"
                    type="text"
                    default=""
                    label="Flickr API key"
                    description=
                    "The API key that allows Flickr searches." />
                <field
                    name="cache_expire"
                    type="int"
                    default="24"
                    label="Cache expire (hours)"
                    description="Number of hours to cache results. Set to 0 to disable module." />
                <field
                    name="num_items"
                    type="int"
                    default="2"
                    label="# of items"
                    description="Number of news items to display" />
                <field
                    name="shuffle"
                    type="int"
                    default="1"
                    label="Shuffle"
                    description="Shuffle item results" />
                <field
                    name="width"
                    type="int"
                    default="400"
                    label="Width"
                    description="Width of containing DIV" />
                <field
                    name="height"
                    type="int"
                    default="300"
                    label="Height"
                    description="Height of containing DIV" />
                <field
                    name="border"
                    type="int"
                    default="1"
                    label="Border pixels"
                    description="Number of pixels for gray border" />
            </fieldset>
        </fields>
    </config>
    <files>
        <filename module="mod_flickr">mod_flickr.php</filename>
    </files>
</install>
```

This module will display the number of requested Flickr images and include the appropriate attribution to the owner of the photograph. Using images can dramatically increase the visual presence of your site.

Conclusion

In this chapter, you've learned how to connect Joomla to a number of web services. Your Joomla site can now surface relevant Twitter feeds specific to the pages where they appear. You can add a Google Map to the site that shows specific geographic information such as store locations or restaurant reviews. You've added a Flickr mashup to show relevant photos for your articles.

Every day, users of the web are becoming more interconnected largely through the use of social networking technology provided by sites such as Facebook and Twitter. Increasingly, these sites are making available widgets and APIs to allow other sites to join with them and share information. Joomla web sites are perfect for taking advantage of some of these integration technologies that are available.

In the next chapter we'll be looking at Joomla security administration. It's maybe not the most exciting of topics, but it's absolutely essential that you understand how to protect your site from malicious users.

CHAPTER 7

■ ■ ■

Joomla Security Administration

For most people, security is one of the least interesting aspects of managing a web site. For this reason, many hobbyist web site administrators either ignore it completely or put only the most minimal protections in place. Paying such scant attention to security is a mistake. An unrefined security policy can make a site more vulnerable to breach and eliminates the possibility of safely working with outside volunteers, contributors, or moderators.

Securing your Joomla site is not a complicated process, so if you follow the simple guidelines provided in this chapter, you will not only have more confidence that your site won't be penetrated and defaced, you'll also be able to easily set up the proper limits for user accounts so you can allow others to contribute to your site without the risk of content loss or site failure.

In this chapter, you'll learn how to:

- Set up user group restrictions properly so adding new users with proper permissions is a fast and easy process.

- Control access to site content to allow some content to only be viewable to particular types of users.

- Configure access groups to allow for safe contribution for others without risk to your core site content or reputation.

- Organize your server structure and configuration to minimize site vulnerabilities that might be exploited by hackers.

In this chapter, we'll examine all of the advanced aspects of administrative and security configuration for the Joomla system. Then we'll review the more universal security concepts and how they apply to the needs of a Joomla site.

Implementing Site Security and Server Security

For a Joomla administrator, there are two primary areas of security configuration that must be managed: *site security* and *server security*. Site security relates to the security settings that are chosen inside the Joomla CMS. Server security relates to setup and configuration of the server that is hosting the Joomla site to make sure the server is secure from attack.

We'll begin with the recommended setup for the Joomla site security, since these selections provide a good starting point. Site security tends to be less technical than server security because all of the security configuration takes place through the Joomla Administrator interface.

Setting up Site Security

Before you begin setting up your security configuration, it is important to understand the fundamental security model used by Joomla. Like the Linux operating system, Joomla security uses an *additive* security model instead of a *subtractive* security model. In an additive model, the top level of the security hierarchy provides almost no access rights and each hierarchical level adds additional rights.

The additive model is counter-intuitive to most people because it means, in essence, that a parent has *fewer* access rights than a child. You can see the additive structure of the Joomla security setup clearly in the User Manager for Groups as shown in Figure 7-1. The Public group—which is the root node of the permissions tree—is the group with the fewest permissions and it sits at the top of the hierarchy. In the Registered group branch, the Author child group has more permissions than a simple registered account, an Editor group has more permissions again, and the Publisher group has even more.

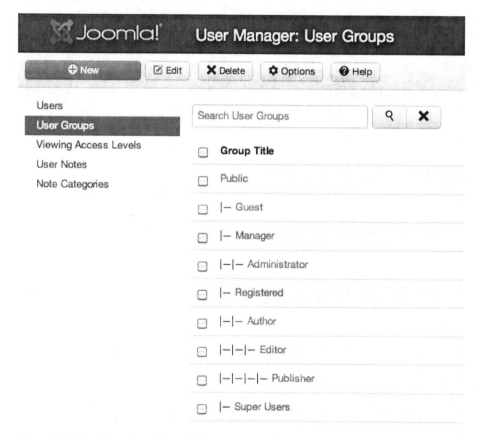

Figure 7-1. The hierarchy of the additive security model shows that child groups have more priveleges than a parent group

Because access to any resource needs to be explicitly granted under the additive model, the model is slightly more difficult to understand and use than the subtractive model. However, it is much more secure because there are no resources that are exposed by accidental oversight.

■ **Note**   Under the subtractive security model, the top level of the hierarchy has privileges to everything and then individual groups add restrictions down the tree. That makes the Super Administrator the top of the hierarchy and progressive restrictions are added until an account such as Guest has the fewest privileges. The subtractive model is less secure than additive, but it is generally easier to understand and implement so it remains a popular security strategy for smaller applications. You can read about both models at `www.forestpath.org/research/platform/linux/security.html`.

The structure of the additive model leads to the logical conclusion that if we want to create a very restrictive group, we want it defined near the top of the hierarchy. If you look at the Guest account in the Joomla User Manager, you'll see that it is a child of the Public group which has essentially no privileges at all.

Now that you understand how the additive model works, let's get started and define a new group.

Creating a Sample Group with the Joomla User Manager

In the Joomla Administrator interface, the User Manager allows the definition of user access settings, groups, and access levels. Users (or groups of users) can be given special permission to access the User Manager itself, which makes it possible for site administrators to share the burden of user management with moderators. User management is often one of the more important, yet time consuming, tasks of a site maintenance when a site has a large number of users.

The most effective procedure I've seen for the setup of professional-grade security (and the one most security experts recommend) is that the structure of the security system be done in the following order:

1. *Define groups*: Create groups first—before individual user accounts—for all the classes of users that are expected to use the site.

2. *Create necessary access levels*: In Joomla, restrictions to various objects (menus, articles, and so forth) are stored as *access levels*.

3. *Assign access levels to groups*: Restrictions are placed on each of the created groups to provide exactly the access level the users of the groups need to complete their tasks.

4. *Assign users to groups*: Users are assigned to the appropriate groups and inherit the permissions specified for that group.

5. *Assign overrides to particular users*: Finally, if special access options are needed for a user, apply those changes to the individual user.

By creating the groups first, you will be sure to address the general case or the most common permission scenarios rather than the special case. Defining permissions at the group level dramatically decreases the amount of time required for system admins to add new users or modify the permissions of existing users. Granting additional privileges to a class of users is often as easy as adding the extra access to the appropriate group. Keeping access privileges on the group level also minimizes mistakes of unintended access granted to a user, which can often occur when each individual requires separate access setup.

Following this methodology in Joomla is straightforward because it is patterned after the best security practices. Let's step through the process of setting up security in Joomla so you can define the security for your own site very quickly.

Defining a Group in Joomla

Open the Administrator interface for your Joomla site. Select the Groups option from the Users menu. The hierarchy of groups is clearly displayed with the same type of indentation system used in the Menu Manager, as you can see in Figure 7-2. The hierarchy shows which groups are sub-groups of others with each child appearing under its parent group. A child group inherits the privileges of the parent and can add additional capabilities available to the group.

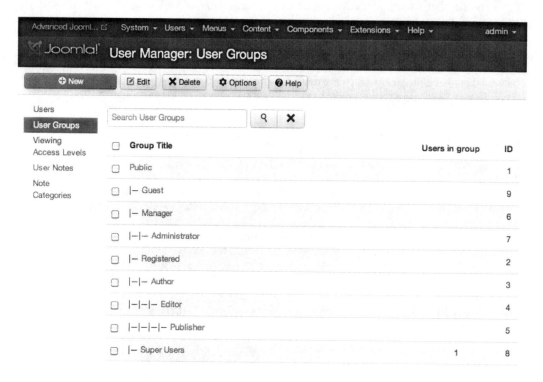

Figure 7-2. *Groups appear organized by hierarchy that represent many of the privilege levels available to that group*

To create a new group, click on the *New* button in the toolbar. When the User Group Details screen is displayed, set the Group Title to Co-brand A and select the Group Parent as Public so the group will not inherit any permissions. This new group will be used for clients that have a co-branded representation on the site. For example, if you administered the web site for the National Football League, you would want to create an area for the individual teams where they could add news articles and edit their team graphics. Each team would have a co-brand login.

■ **Note**   The Joomla security system allows a user to be assigned to multiple groups. For the clients in this example who were logging into the system, we might want to split up the rights among several accounts that parallel the traditional account (for example, "Co-brand A Author," "Co-brand A Editor," and so forth). A user might be added to that group in addition to another general site group, such as "Registered".

For these co-brand users, we need to give them privileges to add categories and menus as they see fit, but they should not be allowed to make fundamental system changes such as installing extensions or creating new users. That would threaten the stability and security of the site. A good place to begin when defining a new group in the additive model is to grant the group simple login privileges.

1. Open the Global Configuration manager from the System menu of the Administrator interface.

2. Click on the Permissions tab and you should see the groups in tabs down the left side of the pane.

3. Click on the "Co-brand A" link to display the permissions for the group.

4. Select the Allowed option for the settings of Site Login (that's front-end login permission) and Admin Login (that's the back-end or Administrator interface login permission), as shown in Figure 7-3.

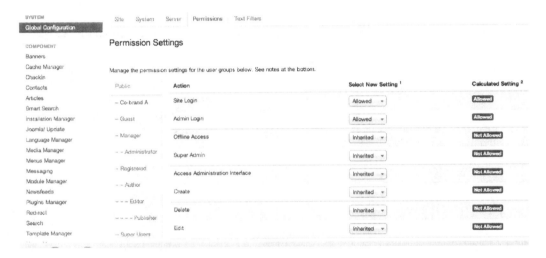

Figure 7-3. *Using the Permissions tab of the Global Configuration to select the actions permitted for your group*

5. Click on the Save & Close button to save the permissions for the group.

To test the capabilities of the Co-brand A group, open the User Manager and create a user named cobrand and under the Assigned User Groups tab, check the Co-brand A group and uncheck the Registered group (which is selected by default).

You may have noticed that we set up the group with only login permissions—nothing else. This provides a good setup so you can see the foundation of a new group setup.

Log in to the Administrator interface with the cobrand user. For testing, I would suggest you log in using a different browser (or using Chrome in Incognito mode or Firefox in Private Browsing mode) than you are using for the administrative configuration so you can have both the Admin user and the test user open at the same time. If everything is set up properly, you should see that the user has no capabilities in the Administrator interface. As shown in Figure 7-4, the interface that the user is shown has no menus and no options.

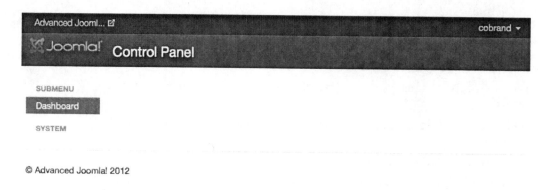

© Advanced Joomla! 2012

Figure 7-4. *The cobrand user has no permissions except login because the user belongs to a group that has only those permissions*

Now that you've created a user that has very few permissions, let's see what actions you can specifically restrict the group to use.

Limiting the Actions of a Group

After you've created user groups that can perform certain types of actions, you may also wish to limit them to the areas of the site where they can make these modifications. Setting up Access Levels provides exactly this type of control.

The available Joomla core actions are:

- Site Login, Admin Login

- Offline Access

- Super Admin

- Access Administration Interface—Whether the Administrator component for the item is available to the group

- Create

- Delete

- Edit

- Edit State

- Edit Own

You can configure these levels for:

- Global configuration

- Components

- Categories/Items

Let's start by taking a look at the setting security for the Banners component in the Global Configuration screen (see Figure 7-5).

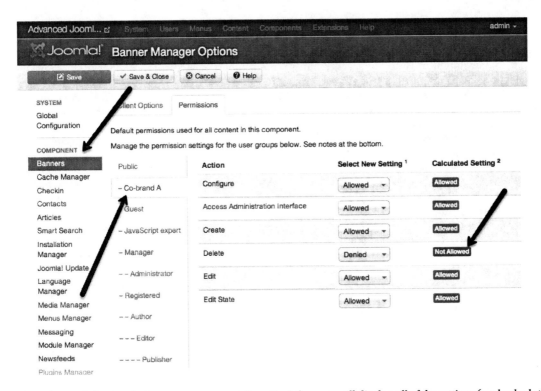

Figure 7-5. *Selecting the Banners component from the left menu will display all of the settings (and calculated settings) for the component*

From this figure, you can see that the Banners component is selected on the left column for the configuration settings. The Co-brand A group has been selected and shows that only the Delete option has been set to Denied (which is the default). All of the other options are Allowed. Note that all of the options have been specifically set. If the Inherited option is selected, the particular setting will be inherited from the global settings.

Instead of accessing the component settings through the Global Configuration, you can reach this same screen for the individual managers with the Options button for that Manager, as shown in Figure 7-6.

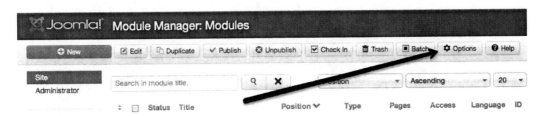

Figure 7-6. *You can set the access level for modules through the Options button on the Module Manager screen*

Click on the Co-brand group tab. For the Access Administration Interface row, select the Allowed option. Now if you log off and log back onto the system, you'll have access to configuring modules through the Administration interface.

So far, we've only modified actions that are available through the Administrator interface. More often, we will want to restrict viewing content on the front end. Viewing is restricted to particular groups using Joomla Access Levels.

Setting up Viewing Access Levels

While modification privileges dominate the security documentation because this is the area where hackers can cause problems, for day-to-day running of a web site, access security is more important. Access levels will help you protect non-hostile users from viewing content that their access level prohibits.

Configuring viewing privileges is the most common security need of a Joomla Administrator. On a very basic level, registered users often have more viewing access to content than unregistered visitors. If your site is more advanced, you will want to create viewing restrictions even differentiated among registered users.

Joomla includes a full access control list (ACL) implementation that allows for configuring user and group designations for access restrictions. The Joomla ACL lets an administrator define custom groups and user types, set access levels for these new entries, and add users to them. With the ACL features of the User Manager, a Joomla administrator can govern how a user views and modifies the web site. By allowing control over such actions as article editing to be granted to specific users, a web site can be more community-driven with various user types given particular capabilities to fine-tune relevant settings.

Access-level selection allows permissions for groups to be set for particular parts of a system (an unlimited number of access levels can be created). These levels include:

- Core
- Content
- Banners
- Newsfeeds
- Trash
- Weblinks

Each of these areas may be restricted from particular user types. By allowing an advertising client group to only have access to the Banners component, you could let them govern the Banners that are displayed on the site. To understand the best way to set up a new group, you can examine the existing groups. Let's look at some of the common groups, including Author, Editor, Publisher, Manager, and Administrator.

Select the Access Levels option from the Users menu of the Administrator interface. You should see a variety of access levels displayed. Click on the Registered level and you should see all of the Groups that are assigned that access level, as shown in Figure 7-7. You can assign multiple groups to each access level. Additionally, you may assign a group to one or more access levels.

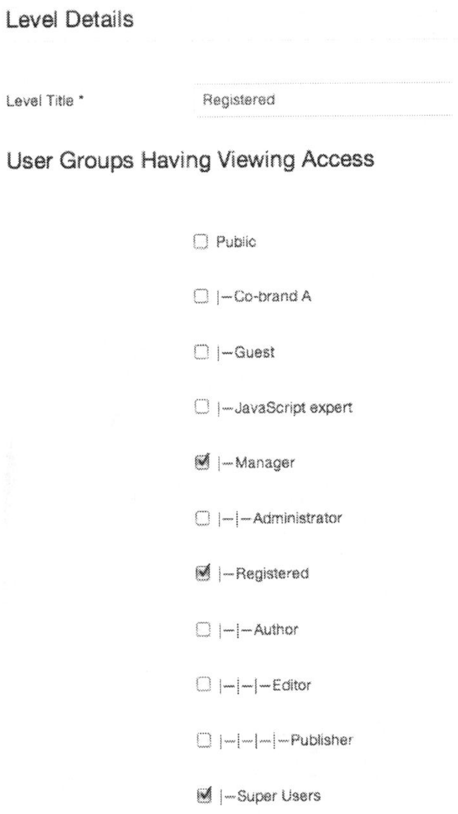

Level Details

Level Title *   Registered

User Groups Having Viewing Access

☐ Public

☐ |—Co-brand A

☐ |—Guest

☐ |—JavaScript expert

☑ |—Manager

☐ |—|—Administrator

☑ |—Registered

☐ |—|—Author

☐ |—|—|—Editor

☐ |—|—|—|—Publisher

☑ |—Super Users

Figure 7-7. *For any access level, you can assign multiple groups to that level*

You may be wondering where this access level will be used. You can assign access levels to any individual piece of content or category holding content. If you select the Category Manager from the Content menu and click on a category, you'll see a drop-down menu labeled Access. By default, Public is selected, giving everyone access. If you select the menu, you'll see all of the Access levels from the configuration screen.

The Access drop-down menu is also available for each individual article so you can apply access restrictions very specifically. To make these access levels apply, you need to place users in particular groups.

Defining User Accounts

Joomla administrators can create users that can be assigned to groups with a simple selection, as shown in Figure 7-8. If the user is added to multiple groups with conflicting access levels, the more restrictive access settings will automatically be used.

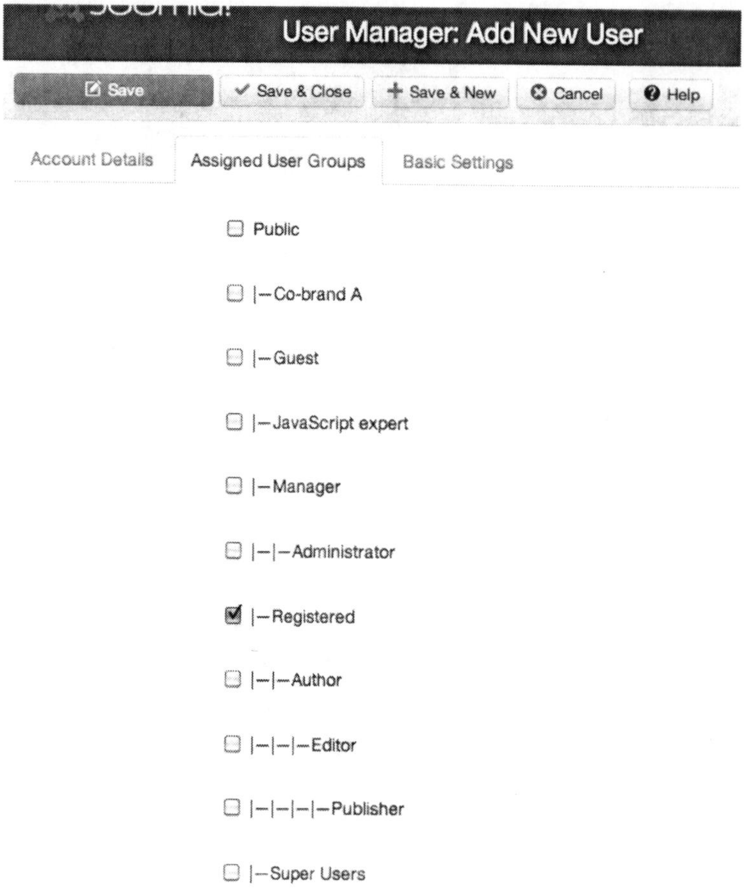

Figure 7-8. *A user can be included in one or more groups with a simple selection*

Only in very rare circumstances will you need to make specific settings for individual users. If possible, make settings to the parent groups so that there will not be special case settings that can lead to security loopholes in the future.

Protecting Against Automated Attacks

Automated attacks are becoming increasingly common. When a security flaw in any type of popular system is discovered, whether that system is ASP, PHP, Joomla, or Drupal, a hacker will set up bots to scan the Internet looking for sites that use the target technology. When a potential site is located, the bot will attempt penetration with the known security flaw. If successful, the bot will often shut down the site and post some type of hacker tag or message on the home page.

In the worst cases, the bot will inject a trojan horse, worm, or other malware so that future visitors to the web site will become infected. Because this type of attack is becoming more common, you need to prepare for such an eventuality. A few years ago, such a bot hacked tens of thousands of Joomla web sites when a flaw was discovered in the login system. The cost of such attacks is difficult to calculate, but the wasted time by individuals and corporations is almost unimaginable.

The best ways to protect against these types of attacks include:

- Ensure that you have the latest versions of various parts of the system upgraded to the most recent versions (both Joomla itself and any third-party extensions). Most organizations (including the Joomla development community) release security patches as soon as they are aware of the potential of security breach in a particular part of the system. Very often, the developers themselves recognize and identify the dangers of a security flaw before any hacker has exploited it. The new release or patch will eliminate the loophole that exists in the application or extension.

- Be sure to regularly check back on the Joomla web sites for the latest updates. You can subscribe to the RSS security alert system at `http://feeds.joomla.org/JoomlaSecurityNews`. For each new upgrade to Joomla, the development team makes available a patch file that you can apply to an existing site. That means that you can quickly and easily apply a patch package to a web site and upgrade it. Normally, you can apply these patches directly through the update capabilities of the Joomla Administrator interface.

- Don't follow system defaults. Automated attacks rely on all the systems that are attacked to be the same. For example, the default administrator account is named `admin`, which the automated script can exploit. If you change the administrator account to `jadmin` or something else, even if there is a login vulnerability, the script will attempt to use the `admin` user name and fail. Joomla changed to random database table prefixes (instead of the previous standard `jos_`) in the installer for exactly that reason—to make it difficult for automated scripts to guess the Joomla table names.

- Always choose strong passwords. Most automated attacks use dictionaries of common words in their attack, trying variations until they find a match.

- Do not use a password that has guessable personal significance. Birthdates are commonly used as passwords and this is a very bad idea—especially in the age of Facebook where birthdates are routinely exposed to various people. A friend recently had his WiFi hacked because he used his phone number as the WPA key. Avoid information that can be harvested from other systems and used to attack your own.

- Use `.htaccess` to block logged attacks. You can modify your `.htaccess` file to block particular IP addresses (you'll learn how to do that in the server security section later in the chapter). If you examine your logs and see suspect hacking behavior, add a block to specific IP addresses and see if the problem goes away.

- When writing extensions, always consider outside input dangerous. Third-party extensions are the most common ways hackers penetrate Joomla sites. When you're writing an extension, be sure to use the Joomla methods (such as `$app->input-get()`) for any values passed from the outside world. Joomla constantly updates their code to protect against possible threats, so using the system methods to clean input will safeguard your extension now and in the future.

Following these basic rules can help you protect against an automated attack. One of the most common methods hackers use is dictionary attacks against passwords. One of the best methods of protection is ensuring that your passwords are complicated or "strong" passwords.

The problem with most strong passwords is that they are difficult to remember—especially with the number of passwords one has to use in the modern world. Here are three suggestions to make this process easier.

1. Use a common phrase with the first letters capitalized and remove the vowels. A phrase like MyJmlRls (MyJoomlaRules) is easy to remember, but very difficult for a dictionary attack to find.

2. Using numbers in place of certain letters (1=L, 3=E, 4=A, 5=S, 0=O) makes things easy to remember but hard to attack (for example 34ch0n3 (EachOne)).

3. Using a mixture of different languages such as StrangeComida (StrangeFood) will make a password that is very unlikely to be listed in a common hacker penetration dictionary.

These strategies should make it less painful to use strong passwords. Remember that using a difficult password will only seem tedious before an attack. Foiling an attack will make you glad you put up with the inconvenience.

■ **Tip**   If you find a security flaw yourself, or your site is penetrated, you can e-mail the Joomla security strike team identifying a Joomla vulnerability at security@joomla.org.

Ensuring Secure Cookie Settings

Cookies have always been the source of potential security problems. Cookies are stored as plain text by the user's browser and also transmitted in plain text. That means if a web application stores sensitive information in the cookie, if the user's system were to be breached by malware or other spyware, that information might be harvested and used. Further, if a hacker were to obtain a session cookie, that session could be hijacked by the hacker because the server can't tell the difference.

Given the number of Joomla sites in government and hosting eCommerce, it is important to make sure that you don't introduce security problems if you create a Joomla extension. Here are some guidelines for using cookies:

- Set any cookies as session cookies. Session cookies are deleted automatically by the browser when it is closed. This practice will automatically remove potential information that could be dangerous.

- Don't store information on the client. Store a session cookie on the client and all other information should be kept on the $_SESSION object on the server. That means private information is never broadcast over a plain text connection.

- Be sure to store cookies at the domain root.

When the visitor browser requests a document, it sends all available cookies with the page request. The PHP script executing can modify or create any cookies that will then be sent back to the browser when the page is returned and the cookies are then stored in the browser's local storage. By default, cookies are stored at the path level where the creation of the cookie is requested by the application. Further confusing the matter is cookie storage in subdomains, so these three URLs will all store separate cookies in different locations:

```
secure.example.com
www.example.com
example.com
```

This creates numerous strange and problems that are difficult to diagnose—particularly with sessions. If you are using Firefox, I strongly suggest that you install the Web Developer Toolbar plug-in (https://addons.mozilla.org/en-US/firefox/addon/web-developer/). In addition to its numerous other features, it provides a cookie examination menu like the one shown in Figure 7-9. The View Cookie Information option will display a web page (as you can see in the figure) of the domain currently being displayed in the browser.

Figure 7-9. *The Web Developer Toolbar has features that make cookie debugging and examination much easier*

You will find that for many web sites, the same cookies will be stored at multiple path levels, so the session cookie may be stored at the root and well as a subdirectory. When the system requests a cookie to be set for expiration, it may expire the subpath cookie but leave the root cookie intact. This can cause confusion for the system as the system itself believes the visitor may have ended the session while the retrieved cookie may tell the server the session is still active.

When you are using vanilla Joomla, you will rarely see these problems. However, I've found these problems with numerous extensions—particularly those that provide bridge access to other systems such as Facebook Connect.

Joomla includes a class named `JinputCookie` (`/libraries/joomla/input/cookie.php`) that you should use to create and set cookies. To retrieve a cookie, you can use code like this:

```
$cookie = $app->input->cookie->get("MYCOOKIENAME");
```

I recommend you always set a cookie at the root so you don't have problems later:

```
$app->input->cookie->set("MYCOOKIENAME","MYVAL",time()+60*60,'/');
```

Remember that these guidelines also apply if you're setting cookies on the client-side through JavaScript. The jQuery Cookie plug-in (`https://github.com/carhartl/jquery-cookie`) can be very useful for setting cookies (including display preference information) by the JavaScript executing within the browser. JavaScript cookie population can be a very effective way to allow the user to interact with the site and you can adjust settings instantly without a server-side reload.

Configuring Server Security

Security is becoming increasingly important as hackers have become more effective—and in many cases vicious. While protecting your site shouldn't be a full-time job, you should consider it thoroughly so you can have confidence in your site. In fact, creating adequate security controls on your site can give you a great deal of peace of mind. There is nothing more disconcerting that having your site hacked or having a disgruntled contributor vandalize your site.

If you completely secure Joomla itself with the proper groups and access levels, the server that hosts your site might not have the optimal controls in place. Some things are out of your control if you are running your site on a shared hosting environment. However, if you have your own server or even a Virtual Private Server (VPS), you have almost complete control (and responsibility) for the security of your site. Start by evaluating the information you will be storing on the server so you can properly choose the amount of time and resources that you should apply to security concerns.

Selecting the Type of Security Setup

The one inescapable fact of safeguarding your web site is this: security is expensive. Security takes time, energy, focus, and often the expenditure of hard-earned money. Additionally, it often requires the sacrifice of performance. If you've ever installed e-mail spam filter software or a system virus scanner, you know the performance hit that occurs on your system. The same penalty (although not as severe) must be paid when you install security on your web server.

Because of the costs associated with adding security, it is important to clearly evaluate the benefits involved in any security strategy. Web sites span the spectrum of security needs and dangers. For example, the following web sites have different security needs:

- *Pentagon/military security bulletins*: While such a site would likely be available on the web (and could be very capably handled by Joomla) and would need broad access to be useful, the danger if the site was penetrated would be high. Therefore, a large expenditure ensuring security would be justified.

- *Twitter or other high traffic volume site*: Although there may not be a great deal of private data at risk of exposure, if the site was compromised and rendered inoperable for any length of time, the monetary loss and loss of trust could be substantial. Spending on security would likewise be a wise investment.

- *Small retailer online presence*: For a boutique eCommerce web site, targeted precautions are a good idea. Protecting the customer's private information would be a priority. However, if the site was brought down by a denial of service attack, for example, the damage would likely be low. Additionally, the small web footprint of the site would not make it an inviting target for notoriety-seeking hackers. A security plan that focused on protecting private data would be the most useful.

- *Hobbyist web site or forum*: This type of web site is often the focus of hacker attacks because the community of dedicated users may be large (so tagging or defacing the site will have widespread recognition) and the technical skill level of the web master is often low, making it an easy target. The security focus of such a web site will likely be a systematic backup process since the hackers will likely be sophisticated and protection will be difficult. The ability to quickly and easily restore a site once it has been compromised is of primary importance.

- *Blog or personal web site*: Security here would likely involve basic steps to ensure the site isn't wide open for attack. Also, a regular backup schedule would be a wise precaution. However, spending a great deal of time on security would likely be a wasted effort and that time would probably be better spent on creating more content for the site.

If you select the proper type of security you need at the outset, it can make performing security configuration much easier.

Security Configuration

Security configuration should not be done from memory because items can too easily be overlooked. By following a standard list of items, you can minimize the chances that a security vulnerability will exist on your system.

This section seeks to enumerate some of the more common security settings that must be in place to have a secure site. It is by no means exhaustive, as that is too large a task for any single book—let alone a chapter. Instead, the details here are intended as a foundation on which you can build your own decision tree to ensure site safety. If you spend a small amount of time per year reading the security journals for current dangers and take the precautions of a regular security scan, you will be protected a majority of the time.

■ **Tip** Anyone watching the Microsoft security updates or update logs will have a good idea of how frequently new security threats appear on the Internet. Scores of security holes are discovered every day and it is frankly too much for an small site administrator to keep up with. I recommend rather than focusing on these constant minor threats, you regularly look at the security bulletins of the primary technology providers behind your site (such as Joomla and PHP). These sites rate threat levels from minor to major. Major threats should be addressed as soon as possible, while most minor ones can be evaluated and remedied if the threat is specific to your site.

Refining Htaccess for Joomla

You probably have activated an .htaccess file to enable the custom Joomla routing for more SEO-friendly URLs. If not, you can look at the sample .htaccess file in the root directory of your Joomla installation for the htaccess.txt file. It contains default settings to perform URL rewrites so that search-engine-friendly URLs can be used on your Joomla site.

However, the .htaccess file can do much more than rewrite URLs. Some of the available configurable options include:

- Custom error routing

- Setup security

- Block users—by IP or referrer

- Change default directory page

- Define redirect behavior

- Add MIME types

- Prevent hot linking

- Configure directory listing

Let's take a look at some of the configuration settings and how they can benefit a Joomla installation. Each .htaccess file contains a number of directives that you can use to override the settings in the core Apache configuration for a specific directory. Modifying these settings in the .htaccess file allows changing the server configuration without requiring a reboot of the Apache server.

Anything you can do in the .htaccess file can also be done in the main Apache configuration file—but not vice versa. In fact, the directives that are allowed in an .htaccess file can be specified in the main configuration. The AllowOverride directive in the Apache configuration specifies what you can configure on a per-directory basis. When the AllowOverride directive is set to All, you can use all available overrides. When it is set to None, no overrides will be available to a directory with an .htaccess file. Specific limitations include AuthConfig (for authentication), FileInfo (for setting headers, error documents, cookies, etc.), Indexes (directory listing), Limit (page access), and Options (such as FollowSymlinks, includes, and so forth).

■ **Note** Web hosting companies can determine exactly which .htaccess directives they will allow you to configure and which are unavailable. Unfortunately, there isn't an easy way to determine the allowed directives. Check the FAQ of your web host for a list of available commands.

The directives in the .htaccess file will affect the directory where it is located and all of the subdirectories below it. Note that enabling .htaccess controls can very slightly slow down performance of the server because each directory access will try to read the .htaccess file. For most sites, this speed penalty (which adds milliseconds to load time) can be ignored, but larger sites need to recognize it is happening. On the bright side, the fact that the file is loaded with each page access means that changes to directives in the .htaccess file should be immediately live.

■ **Note** In Apache configuration files, like .htaccess files, lists are generally delimited by spaces instead of commas as in other configurations. For example, to use the AuthConfig and Indexes options, the directive will look like AllowOverride AuthConfig Indexes and further options will be added with additional spaces. Also note that comments are made by starting the line with the pound or number sign (#) unlike the double slash (//) used by PHP.

Let's do a practical hands-on lesson to .htaccess configuration on a local Apache server (don't do this on your production server). Start by backing up your main Apache configuration file (either httpd.conf or apache2.conf) and then editing the access section to match the following:

```
#
# Each directory to which Apache has access can be configured with respect
# to which services and features are allowed and/or disabled in that
# directory (and its subdirectories).
#
# First, we configure the "default" to be a very restrictive set of
# features.
#
<Directory />
    Options All
    AllowOverride All
    Order allow,deny
    Allow from all
</Directory>
```

By default, this section has directives such as AllowOverride None, which defaults to allowing no overrides. The change we have made allow any folder with an .htaccess file to use all available directives. Reboot your Apache server so the changes will take effect. Next, create a simple file called index.html in the root of your localhost root directory and add the following text:

```
<h1>Hello .htaccess</h1>
```

Access it in your browser (http://localhost) to make sure it displays properly. Now create an .htaccess file in the root folder and add the following directive to deny all access:

```
<Limit GET POST>
order deny,allow
deny from all
</Limit>
```

If you refresh your browser, you should receive a forbidden message like this:

```
Forbidden
You don't have permission to access / on this server.
```

If that worked, excellent! The .htaccess file was set to deny accesses for all, so the forbidden message was displayed. If it didn't, check the Apache logs for errors. You should be able to see a problem there. Correct the problem, reboot the server, and try again. Even debugging these types of problems can be useful. If you still can't find the problem, look through your configuration file—you probably have a later directive that overrides the section that you modified to grant .htaccess all available options.

Blocking Specific IP Addresses

Now that you have a good testbed for experimenting with configuration, let's start by blocking particular IP addresses, which can be an effective technique to block spammers. Modify your .htaccess file to read:

```
<Limit GET POST>
order deny,allow
deny from 127.0.0.1
</Limit>
```

Try to refresh again from your local browser. You should be forbidden access. For the next test, you'll need a second computer, tablet, or cell phone that is connected to your local area network. First, you need to determine the IP access of your development server. For Linux or MacOS, you can typically enter the ifconfig command at the console and it should list the IP address. For Windows, use the ipconfig command at the command prompt. In most cases, the IP address should read something like 192.168.1.113.

Enter this address into the browser of your second computer (or mobile device). You should be able to see the Hello .htaccess message! In this example, you've blocked a browser on the same machine from accessing the page, but let through remote access. That's generally the opposite of what you want, so let's reverse it.

Look at the end of your Apache access logs. You should see the access entry of your secondary device like this:

```
192.168.1.113 - - [23/Apr/2013:14:33:55 -0800] "GET / HTTP/1.1" 200 25
```

Change you .htaccess to block that address like this:

```
<Limit GET POST>
order deny,allow
deny from 192.168.1.113
</Limit>
```

Try to access the server from the secondary device—you should be forbidden. Use your local browser again and the page should be available. Now you know how to block an IP address. What if you want to block a whole range of IPs? Or block all IPs from a range, but make an exception for a single IP? Or what about blocking any request from a specific domain? You can do that, too, with directives like this:

```
<Limit GET POST>
order deny,allow
deny from 192.168.1.0/8 # Works the same as wildcard 192.168.1.*
deny from 192.168.1.0/16 # Works the same as wildcard 192.168.*.*
allow from 192.168.1.113 # Allow from one IP in the denied range
deny from example.com # Denies accesses from the example.com domain
</Limit>
```

This type of range blocking gives you great power in limiting hackers and (in particular) spammers. Be careful, however, not to make blocked range too large or you'll block valid visitors. The more effectively you can target an IP access denial block, the less likely that you will block safe visitors.

Allowing Index Listing

Most of the primary configurations are specified with the `Options` directive. Let's allow a folder underneath our main folder to show the directory of files. To allow listing of directories in the user's browser, add this directive to the top of your `.htaccess` file:

```
Options Indexes
```

This option will specify that the Indexes AND ONLY the Indexes option should be enabled for the current directory and any child directories. If you want to add the Indexes option to any other existing options inherited from parent directories or the Apache configuration, use the plus (+) sign like this:

```
Options +Indexes
```

If you want to block directory listing of directories, use the minus (-) sign:

```
Options -Indexes
```

Create a new directory called `test/` at the root of the web server and create a few other folders or files in that folder. Don't name any of those files `index.php` or `index.html`, otherwise the directory listing won't be displayed. Access the directory from your browser (`http://localhost/test`) and you should see the directory listing as show in the Figure 7-10.

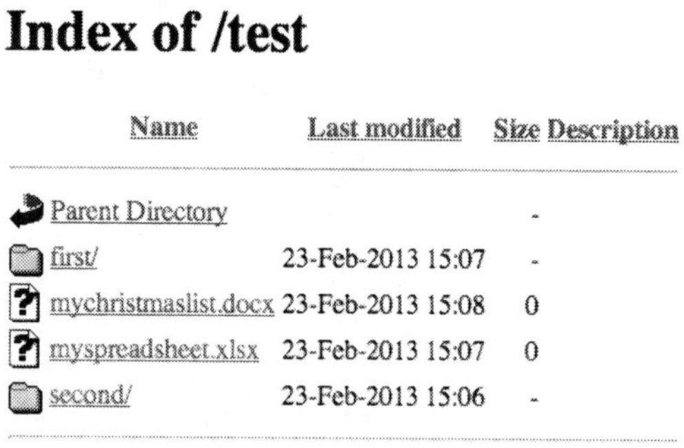

Index of /test

Name	Last modified	Size	Description
Parent Directory		-	
first/	23-Feb-2013 15:07	-	
mychristmaslist.docx	23-Feb-2013 15:08	0	
myspreadsheet.xlsx	23-Feb-2013 15:07	0	
second/	23-Feb-2013 15:06	-	

Figure 7-10. *The directory listing of the test/ folder should be displayed*

For Joomla installations, it's unlikely you'll want to enable the listing of directories without some other type of security. For example, you might accept contributions to your site and want to make available licensed clip art or CSS files. Or want to provide moderators with guidelines in formatted PDF files. By adding `.htaccess` security to this directory (and providing specific passwords to those who needed access), you could add a place where contributors could go and easily download whatever they need. Before you opened up this type of directory browsing, however, you will want to add the proper security.

Adding Password Access to the Administrator Ddirectory

The previous example showed adding directory listing through the `.htaccess` file. More commonly, you will want to add htaccess security to the `/administrator` directory. If a hacker finds a security hole in Joomla (which they have in the past) and gains complete access to the Administrator interface, they can essentially do anything to the site from modifications to stealing user information. You can prevent many of these penetrations by simply making the

Administrator interface inaccessible. One method of securing the Administrator interface is changing the default name of the directory so a hacker doesn't know the route—but this can be a problem for Joomla upgrades. Another is adding access security to the directory that contains the interface.

You have probably already seen .htaccess security on web sites before. Before you can access content at a URL, the browser itself displays a login dialog box, as shown in Figure 7-11. If the user fails to enter a valid username and password, the web server rejects access to those site resources. That means the system is never exposed to possible security loopholes that exist in a web application (such as Joomla). Once the user logs in, they will remain logged into that protected directory until the browser is closed. If this type of security is added to Joomla, it means you will need to log in twice (once for the .htaccess security and again for the Joomla system), but you will be protected from many more forms of security penetration.

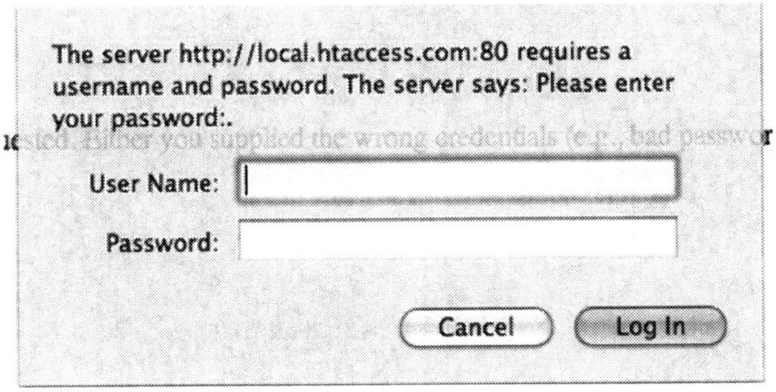

Figure 7-11. *Putting .htaccess security on a directory causes the browser to display a login dialog*

To add an .htaccess password, you need to add a few directives to your existing file. You will also need to generate a password file that will contain any of the logins that you want. Generally, you will need to do this from the command line or console (unless your service provider offers a web-based equivalent).

Start by adding the following directives to your .htaccess file:

```
AuthType Basic
AuthName "Please enter your password:"
<Limit GET,POST>
require valid-user
</Limit>
```

Try to access your localhost from a browser and the login dialog box should display. The directives tell the server system to require the login through the server's password system. Let's add one additional line and specify a file that contains the passwords:

```
AuthUserFile /etc/apache2/.htpasswd
```

That will keep web authentication passwords in a separate place from general server login credentials. However, now we need to create that password file because right now, no one can log into the system because there is no password file and no entries in it. If you have command-line access to the server, you will need to create a user account on the system and set a password.

To create a new password, make sure there is an /etc/apache2 directory (with a mkdir /etc/apache2 command) and then execute this command to create a user and set the password:

```
sudo htpasswd -bc /etc/apache2/.htpasswd jadmin AdvncdJml
```

This will create a login with the name jadmin and set the password to AdvncdJml. Once you have set up the password, you should be able to use it immediately to log in. Keep in mind that this login is completely separate from the Joomla system, so if you change the password in the Administrator interface, it will not automatically change on the server. If you can live with the inconvenience, it is probably a good idea if you were to use different passwords for .htaccess and the Joomla Administrator account. That would double the security for the site.

Implementing SSL on Your Server

Joomla is well-suited to creating a secure site because it has built-in routing capabilities for the Secure Socket Layer (SSL). While SSL doesn't secure the site itself, since it encrypts traffic to and from the server, it can prevent eavesdropping. SSL is an HTTP-based method of providing the secure exchange of data between a browser client and a server. Using SSL can be very useful if you are accepting private data (such as birthdates or Social Security Numbers) on submitted forms or providing some type of eCommerce solution. When communication occurs over the SSL channel, data between the client and server is well-encrypted, making interception and decoding of data a minimal concern.

Recognize that an SSL session requires a fair amount of processing overhead on both the client browser and the web server. All traffic between the browser and the server needs to be encrypted at one end and decrypted at the other, which requires a large number of mathematical calculations. Even images in an SSL session are encrypted.

■ **Note** Computers continue to become more powerful and the execution overhead of SSL has become a smaller drawback. The decreasing processing burden of encryption is the reason many popular web sites such as Google, Gmail, GitHub, and eHow Now simply encrypt all of their traffic and make https:// access to the server the default.

This processing overhead is the reason that the Joomla interface allows you to limit encryption on specific pages via the Secure option in the Administrator interface (see Figure 7-12). You can specify particular menus that will automatically use SSL and others that will not. Note that this setting just affects the links that are created for the particular menu of the site—they don't perform routing redirection.

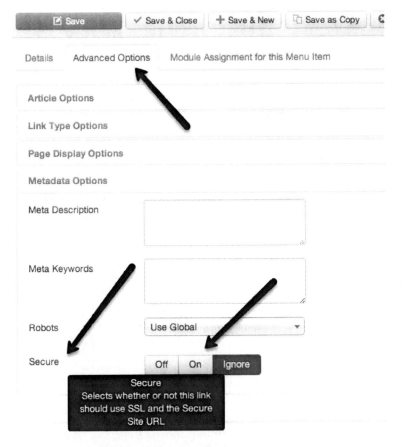

Figure 7-12. *Through the Advanced tab, you can set a menu to use SSL security*

If a menu is set with Secure to Off, then whatever the site policy, the specified menu will have links that are not https. For a menu that is set to Ignore, the menu will use the default policy (and this is the default setting). If set to On, then the link will always use the https prefix.

You can configure Joomla to force the redirect pages that are referenced without a secure header—but you can only perform this on the whole site or the whole Administrator interface. If you select the Global Configuration option from the System menu, click on the Server tab to show the Force SSL options. From the menu, you can select the force to affect the entire site or only the Administrator interface.

Before you can use SSL capabilities, however, you need to configure your server to use a secure certificate. In the following sections, I'll explain the basics of the SSL setup and you'll learn how to create your own certificate on a development server so you can test how it works before you implement it on your production site.

▓ **Note**   Normal web page interaction occurs on port 80. For SSL sessions, all communication happens on port 443.

Registering a Secure Certificate

To make a web server secure, you need to have a file called a certificate on the server (or provided by a load balancer) so when a browser visits an https address, it can request the certificate. That certificate is then verified by a certificate authority (a trusted third-party company, such as Network Solutions) that confirms the site is the same one it claims to be. If so, an encrypted session is set up between the browser and the server.

All of this happens automatically—the visitor never sees anything beyond the secure icon if the certificate is valid and the certificate authority is recognized. To secure your site, you need to purchase or create a certificate that the server can send to the browser when the server is accessed.

Most web host providers have a service that allows you to buy various types of certificates that you can apply (through an Administrator GUI interface) to individual sites hosted on their servers. You can even purchase bundles of certificates for a discount when securing multiple domains. Look at the available options with your current hosting provider.

Keep in mind that you need a separate certificate for each URL. For example, you may have a certificate for:

```
https://www.example.com
```

This certificate is not valid for:

```
https://secure.example.com
```

Therefore if you have multiple domains, you will need a separate certificate for each URL. This is another reason to limit the security that you need to specific areas of your site. By centralizing the secure traffic at a particular place on your site and with a particular URL, you can minimize the amount of money you will need to spend on certificates.

To gain some experience relating to how certificates work, you can generate your own.

Creating Your Own Certificate

Creating your own certificate can be useful, especially for internal web sites. The reason you generally don't want to use self-created certificates with eCommerce site is that the creator is not a "recognized certificate authority," which means that every time a user accesses the site, they will be presented with a dialog that informs them that the certificate is not from one of these providers (as see in Figure 7-13).

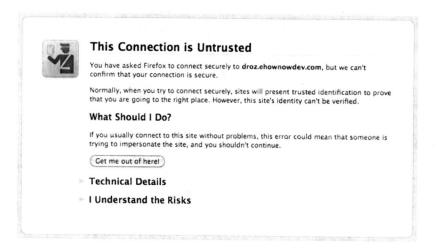

Figure 7-13. *A certificate from an unrecognized certificate authority causes a browser to display a special dialog box in the user's browser*

However, if this isn't a concern (as it isn't on an organization's internal web site), you can create as many certificates for as many domains as you might need. The process is fairly straightforward on Linux or MacOS and you can use the following instructions. Windows requires a bit more work and changes with new Windows version releases. Search on the web for "generating SSL certificate on Windows" to find tutorials and guidelines.

■ **Note** To use the SSL features effectively, the domain name with the secure certificate and the unsecure domain name must match. For example, if you have a domain name `http://www.example.com`, your secure site name should be `https://www.example.com`. If the secure version of the site has a different domain name (for example, `https://secure.example.com`), the Joomla system can become confused and unexpected situations can occur such as the entire site (instead of the specified pages) may be accessed through the SSL. Because the SSL certificate is directly related to the subdomain, you may also want to create a `mod_rewrite` rule that redirects any attempt to access a URL without a subdomain (such as `https://example.com`) to the proper subdomain (such as `http://www.example.com`).

To set up the secure server, you first need to create a directory where you're going to keep your certificates. On Linux or MacOS, create the directory and switch to it:

```
mkdir /etc/httpd/ssl
cd   /etc/httpd/ssl
```

Now run the `openssl` command to generate a certificate there:

```
openssl req -new -x509 -days 3650 -sha1 -newkey rsa:1024 \
-nodes -keyout server.key -out server.crt \
-subj '/O=Company/OU=Department/CN=www.example.com'
```

Change the `CN=www.example.com` reference to match the hostname of your current server. You can obtain the hostname with the command:

```
hostname
```

In my case, the hostname on my local machine returned `MacBook-Air.local`, so I set this reference to `CN=MacBook-Air.local`. When the `openssl` command is run, it should output the status that confirms the generation of the certificate:

```
Generating a 1024 bit RSA private key
.....++++++
.......................................++++++
writing new private key to 'server.key'
-----
```

There are two key files generated (`server.crt` and `server.key`) for a certificate. Once you have these files generated, you need to create an Apache configuration file to use them. With your favorite editor, create an `ssl.conf` file in your `/etc/httpd/conf.d` directory and add the following text to the file:

```
LoadModule ssl_module modules/mod_ssl.so
Listen 443
```

```
NameVirtualHost *:443
SSLRandomSeed startup file:/dev/urandom 1024
SSLRandomSeed connect file:/dev/urandom 1024
SSLSessionCache shm:/usr/local/apache2/logs/ssl_cache_shm
SSLSessionCacheTimeout 600

<VirtualHost *:443>

    VirtualDocumentRoot /var/www/%0/docs
    ServerAlias local.*.com
    ServerName local.*.com:80

    SSLEngine on
    SSLOptions +StrictRequire

  <Directory "/var/www/">
       SSLRequireSSL
       Options -Indexes MultiViews FollowSymLinks
       Order allow,deny
       Allow from all
       AllowOverride All

  </Directory>

    SSLProtocol -all +TLSv1 +SSLv3
    SSLCipherSuite HIGH:MEDIUM:!aNULL:+SHA1:+MD5:+HIGH:+MEDIUM

    SSLCertificateFile /etc/httpd/ssl/server.crt
    SSLCertificateKeyFile /etc/httpd/ssl/server.key

    SSLVerifyClient none
    SSLProxyEngine off

    <IfModule mime.c>
        AddType application/x-x509-ca-cert        .crt
        AddType application/x-pkcs7-crl           .crl
    </IfModule>
</VirtualHost>
```

This configuration file firsts loads the SSL module and sets off the server to listen on port 443. The directives that follow set up the random seed and the location of the session cache files. The remaining options setup the wildcard directory structure and variable vhost options. Note the SSLCertificateFile and SSLCertificateKeyFile directives that specify the location of the certificate files that we generated earlier.

Once you have the file created, test to make sure it works properly with the configtest command:

```
apachectl configtest
```

If the test reveals that the SSL module is throwing an error or the SSLRandomSeed directive is not found, you may not have the SSL module installed. Check the active Apache modules with this command:

```
apachectl -M
```

You should see `ssl_module` in the list if the module is installed. If not, install it in the method necessary for your operating system. For CentOS, you can use the `yum` utility:

```
yum install mod_ssl
```

Run the `configtest` command again. If the `VirtualDocumentRoot` directive returns an error, you probably don't have the `mod_vhost_alias.so` enabled. On CentOS, it should already be installed—you just need to activate it in your main configuration file by uncommenting the reference to it. On Ubuntu, you'll find it in the `/etc/apache2/mods-available` folder and you just need to move it to the `/etc/apache2/mods-enabled` folder. On MacOS, Apache modules are typically located in the `/usr/libexec/apache2` folder. On Windows, you'll find modules in the `modules\` folder in the root of the Apache install (for example, `c:\apache22\modules\`).

Run the `configtest` command again. You should have no errors now. Reboot your Apache server and check your Joomla installation using your web browser:

```
https://local.joomapples.com
```

You now have a secure test server! If you're running SSL on your production server, you want your development server as close to parity as possible, so running your server on `https` is a good idea. If there are any problems, check the access and error logs.

Examining the SSL Logs

Many users new to SSL don't realize that logs for secure sessions are kept separate from the traditional Apache access and error log files. The SSL logs have the prefix *ssl_* appended, so if the normal access logs have the file names `access_log`, the SSL logs will have names such as `ssl_access_log` and can be found in the same folder as the normal logs.

Generally, the SSL configuration creates three log files:

```
/var/log/httpd/ssl_access_log
/var/log/httpd/ssl_error_log
/var/log/httpd/ssl_request_log
```

The `ssl_request_log` stores all of the SSL requests including the session setup requests. That means that the files can grow much larger than the traditional access logs. That generally means if you have a popular site, you will need to rotate these files so you can archive or delete older files. The Whitehorses blog (`http://blog.whitehorses.nl/2010/04/16/rotating-ssl_request_log-in-ssl-conf/`) has an excellent article describing how you can set up this rotation.

Summary

In this chapter, you've learned how to perform both site security and server security setup for Joomla. For site security, you learned how to create and configure groups and access levels that will allow you to secure your site at the same time you can confidently allow third-party access—restricting those users to areas and actions appropriate to their needs.

Server security includes refining the server configuration for specific access security (through `.htaccess` controls), directory listing services, and setup of SSL certificates to allow https sessions on your Joomla server. You also learned how to use the `.htaccess` file to block particular IP addresses or IP ranges to prevent hacker attacks from specific routes.

In the next chapter, you'll learn how to access the Joomla database directly so you can take more control of your system.

CHAPTER 8

■ ■ ■

Joomla Database Administration and Configuration

At the heart of every content management system is the database that stores and serves the material that makes up the site. Maintaining this database is essential to your Joomla site and the more you learn about the database structure and functionality, the more effective administrator you will be. Fortunately, the database structure (schema) that serves the Joomla CMS is very well designed, which makes it easy to administer and possible for any advanced Joomla user to leverage through direct access.

Nearly all Joomla sites use the powerful MySQL database as the back-end to store their content. Most Joomla administrators simply let Joomla take care of the details of the database. This hands-off-the-database approach has traditionally limited the power of administrators since operations such as batch content modifications or custom reporting are not generally available through the standard Joomla installation.

For example, transferring all articles associated with one user account to another user account can be very difficult and time-consuming using the Administrator interface. Third-party extensions may or may not be available to fulfill a particular administration need. However, these types of global operations are often quick and convenient when performed through direct database access. Further, you can create and run ad hoc reports (such as a report that shows which contributors have the articles with the most page views) in seconds. As you begin to become comfortable with direct database access, you will find that it opens up a world of possibilities. In this chapter, you'll learn how to directly query the database for reports such as article statistics and how to make global modifications such as changing the database engine of all the tables to save you time and frustration.

■ **Tip** Before performing any bulk changes to the database, be sure to back up either the entire database, or, for multi-record update commands, back up the specific tables being modified. It is very common—even for advanced users—to create an update or delete command that has unintended consequences. Perhaps most often (and most disastrously) a bulk update is applied to a table where the author of the query doesn't realize that the identifying id (such as user id) contains multiple records associated with it. Instead of deleting a single article by author #1101, all articles by that author are deleted. Without a backup, this can be a catastrophe. On most hosting platforms, you can use phpMyAdmin to do the backup and there are instructions later in the chapter describing its use. If you have direct command-line access to the MySQL server, you can use the powerful `mysqldump` utility that can dump in a variety of formats and even directly from server to server.

SQL (Structured Query Language) Primer

Most database servers use a language called *SQL* (or Structured Query Language) to allow retrieval and modification of data. Joomla communicates with the MySQL server using SQL, and this small primer will introduce you to the query language. The purpose of this primer is not to teach you how to write advanced code in SQL—entire books are devoted to the subject—but instead to make you comfortable enough with the language to modify the reports included in this chapter.

Unlike procedural execution programming languages such as PHP that execute statements sequentially (line 1 is executed, followed by line 2, and so on), SQL is a results-oriented language. In SQL, you tell the database server what you want as an end result set and the server itself figures out the most effective sequence of commands for fulfilling that request and executes them. That means SQL code tends to contain very few lines because you only need to tell the server *what* you want, not *how* to collect and process it.

Examining Some Simple Query Examples

For example, a very simple query that can request all the data of an article that has an article ID of 1 would look like this:

```
SELECT * FROM jos_content WHERE id = 1
```

The query, when executed against a Joomla database server with the sample data installed, will return the information about article #1 with data broken into separate columns (here displayed as rows for easy reading):

```
id: 1
asset_id: 27
title: Joomla!
alias: joomla
title_alias:
introtext: <p>Congratulations, You...
fulltext:
state: 1
sectionid: 1
mask: 0
catid: 29
created: 2008-08-12 10:00:00
created_by: 42
created_by_alias: Joomla!
modified: 2010-07-05 13:46:40
modified_by: 42
checked_out: 0
checked_out_time: 0000-00-00 00:00:00
publish_up: 2006-01-03 01:00:00
publish_down: 0000-00-00 00:00:00
images:
urls:
attribs: {"show_title":"","link_titles":"",...}
version: 37
parentid: 0
ordering: 1
metakey:
metadesc:
```

```
access: 1
hits: 121
metadata: {"robots":"","author":""}
featured: 1
language: *
xreference:
```

Let's take a look at the SELECT statement again:

```
SELECT * FROM jos_content WHERE id = 1
```

The SELECT statement specifies that this SQL command is a query—not an INSERT or DELETE. Following the SELECT command is the wildcard asterisk (*) character that specifies all of the columns (fields) for the selected record(s) will be returned. If you imagine each database table is like a spreadsheet with rows and columns, it will be much easier to understand the database structure. In this spreadsheet metaphor, rows are the individual records (for example, article #1, article #2, and so forth) and the columns are the fields for each article (for example, title, publish data, article text, and so forth). You can interchangeably use the terms *rows* and *columns* with *records* and *fields* when describing a database.

In Joomla, articles are stored in the jos_content table. The SELECT statement uses the FROM command to specify the table that holds the requested data.

░ **Note** Older versions of Joomla used the jos_ table prefix as the default, so the content table, for example, would be named jos_content. Joomla now defaults to a random five-letter prefix that is available for editing during the initial Joomla installation. The table names on your installation, therefore, are likely to have a different prefix than the jos_ one used here. For consistency, this chapter will always use the jos_ prefix, but when you use the queries on your own server, please substitute your site's actual prefix. You can look in the database schema itself to determine the current prefix, or look at the $dbprefix value in the configuration.php for your web site installation.

Finally, the WHERE command specifies the query criteria, which in this case requests data where "id=1", so only an article with an ID of 1 will be returned. What would a SELECT statement look like that wanted the data for article #2?

```
SELECT * FROM jos_content WHERE id = 2
```

How about a query that only returned the id, title, and introtext of article #3? For this SELECT statement, you would specify the column names you want returned rather than use the asterisk wildcard in the column request:

```
SELECT id, title, introtext FROM jos_content WHERE id = 3
```

How about the article id, title, and alias for all articles modified during the month of December? You can add the AND Boolean to specify more than one condition in the WHERE clause:

```
SELECT id,title,alias FROM jos_content
WHERE modified>='2012-12-01' AND modified<='2012-12-31'
```

From these simple examples, you can probably get a sense of how powerful querying the database can be. I keep a large set of commonly used queries in the Leo Outliner (http://webpages.charter.net/edreamleo/front.html) that lets me quickly search and find queries that I can tweak to my particular needs and execute. I would suggest that if you start using SQL regularly, you also create a "cheat sheet" document in which you can store common queries where you can easily reference them.

Using More Complex Queries for Reporting

You can use the SQL SELECT statement for everything from very simple record retrieval (such as that shown in the preceding example), to complicated grouping and data aggregation. The following query groups all of the articles by category, counts them, and then relates or "joins" the category ID to the jos_categories table in order to report the category title:

```
SELECT c.catid, cat.title, count(1) numArticlesInCat
  FROM jos_content c
  JOIN jos_categories cat ON c.catid = cat.id
  GROUP BY catid
  ORDER BY numArticlesInCat DESC;
```

This query is quite a bit more complicated than the earlier ones, but you should recognize the same key elements. The SELECT statement is followed by the columns or fields that you want returned for the data. In this case, there will be three fields returned: catid from the jos_content table, title from the categories table, and numArticlesInCat, which is an aggregate count of the number of articles in a particular category.

The FROM statement contains the same table name as earlier queries (jos_content) with one difference—this table name is followed by a table *alias* that provides an alternate, shorter name for referencing the table, which in this case is the letter c. The alias can be any unique word you want to use because it is only temporary and lasts only for the execution of this query. For example, you could have used the alias cntnt instead of the single letter c if that would make your query easier to read.

Did you notice that in the fields, there was a column requested called c.catid? This reference requested the field catid from the jos_content table. If we hadn't used the alias, the catid could have been addressed as jos_content.catid and it would have had the same effect (although selecting many columns without shorter aliases makes things difficult to read).

The rest of the SQL code specifies how the aggregation will occur to return the results that we want. The JOIN connects two tables together (jos_content and jos_categories) by category ID. The GROUP BY specifies which field should be used for the grouping and aggregation. Finally, the ORDER BY statement requests that the data be returned in descending order by total number of articles in category.

When executed, this query returns rows of data—one for each category that contains articles. When you execute this query on the sample data, the returned results will look like this:

```
40, 'Modules', 27
31, 'Joomla!', 9
43, 'Plugins', 8
39, 'Components', 7
41, 'Templates', 5
36, 'Scenery', 4
37, 'Animals', 4
35, 'Park Blog', 2
```

You can see from this query that the Modules category ID of 40 is pretty congested with 27 articles—three times more than the next largest category, which has 9 articles. After that, the drop-off is fairly rapid with the eighth most populous category only containing two articles. If this was a production site, it would be easy to see that some reorganization was required when a majority of the articles are going into what must be becoming a "catch all" category in the system.

At the time of this writing, there is no built-in method to determine category congestion through the Joomla Administrator interface—without manually selecting each category and counting the articles that are contained there. This example should provide you with some sense of the power available to an administrator who can directly access the Joomla database.

■ **Note** For most Joomla database work, the SQL SELECT statement will be the only SQL statement you will need because it searches and returns data. The SQL modification commands (such as INSERT, UPDATE, and DELETE) are best used indirectly by calling the appropriate methods in the Joomla Framework (see Chapter 12). Many of the Joomla modification operations make adjustments to several tables, so if you make a custom modification to database records, you could alter something that would throw the Joomla system out of sync. If you do perform batch operations, use care before executing the SQL command and, once again, be sure to back up your database before you run anything.

You might be asking, "How would I run these SQL commands?" Most commands of this type are executed once or at non-regular intervals. You'll find you often want to tweak them to provide specific information, so they are generally not something you would build into a custom extension. Instead, you would use one of the many query tools available to execute the query for you. One of the most popular MySQL database management tools is a web-based open source tool known as phpMyAdmin, or PMA for short.

Using phpMyAdmin (PMA) for Database Administration

The web application known as phpMyAdmin (or PMA for short) is a web-based database administration application that contains hundreds of features to examine, manipulate, back up, and maintain a MySQL database. Because it uses a web-based interface, you can access it through any modern web browser and use it to easily maintain one or more remote databases.

The PMA application has these features:

- Carry out any SELECT, INSERT, UPDATE, CREATE, DELETE, or RENAME operation against a database

- Execute a SQL query or a sequential batch of queries

- Manage stored procedures and triggers in MySQL (note these operations are only available to the root or super user even if routines are specific to a database where you have full read-write access)

- Import new data using either SQL or CSV files

- PMA also has advanced features including:

  - Create complex queries using the Query by Example (QBE) interface

  - Create a schema graph PDF file of the Joomla database structure (schema)

  - Transform data stored in fields using pre-defined functions, such as BLOB fields to images

  - Multi-server administration from the same console

  - Global server for all tables in a database or specific selected ones

The user interface is pretty friendly for beginning users, as shown in Figure 8-1. PMA makes it easy to examine either the data structure (known as the database schema) or the data it contains.

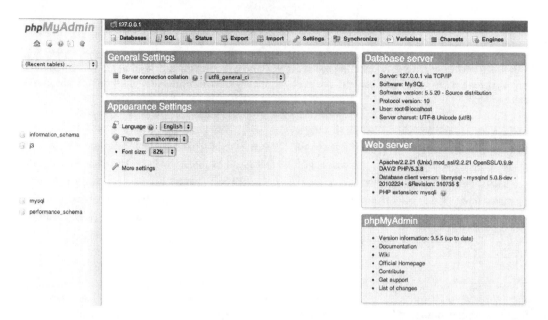

Figure 8-1. *The PMA interface is a web-based GUI that makes MySQL administration easy and accessible on many web hosts*

■ **Tip** Some of the other popular MySQL administration tools require direct access to the MySQL port 3306 to perform management operations. Most ISPs don't grant access to the MySQL port outside the server workspace itself for security reasons. Therefore, a web server and PHP executing within the host environment can access the MySQL instance, but a MySQL client utility running on your desktop machine cannot. That's one of the reasons for the popularity of PMA. Because it runs on the web server itself, if your web application can access the MySQL server, than PMA can as well—making it the only admin tool available for use in those circumstances. If you do have direct access to the MySQL instance, you may find free tools such as MySQL Query Browser (http://dev.mysql.com/downloads/gui-tools/5.0.html), MySQL Workbench (http://dev.mysql.com/downloads/workbench/), or SQL Workbench/J (www.sql-workbench.net/) a little more responsive, powerful, and flexible.

PMA generally comes pre-installed by most ISP vendors. If not, or if you want to use it on your development machine, downloading it from the PMA homepage (www.phpmyadmin.net) and installing it yourself is a straightforward process. In the following section, I'll walk you through the basic installation steps so you can get started using it right away.

Setting Up PMA

If you're running Joomla on a localhost or dev server, you will need to set up your own copy of PMA to interface with the database. Even if your web host supplies it, you may want to perform a manual install so you can use the latest version. This is a very simple and quick process in most cases.

Go to the web site (www.phpmyadmin.net) and download the latest version, which is available in ZIP format (useful on all operating systems) or .gz format for Linux-based machines. Extract the files from the archive to a location that can be accessed from web server, such as the htdocs/ folder. The path might be something like htdocs/pma.

■ **Note**   If you want to set up login through the PMA system, follow the configuration instructions on the PMA web site. In most cases, I set up an .htaccess in the folder containing the copy of PMA and let the Apache system handle the access security. Whichever method you choose, **make sure** you set up the necessary security so no hackers can harvest the content of your site or cause destruction directly to the Joomla MySQL database.

To configure PMA to access the database, first duplicate the config.inc.sample.php file in the root directory of the PMA install. Rename the copy of the file to config.inc.php so the system can find and use it. Next, change the default auth_type line (which is set to "cookie") to use configuration like this:

```
$cfg['Servers'][$i]['auth_type'] = 'config';
```

Then add two lines to specify the username and password to your MySQL server:

```
$cfg['Servers'][$i]['user']         = 'root';
$cfg['Servers'][$i]['password']     = 'MYSQLPASSWORD';
```

If you aren't running the MySQL server on the same machine as the web server (localhost), you will need to set the host setting to the URL or domain of the site:

```
$cfg['Servers'][$i]['host'] = '128.128.0.128';
```

Alternately, if the localhost DNS record isn't configured for MySQL, you might have to put in the localhost IP address like this:

```
$cfg['Servers'][$i]['host'] = '127.0.0.1';
```

That's it! Simply access the proper path in your web browser. I set the folder name to PMA, so the URL I can use is:

```
http://localhost/pma/
```

You will see a home screen like the one shown in Figure 8-2. Clicking on the Databases tab at the top will show all of the available databases on the current MySQL server. This screen will also allow you to create new databases (called database schemas) and set various configuration options including the database collation, default language, and the PMA color scheme.

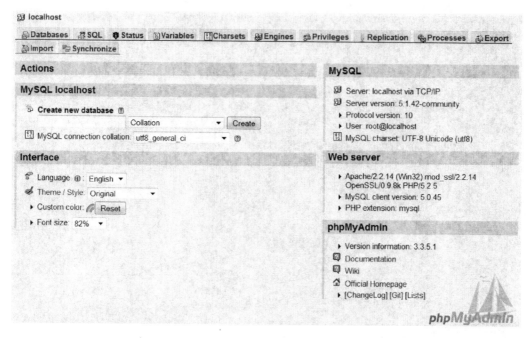

Figure 8-2. *The PMA interface when initially accessed via the browser will show the home screen with tabs running across the top*

Using PMA to Examine the Joomla Database

The Joomla database consists of around 40 tables stored in a database of any name set during initial Joomla installation (although most administrators name that database joomla for simplicity). Historically, all Joomla tables have the prefix jos_ although during setup any alphanumeric prefix may be selected.

If you open the Joomla database in PMA, it will likely look something like the interface shown in Figure 8-3. Down the left side of the main window you will see all of the Joomla tables with the jos_ prefix. By default, the Structure tab in the right pane is also selected so all of the tables with their various attributes will be displayed there.

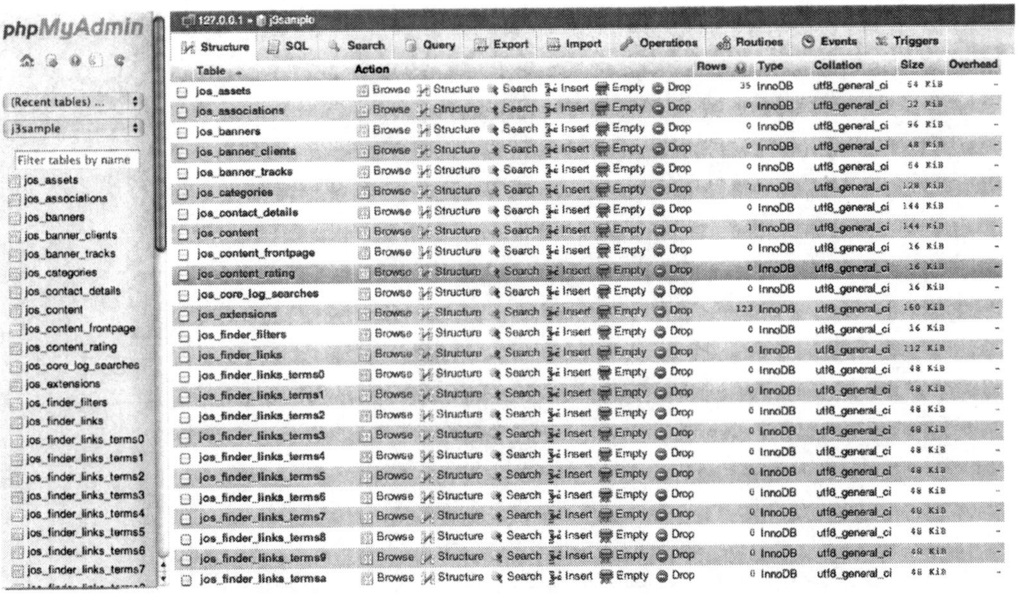

Figure 8-3. *Opening PMA to display the Joomla database will show you the jos_ prefixed tables that make up the Joomla schema*

The Structure tab provides you with valuable information such as the number of records in each table, the type of each database table (which we will change later), the size in bytes taken up by the table for storage, and other items.

■ **Note** The number of records displayed for a table is an approximation and should not be relied upon—especially for table imports. The number is generated by the MySQL server using a shorthand method of calculation and may not contain the latest row updates and deletes. It is very common for beginning DB administrators to use this value to confirm the size of a table, but it is more often wrong than right—commonly off by a few rows in small tables but as much as hundreds of rows in large tables. To determine the true number of rows for a table, execute a count query such as SELECT count(1) FROM jos_content. The count(1) in the query will perform an aggregate and add up the sum using a one for every row it finds.

Let's start using PMA by simply executing one of the SQL queries that was detailed earlier. Click on the tab labeled SQL and in the text box that is displayed, enter the following query:

```
SELECT * FROM jos_content WHERE id = 1
```

Remember to modify the table name to match the table prefix your site uses (you can find the prefix as the $dbprefix in the configuration.php file). Click the Go button to run the query and you should see the results for article 1 in the results table, as shown in Figure 8-4.

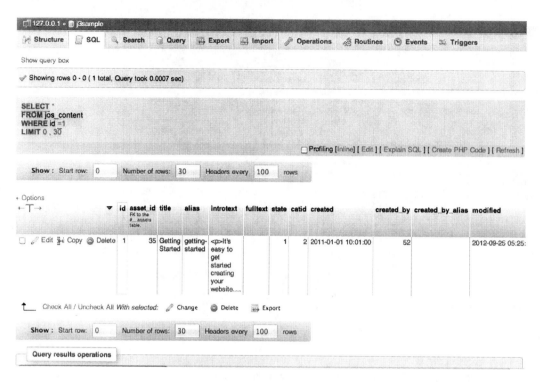

Figure 8-4. *The PMA results table will display the results of a SQL query after execution*

If no results are returned, try removing the WHERE clause. The SELECT statement uses this WHERE clause to filter the records returned, and your Joomla database may not have an article with an id field that is equal to 1. Use this query to return all rows of the table:

```
SELECT * FROM jos_content
```

PMA will automatically paginate the query so you won't have to worry about too many rows being displayed on a single screen. You can click on the Edit link in the top-right corner of the window to edit the current query in a pop-up window. Edit the query and re-execute it. You should now see many rows—each one representing one Joomla article. If the SELECT statement that filtered for the article ID of 1 didn't return a single row, you might notice that the results from the query that returned all of the articles in your table show that your id field values don't begin with the number 1, but something greater instead.

Using the Query by Example Interface for Reports

While the simple queries you just executed are good for examples, you will probably want to construct more specific queries to aid you in reporting on your site. At the same time, you might not want to devote the time necessary to become an expert at writing SQL code. The PMA application has an extremely useful feature known as Query by Example (QBE) that lets you construct complex data queries using simple examples of different searches.

The QBE interface is helpful enough that even a user not familiar with SQL can create a complex query against multiple tables. As you can see in Figure 8-5, the query interface lets you specify columns/fields and tables to query and build your SQL statement progressively. You can easily select Boolean conditions for the query and they will be introduced into the SQL statement that you can execute.

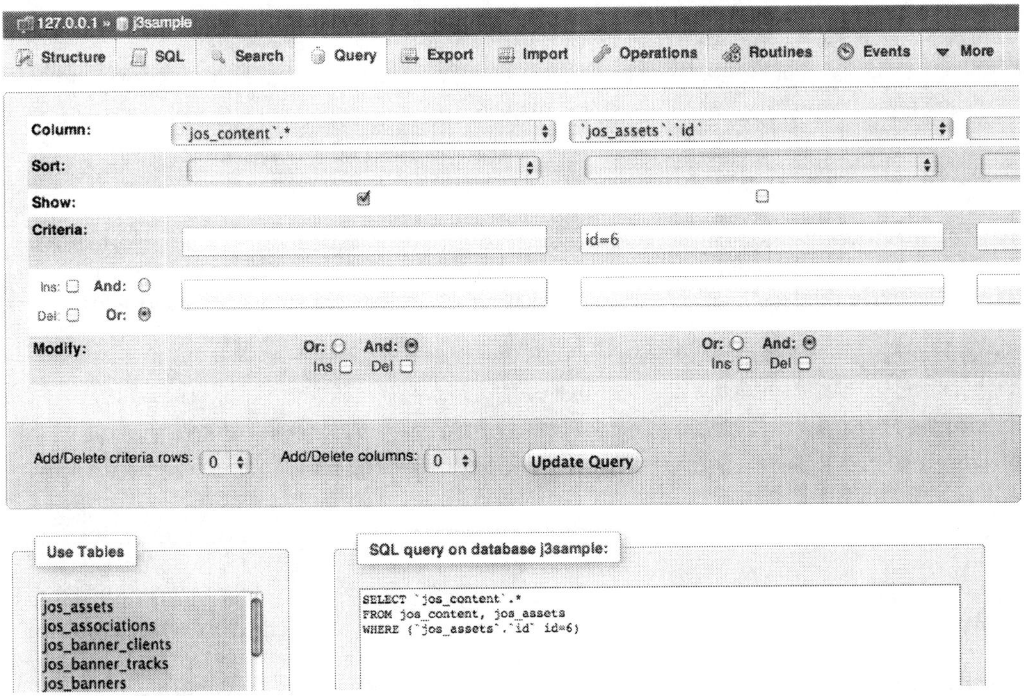

Figure 8-5. *The PMA Query by Example interface lets you easily create a query through drop-down interface selections*

To get to the QBE interface, click on the Query tab in the interface. The query interface will be displayed allowing you to select various fields and criteria for the search. To display all of the articles in the Joomla database, click on the first field drop-down menu and select the entry labeled 'jos_content.*', which uses the wildcard to select all of the fields of the content table.

Click on the Show checkbox and then click on the Update Query button, which will generate a SQL statement based on the options you've selected in the QBE interface. Click on the Submit Query button and the query will be run on the database and display all of the results.

To show only the article with an ID of 6, you can set the first field as you did in the first example, and the add a second field with the 'jos_content'.'id' selected. For the criteria, enter "id=6" and click the Update Query button. The SQL that is rendered will look something like this:

```
SELECT 'jos_content'.*, 'jos_content'.'id'
FROM 'jos_content'
WHERE ('jos_content'.'id' id=6)
```

Executing this query will show the row for only this particular article. You can use QBE to create complex queries by adding additional rows of criteria (with the Add/Delete Criteria Row option on the control panel) or using the Add/Delete Field Columns on the control panel to add additional fields to be queried beyond the default of three fields shown (this option will not add or delete anything from your database).

The QBE can be an extremely useful tool if you want to learn how to construct SQL statements. By selecting the parameters in the easy-to-use graphical interface and then seeing the resulting query, you can quickly grasp the proper syntax for a SQL query and begin writing them on your own.

While you can use PMA to simply access and modify a MySQL database, it also comes with more advanced features that allow you to document and monitor the core structure of the database itself. These features can aid you in understanding how a database is engineered and are particularly helpful in learning about a database you didn't author—such as the Joomla database we're examining in this chapter.

Setting Up Special PMA Tables

To use the advanced database documenting and monitoring features of PMA, you need to create special tables that are used by PMA to hold metadata (data about data) about the various relationships within the database. PMA can use these tables whether they are located inside your Joomla database or in a separate database created specifically to hold this data.

■ **Tip** I would recommend you create a separate database for the PMA tables if your ISP doesn't limit your database creation abilities. This makes it so the Joomla database contains only Joomla data—not miscellaneous information about the database that can be reconstructed if need be. It also means your Joomla database backup will be smaller because it doesn't include this extra data.

Every database has a structure known as a database *schema*. The schema defines what tables are in the database, how they are organized, how different fields/columns relate to each other, the type of data held in each field/column, and what types of indexes make searching the content faster. While MySQL can dump a text-only version of a database schema, it is difficult to gain a high-level understanding of the structure of a database from the dump file.

PMA can create a visual representation of the Joomla database schema by creating a PDF file that shows the various tables of the system and the relations between them. PMA also allows you to import data from a CSV file directly into a database. This can be useful especially when importing data from another system (such as database content).

The PMA application lets you perform some advanced database operations including the generation of a complete schema diagram of tables and table relations of a database.

To activate the advanced functionality, you'll need to start by editing the PMA configuration file (/config.inc.php) that you created when you first installed PMA. If you open the configuration file, you'll see a number of commented lines like this:

```
/* User used to manipulate with storage */
// $cfg['Servers'][$i]['controlhost'] = '';
// $cfg['Servers'][$i]['controluser'] = 'pma';
// $cfg['Servers'][$i]['controlpass'] = 'pmapass';

/* Storage database and tables */
// $cfg['Servers'][$i]['pmadb'] = 'phpmyadmin';
// $cfg['Servers'][$i]['bookmarktable'] = 'pma_bookmark';
// $cfg['Servers'][$i]['relation'] = 'pma_relation';
// $cfg['Servers'][$i]['table_info'] = 'pma_table_info';
// $cfg['Servers'][$i]['table_coords'] = 'pma_table_coords';
// $cfg['Servers'][$i]['pdf_pages'] = 'pma_pdf_pages';
// $cfg['Servers'][$i]['column_info'] = 'pma_column_info';
// $cfg['Servers'][$i]['history'] = 'pma_history';
// $cfg['Servers'][$i]['table_uiprefs'] = 'pma_table_uiprefs';
// $cfg['Servers'][$i]['tracking'] = 'pma_tracking';
// $cfg['Servers'][$i]['designer_coords'] = 'pma_designer_coords';
// $cfg['Servers'][$i]['userconfig'] = 'pma_userconfig';
// $cfg['Servers'][$i]['recent'] = 'pma_recent';
```

If these configuration settings do not appear in your configuration file, you may have an old version. You can try entering these items and see if the functionality will activate, or you may need to go to the PMA site and download the current version.

Remove the double slash (//) comment marks that are in front of all of these $cfg variable settings. These settings allow PMA to write metadata about databases into its own information store. Set the controlhost, controluser, and controlpass entries to match the earlier entries you configured for host, user, and password, respectively.

If you leave the pmadb parameter set to PMA (the default), you'll need to create that database on your MySQL server. If you're going to store the information in your Joomla database, change this setting to the name of your existing database.

Next you will need to create the PMA tables. There is a script in the phpMyAdmin /scripts/ directory (or /examples/ directory depending on your PMA version) called create_tables.sql that you will need to execute on your database server. You can do that through PMA itself by clicking on the Home icon and then clicking the Import tab. You can browse to the file and click the Import button to execute it on the server.

Note that this script begins with the command to create the PMA database and use that for the import. If you want to use a different DB, comment out that section and set the use command to your database like this:

```
USE myjoomladb;
```

After you execute the script, make sure the tables have been generated by browsing to them in the PMA interface. If they were created properly, you should see a confirmation screen like the one shown in Figure 8-6.

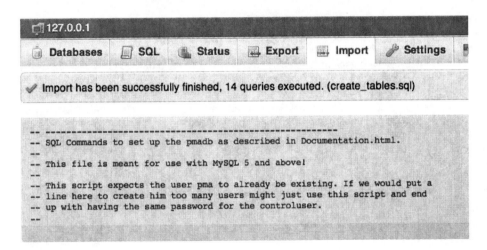

Figure 8-6. *The PMA execution of the table creation script should show the import worked correctly*

Now you're ready to start generating schema diagrams!

Generating a PDF of the Joomla Schema

The newer versions of PMA include substantial database designer capabilities. The GUI design lets you graphically lay out tables and relations between them for better understanding and schema building.

As shown in Figure 8-7, I've begun the process of mapping the Joomla schema. Creating this type of map is an excellent way to learn the structure of a database that you didn't originate. It can help you envision the tables of the database spatially so it is easier to understand and remember the import tables in a way that is impossible with a simple linear list of table names.

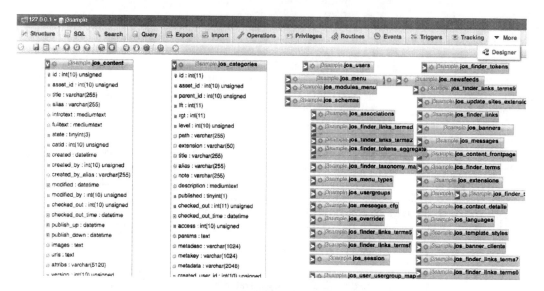

Figure 8-7. *You can graphically map the Joomla database schema in the PMA Designer*

In an advanced database like Joomla, the database structure is "normalized" or designed to minimize the duplication of data. For example, each article in the Joomla system has a designated category. Each category has a number of pieces of information associated with it, such as name, title, alias, whether it is published, and so forth. If all of this category information was stored with each article record, not only would the database grow very large, but if you ever wanted to change a category name, the record for every article record would need to be updated.

Instead, categories are stored in one table and articles are stored in another table and a numeric value is used to create a relation between the article and its associated category. For example, a category named Animals might have a category id of 37 and all of the articles for that category will store this single number 37 in each article record. To get the category information for the article, the database simply takes the category number (in this case, 37) and performs a lookup on the category table to find the associated category information.

In this scenario, the *reference key* is the main id of the category that is the column/field named id in the jos_categories table. The column in the jos_content table that stores a value for each article that associates an individual article to the category is called the *foreign key* because it references a table outside itself. In our example, the foreign key for the category id is named catid, which you can see in Figure 8-7.

Let's create a relation in the schema diagram between these two fields so you can understand how such a diagram is constructed.

1. Open the Designer view in the PMA window using the More menu. On the far right side of the top menu (following the Tracking tab), you should see a More drop-down menu. This menu should have the option of Designer. If you don't see it, try opening PMA in another browser. PMA seems to reload settings once per browser load and the designer requires the pmadb we set up in the last section.

2. Reorder the tables until the jos_content and jos_categories tables are clearly visible, as shown in Figure 8-8. When you first enter the Designer, the tables are usually stacked one atop another. You need to drag and drop the tables until you clear a working area.

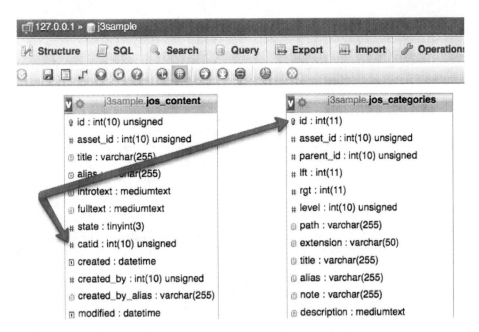

Figure 8-8. Clear space so you can work with the content and categories tables

3. Click on the "Create relation" icon in the Designer toolbar to set up the relation between these two fields.

4. A popup will tell you to select the reference key, which you can do by clicking on the id field of the jos_categories table.

5. A second popup will ask you to select the foreign key, which you can do by clicking on the cat_id column in the jos_content table.

6. A popup will ask you to confirm the relation and, after clicking the OK button, the graphical representation of the relation will be created.

You have now created your first relation. You can create other relations, such as a relationship between the reference key id for the jos_content table and the jos_content_frontpage and jos_content_rating foreign keys. You can export this graphical design as a PDF so you can print it or use it for reference later.

■ **Note** To create relations in the Designer, the field types must match EXACTLY or the relation can't be created. When you try to create the relation, a nondescript error such as "Error: The relation could not be created" is displayed. Unfortunately, at the time of this writing, Joomla has many field type mismatches that make creating relations a problem. In Figure 8-7, you should be able to see that the foreign key field catid is an int(10) unsigned while the primary key field id is an int(11). If these problems have not been resolved yet, you can correct them yourself with an ALTER statement, such as ALTER TABLE jos_content MODIFY catid int(11); that will match the primary and foreign key types.

Now that you've examined the Joomla database thoroughly, you might want to make a few changes. One change many advanced MySQL users make to existing databases is changing the database engine type from MyISAM to InnoDB for more reliability and the availability of additional features.

Using PMA to Convert Joomla Tables to InnoDB

Depending on your web hosting, Joomla may create the tables it uses as type *MyISAM*. This specifies the database engine that will be used to read and write data (MySQL includes several database engines you can select). MyISAM is the database engine that is often selected for its speed on smaller web sites. However, MyISAM has the following substantial disadvantages:

- Table locking: With any update or insert to a table (such as incrementing the number of views for an article), the entire table is locked for other changes. Therefore, if 10 articles were accessed at the same time, even though the changes are occurring to different rows, these updates would stack up because the entire table is locked until each update is complete. InnoDB, in contrast, can lock by individual row so only updates to the same article will queue up.

- Poor crash recovery: MyISAM tables can be corrupted in a crash. InnoDB has advanced features to prevent any data loss or corruption in all but the most severe circumstances.

- Lack of data integrity mechanisms: Certain operations need to be treated as a set for all or nothing updates. For example, a money transfer at a bank might subtract a sum from Account A and add a sum to Account B. If the power would fail after the sum was subtracted but before the other sum was added, that amount of money would be unaccounted for. By encapsulating multiple operations in a "transaction," data integrity is assured. While not critical for most Joomla sites, eCommerce sites in particular are safeguarded by transaction features.

No medium to large site would want to use MyISAM for the primary tables because of locking problems and the potential of data corruption. Because MyISAM and InnoDB are almost entirely compatible, you can convert existing MyISAM Joomla tables to InnoDB easily.

We can begin converting a single Joomla table to InnoDB using the PMA GUI so you can see where to access the database engine selection. Afterward, we will use a bulk `alter` statement to change all of the remaining Joomla tables to InnoDB. At the main structure pane, for the first table `jos_assets`, click on the Structure icon (see Figure 8-9) in the table.

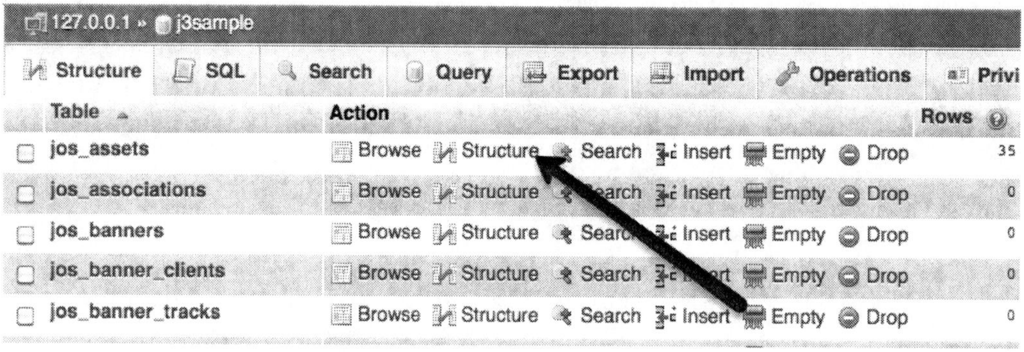

Figure 8-9. *Begin table conversion by clicking on Structure*

Once the table is selected, click on the Operations tab. You will see the screen with all of the overall settings for the table. If the Storage Engine drop-down under the Table Options section has MyISAM, you should change it to the InnoDB engine. Select InnoDB instead and click the Go button. You should see a message appear at the top that reads "Your SQL query has been executed successfully" and directly below that message you should see this SQL code:

```
ALTER TABLE 'jos_assets'  ENGINE = InnoDB
```

That is the SQL statement that changes the storage engine used by that table. Now if you return to the database structure by clicking on the database entry on the breadcrumb at the top of the PMA screen, you will see that the table has been changed to an engine of InnoDB.

To convert all of the tables, you can execute the MySQL SHOW TABLES command in PMA to list of all the tables. If you export the list of table names to your favorite text editor, add a text prefix ALTER TABLE ' to each line and the suffix ' ENGINE = InnoDB to each line you will have a multi-line macro to do the complete conversion of all the tables.

Paste the macro into the SQL textbox of PMA for execution. That is one simple technique to complete the task. More commonly, a database administrator will write a standalone script to perform this type of macro operation. Let's create just that type of script as an example so when you need to construct a macro to do most complex modifications, you have a foundation that can be built upon.

Scripting the Conversion of Joomla Tables to InnoDB

Given that Joomla has more than three dozen tables, changing the database type for each can be very tedious. Additionally, various extensions may have created tables that likewise could need conversion to InnoDB. Instead of performing all of these alterations manually, it would be quicker to write a script to simply loop through all of the tables and execute the proper ALTER statements to the database server. In addition to creating a script that you can re-use on multiple installations, you will also have a basic script that you can modify to use for your other batch operation needs.

Following is an implementation of a script that will convert all of the tables from the MyISAM engine to InnoDB. Modify the line that calls the mysqlConnect() function to include your username, password, and the name of your Joomla database.

```php
<?php
function mysqlConnect($username,$password,$dbName='',$host='localhost') {
        $success = false;
        $link = mysql_connect($host, $username, $password);
        if (!$link) {
                $success = mysql_error();
        } else {
                if(!empty($dbName)) {
                        $result = mysql_select_db($dbName,$link);
                        if($result) {
                                $success = $link;
                        } else {
                                $success = mysql_error();
                        }
                } else {
                        $success = true;
                }
        }
        return $success;
}
define('NL','<br/>');
mysqlConnect('USERNAME','PASSWORD','joomla16');
// Turn off unique checks during conversion to lower disk i/o
$sql = "SET unique_checks=0;";
$result = mysql_query($sql);

$sqlGetTables = "show tables;";
```

```
// Get list of all Joomla tables
$result = mysql_query($sqlGetTables);
while($row = mysql_fetch_row($result)) {
        $sql = "ALTER TABLE '{$row[0]}' ENGINE = InnoDB;";
        $resultAlter = mysql_query($sql);
        echo $sql.NL;
        if(!$result) {
                echo mysql_error().NL;
        }
}
$sql = "SET unique_checks=1;";
$result = mysql_query($sql);

?>
```

To execute the script, simply place it in the root folder of your web site and access it with your browser. If you name the script changedb.php, for example, accessing the URL such as http://localhost/changedb.php would make the modification. Be sure to remove the script from your site as soon as you execute it to make sure there isn't a security vulnerability that a hacker could exploit.

Managing the MySQL Database Server

The modification script may have been your first substantial foray into database administration. DB administrators are responsible for the health and proper functioning of the databases and database servers. Joomla does most of the basic DB administration such as table creation and content maintenance, but leaves the full administration to other tools. You've been using PMA for queries and basic modifications to the database. You can use it broader administration including database backup, full text search, and multi-server synchronization.

Using PMA to Back Up Your Joomla Database

There are many excellent Joomla extensions for database backup. Some will extract the data from the tables, concatenate it, compress it, and then e-mail the backup to a specified address. Some will synchronize with another database like the PMA synchronize feature (see the Synchronizing Remote Databases section later in the chapter). Others will dump the data to a backup file on the web server.

All of these solutions are useful. However, it is good to know how to perform these operations yourself so if your needs are more specific, you can back up or restore the data you need. The restoration phase is the most important—it doesn't matter if you have a backup of your data; if you have problems reloading it, then you're in trouble. For that reason, it is good to perform a manual backup and restore at least once.

Additionally, your backup needs may be more exacting than that allowed by the various off-the-shelf solutions. For example, perhaps instead of a complete database backup, you only want to back up the content added in the last 14 days. Or maybe you only want to back up the users that didn't log in through an LDAP system. By performing the database backup yourself, you can restrict the backup to any number of parameters that are required.

Backup and restoration through the PMA interface is completed using the Export and Import tabs. The Export tab allows you to pick a large variety of export formats. These formats include CodeGen, CSV, CSV for MS Excel, Microsoft Word 2000, JSON, LaTeX, MediaWiki Table, Open Document Spreadsheet, Open Document Text, PDF, PHP array, SQL, Texy! text, XML, and YAML.

The Export screen allows you to select specific tables, columns, and a variety of other export factors. Clicking on the Export tab will allow you to select either the Quick Export method, which displays only minimal options, or the Custom Export, which lets you select everything from columns to specifying INSERT statements.

Let's back up the jos_content table so you can see how it works. Follow these steps:

1. Select your database in PMA.

2. Click the Export tab to display the Exporting Tables screen.

3. For the Export Method, choose the Custom option so you can select specific tables to export.

4. Select only the jos_content table.

5. Set the file name for the export. By default, it is the name of the database. Because we're only exporting a single table, add the table name to the file name (e.g. @DATABASE@-jos_content).

6. Click the Go button to create the exported file.

You can now import just the jos_content table if you want to load the content into another site.

Using PMA to Search the Entire Database for Text

When you do a basic SELECT query, generally you specify the exact table and column you want to search with the query. This is perfect when the data set is well-understood and you know where to look for the data that you're trying to locate. However, if you have a complex database or one that was created by other people (in this case, the core Joomla development team), it is helpful if you can do a global search across all the tables of the database. The Search tab in the PMA interface lets you perform a global search for values across tables.

Clicking on the Search tab will display the search box where you can enter search text with wildcards, as shown in Figure 8-10. The "Inside table(s)" list box allows you to select one or more tables where the search will be performed. The Select All link will select all of the tables in the current database. The "Inside field" text box will also allow you to restrict the search to a specific a field/column.

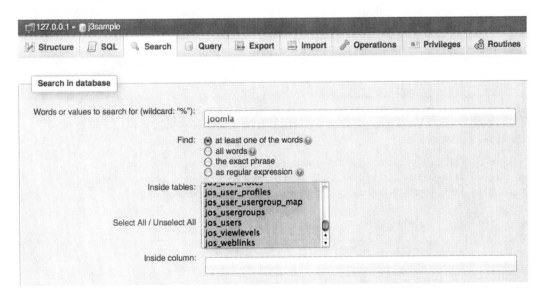

Figure 8-10. *The Search screen lets you search for values across tables in a database and use specific terms or terms with wildcards*

Clicking the Go button will execute the search, which will then display a table of search results. Each table in the search will be listed along with Browse and Delete buttons that will let you browse the matches or delete the rows that contain the matches, respectively.

▪ **Tip**   When you are developing in Joomla, you can often use this search to more quickly find database code related to particular functionality. If you can navigate to the part of the web site that contains the functionality that you want to adjust, look for a unique piece of text (such as the phrase "Milky Way"). Search for this text in the database to find out the table and column where the related data is stored. Then you can search the source code for references to these database structures and often quickly pinpoint the code that displays or modifies the data.

Synchronizing Remote Databases

One amazing feature included in PMA is the ability to synchronize databases across servers. That means that you can synchronize a remote production database (running on a web host, for example) to a local database (perhaps for development), or vice versa. The ease of synchronizing means that you can quickly keep two or more copies of a Joomla site coordinated.

Synchronizing a database is as easy as setting up the source and target of the synchronization. Follow these steps:

1. In PMA, start by clicking on the Home icon to take you to the top level of the application.

2. Click on the Settings tab.

3. When this window is displayed, in the More Settings pane, there is a link to the Setup script—click that to edit the `config.inc.php` that you created when first performing the PMA setup.

4. On the Setup page, click the New Server button to add additional servers.

▪ **Tip**   Alternately, you can add additional servers to the setup configuration file with your text editor. In some ways, that is preferable because it means that you don't have to make your config.inc.php editable.

---

5. Once you've set up the necessary target servers, return to the home screen in PMA and click on the Synchronize tab.

6. When you click on the Synchronize tab, the synchronize form will display, as shown in Figure 8-11. This first screen lets you set the access information for the two databases to be synchronized. Both servers must be accessible from the server that is running PMA.

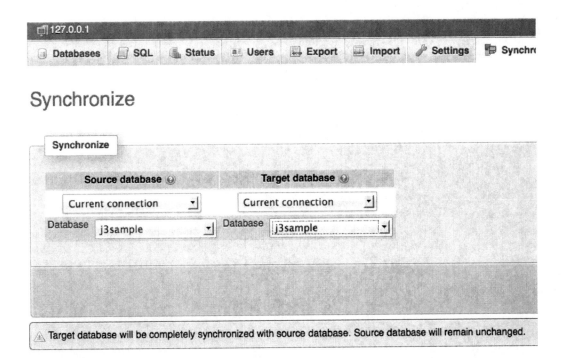

Figure 8-11. *The Synchronize form provides selections for a source and a target database*

By default, the database location for each is set to Current Connection on the drop-down menu. For a
emote server, you can set the host, port, socket, and database of both the source and target databases. Once this
information has been entered, clicking the Go button will take you to the next admin screen—it will NOT begin the
synchronization process. The target database must exist before you can access the next screen because PMA will not
create the database for you.

When you click on the Go button, the synchronization screen will display a table showing the source information
in the left column and the target information in the right column. The middle column has buttons for *S* and *D* that
signify Structure and Data, allowing you to synchronize structure or data or both by individual tables. The buttons are
color-coded with a green background on each button, showing there are no changes to synchronize, while the red
background indicates that there is a difference between the two.

Clicking one of these buttons will turn the background gray, indicating that the table option has been selected
by the user for synchronization. Additionally, the table below the three column table will display a row-by-row list of
the syncs that will occur. For example, one row will have the structural synchronization changes that will occur. If the
data sync for that same table is selected, the next row will show that selection and display the number of rows that
will be affected.

There is an option checkbox that reads "Would you like to delete all the previous rows from target tables?" and
will let you preserve the existing table data—if there are no key conflicts. Unfortunately, the structure of most database
tables including most Joomla tables includes an id that must be unique, so trying to synchronize additional records
into a populated target generally fails because of duplicate key conflicts.

Clicking the Apply Selected Changes button will execute the code to perform the synchronization. The PMA
application will examine both databases and display a list of differences including schema changes and data changes,
as shown in Figure 8-12. You can click on the individual differences (such as the "S" structure change icon) and that
change will appear in the change list directly below the synchronization report.

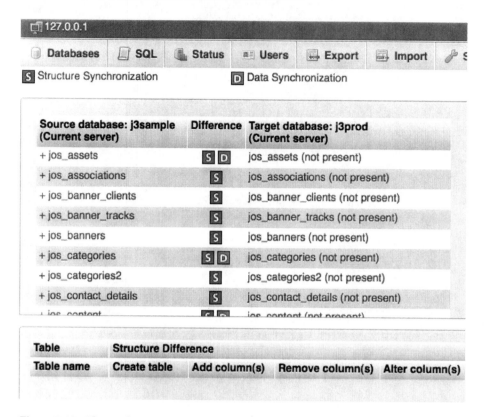

Figure 8-12. *The synchronization report will show you the changes that exist between the source and target databases and allow you to select specific changes*

You can use Apply Selected Changes to make individual synchronization changes or click the Synchronize Databases button to completely synchronize the changes. There is also an option to truncate the table data before the synchronization process so that the process will complete more quickly.

When the synchronization is complete, the report screen will display the success or report any problems that occurred with the synchronization. It will also list all of the SQL statements that were attempted for execution. This report is very useful to examine the individual changes for quality control after the synchronization process has been used.

You can use the Synchronize operation to synchronize the database schema as well as the data contained in the database. Note that this command performs no data merging—it simply replaces the data on the target with the data from the source. Therefore, any extra data in a target synchronized table will be lost.

■ **Tip** Like many other database operations, there is no undo option with this feature. Be sure to back up your target database before you begin the synchronization process. This file can easily be deleted after synchronization is complete. I usually name my backups with a delete date that is seven days into the future, so my backup file might have a name like "del12092013_joomlabu.sql" so I know when I can delete the file. By simply looking at the filename, I can see that the temporary backup is old and can be removed. Compare this file name to one often used by DB administrators such as "bu1.sql", which provides little or no information about the state or contents of the backup.

Refining the MySQL Server Configuration

There are many adjustments that you can make to your MySQL database server to improve performance and make it easier to use. You definitely want to optimize your development server to provide additional reporting and logging so you can examine and address problems in your development environment before pushing to production.

If your ISP doesn't allow you to modify the MySQL configuration (most don't because it requires a reboot of the server), it can be to your advantage to run a profile so you can determine if any site slowdown is actually occurring on the server. If it is, you can sometimes request access to a different server that has performance characteristics that more closely match your needs.

Start by clicking the Home icon and then selecting the Variables tab in PMA, which will display a list of all the configured variables of the system (see Figure 8-13). Most of these variables can be very useful to determine the exact functioning of the system, but are beyond the scope of this book. We'll examine a small subset of the available variables that will have the greatest impact on your web site performance.

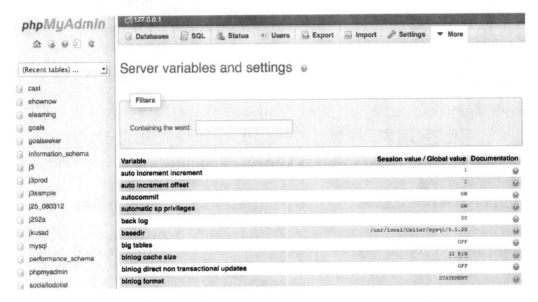

Figure 8-13. *From the Home screen, the Variables tab will display all of the current settings on the MySQL server*

The MySQL variables are displayed in alphabetical order. Scroll down to the entry that says slow query log and make sure it is marked as ON. This log will record any queries that took longer than a specified interval to execute and allows you to modify either the database or the code to address performance issues. The variable directly below it reads slow query log file, which contains the path to the slow query log. This log is a text file and will record the SQL statement of every slow query. This log can get quite large on an active site, so be sure to clear it regularly.

To see how long the query execution time must be to be recorded in the slow query log, look at the long query time variable. By default, it is set very high—usually some time like 10 seconds. In a production environment, that would be a *very* slow query. Often you will want to lower this threshold to two-three seconds so you can see queries that are affecting the user experience.

If the slow query log isn't active and you have the ability to modify the MySQL configuration, you can activate the log by modifying the my.ini or my.cnf file, which contains all of the MySQL settings. This file can generally be found in the base directory of the database server. Look at the basedir variable to find the file path to that directory. On a Windows installation, it will be something like this:

```
C:\Program Files\MySQL\MySQL Server 5.1
```

Open the my.ini or my.cnf file in your favorite text editor and add the following two lines:

```
slow_query_log = 1
long_query_time = 2
```

The first will activate the slow query log and the second sets the long query threshold at two seconds. You will need to restart the MySQL server for this change to take effect. From the command line, you can do it like this:

```
service mysqld restart
```

On a remote site, the restart procedure will vary based on the type of control panel available through your ISP. If you reference the variables display in PMA, you should see your selected changes.

A large number of things can cause slow queries, from poor query programming to the lack of an index. Because the Joomla developers are very good at tuning the database interaction, you won't generally see any big problems with the query code. Most often, the database server configuration will cause the bottlenecks.

There are a few key variables that you should examine to make sure they are within the best performance ranges for a Joomla system:

- query cache size
- open files limit
- table open cache

Tuning these variables properly requires a fair amount of knowledge of MySQL. However, there is an excellent script called MySQL Tuner (https://github.com/rackerhacker/MySQLTuner-perl) that will examine the configuration of MySQL and make fairly accurate recommendations of the best settings for the server. Unfortunately, the script is written in Perl and needs to be run at the UNIX command line.

If you don't have the skills to execute the script, locate someone who you trust that can run it for you. The script only needs to be run once (or at most, periodically) for you to get a pretty solid understanding of the best parameter settings for your server.

If the database settings already match or exceed the settings recommended by the MySQL Tuner script, your Joomla system is probably functioning optimally. If they are far below these recommendations, you probably have a few things that you need to address for best server performance.

Tracking Database Changes

With advanced use of Joomla, you will find that you will often need to make slight adjustments to the database tables. Perhaps you need to add an extra ID field to the users table to integrate or synchronize it with your contact manager. Maybe you want to track how often an ad is clicked from a particular article so you can find your top monetizing content, so you want to increment a counter with each ad click.

If you're making changes to the Joomla database, there will come a point in the future that you will want to upgrade your version of Joomla and that new version will have an altered database schema. PMA allows you to track changes made to the database. By using this tracking feature, you can record your changes and even re-apply them to a new schema of the updated version of Joomla.

Whatever the requirement, in the past it has been problematic to track and replicate these changes when a virgin installation of a Joomla database is created or a new version of Joomla forces a database update. Thankfully phpMyAdmin has added a database schema versioning system similar to Git or other version control that let you track different versions and the changes made to the different tables. When you modified the PMA configuration earlier to activate the advanced features such as the Designer, you also activated the ability to track database changes.

There is a tab labeled Tracking in the PMA interface. If you click the tab, you will see a list of all of the tables that are currently untracked in the database, as shown in Figure 8-14. Let's add an additional column to the jos_content table so you can see how the tracking works. Start by creating an initial revision of the table by clicking the Track table link to the right of the table.

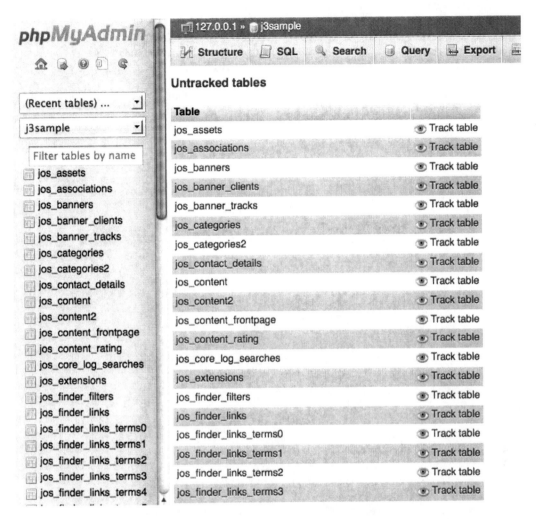

Figure 8-14. *The PMA tracking tab will show all of the currently untracked tables in the database*

The version creation screen will display, which shows the changes to the schema that can be tracked in the system. These include the data definition statements (ALTER TABLE, RENAME TABLE, CREATE TABLE, DROP TABLE, CREATE INDEX, and DROP INDEX) as well as the data modification statements (INSERT, UPDATE, DELETE, and TRUNCATE).

On a production web system, this tracking can be essential because you will have a log of any changes made to the database through PMA, so overrides are all documented. The tracking is even more useful if you have multiple administrators working on the same system. If an administrator makes an explicit change, the log will show the change, making the history of interaction much clearer.

■ **Note** This tracking only applies to interaction through the PMA interface. If an author modifies an article through the Joomla Administrator interface, it will be invisible to the tracking system.

For the example of tracking the jos_content table, leave the defaults to track everything and click the Create Version button. The screen will refresh and you will see the version line item with the first version. For a production system, I would suggest clicking the Create Version button again. That is useful because you then have an initial default version that was created by Joomla so you can compare later modifications made by a new version of Joomla with the initial revision.

Use the Insert or Search interface to make a change to the data of the content table. Then use the Structure tab to modify the table structure. I went to the control panel directly under the table to add an additional field and clicked the Go button, which displayed the field/column definition screen. There, create a VARCHAR field for wiki_id so an article can be linked to its related piece of content in a wiki system.

If you return to the Tracking tab and click on the "Tracking report" link for the current revision, you should see your change to the table, as shown in Figure 8-15. The data definition and modification sections are kept separate for easy examination. You can also use the Show Structure and Data drop-down menu to show only one type of change or the other as well as restrict changes displayed to a particular date range or user.

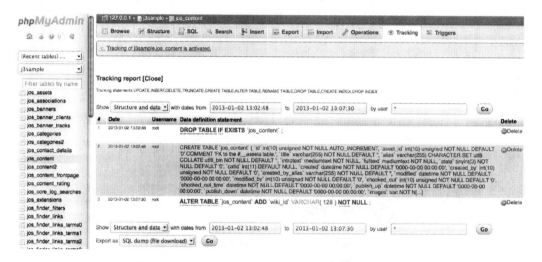

Figure 8-15. *The Tracking report will display all modifications to the structure or data made through the PMA interface*

In addition to the Tracking report, you can also click on the Structure snapshot link to show the schema of that table in the current revision. If you created an initial revision before you made changes, the Structure snapshot will show the initial table schema that was created by Joomla.

Conclusion

In this chapter, you've had a small glimpse of the power of direct access to the database. An advanced Joomla administrator can simplify difficult tasks and promote data integrity by harnessing the power of the database server. Although Joomla makes most routine tasks addressable through the user interface, to take true control of your Joomla site, you can query and update the CMS data directly.

The queries presented in this chapter will allow you to examine the workings of your site. You should now be able to modify these queries to obtain the information you want. These can help you know your site from the backend. To know the site from the visitor's perspective, the next chapter will demonstrate professional testing tools that can ensure your site is functioning properly.

CHAPTER 9

■ ■ ■

Testing a Site with ApacheBench, JMeter, and Selenium

Automated testing—the process of having a computer run a scripted set of commands and checking the results—has come a long way in recent years. In the 1980s, the widespread adoption of graphical user interfaces (GUI) put a damper on the promise of automated testing. It was difficult and expensive to create tests that could accurately and reliably navigate a GUI. Small changes in position or functionality of the screen elements would often break existing tests and substantial resources would be required to correct the tests so they worked under the new conditions. This made testing more expensive than it was worth. The growth of the Web and standardization of HTML-based web applications has breathed new life into the field of automated testing.

Not only is it much more cost-effective to create tests (because even GUI components are accessible as web page elements through code), but it has become essential with the growing complexity of web-based applications. At the lowest level, automated testing can verify the baseline functionality of a web site or web application. As a site changes, additional tests can be added to the group of tests used on the site.

A thorough set of tests can do an excellent job of peering into the dark corners of an application, ensuring that the more rarely used features are tested. Further, load testing can tell you the maximum number of concurrent users that can address your site without considerable access slowdown. Load testing can also provide early warning by showing you which parts of the site will break under a heavy load so the problems can be corrected before real users are subjected to them.

If you're an individual or member of a small team that maintains a Joomla web site, automated testing can be critical. You probably don't have time to check every facet of the application each time you make a change. Further, if you don't visit your site or parts of your site regularly, you can set up scheduled automated tests that can ensure that the site is functioning properly and hasn't faulted because of system failure or a hacker attack.

Until recently, automated testing tools have been extremely expensive, often running into the thousands or even tens of thousands of dollars. The efforts of the open source community have resulted in an increasing number of industrial-grade tools available for free.

In this chapter, you'll learn how to test your Joomla site using three important open source tools:

- *ApacheBench*: ApacheBench is a basic load-testing tool that you can use to quickly and easily to put a load on your server and examine the site performance at various levels.

- *Selenium*: One of the most popular testing tools, Selenium is a suite of tools that provides everything from browser-based GUI test creation (using Selenium IDE) to cross-browser distributed execution of tests on various browsers and operating systems.

- *Apache JMeter*: A professional-grade tool that you can use for most aspects of testing—including directly accessing your MySQL database connection and creating graph reports of increasing user loads on a target server.

When these three tools are used in conjunction, you can run almost every primary test against your Joomla site.

■ **Note** Selenium performs a type of testing known variously as "acceptance testing" or "black box testing" or "functional testing" on a web application. This type of testing simulates a real user or customer performing operations on an application and tests the application as a whole—including the user interface. Other types of testing such as "glass box testing" or "white box testing" are tests that are performed at a lower level on the code itself such as the unit testing. The Joomla framework itself is increasingly adding unit tests that you can run yourself with PHPUnit (see instructions at `http://docs.joomla.org/Running_Automated_Tests_for_the_Joomla_CMS`).

Testing Overview

Before you dive into the world of testing, it is useful to review a few concepts and some of the terminology used in the field. When listening to professional testers (or reading articles they've written), it can sometimes seem like they're speaking a different language. Because the results of testing are so fundamental to standard application use, however, a small amount of explanation can make most of the seemingly indecipherable text as plain as day.

To begin, the most basic question in testing is: what are we trying to test? Tests are broken down into a few basic areas. Although there is some overlap (and some tests cover multiple areas), the primary areas include functional testing, integration testing, regression testing, unit testing, and performance testing.

Functional Testing

As it sounds, functional testing tests the functions of a system. For example, when the New Task button is clicked, is a new task created by the software? When the print option is selected, does the page print? These high-level tests are relevant to Joomla installations in the areas of preventing broken links and making sure extensions are executing as they should.

Because functional testing is an attempt to simulate user interaction, most web-based functional testing needs to be executed within a browser. Many Joomla sites use JavaScript or Flash to add additional site functionality. You can only test portions of the site that use this technology if the code (JavaScript or Flash/ActionScript) is actually executed.

■ **Note** At a professional level, there are a growing number of so-called "headless browsers" that allow QA automation to run tests on JavaScript and other code without requiring the overhead of actually launching a graphic-intensive browser application. Google is using their V8 JavaScript engine (`http://code.google.com/p/v8/`) to crawl sites with this technology. This technology is evolving rapidly, so if you're interested, you should perform a web search for `headless browser` to find the most robust technology in this field.

Integration Testing

Integration testing assures that multiple components work together properly. Many of the problems with Joomla sites result from the failure of integration testing. When the new shopping cart was installed, was the site search component tested to make sure it could see items held in the product catalog? If a new template is set as the default, do all of the existing pages display properly?

The modular nature of Joomla makes it particularly susceptible to integration failure. Site administrators regularly add new templates, modules, and components. All major parts of the site should be subjected to integration testing when additional Joomla extensions have been added to make sure the new technology is working properly with the existing site technology.

Regression Testing

These tests make sure that the site hasn't "regressed" after the addition of new features. For example, did installing the new animated drop-down menu module break the JavaScript of the tooltip module that was working before? Regression testing seeks to make sure that new changes don't damage existing systems.

Regression testing is generally performed during stages of integration testing as the integration of new technology is the most common reason for previously working parts of the system to fail. This form of testing can be tedious because it requires you to constantly review the same subsystem again and again—subsystems that generally WON'T be broken by the new technology. For high-volume sites, however, this form of testing is perhaps the most important because of the ripple effects that can occur if one piece of code breaks another.

■ **Note**   Regression problems can have a tremendous impact on revenue. On the site where I work (www.ehow.com), a developer accidentally pushed a new module to production that added an erroneous closing tag to the HTML code. This problem prevented a set of Google advertisements from appearing on the page. If regression testing had not caught the problem, the flaw would have been live on the site over the weekend and caused untold loss of revenue. For smaller sites, a similar problem might not even be caught until a monthly AdSense check arrives with a fraction of the normal payment.

Unit Testing

These are programmer-oriented tests that are written to test a very small part (or unit) of the programming code. While unit testing is very popular in some areas of the computer world (such as the Java world), Joomla developers haven't widely adopted the practices of unit testing. Increasingly, the developers of Joomla have been adding unit tests to the source code so they can test the core code before each release.

Unit testing has proven most effective in particular specialized areas such as frameworks (the Joomla platform, for example), driver creation, and certain automated processes. Most Joomla developers, even extension developers, will find the maintenance of tests prohibitively time-consuming. For this reason, unit testing won't be detailed in this book. If you want to learn unit testing, Joomla is a great place to start! You can access all of the Joomla unit tests on GitHub at https://github.com/joomla/joomla-platform/tree/staging/tests.

Performance Testing

You can test the performance of the site or application in many different ways and from many perspectives. Performance testing is both difficult and very important. This type of testing will show you what the user will experience in terms of load times and site speed. Performance is even becoming important for SEO reasons as a slow site will be spidered much less often by the search engine crawlers, which means that it will take more time to detect and index new content.

One of the most common forms of performance testing—load testing—will determine the performance of a site when many simultaneous users access it. However, this may not be as straightforward as it seems. If the performance is bad, these questions immediately pop up in an attempt to determine the bottleneck:

- Is the server itself slow (a slow processor) or is the server starved for resources (not enough RAM, slow drive performance,and so forth)?

- Is the Internet connection slow?

- Is the firewall creating a fail-down condition?

You must also examine a good performance test closely. It could mean the site is performing well, but it could alternatively mean that the test...

- ... wasn't representative. For example, the performance test may have been run on a local network and is not a representation of the experience of a normal user accessing the site from across the country.

- ... received a "false positive" where the test failed but appeared to return a good performance result. For example, if the test checks for server responsiveness, it might get the fastest response when the server can't find the requested web page (a 404 error). If this error response is not being checked, the overall performance figures will be contaminated.

- ... didn't check for the proper things. For example, it is very common to use a JavaScript library such as SWFObject to load and play Adobe Flash content. However, most test software (including Apache AB and Apache JMeter) don't execute Flash code. This means that the Flash content is invisible to the standard load tests in these applications. Therefore, if your home page consists of 130K of HTML code, but a 3-megabyte Flash movie, the standard load tests will not reflect the slow loading experience of an average viewer accessing your site for the first time.

- ... addressed overly optimal conditions. Most advanced web applications (including Joomla) provide some form of caching of pre-rendered content. The cached content also generally has an expiration date or time (often as short as 15 minutes). That means most load-testing tools, if the cache remains enabled, will not provide representative processor load or response speed. All of the simulated user requests for the same page will return the same cache file, which may not accurately simulate the average user who will request an uncached page. This is a very common difficulty when creating performance tests because caching occurs throughout the system—including temporary tables on the database server.

Examining performance testing results carefully ensures that the information on performance that is being sought is effectively checked in the test.

Understanding Testing Terminology

The terminology used by testers provides effective shorthand with which they can communicate common ideas that need to be covered very often. Some of the terms you are likely to come across include:

- *SUT*: The System Under Test is the system that is being tested. For a Joomla site, this generally refers to the actual server where the site is deployed.

- *AUT*: The Application Under Test is the application or site that is being tested. For Joomla users, the AUT will mean the Joomla application and extensions regardless of whether it is deployed on a staging or production server.

- *Test coverage*: The amount of a desired area that is accessible by a particular test or set of tests. For example, if a Selenium test for menus checks all of the top-level menus (of which there are 12), but doesn't test any of the left menus (of which there are 24), the test coverage for menus is said to be 33%—only 12 of the 36 menus are covered by testing. This doesn't mean that 33% of the tests pass or fail; it specifically refers to the amount of the particular area that are *covered* by tests. All of the 36 menus may work or all of the 36 menus could fail and the test coverage number would not change.

- *White box/Glass box testing*: Testing of a system by testers that know the code and how it is supposed to operate. For example, when a programmer performs white box testing, the inner workings of the routines are known to the tester. This form of testing has the advantage that the developer understands all of the features of the AUT and so can perform more in-depth testing of particular functionality. The drawback is that the developer knows how it is "supposed" to work, meaning that a user who doesn't know the inner workings will often try something unplanned and therefore expose a break in the system that will be invisible to the white box tester.

- *Black box testing*: When the tester doesn't understand the inner workings of the SUT or AUT. The tester treats the system as a black box and expects when specific input is applied, the functionality or output will be as expected.

- *Test harness (or test fixture)*: The testing tools, testing data (input and output), and configuration are referred to collectively as the harness.

The more you work with testing systems, the more you will come across this terminology. Knowing these basics will help you to read the QA testing literature and have a conversation with a QA engineer with a basic shared understanding of the concepts to be discussed.

We've now covered enough generalities about testing. You're ready to get started. Most web testers begin testing a site with ApacheBench because it is very easy to use and provides some really useful statistics that show the basic performance of a SUT.

Using ApacheBench for Performance Testing

Installing the Apache web server will also install the excellent (although basic) load-testing tool known as ApacheBench (ab). It can be very useful in quick and simple load testing and creating a basic benchmark for system performance. This can be particularly helpful when you're trying to determine your production web server's connection performance.

On Windows, you'll likely find ab in your bin\ path, like this:

```
C:\Program Files\Apache Software Foundation\Apache2.2\bin\ab.exe
```

On Linux, you'll find it in a path like this:

```
/usr/bin/ab
```

On Mac, your path might be:

```
/usr/sbin/ab
```

or

```
/applications/mamp/library/bin/ab
```

The ab program is run at the command line and includes the following command-line parameters:

-A	auth-username:password
-c	Set the number of concurrent users that the ab will simulate accessing the site
-C	Add a cookie to the page request
-e	Write output data to a comma-separated-value (CSV) file
-k	Enable HTTP keep alive feature to perform multiple requests on the same HTTP session (default setting for keep alive is disabled)
-n	Number of requests to attempt; this defaults to a single request that is not useful for any type of benchmarking

-p   Send an HTTP POST command using the post-data found in the specified file

-q   Quiet mode will suppress the progress count reporting

-t   Specifies the time limit for benchmarking; the default is no limit

-w   Output results as a HTML table

To test with 100 connections and 15 simulated simultaneous users, you can execute this command line:

```
ab -n 100 -c 15 http://www.example.com/
```

It will return statistics like this:

```
Server Software:        Apache/2.2.3
Server Hostname:        www.example.com
Server Port:            80

Document Path:          /
Document Length:        2018 bytes

Concurrency Level:      15
Time taken for tests:   5.565972 seconds
Complete requests:      100
Failed requests:        0
Write errors:           0
Total transferred:      232200 bytes
HTML transferred:       201800 bytes
Requests per second:    17.97 [#/sec] (mean)
Time per request:       834.896 [ms] (mean)
Time per request:       55.660 [ms] (mean, across all concurrent requests)
Transfer rate:          40.60 [Kbytes/sec] received

Connection Times (ms)
              min  mean[+/-sd] median   max
Connect:        9   80  498.1     10    3919
Processing:    63  366 1088.9     70    5066
Waiting:       62  346 1089.9     68    5064
Total:         73  446 1179.2     80    5075
```

You can examine these statistics to determine the basic response speed of the web server. The most important basic number will be the *Requests per second* or RPS. This number tells you what number of concurrent requests the site can handle under the load you placed on it. In this case, the site can perform with almost 18 simultaneous requests or if 1,000 users accessed your site in the same minute, they would have a reasonably speedy page response. As a general guideline, 8 RPS is too slow, 12 RPS seems average for GoDaddy Joomla sites, popular news sites run at about 17 RPS, and sites with full caching solutions (such as Varnish or Akamai) can run as fast as 40 RPS.

Keep in mind this is the RPS of the page itself—none of the sub-files such as images, CSS, JavaScript, Flash, and so forth that are on the page were loaded in these requests. That means you have a baseline of what the server can do (including executing the Joomla PHP code), but it doesn't reflect what a full page load would look like.

You also want to look closely at the maximum connection times. If you run the test once and the maximum times are high, and then run the same test again and the numbers are much lower, this probably means a cache is being used in the second run. For Joomla testing with ApacheBench, it is a good idea to run a set of tests with caching turned off so you can get a worse-case scenario of your web site response.

■ **Tip**   If you want a more in-depth explanation of examining the various statistics output by Apache AB, I've posted an article on my web site (www.joomlajumpstart.com/general-joomla/13-joomla-resources/63-testing-joomla-with-apache-ab) that examines the numbers in detail and how they relate to Joomla testing.

Using ApacheBench for performance testing isn't something that you generally perform too often on a Joomla site unless you have a very high traffic growth. You generally want to perform such analysis when you first launch your site so you can correct any clear problems with the server or server setup. Thereafter, periodically running Apache AB on your site will give you an idea if something is going wrong.

■ **Note**   For testing of page load speed, Joomla administrators would benefit most by optimizing the template or module-loading aspects of the page. There are two popular browser plug-ins: YSlow from Yahoo (http://developer.yahoo.com/yslow/), which is available for most browsers, and Page Speed from Google (https://developers.google.com/speed/), which is available for Firefox and Chrome. These tools analyze a page load and tell you not only what is making page load slow from the front-end perspective, but they each make suggestions for page optimization.

Introducing the Selenium Suite

Selenium is actually a number of different programs that work in concert to provide various aspects of automated web testing across many platforms. At the time of this writing, there were four primary tools in the Selenium suite:

- *Selenium IDE*: A browser plug-in that's used to record and edit test scripts. Use it to group sets of tests into a test suite. Selenium IDE can also replay scripts and save scripts in a variety of language formats (such as Java, and so on) for execution on Selenium Server. At the time of this writing, the IDE is only available for the Firefox browser.

- *Selenium Core*: A PHP/JavaScript web application that can run individual test scripts and test suites in any browser (including Google Chrome, Internet Explorer 6 and above, Firefox 2 and above, Safari 2 and above, Opera 2 and above, and others). Because of security restrictions on web servers, the Selenium Core must execute on the web server of the site being tested.

- *Selenium Server (until recently known as Remote Control (RC))*: A Java-based application server that can open and close browser windows and execute scripts automatically. This allows test suites to be fully automated and tested across a variety of browsers with no required user intervention.

- *Selenium Grid*: A controlling application for Selenium Server that allows coordinated parallel control of multiple distributed instances of RC. You can distribute test execution across multiple machines to scale up the testing process.

Although you can deploy the full Selenium suite (http://seleniumhq.org/download/) at even large organizations, most Joomla webmasters are likely to mostly use the IDE and Core for browser compatibility testing. Organizations using Joomla will gain the most benefit from the regular use of the RC and Grid applications.

Selenium IDE

Selenium IDE is a browser-based plug-in that, in its simplest form, acts as a macro recorder for web sites (you'll learn how to set it up in a later section). It can record the actions of a user as a web site is browsed. Each step of the interaction with the web site (such as clicking a button or entering text into a field) is stored as an entry in the Selenium test. In Figure 9-1, you can see the Selenium IDE that has stored the procedure for a simple search of the Google web site.

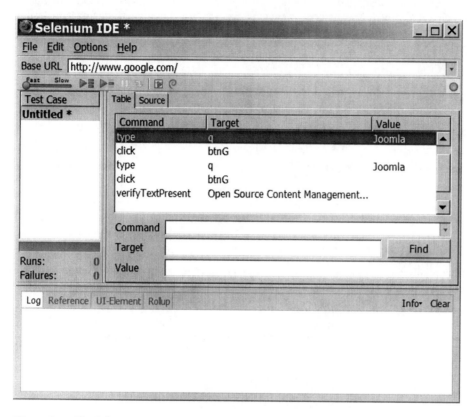

Figure 9-1. *The Selenium IDE records each event that occurs in the browser as a separate line entry*

For simple tests, you can simply save the recording and later manually run it to re-test the operation of a part of the web site. Selenium, however, is much more powerful than a simple macro recorder. It lets you:

- Test elements on the web page to make sure the events are causing the expected results. For example, a login test might enter a username and password and Selenium can check text on the web page to make certain the login was successful.

- Embed JavaScript in tests to allow the execution to dynamically supply or store conditions. For example, the Joomla login system will not allow duplicate usernames so a static script will fail the second time it's executed. Using JavaScript, the new username can be randomly generated, allowing the script to execute properly each time.

- Set up test suites (groups of tests) that will be run sequentially so you can test the entire site or multiple conditions in one run. The tests are also timed, so the execution speed and performance for multiple executions can be determined.

- Automate the execution of tests through a variety of languages such as Java, Python, and PHP so you can run the tests automatically on a regular basis with the results reported via email.

By default, tests are stored in a standard formatted HTML table for easy editing, modification, combination, and splitting. You can easily convert tests to any of the other languages that Selenium supports. Additionally, the conversion process is a straightforward set of JavaScript functions so you can write a converter for nearly any language in a small amount of time.

Selenium Core

The Selenium Core has a fairly rudimentary interface since it is designed specifically to execute tests that have been recorded on the Selenium IDE (which has limited browser support) on nearly every popular browser.
In Figure 9-2, you can see that the primary screen duplicates a number of the buttons and the general display of the main IDE interface. It can run one test, all tests, push the test run, and report the log and error findings.

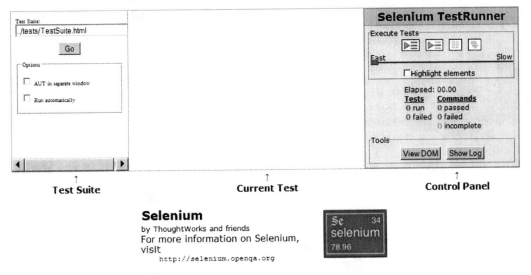

Figure 9-2. *The Core interface resembles a boiled-down version of the IDE execution interface*

The real power of the Selenium Core lies in its ability to execute on any browser. While the IDE can only run in Firefox, you can literally run the Core in any browser that can access it and execute JavaScript. This means that you can check even mobile browsers such as Mobile Internet Explorer and iPhone's Safari for site compatibility.

Therefore, Selenium Core can replay the test scripts in nearly all browser types including Internet Explorer 6 and above, Mozilla Firefox, Safari, Opera, and others. If the browser supports JavaScript and access to the Document Object Model (DOM), it can very likely run the Selenium suite.

■ **Tip** There is a fair chance that you will have to make some modifications to your tests to allow them to run properly on the different browsers. For example, Internet Explorer seems to render linefeeds differently than Firefox (even on the same Windows machine), so a `verifyText` command that passes on a multi-paragraph block of text in one browser may fail on another. Typically, slight modifications to the test will make it accurately determine a pass/fail.

Unlike the IDE, the Core must be located in a browsable path on the web server that hosts the web site. Due to security restrictions, this also means that the tests run on the Core can only address pages on that server.

Selenium Server (Formerly Selenium Remote Control or RC)

The Selenium Server system is a Java-based application server that can execute various browsers and run the Selenium tests within each browser instance. Additionally, RC can execute tests scripted in a variety of languages, which means you can use the programming system that you are most comfortable using (PHP, Python, Java, and so forth) to execute tests. The real power in this lies in the ability to make programmed tests that include loop logic and use `if...then` data execution control.

The RC system is the part of the Selenium suite that lends itself best to automated execution of the test suites. This can be useful to system administrators not only to ensure that the site is functioning properly at all times, but provides an excellent notification service in case the site is attacked and penetrated by a hacker. Even a basic title assert and a content check will warn you that your site was defaced. Comprehensive content checking can help detect subtle modifications.

Selenium Grid

The Selenium Grid allows you to distribute execution of Selenium Server tests across multiple computers. This means that you can execute a set of tests that would normally take a long time to execute simultaneously in multiple places, allowing magnitudes of timesavings.

Because of the resource requirements for setting up a grid (multiple computers with enough RAM to run scores of browser instances), most Joomla sites won't need to deploy a Selenium Grid for testing. However, if your site were to achieve the traffic loads that the central Joomla site experiences, the Grid should certainly be investigated.

Using the Selenium IDE on a Joomla Site

Joomla sites are perfect for testing using Selenium. Because they have a standardized presentation through the Joomla menuing system, you can create general tests that are used in a variety of tests in the suite.

For example, if you wanted to test all of the registration features of the Joomla site, you could make a test that performs and verifies a test login. You may use one script to test to make sure the desired modules are on particular pages. You could use another script to log out the test user. You could use this script to bracket any of the registration execution of the site. A third script may check the metadata information in the page headers to make sure appropriate description and OpenGraph Facebook tags are present.

What makes Selenium so compelling for Joomla site administrators is the ease with which it can be set up, configured, and used. From the moment you begin to download the browser plug-in to executing your first test should be under 10 minutes.

Installing Selenium IDE on Firefox

At the time of this writing, the Selenium recorder, or Selenium IDE, is only available for Firefox. Although the recorder is limited to a particular type of browser, you can play back and test the recorded tests on nearly any browser (using Selenium Core), so tests can confirm basic browser compatibility across a wide range of browsers.

In this section, you'll learn how to install Selenium on the Firefox browser. Installing Selenium is as easy as installing any other Firefox add-on. It is probably easiest to go directly to the Selenium site to get the latest version.

Alternately, you can use the Firefox Add-ons manager by selecting the Tools ➤ Add-ons menu that will display the Add-ons window. Click on the Get Extensions link at the bottom-right corner that will take you to the Firefox add-ons page at this URL (for the English-language Firefox site):

`https://addons.mozilla.org/en-US/firefox/`

In the search box, type "Selenium" and you should see the Selenium IDE entry. Click on the Add to Firefox button and the Selenium IDE will download and install. You will need to restart Firefox to enable that add-on. Optionally, you can go directly to the Selenium site (`http://seleniumhq.org/projects/ide/plugins.html`), download the XPI file, and double-click the file to install it on your browser.

Once it is installed, Selenium IDE should appear as an option in the Tools menu in Firefox. Selecting that menu option will display the Selenium window where you can open, create, and execute tests.

Recording Tests

Recording a test is a simple process with Selenium's IDE. You might start out recording an example of a popular web site that you know doesn't heavily use JavaScript (which can potentially get in the way of Selenium). In this example, we'll start with Google.

Navigate to the web site you want to test and copy the URL out of the browser address bar. Select the Tools ➤ Selenium IDE option to display the Selenium window and paste the URL into the Base URL box at the top of the window. Your window should match the one shown in Figure 9-3.

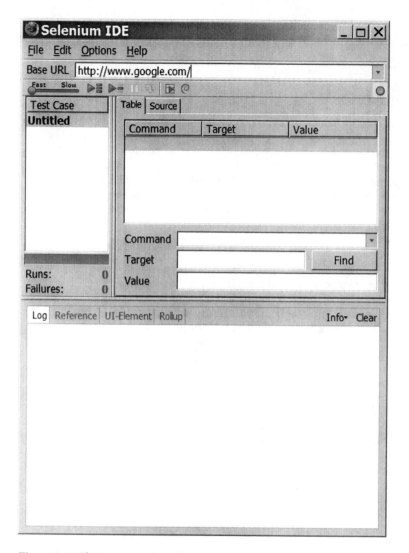

Figure 9-3. *The Base URL should match the URL of the site you want to record*

Click on the red record button in the right corner if it isn't already recording. You can mouse over the button and a tool tip will appear stating Now Recording if it is recording. Any actions related to the web browsing will now be recorded as line items in the IDE.

Let's start with something very simple. Search for Joomla on Google. Once the search page appears, you should see the first entry is the Joomla.org site.

There will be a site description, such as Open Source Content Management System. [Open Source, GPL] directly below the link to the site. Move the mouse pointer to the beginning of this text, click and hold down the mouse button, select the text of the description, and release the mouse button. Move the pointer back over the selected text and click the right mouse button (or, on the Macintosh, hold down the Ctrl key and click). This will display the context menu that has some Selenium-added options.

As you can see in Figure 9-4, there are a number of options at the bottom of the menu related to Selenium commands. You will see that one option states verifyTextPresent followed by the text you selected. Click on this option to add the text verification to the script.

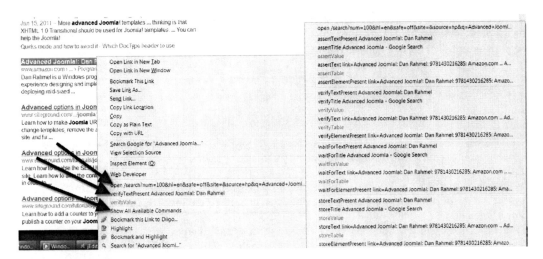

Figure 9-4. *The context menu in Firefox has additional options created by the Selenium add-on*

When you return to the Selenium window, you should see all of the line items recording the various execution items. Click on the red record button to stop the recording. On the toolbar, you will see two play buttons: on the left for `Play entire test suite` and on the right for `Play current test case`. Click on the `Play current test case` and watch the browser window (see Figure 9-5).

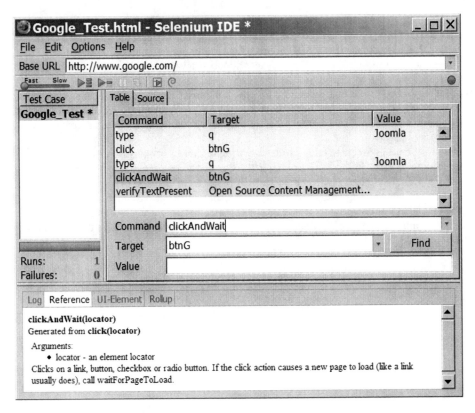

Figure 9-5. *Click on the Play current test case option to execute the current test*

You should see Selenium address the main page of the IDE, enter the search text, click the button, and attempt to verify the text on the page. If everything ran properly, the log pane at the bottom of the window should have displayed all of the execution steps and all of the line items at the top should now have a lime green background color.

■ **Note** You may have to clear the tab in Firefox before clicking the play button if you already have the search page open.

If the final text verification failed, you will see red error text in the log pane that reads [error] false and the verify item will have a red background. If you did get this error, you may be puzzled because the text seems to be on the browser screen.

The error was likely caused by a timing issue with the execution of the script. You may have noticed that the script executed very quickly. In the next section, we'll make a modification to the script to make this a non-issue. For now, let's do something a little different.

In the top-left corner of the window, you may have noticed a slider with a green oval that is labeled Fast at one end and Slow at the other. This slider determines the speed of the execution of the test. By default, it is set to the fastest speed.

Click and drag the slider all the way to the right so it is set to execute the slowest. Then click the Play current test case to run the test again. Did it work correctly that time with all entries green and no errors? The problem earlier was caused by the test executing too quickly so the text verification was attempted before the page loaded. Instead of slowing down the script, however, we can make Selenium wait until the page returns.

Modifying the Script

You will find that you will often need to modify a script after the initial recording so it will execute and check for the items on the page that you want. This is especially true when you have Ajax implemented on the site. Scripts for executing Ajax will typically need pause commands added to the execution to allow the Ajax requests time to return data from the server.

In the last script, when you clicked on the Google Search button, the IDE most likely recorded a click command. When you attempted to re-execute the script, the search didn't have enough time to return the page and load into the browser, causing the subsequent test failure. You can make a simple modification to the script to make it pause execution until the page has returned to the browser.

In the Selenium IDE window, the list of executed commands shows the sequence of execution. Directly above the text verification, you should see a row that has the value click in the Command column and btnG in the Target column. This is the command you want to change. If you change the command from click to clickAndWait, script execution will wait until the page has loaded completely before continuing the execution sequence.

Click on the line with the click command and the three text boxes below the command list should display the values of that entry. Change the command to read clickAndWait, as you can see in Figure 9-6 and set the execution speed slider back to the fastest position.

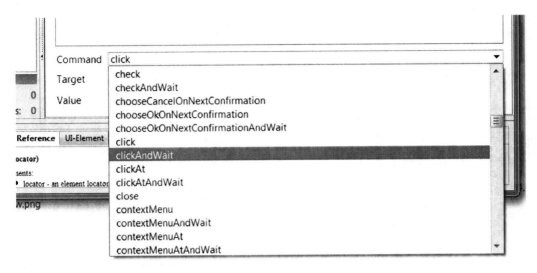

Figure 9-6. *Change the click command to the clickAndWait command for that entry*

Execute the test case again. This time, the test should have executed very quickly and yet the text still verified properly. This simple example of a test script modification is very common.

Once the script is working properly, save it by using the File ➤ Save Test Case option in the Selenium IDE. For a filename, type `Google_Test1.html`. The test code is actually stored in HTML table format. You can edit the code with any standard text editor.

Examining the Script Code

It can be useful to modify the Selenium code directly, especially when you begin putting together groups of tests known as test suites. If you open the file that you just saved using a text editor such as Notepad, your script might look like this:

```
<?xml version="1.0" encoding="UTF-8"?>
<!DOCTYPE html PUBLIC "-//W3C//DTD XHTML 1.0 Strict//EN"
"http://www.w3.org/TR/xhtml1/DTD/xhtml1-strict.dtd">
<html xmlns="http://www.w3.org/1999/xhtml" xml:lang="en" lang="en">
<head profile="http://selenium-ide.openqa.org/profiles/test-case">
<meta http-equiv="Content-Type" content="text/html; charset=UTF-8" />
<link rel="selenium.base" href="http://www.google.com/" />
<title>Google_Test</title>
</head>
<body>
<table cellpadding="1" cellspacing="1" border="1">
<thead>
<tr><td rowspan="1" colspan="3">Google_Test</td></tr>
</thead><tbody>
<tr>
        <td>open</td>
        <td>/</td>
        <td></td>
</tr>
```

225

```
<tr>
        <td>type</td>
        <td>q</td>
        <td>Joomla</td>
</tr>
<tr>
        <td>click</td>
        <td>btnG</td>
        <td></td>
</tr>
<tr>
        <td>type</td>
        <td>q</td>
        <td>Joomla</td>
</tr>
<tr>
        <td>clickAndWait</td>
        <td>btnG</td>
        <td></td>
</tr>
<tr>
        <td>verifyTextPresent</td>
        <td> Joomla! - the dynamic portal engine and content management system </td>
        <td></td>
</tr>

</tbody></table>
</body>
</html>
```

If you're used to reading HTML code, you can see that this is a very simple file. You can edit it manually if you ever need to make changes when the Selenium IDE is not installed on a machine.

Creating and Running a Test Suite

The test we created was very basic and was meant to get you started. Now that you have a basic understanding of the Selenium execution, you can begin to make it address your Joomla site. The following demonstration takes you through the process of creating a test suite that will allow you to test your entire Joomla site with each test execution to focus on a particular area.

In these examples, I'll be running a copy of Joomla out of the folder `http://localhost/joomlaadv` that has a generic site setup. We'll create a test suite that tests a menu that is only available to registered users. To make this possible, we'll record several different test scripts:

- *joomla_login*: This script will perform the login of the registered user to the system.

- *joomla_logout*: This script will log out of the system.

- *joomla_menu1*: For a logged-in user, this will ensure that the menu is available and accessible.

- *joomla_nomenu1*: After logout, this test will make sure the menu isn't present.

A suite of tests, as you'll soon see, can execute multiple test scripts sequentially. By breaking down the execution pieces into separate scripts, you can re-use the scripts such as the login and logout scripts across multiple situations. For example, you can use the same login script to run one registered user script and then, later in the script execution, you can use the same login to test another registered user feature.

1. Open the Selenium IDE and select the File ➤ New Test Case option. To the left of the area that shows the Table and Source tabs is a list of current tests in the active test suite. By default, you can't see this area, but if you move your mouse over to the left side of the Table tab, you'll see it change into the resize area pointer.

2. Click and drag the left side of the Table tab to the right side of the window until the test suite list appears. At the top of the column, you should see the text Test Case and the entry for the new case you just created should read Untitled.

3. Right-click on the case and select the Properties option. A dialog will appear allowing you to rename the selected script, so enter joomla_login and click the OK button.

4. Follow the same process you did last time. Copy the URL for the site into the Base URL text box.

5. Click the red button to begin recording.

6. Type your username and password into the login box in Joomla and click the Login button. When the login is successful, select the greeting text (such as "Hi, Charley") and insert a verify text test into the Selenium test using the context menu.

▧ **Tip**   If you have typing completion active on your browser (that will auto-complete a text field if you have entered it previously), it is a good idea to deactivate it before you begin recording a test. Generally, Selenium can't record text selected from an auto-complete add-on.

---

7. Return to the Selenium IDE and click on the red button to stop recording. In the browser window, click the Logout button so you can test the script. Play the script once to make sure it works and make any necessary adjustments.

8. Using the File ➤ Save Test Case option, save the test as joomla_login.html. After it has saved, select New Test Case and name it joomla_logout. Click the record button, return to the browser window (you should be logged in from the test run of the login script), click the Logout button, and do a verify text on the vanilla login greeting that should now display.

9. Save this test as joomla_logout.html. You now have the first of a series of tests that you can reuse for all your site testing.

10. Create another Test Case that checks for a menu that should only be available to a registered user. Use a verifyTextPresent to confirm that the menu text is on the page. Save this test as joomla_menu1.html.

For the joomla_nomenu.html, begin a new test. Make sure you're logged out. This time your test will verify that there is NOT text on the page. To create this type of test, it is usually easiest to begin by creating a basic test that verifies text that will be on all pages. Once the fundamental two or three commands have been established in the Selenium test, click the red record button to stop recording.

1. In the Selenium IDE, in the column labeled Test Cases that shows all of the cases in the current Test Suite, select the joomla_menu1.html test. The commands for that test should be displayed in the list box.

2. Right-click on the verifyTextPresent command and select the Copy option.

3. Reselect the joomla_nomenu test.

4. Right-click on the empty list item below the last command and select the Paste option.

5. Click on the item you just pasted into the test and the command text box should be filled (with verifyTextPresent) and the Target box should fill with the menu text.

6. Just to the right of the command text box, you'll see a drop-down arrow. Click on the arrow and you should see a list of all of the available Selenium test commands. Scroll down until you see the verifyTextNotPresent command and select that. Now the item in the script will confirm that the menu text is NOT on the page.

7. Make sure you are logged out and run the test. It should pass. Log in and try it again. The test should fail. You now should have all four test cases that you can use in the first small test suite of the site.

8. Save the suite of four tests by selecting the File ➤ Save Test Suite option and name the file TestSuite1.html. You need to rearrange the tests in the proper order and tests. Some versions of Selenium IDE allow you to drag and drop to rearrange the tests. If you can't rearrange your tests from within the Selenium IDE, you'll need to open the suite file in a text editor.

Like the formats of the tests, the execution of test suites are arranged as rows in a standard HTML table. You will need to arrange the tests so that they execute in this order: joomla_login.html, joomla_menu1.html, joomla_logout.html, and joomla_nomenu.html.

When you open the suite again in Selenium IDE, you should be able to execute the full set of tests to confirm proper functioning of a menu for both registered and unregistered conditions. You should begin to understand how you can create an entire battery of tests that will examine all of the menus and options of your Joomla site. It should also be apparent how you can reuse the login and logout scripts for many other tests.

Although static scripts such as this are very powerful, Selenium tests perform much more complicated tasks. For one thing, you can embed JavaScript in a test to make the test perform on-the-fly calculations. You might use JavaScript to create unique fields for forms such as the registration system that may require them.

Embedding JavaScript for a Dynamic Registration Test

In Joomla, each user name must be unique, which makes it difficult to create a static test that checks the registration system. With such a static test, the tester would need to change the username for the test each time before the test is run. However, what if you could use JavaScript to randomize the username each time? That would avoid the duplicate problem.

To create such a dynamic test, first record a standard static test where you enter all of the fields for registration. It would be useful if you enter some common field such as a name that always begins with Test so these users will be easy to locate and delete from the Joomla Administrator interface.

Make sure you perform a verifyTextPresent at the end of the test that confirms the registration has been successful. Once you have finished the last step, open the Selenium IDE and click the red button to stop recording.

In some versions of Joomla, the JavaScript for the e-mail validation makes the e-mail text boxes invisible to the Selenium IDE recorder. In this case, you will need to manually add these fields. On the version of Joomla at the time of this writing, the e-mail field names had element IDs of jform_email1 and jform_email2. With your recording, right-click on the final command (which should be clickAndWait) and select the Insert New Command option from the drop-down menu. Mirroring the commands above it, set the command to *type*, the target to id=jform_email1, and the value to whatever e-mail address you're using for testing. Do the same for the second e-mail field, changing the target to id=jform_email2. Now the test should execute properly.

If you run the test again, you should receive an error because the same username was attempted again. The page should show an error like this:

```
This username you entered is not available. Please pick another username.
```

Locate the line in the script with a command of *type* that enters the username field. Click on the command to bring up the variables for it in the text boxes at the bottom of the screen. The Value text box should display the entry that you made for the username. Replace that text with the following value:

```
javascript{"t"+Math.ceil(Math.random()*10000)+"test"}
```

This test inserts a random number between 0 and 10,000 into the username field, making it unlikely to generate a duplicate. If you execute the test again, it will fail at a different point. In this case, it will say the e-mail address is already used. Because the same value must be placed in both the e-mail address and the e-mail confirmation field, we can't just use a random value each time—we'll have to randomize and then store it.

Right-click on the row where you enter the username and select the Insert New Command option. Set the command to *store*, set the value to *myrand*, and enter the following in the target field:

```
javascript{"t"+Math.ceil(Math.random()*10000)+"test"}
```

After that is executed, the random text will be stored in the *myrand* variable. Modify the value of the username row to ${myrand} and the value of both of the e-mail fields to ${myrand}@sogetthis.com so they hold the same value.

■ **Tip** If you've never heard of the Mailinator site (www.mailinator.com), you've been missing out. Mailinator is a free service that accepts e-mail from any source and lets you view it. There is no blocking. E-mail is stored in memory, so it only stays for around 48 hours. This service is fantastic for testing because you have unlimited e-mail addresses and the mail doesn't hang around clogging up an e-mail box. Mailinator has many alternate domain addresses and one of them is sogetthis.com as used in the preceding example.

The test should now operate properly each time you run it! If you save the test to HTML and open it in a text editor, the body of the code should look something like this:

```html
<table cellpadding="1" cellspacing="1" border="1">
<thead>
<tr><td rowspan="1" colspan="3">joomla_registration</td></tr>
</thead><tbody>
<tr>
        <td>open</td>
        <td>/joomlaadv/</td>
        <td></td>
</tr>
<tr>
    <td>type</td>
        <td>id=jform_name</td>
        <td>lover</td>
</tr>
```

```
<tr>
        <td>store</td>
        <td>javascript{Math.ceil(Math.random()*10000)}</td>
        <td>myrand</td>
</tr>
<tr>
        <td>type</td>
        <td>id=jform_username</td>
        <td>${myrand}</td>
</tr>
<tr>
        <td>type</td>
        <td>id=jform_password1</td>
        <td>lover1</td>
</tr>
<tr>
        <td>type</td>
        <td>id=jform_password2</td>
        <td>lover1</td>
</tr>
<tr>
        <td>type</td>
        <td>id=jform_email1</td>
        <td>${myrand}@sogetthis.com</td>
</tr>
<tr>
        <td>type</td>
        <td>id=jform_email2</td>
        <td>${myrand}@sogetthis.com</td>
</tr>
<tr>
        <td>clickAndWait</td>
        <td>css=button.validate</td>
        <td></td>
</tr>

</tbody></table>
</body>
</html>
```

This is a simple example of some of the capabilities that are possible with live JavaScript execution. In addition to generating test fields, the embedded JavaScript can use regular expressions to process strings and use the DOM to navigate the page elements and actively examine or manipulate the current page. You can even use the Selenium `store` commands to write values into JavaScript variables.

▨ **Tip**   It would be preferable if you wouldn't send hundreds of junk e-mails to some miscellaneous e-mail domain. If you have your own domain, I would suggest you use that domain name for your test e-mail account.

Refining the Selenium Tests

The Selenium IDE has many useful features that help you build proper tests. You can set breakpoints and use a variety of other commands within your script for proper execution.

You can right-click on any line in the Selenium IDE and set a breakpoint at that location. When you next execute the test, the execution will halt at that point so you can manually step through the code. You can also press the X key after selecting any line in the test to execute that individual command.

Please review the manual for Selenium commands that can be useful in creating tests. Some of the most helpful that I use frequently include:

- *pause*: Halts test execution for a specified number of seconds. This is useful if the page has to perform some operation such as an Ajax request or JavaScript event that will take time before the page will be ready for testing.

- *deleteCookie*: Can delete a cookie so programs that insert a cookie in the browser can be effectively tested.

- *assertElementPresent*: Check for the presence of an image or other page element. This is very useful if you need to check a non-text item such as a Flash object.

- *handleAlert*: Intercepts a JavaScript alert dialog and can report the contents. This is very useful for performing failure testing on form fields.

You can find a reference of all of the available Selenium commands as part of the Selenium Core installation. In the Selenium Core folder, you'll find the reference file here:

```
<selenium installation root path>/SeleniumCore/reference.html
```

Other Selenium IDE Options

In this chapter, we've only scratched the surface of the power available through the IDE. Take a look at some of the options available for special configuration under the Options ➤ Options menu item. The Options dialog has a number of check box options including:

- *Remember base URL*: This is useful in some circumstances and trouble in others. If you have many stage and production sites, you might not want to record the base URL so the tests can be used on any site.

- *Record assertTitle automatically*: I always use this option so that there is a baseline check on every page the test script will access.

- *Record absolute URL*: Stores the absolute URL (instead of the default relative URL) for each location in the test.

- *Enable UI-Element*: Allows the UI-Element location code to execute for abstraction of page element names for more durable tests.

You might notice that there is an option to configure the location of the directories that hold these Selenium extensions. There are a number of extensions available that you can download from the Selenium web site that add better locator functionality to find elements on a page, supplement the test logging function, and other enhancements.

Working Through Selenium's Limitations

There are a number of actions in Selenium that, when the test is replayed, break because they weren't recorded by the application properly. The back arrow, for example, often causes a problem. Selenium allows you to manually edit tests and direct action input so there is nearly always a way to work around the broken test. The best method is to try and find an alternate method of doing the same operation.

For example, if you need to return to the home page of a site, and recording the back button doesn't work properly, usually the top banner on a web site provides a link to the home page and you can use that instead.

Selenium Extensions

Selenium features an extension plug-in system, so if you want to add a missing feature and you know JavaScript, you can easily add this feature to the system. One popular extension is the UI-Element that allows mapping between a list of custom-defined reference names and elements on the HTML page.

For example, if the page contained references to a text input field that held the first name of the user that was named id66182, you can create a UI-Reference that calls that element txtFirstName so the tests you create would be easier to read and understand.

Using UI-Reference can also be helpful for pages that change often—particularly during a development cycle. You can create a single reference that all of your tests can use. When the elements of the page change, a single update to the reference file will allow the tests to work properly again.

This extension is a useful one to study because it contains many of the common operations that are needed in a file, including the ability to read a formatted data file. The reference file is stored in JSON (JavaScript Object Notation) format, which is a very lightweight but powerful way to organize hierarchical data. The extension is comprised of a single JavaScript file named *ui-element.js*.

There are a number of additional commands that you can add to the Selenium system, including:

- Recording image titles

- Assertions for right-click context menus

- Check for an Ajax-built table

- Verify editable or non-editable field

- if . . . then test control

- while looping in tests

- Locators used to locate page elements for testing

All of these extensions are programmed in JavaScript, so you can also use them as a foundation for developing your own custom functionality. You can access these plug-ins on the Selenium site (http://seleniumhq.org/projects/ide/plugins.html) with instructions for installation and execution.

Adding Language Formats

Selenium can output tests in many language formats. Although by default, tests are stored as HTML (as you have seen), there are a number of other languages that the Selenium IDE can export including PHP, JUnit, Ruby RSpec, and others. To add additional language support, you can either download additional JavaScript files (.js extension) or even create your own. You will have to open the .js file in a text editor, select all of the code, and select the Edit ➤ Copy option to save the text to the clipboard.

Select the Options ➤ Options menu item and click the Add button on the Formats tab. Paste the code into the body text box. There is a default template there by default, so you'll likely want to select that existing test and paste over it. Set the format name in the top text box and click the OK button.

You should immediately see the format added to the listbox on the Formats tab. It will also be available in the Format submenu of the Options menu.

Setting up Selenium for Flash Recordings

If you have Flash on your site, you can even test that Flash with Selenium, although you have to adjust the Selenium system to record events not just on DOM elements, but also general clicks. Because Flash is not actually part of the DOM, you will need to record click events that will then be replayed by the Selenium script.

You can add the following JavaScript code to the page that contains Flash in order to record the clicks for inside the Flash stage for testing:

```
Recorder.removeEventHandler('click');
Recorder.addEventHandler('clickAt', 'click', function(event) {
var x = event.clientX - editor.seleniumAPI.Selenium.prototype.getElementPositionLeft(event.target);
var y = event.clientY - editor.seleniumAPI.Selenium.prototype.getElementPositionTop(event.target);
this.record('clickAt', this.findLocator(event.target), x + ',' + y);
}, { capture: true });
```

Modifying and Customizing the Selenium IDE

The Selenium IDE is written in JavaScript, so if you see a limitation in the Selenium system or want to add a feature that cannot be effectively created with an extension, you can directly access the Selenium code. The Selenium plug-in is located in this directory on a Windows system:

```
C:\Documents and Settings\<USER_NAME>\Application Data\
  Mozilla\Firefox\Profiles\<???>.default\extensions\
  {???}\chrome\Selenium-ide.jar
```

Replace the ??? with the directories you find there. A .jar file is simply a zip-compressed file with a different extension. Most zip-compatible systems will recognize the .jar extension and natively uncompress the files there. If not, simply change the extension to .zip and uncompress the archive. You can then examine the JavaScript files contained in the archives and make any desired changes.

Using Selenium Core

The tests that you have executed in the Selenium IDE have been limited to execution on the Firefox browser. With Selenium Core, however, you can execute the Selenium tests in nearly any browser. You can download the Selenium Core here:

```
http://seleniumhq.org/projects/core/
```

To install it, simply uncompress the files into a directory on your web server and copy your saved Selenium IDE tests there. If you install the Core on localhost, you can access it at a URL like the following:

```
http://localhost/SeleniumCore/core/TestRunner.html
```

Enter the URL of your test suite in the text box, as shown in Figure 9-7. Once you click the Go button, the test suite will load. You can then execute individual tests or the entire suite.

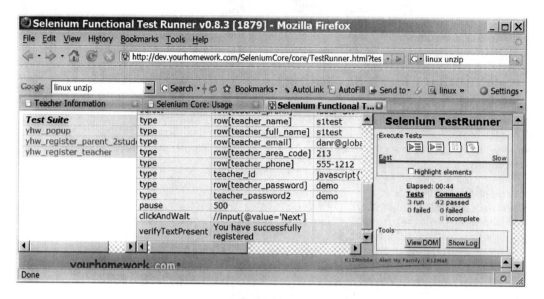

Figure 9-7. *Enter the URL of your test suite HTML and click the Go button to execute the tests*

You should be able to execute the tests on any browser that can access the web server and can execute JavaScript. Note that tests that perform on one browser may not perform the same on another browser or platform. You may have to slightly modify your tests to get them to execute properly. This is particularly apparent with Internet Explorer when verifyTextPresent values have line feeds as they are handled differently between the browsers.

■ **Note** You may need to change the header of a script for it to run properly in Core. The IDE recordings generally use the XML header to signify that they conform to the XML standard (are well-formed HTML). You may have to remove the XML header line from your test files to get them to execute properly in a browser when executing the script on Selenium Core. They sometimes cause a syntax error when the Selenium core reads them for execution. That means that the files will begin with an XML declaration (e.g. `<?xml version="1.0" encoding="UTF-8"?>`). At the time of this writing, the Core would fault when it encountered this header generating a syntax error. If your system generates such an error when you execute your IDE tests on Selenium core, try removing this first line and your test will most likely execute properly.

Using Apache JMeter

Apache JMeter has so many features that an in-depth examination of the program is beyond the scope of this book. However, even using a small portion of JMeter's features can generate critical information useful to any Joomla administrator. Additionally, if you create an enterprise-level Joomla site, there are better than average chances that JMeter will be your choice of testing tool.

JMeter provides the following testing features that are relevant to Joomla users:

- GUI interface for easily creating functionality tests

- Performance testing capabilities for many server types, including HTTP, HTTPS, SOAP, Database (including MySQL), LDAP, POP3 e-mail, and IMAP e-mail

- Multi-platform Java implementation that will run on Windows, MacOS, and Linux

- Multithreaded execution for effectively simulating a large number of simultaneous users

- Built-in proxy server to capture a web browsing session live (like Selenium IDE)

- Load statistics, including line/point graphs for visualizing performance results

JMeter is an application written in Java that you can run as either a standalone GUI application, as shown in Figure 9-8, or directly through the command line.

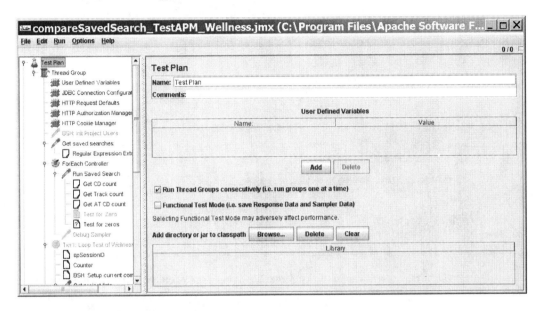

Figure 9-8. *The JMeter interface makes maintaining tests extremely easy*

Perhaps that best way to get a basic understanding of JMeter is by creating a quick load test and executing it. After you have created a foundation test plan (which you will likely use as a template for other test construction), you'll see how easily you can use the proxy server functionality included in JMeter to capture a live browser session.

You can download JMeter from the Apache Jakarta project web site (http://jakarta.apache.org/jmeter/) and simply expand the archive—no installation is required. JMeter does require a current version of Java that you can download from the Sun web site (www.java.com/en/download/).

You can execute JMeter on Windows by double-clicking the batch file that you'll find in the bin\ folder (jmeter.bat) or double-clicking on the jar itself (ApacheJMeter.jar). From the Linux or Mac GUIs, you can double-click on the jar, or from the command line you can use the bash script instead (jmeter.sh).

Creating a Simple Load Test

When JMeter is first launched, it displays a window split into two vertical panes. The left pane contains a basic hierarchical tree list that holds all of the nodes of the currently loaded test plan. Selecting a node in the left pane will populate the right pane with parameters and controls reflecting the selected item.

Every new JMeter test begins with a least one node titled *Test Plan*. All other test nodes are organized as children of this header node. It contains the overall configuration of the plan.

Let's begin creating our load test. Click on the *Test Plan* node in the left pane and the properties of the plan will be shown as in Figure 9-9. In the right pane that shows the properties of the node, change the name in the text box labeled Name: to read *Joomla Load Balance*. In the Comments: field, enter text such as *This test will load test the Joomla server*.

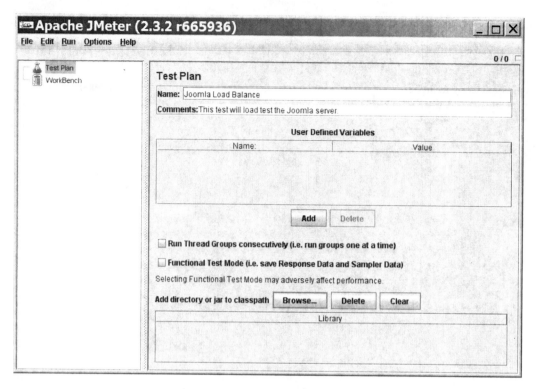

Figure 9-9. *The two panes of the JMeter interface with the left pane displaying a tree of all the nodes of a test plan and the right pane showing the properties of the selected item*

Most of the options that are used to add nodes to the test plan are accessed by right-clicking on one of the existing nodes. This will display a context menu of items relating to that node.

Right-click on the node that was previously labeled Test Plan (it will have updated to reflect the new Name property you entered previously), select the Add submenu, and then select the Thread Group option as shown in Figure 9-10. You will see a thread group node added as a child node to the test plan.

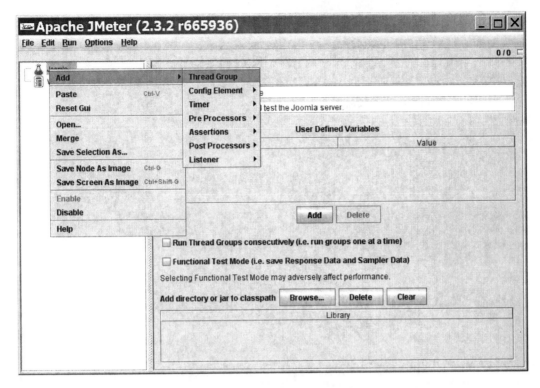

Figure 9-10. *Add a new Thread Group by right-clicking on the first node and selecting the Thread Group option*

All tests must be added to a thread group, so each test plan must have a minimum of one thread group. Some of the options that you will see with the current thread group selected include:

- *Action to be taken after a Sampler error*: You can halt all further tests when one error occurs, but usually the default setting of continue is best.

- *Number of Threads (users)*: This property determines the number of simulated concurrent users. This is the main variable that you will set to perform load testing. However, for the first test runs and setup of your test, it is best to leave this set to the default of 1 so you can complete repeated test executions quickly.

- *Ramp-Up Period (in seconds)*: This is the number of seconds to wait between the creation of one thread (user) and the next. Setting this option to zero will make the program attempt to start all threads at the same time. This is useful for simulating a burst access condition. Often you will want to increase this setting so you can easily see the graphic visualization of increasing load as new users are added to the request pool.

- *Loop count*: The count determines the number of loops that will be executed of the current thread group. Because a thread group can contain multiple page (or other) requests to simulate a session, you can use this to simulate multiple sessions for each user. Therefore, if the Number of Threads property was set to 10, the Loop count set to 5, and the number of page requests in the Thread Group is 6, then the complete test run would request 300 pages (10 x 5 x 6).

Leave all of these settings at their defaults for the moment.

Add User-Defined Variables

User-defined variables allow you to set variables in one place that you can use with other parts of the JMeter test. In this example, we're going to create three variables for items that you will likely want to change for various testing scenarios:

- *Log file*: The location of the log file where the data from the test will be recorded as an XML file

- *Log summary file*: The location of the log summary file where the summary of the test execution will be recorded in a comma-delimited CSV file

- *Base path*: The base path of the web page where the test will be run; changing this parameter will let you run the test on various parts of your site

You can use variables for many more items than configuration parameters. They can specify information to be passed in a GET or posted with a POST command, added to strings, or included in almost any parameter in the system.

1. Right-click on the Thread Group node, select Add ➤ Config Element ➤ User Defined Variables. This will add the node as a child of the thread group. In the right pane of the window, click on the Add button at the bottom of the screen and you should see a line item added in the User Defined Variables list area.

2. Click on the box in the Name column of the list area and type logfile and you should see that text appear in the box. Hit the Tab key to move the focus to the value column and enter the path where you want the log file to be saved. As you can see in Figure 9-11, I've entered a path to save the log file at my drive root.

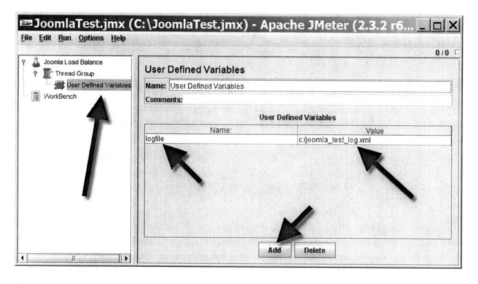

Figure 9-11. *Create a variable to store the log file name*

3. Create another variable and set the name to logsummaryfile and the value to the desired path such as c:/joomla_test_summary.csv to store the summary information. Add one more variable with a name basepath and the value to the base URL path of the page of your site to use. To simply test the front page of the site, you can set the value to / so the test will load the base page.

Access these variables in other parts of the system by encapsulating the variable name with the prefix ${ and the suffix }. We'll be using the base path in the next step.

■ **Tip**   The User Defined Variables node is the best place to locate configuration data that may change from time to time. In the preceding example, the base path is held in this node so you can easily change it to test another copy of Joomla located at a different server path. Also, if you're going to give this test to someone else to run (such as QA department personnel), I would suggest that you always have this node as the first one in the test plan and then name it something like ___CONFIG VARIABLES___ so that someone who didn't author the test can easily spot it.

Add HTTP Request Defaults

Right-click on the Thread Group again, but this time select the Add ➤ Config Element ➤ HTTP Request Defaults option. In the Web Server frame, you'll see a text box to enter Server Name or IP. Enter the domain name that you want to test without the `http://` prefix. For example, you can enter "`www.example.com`" to test a site located there.

In the HTTP Request frame, put `${basepath}` in the Path text box. At the time the test is run, the value contained in the `basepath` variable will be substituted for this entry. Check the *Retrieve All Embedded Resources from HTML Files* box so that when the page is loaded, the extra files such as the images and the CSS files are loaded as well.

Add HTTP Authorization Manager

If you have an .htaccess setup with access limitations (only users with the proper passwords can access a particular page or pages), you will need to set up the HTTP Authorization Manager. This manager will hold URL routes and their proper username and password settings. You can set these once in a test and they are automatically applied when restricted pages are requested.

Right-click on the Thread Group again, but this time select the Add ➤ Config Element ➤ HTTP Authorization Manager option. By default, this list will be empty. Click on the Add button to create a row entry. In the first box, enter the entire base URL to the site (for example, `http://www.example.com`) that uses .htaccess access limiters. Enter the username and password of the login in their appropriate boxes. Finally, in the domain box, place a single forward slash (`/`) if the access permissions begin at the root folder.

Your setup should look like the one shown in Figure 9-12. If your test will access multiple hosts with .htaccess restrictions, add them here now. The access name and passwords in this node will be used automatically for all authentication challenges from the servers that the test accesses.

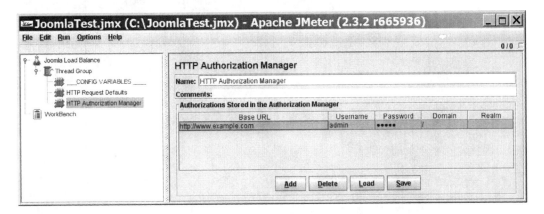

Figure 9-12. *Set up an entry for each area of the web site where an .htaccess username and password will be required*

Add HTTP Cookie Manager

If your session needs to simulate cookies (and most do), simply adding the HTTP Cookie Manager node to your test plan will automatically simulate cookies. Normally, adding this node is good enough for most tests. However, if you have some advanced tests that need to simulate pre-defined cookies, you can simulate explicit cookies and their values with this node.

Right-click on the Thread Group again, but this time select the Add ➤ Config Element ➤ HTTP Cookie Manager option. No configuration is required unless you want to manually specify various cookie variables that can be populated with constant values before the test is executed.

Add an HTTP Request Sampler

The Sampler nodes are perhaps the single most important part of a test because they perform the actual "sampling" of a System Under Test (SUT). A sampler sends a request (which may be an HTTP request, a database query, an LDAP lookup, or numerous other types) and stores the return reply. If a test is run that fails, JMeter makes it easy to examine the actual request that was sent as well as the data returned to the sampler. Having the request and the reply in one place can drastically shorten the time required to debug test problems.

Right-click on the Thread Group again, but this time select the Add ➤ Sampler ➤ HTTP Request option. The node added has a small eyedropper icon and is titled HTTP Request. Change the Name to Front Page. Set the path to a single forward slash (/) so the sampler will get the front page of the Joomla site. Your test plan should resemble the one shown in Figure 9-13.

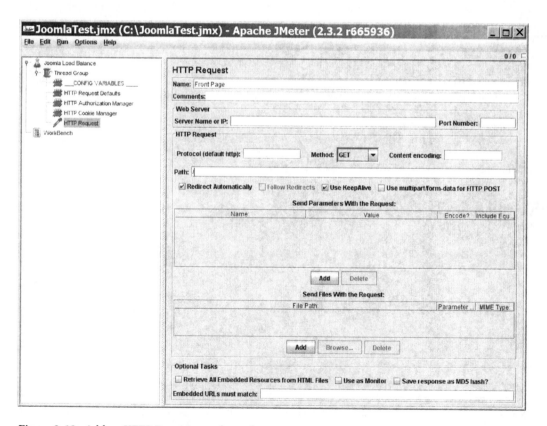

Figure 9-13. *Add an HTTP Request sampler to the current test*

Add a View Results Tree

All of the logic we've put into the test so far has been the setup of the actual test execution. However, there are other nodes that let you examine the results of the tests—either individually or as a summary. One results node type, the View Results Tree, will let you examine any single item executed in the test. This can be done hierarchically so that just as nodes in the test are organized with child nodes, so too the results are organized for easy navigation.

Right-click on the Thread Group again, but this time select the Add ➤ Listener ➤ View Results Tree option. You can put the path to a file name if you'd like to record all of the results of the test. By default, these are stored in an XML-formatted file, but other options including CSV format are available.

Add a Summary Report

The Summary Report works much like the View Results Tree, although instead of individual test results, it shows the results of test executions in aggregate. This report is particularly useful when performing load balancing as it allows a bird's-eye view of the execution.

Right-click on the Thread Group again, but this time select the Add ➤ Listener ➤ Summary Report option.

Add a Graph Results Node

Graphing results can help you spot trends in performance—especially peaks and valleys. It also helps you spot caching when the initial response time is very slow and when there is a precipitous drop in the response latency.

For the last node, right-click on the Thread Group again, but this time select the Add ➤ Listener ➤ Graph Results option. This will provide a graph or point chart of access speeds when the number of users is increased for load testing. It will allow you to visually examine the execution results.

Running the Test

Everything is ready for the first test, so let's run it! In the left pane, click on the View Results node. On the menu bar at the top of the window, select Run ➤ Start. Note the Stop menu option under the Run menu. This is very useful if you've started an elaborate load test and then realized there was some configuration error or other mass failure.

When this simple test completes, you should see the Front Page item in the results tree list, as shown in Figure 9-14. This list will show you every execution item of the test. In this case, we only have a single sampler that executed one time. If you configure the system for 5 users each with a loop count of 5 and added another sampler, you would see 50 items in this results tree (5 x 5 x 2).

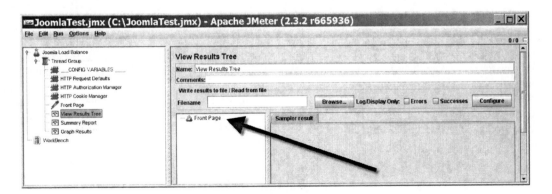

Figure 9-14. *The Front Page item will appear in the response list*

Click on the single result and you'll see the Sampler Request tab fill with information about the request execution. The text for the Sampler Request should look something like this:

```
Thread Name: Thread Group 1-1
Sample Start: 2009-07-26 17:18:56 AKDT
Load time: 299
Latency: 299
Size in bytes: 438
Sample Count: 1
Error Count: 0
Response code: 200
Response message: OK

Response headers:
HTTP/1.1 200 OK
Date: Mon, 27 Jul 2009 00:20:45 GMT
Server: Apache/2.2.3 (CentOS)
Last-Modified: Tue, 15 Nov 2005 13:24:10 GMT
ETag: "b80f4-1b6-80bfd280"
Accept-Ranges: bytes
Content-Length: 438
Connection: close
Content-Type: text/html; charset=UTF-8
```

From this information, you can see the load and latency times in milliseconds, the number of bytes returned to the request, the response code, and the information returned in the headers. If there was an error generated by the request (such as a 404 error), you can instantly see it here.

The Request tab is generally more useful if you have a failure. Click on the Request tab and you should see code like this:

```
GET http://www.example.com/
[no cookies]
Request Headers:
Connection: keep-alive
```

In this simple test, this information isn't very useful. However, in a more elaborate test, this will show the complete request string (that is, `http://localhost/joomlaadv/index.php/article-anatomy/testarticle`) so it can quickly lead you to the location of the error. If you use JMeter extensively, you will commonly adopt user-defined variables to build the request string dynamically. This will let you see any problems with the request URL.

Finally, click on the Response Data tab. This will display the actual data returned by the SUT and makes it easy to spot errors or problems. As you can see in Figure 9-15, the example request returned some basic HTML from the web page. If the sampler used had been a database sampler, the result set from the database query would be displayed in this pane.

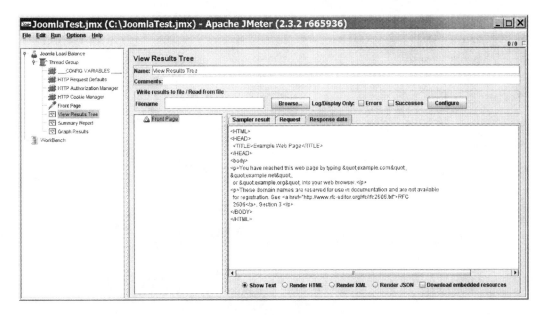

Figure 9-15. *The Response Data tab will show the actual data returned by the request*

You can probably already understand why this system is so powerful for testing. You can set up complete simulated sessions that request pages, check content, and report summary data. Let's scale up this simple test to see how a load-testing scenario for a web site might be accomplished.

Ramping Up the Users

To see a real load test, we need to increase the number of concurrent users accessing the site and also have them access it multiple times. By increasing the load, we should be able to see how the web server holds up (or bottlenecks) given a particular number of users.

Click on the Thread Group icon and increase the Number of Threads from 1 to 50. Set the loop count to 20 so each of the 50 simulated users will make the page request 20 times. This means a total of 1,000 page accesses.

Click on the Summary Report item and then use the Start option on the Run menu. In the top-right corner of the window, you should see a number that starts at 0/50 and increases until 50/50 is reached, as shown in Figure 9-16. These are the concurrent simulated users. JMeter will create a separate thread for each simulated user until all of them are created. When each simulated user has completed the specified number of loops, that thread will be killed and the number will decrease. When the number once again reaches 0/50, all the tests will be complete.

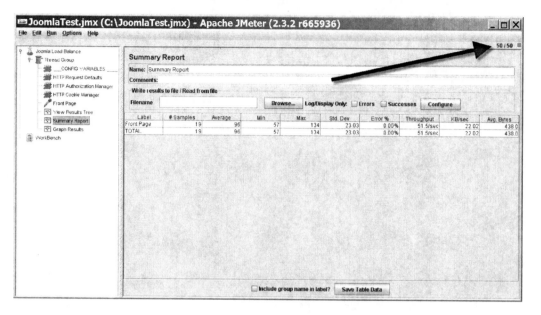

Figure 9-16. *The number of concurrent users requesting pages is shown in the top-right corner*

In the Summary Report table, you should see the # Samples column gradually increasing. The Error % column will show how many of the requests have failed. The Throughput column will tell you how many requests per second to which the server sent a response. The Avg. Bytes column is also useful because it shows the available page load for that URL in bytes.

To see how the server performed, click on the Graph Results node and you'll see a display like that shown in Figure 9-17. You can see each of the various factors such as average response time and throughput for the test. Note that the graph displays in milliseconds on the vertical access, so the higher the point or value that is displayed on the graph, the slower was the execution.

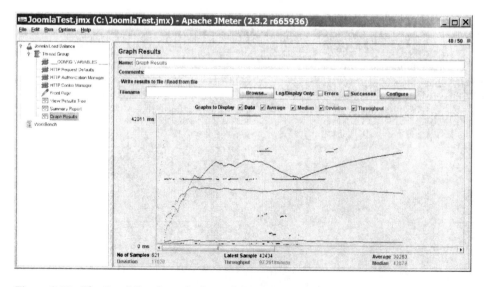

Figure 9-17. *The Graph Results node shows the execution results visually*

A single machine can often test more than a hundred simulated users. For a larger test, you can simply copy JMeter to another computer and run the test there at the same time.

Using the Proxy Server to Capture a Web Session

JMeter has a built-in proxy server that can sit between your browser and Internet connection and record all of the pages that the browser accesses. This allows you to create a list of sampler items quickly and simply.

1. Right-click on the Workbench icon in the left panel and select the Add ➤ Non-Test Elements ➤ HTTP Proxy Server option, as shown in Figure 9-18.

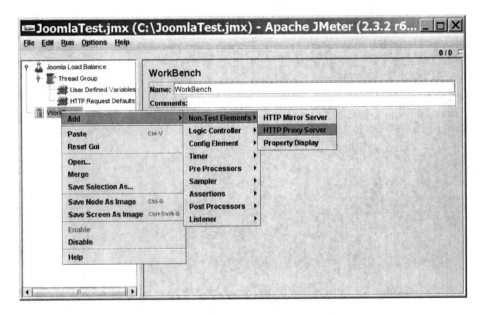

Figure 9-18. *Add an HTTP Proxy Server node to the WorkBench*

2. Set the port to 8080. Select the Destination where the new nodes with be recorded. In this case, select the Thread Group. In the Grouping drop-down menu, select the *Put each group in a new controller* option.

3. In the Content-type filter frame, enter `text/html` in the Include text box to include all HTML files.

4. In the Exclude text box, type `.*\.jpg  .*\.png  .*\.gif  .*\.js  .*\.css` to exclude image, CSS, and JavaScript files.

5. Click the Start button at the bottom of the window. Once the Proxy Server has started, the Stop button will be activated. Now you need to point your browser at the server to record your browsing activities.

After you've started the Proxy Server, you need to configure your browser to access the web through the JMeter proxy server. How this is done varies from browser to browser. Here are instructions for the popular Firefox and Internet Explorer browsers.

Configure Firefox to Use the Proxy Server

To configure the Firefox browser, select the Tools ➤ Options item to display the Preferences dialog box. Click on the Advanced icon and select the Network tab. In the Connection frame, click on the Settings button (see Figure 9-19).

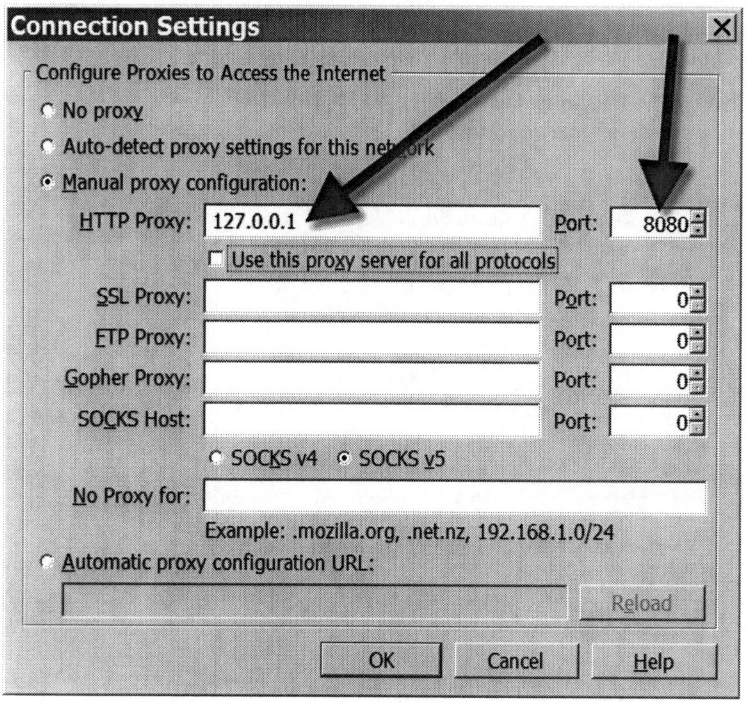

Figure 9-19. *Setup the Firefox browser to access the web site through the JMeter proxy server*

You need to set the proxy server settings to reference localhost (127.0.01) through port 8080, as shown in Figure 9-19. This will make the browser contact the JMeter proxy server that is running on localhost and use it to request all pages for browsing. With the browser accessing the JMeter proxy, it acts as a go-between for the Internet and can record all requests in the test.

Configure Internet Explorer to Use the Proxy Server

To configure the Internet Explorer browser, select the Tools ➤ Internet options item to display the dialog box.

On the Connections tab, click on the LAN settings button. The Local Area Network (LAN) Settings dialog box will display. There you can check the *Use a proxy server for your LAN* box and then enter the information for the JMeter proxy server. Typically this means a URL address of 127.0.0.1 (which is the same as localhost) and a port setting of 8080.

Editing a JMeter test

JMeter tests, even though the files have a .jmx extension, are actually XML files. Because they are plain text files, you can load them into a standard text editor. This provides a simple way to perform operations like search and replace. This capability is particularly useful with tests recorded using the Proxy Server. Often, the samplers recorded through this tool include full URL references, which make the tests less portable than if the URL was stored in the HTTP Defaults nodes.

Conclusion

In this chapter, you've learned how to use a variety of automated testing tools to profile and safeguard your Joomla site. You used Selenium to create fully automated acceptance tests for your Joomla site, ApacheBench to perform load testing, and JMeter to provide functional testing. The power of such automated testing tools will be apparent when you begin catching errors, page not founds, and other items when you make slight modifications to your site that—on the surface—should not affect other content.

Time spent creating tests pays great dividends in the long term. It takes some work to understand these tools and create tests that will look properly at your site. Once you do create these tests, however, they will serve you well and provide confidence that your site looks correct on a variety of browsers and over the long evolution of a web site. In the next chapter, we'll look at optimizing your development process with advanced development tools.

CHAPTER 10

■ ■ ■

Using Development Tools

When developing in Joomla, using the proper tools can make your life a lot easier. Finding the right tool for the job is one of the most important aspects of being an effective developer. There are some key tools such as Git, Eclipse, NetBeans, and jEdit that, once you use them, you won't want to develop without them. The tools introduced in this chapter will help expedite your Joomla development and provide a safety net (through source code control) against making mistakes.

In this chapter, we'll cover:

- Using Git for source code control

- Developing with Eclipse as your standard Integrated Development Environment (IDE)

- Using NetBeans for your IDE

- Remote editing with jEdit

For the modern developer, the one tool that is used regardless of the programming language or size of the development team is source code control.

Using Git for Source Code Control (SCC)

Source code control (SCC) (also known as version control, source code management (SCM), or revision control) is software that maintains a history or changelist of all files that are managed within the system, enabling designers and developers to keep a clear history of the changes to their files.

You can store everything from text-based HTML, PHP, and CSS to binary formats such as GIF, JPEG, and Adobe Photoshop files in a version control system (although text-based files are the easiest to manage). The software also helps in the process of merging changes that have been made to the same file—changes made by a single developer or a team.

Currently, Git (http://git-scm.com/) is the dominant open source tool used to manage source code. It was invented for managing the hundreds of thousands of lines of source code for the Linux operating system and is now used for thousands of development projects, including the Joomla platform.

▇ **Note**   Git was created by Linus Torvalds for managing Linux development. It was made to be fast, flexible, and distributed. Its origins in the Linux operating system make Windows updates less frequent than the Linux version. Therefore, if you want to use the under-development version of Git (not recommended for most users) or you would like to run other Linux-based tools such as sed or awk on the Windows operating system, you might consider using Cygwin (www.cygwin.com). Cygwin is roughly a command-line–based Linux operating system that runs inside Windows (it's not a virtual machine like VMWare or VirtualBox). Although it can't directly execute programs compiled for Linux, it allows Linux source code for programs to be compiled for execution on Windows. The default library of pre-compiled programs already includes most Linux applications (including Git). If you want to use Git for command-line source code control, Cygwin Git may be a good choice.

For the Joomla user, a source code tool such as Git can aid in everything from development effectiveness to deployment control by helping you:

- Keep different versions of a template, module, component, or plug-in

- Track your changes to all files including modifications to Joomla core files

- Back up all of the source code for your complete Joomla site

- Simplify merging Joomla platform upgrades with any customization that you've performed

This chapter will introduce basic version control concepts and provide direct examples using Git. By adopting version control for your Joomla system, you can have a lot more confidence during the development and update phases of your efforts.

Advantages of Source Control

Many beginning designers and developers either haven't heard of SCC systems or don't understand the advantages of using one. Even the SCC name can be off-putting because designers don't think of their style sheets and graphic files as "source code." With overly technical documentation and a steep learning curve, many people simply avoid or ignore these tools. Finally, most SCC systems are portrayed as systems for team development.

While version control is most effective (and nearly essential) for team or collaborative development, the benefits to a sole developer are nearly as great. Perhaps most of all, the beginning developer can benefit from using an SCC. Let's take a look at the most obvious benefits to even a beginning Joomla developer:

- *Unlimited undo*: Every time you "commit" files into the SCC, you create a new version. Any file can be reverted to a previous version, so it creates essentially an unlimited undo feature.

- *Comparison with previous versions*: An SCC can do a "diff" or difference between any version and any other. So if things that were working last week aren't working now, you can very easily compare the current non-working version and the previous version and see exactly what changed.

- *Safety net that encourages experimentation*: Because multiple versions of the same file are kept and files are easily reverted to their original form, an SCC system removes most of the risk from experimentation and trying new approaches.

- *Easy change backup*: It is very easy to create a remote copy of your source code. When you want to back it up, a simple "push" command will push only the changes. That means even if your codebase is very large, since only the changes are synchronized, the backup will be fast.

Here are a few examples of circumstances that range from inconvenient to disastrous that can be solved with a properly used version control system. I'll use Sally the Developer and Paul the Designer to illustrate a few situations:

- *Paul the Designer accidentally deleted one of his key graphic logo files*: With SCC, Paul doesn't even have to look for a backup (if there is one). A single command will restore the last version of the file committed to the system.

- *Sally's new Joomla component won't properly save to the database although the last version did*: Some change (Sally doesn't know where) was made to a file and it doesn't work anymore. With SCC, executing the difference command (known as diff) will show the differences between the versions. Instead of spending countless hours trying to find the single line that broke the routine, Sally is able to find it in moments.

- *Sally needs to make changes to a file she hasn't touched in over a year*: When she looks on her drive, there are six different copies of the file and she has no idea which is the most current. In fact, she can't even find a single copy of the configuration file for the system. Because the project used SCC, Sally simply goes to the central repository and clones a complete copy to her drive along with the logs of the last changes made to the files.

- *Paul's wife had a change of heart and has decided to return to the store logo that she was using three months ago rather than the new one*: Paul simply loads up the logo from three months ago without digging through backups or perhaps finding that he overwrote the original file after the new logo was in place for a month.

- *Another graphic designer made changes to Paul's style sheet file and he needs to know what they were*: Although the new parts of the site look fine, some of the old parts are displaying incorrectly. Paul uses the diff command to see the changes from the last version instantly.

- *For a new site, Sally has to work with a developer in New York who will be emailing file changes to her*: Even though only Sally is using the SCC, she can receive the files and commit them into her own system to track changes and examine differences. An SCC helps Sally integrate and merge changes to files.

- *Paul's file got corrupted on Thursday night and he realizes that he forgot to make his weekly backup last Friday*: Fortunately, he performs a commit to SCC every time he makes a major change to a file (often 8-10 times a day), so his Thursday commit means he only lost 2 hours of work. In contrast to the tedious process of performing regular backups, committing changes to an SCC takes moments and can often be performed with a single right-click on the modified file.

- *Twenty lines of Sally's code that took weeks to write were deleted by another developer and a backup of the original can't be found*: Because Sally committed her changes to the SCC system, she simply views the older version, and copies and pastes to restore the missing code.

- *Paul wants to backup the eight projects on his laptop computer before he travels to a conference, but the files are in many different folders*: Because Paul has all of his files under SCC, he simply performs a backup of the SCC repository where all of the files for all of the projects are stored.

There are thousands of other situations where SCC will save the day. I hope I've sold you on some of the advantages of using an SCC system even if you're an independent, individual Joomla developer. And the news gets better—some of the most powerful SCC systems are free!

■ **Note** Most of the popular version control systems are open source. Besides Git, Subversion/SVN (http://subversion.tigris.org/), CVS (www.nongnu.org/cvs), Mercurial (http://mercurial.selenic.com/), and Bazaar (http://bazaar.canonical.com/en/) are all popular source code control systems. While they vary in basic interface and implementation details, they share most general concepts in common such as committing, versioning, branching, and merging. You can adapt the techniques you learn in this chapter to use with almost any SCC system.

Let's quickly review some of the basic concepts before we start with hands-on examples.

Version Control Is Like a Recorder of Deeds

Version control systems, unlike traditional backup systems, are designed to allow you to quickly revisit (and restore if necessary) older versions of the files and perform comparisons between versions. They are also meant to be fast. Where backup software is understood to execute for minutes or hours, most version control operations take seconds.

I have often read descriptions of SCC systems that are depicted as a metaphorical library, particularly, I think, because of the *check out* and *check in* terminology associated with SCM operations. For myself, I tend to think of SCC like a recorder of deeds, county recorder, or land title recording office. For example, a piece of land has a current owner that is the most recent title transfer entry in the records. Although the most recent entry is the most relevant, it is simple to look back through the journal of recordings to see the exact history of the property ownership.

Likewise, each file in an SCC system is monitored for changes that are recorded and can be easily examined. The process by which the changes between two versions of the same file are compared is called a "diff" or "diffing." You can request an SCC to show all of the differences between the current file and the changes that you made last week or any time.

Source code files are stored in a *repository*. A repository can be a local file folder or files stored remotely on an SCC server. The basic work process for using SCC is something like this:

1. The Joomla developer creates a new repository or does a *check out* or *clone* of the current version of the source code from a repository.

2. The developer edits the files.

3. When enough progress is made, the developer *commits* changes to the repository. Committing is a fast and easy process, so you are encouraged to commit often—don't wait until a feature is complete. Each commit creates a new version, so that means it creates something you can return to examine or revert. Because only changes are stored, very little disk space is used for each commit.

4. If bad code is committed, the file can be reverted. If another developer has made changes to the same file or files, the changes are merged together. If the history of a file or even individual lines of a file need to be examined, the developer can do that with a single command.

That's it! The simplest use case for an SCC. Subsequent actions might include pushing a completed feature to a production server, pushing the working feature to a remote or shared repository, or resolving conflicts that appear when merging your changes with those made by other developers.

Now that you understand how the system works, let's get started by using Git to create a repository and commit some changes.

Creating a Repository and Committing Files to Git

There are many different version control systems available, both in the commercial and the open source communities. The most popular open source version control system is Git. Each system has certain advantages, but Git is increasingly becoming the standard because of the more advanced features it offers, including distributed version control. Most development for Joomla occurs in Git because the actual Joomla platform is being developed with that version control system.

Let's get started. Download a free copy of Git from the open source site here:

```
http://git-scm.com/
```

If you are running Windows, you might consider installing Git for Windows:

```
http://msysgit.github.com/
```

Install Git on your local system and verify that it's working from the command prompt on a Windows, the Terminal window on Mac OS (Command-Space, and type Terminal), or the console on Linux. At the command line, simply type:

```
git
```

That should generate a list of the most common Git commands. With Git installed, you're ready to get started. Git can operate with remote servers but doesn't require them, so anywhere Git is installed, it can be used effectively.

The concepts that govern version control in Git are generally the same for any system you might choose. The files that are managed by the system are held in a *repository*. A repository acts like a custom filing system. Rarely do you access repository files directly. The repository is addressed through a command-line program or another program that interfaces with the repository (such as Tortoise GIT or an Eclipse plug-in).

Let's create a sample repository with Git so you can see how it works:

1. Create an empty folder called mod_demo/ on your system. You can create the folder through the OS GUI or directly at the command line (`mkdir mod_demo` in Mac OS/Linux and Windows).

2. At the command line, navigate into the folder with `cd mod_demo`.

3. Initialize a new repository by typing `git init`. This command will create a new, empty repository at the current location. It will create a folder called `.git` inside the main directory. Most systems hide directories that begin with a period(.), so if you want to make sure it's there, on Linux/Mac OS type the command `ls .git`; on Windows, type `dir .git`. You should see various files and folders.

4. Use your favorite text editor to create a simple text file called mod_demo.php in the folder and type the code `<?php echo 'Demo module'; ?>` into the file.

5. After saving the file, return to the command line and type `git status`. You should see the file listed under the "Untracked files" header. That means the file hasn't been added to the repository yet, so it isn't being tracked.

6. Add the file by typing `git add mod_demo.php` so it will be written into the repository on the next commit.

7. Type `git status` again and you should see the file listed as a "new file."

8. Commit the file to the repository by typing `git commit -a -m` "This is my first commit". The -a switch specifies that all new or changed files should be committed (so they don't need to be listed individually). The -m switch lets you provide a commit message that will be recorded with the commit so you can understand the changes made when you read the log. When the commit has finished executing, the output shows a summary of the changes and now your file is in the repository! Now, the fun part—let's change the file and see the modifications.

9. Edit the file and change the code to read:

```php
<?php
echo '<h1>Demo module</h1>';
$version = 11;
echo "<p>Current version: {$version}</p>";
?>
```

10. Type `git status` again and this time the file should be reported as modified. Want to see the changes?

11. Type `git diff` to show the current changes. The list will show what lines have been removed (denoted by the line beginning with a minus (-)) and those that have been added (beginning with a plus (+)). These changes have been made to the local file and HAVE NOT been committed to the repository yet. You will see the output like this:

```
index 2acacca..7fc2a69 100644
--- a/mod_demo.php
+++ b/mod_demo.php
@@ -1 +1,6 @@
-<?php echo 'Demo module'; ?>
+<?php
+echo '<h1>Demo module</h1>';
+$version = 11;
+echo "<p>Current version: {$version}</p>";
+?>
```

12. Type `git commit -a -m` "Added version number display". When this operation completes, your newest changes have been committed. A `git status` and `git diff` will both show the directory as "clean" since there are no new files and no new modifications.

13. Type `git log` to see what commits have been made in the past. You should see your two commits with the commit messages, a timedate stamp when the commit was made, the author of the commit, and a long alphanumeric string called a *commit hash* (e.g. 92e8f6dac0db0f8ee8ae6428928f29a89d47957d). This commit hash is the reference that you use to specify a commit for a `diff` or other operation. Let's use the commit hashes to see the difference between two versions. Your commit log should look like this:

```
commit 92e8f6dac0db0f8ee8ae6428928f29a89d47957d
Author: Dan Rahmel
Date:   Sat Sep 15 14:42:16 2012 -0500
    Added version number display

commit 17472f40e9cd64c588e3d73d2e9d956f7fef7595
Author: Dan Rahmel
Date:   Sat Sep 15 13:59:53 2012 -0500
    This is my first commit
```

14. Type

```
git diff 17472f40e9cd64c588e3d73d2e9d956f7fef7595...\
92e8f6dac0db0f8ee8ae6428928f29a89d47957d
```

Replace the commit hashes with your own that were displayed in the log. You should see the same `diff` that was displayed before you committed. In that case, you requested the difference between the last commit and the current state of the file. Using this same command but selecting other commit hashes, you could compare ANY two previous commits.

Hopefully you can already recognize the power of such a system. Commits happen in a fraction of a second, so there is no reason not to commit often. The more descriptive you make your commit messages, the easier it will be to find specific last commits.

■ **Tip** You can create a repository on any drive—and that includes flash/jump/thumb drives. For documents that I work on at home and work, I've created a repository on my drive. I then have checkouts of the documents folder on both my home drive and work drive. At the end of the workday, I can simply plug the drive into my work machine and push the changes from my working directory on my desktop machine to the repo on the flash drive. When I get home, I can pull the changes from the drive to my working copy on my home computer. This works especially well with text-based files because Git can merge the modifications. On Windows, make sure that you've set a permanent drive mount letter for the flash drive (for example, I use `R:\` for my flash drive). Because working copies rely on a consistent path, if the drive letter changes it can confuse the checkout.

Some Basic SCC Terminology

Before we continue, it is important to know some of the basic terminology used to describe GIT operations:

- *Repository*: The place where all of the current and past versions of all of the files are stored. If you use a repository browser, the repository appears almost like a traditional file system with files and folders organized hierarchically.

- *Working copy/Checkout*: When a folder from the repository is downloaded to a local drive, this download is known as a *working copy* or *checkout*. Each checkout has a `/.git` folder that includes version control information for every file and folder of the checkout. The folder also contains pointers to the source paths on .he remote repository. Using these paths, the Git system can synchronize local modifications with the source repository. Other users can update their working copies from the source repository to receive the changes.

- *Commit*: When changes are made to a file, those changes are written to the repository by executing a *commit*. Each commit is assigned a commit hash (that acts like a version number) and records a log entry with all of the changes to the file.

- *Commit hash*: Every commit is assigned a statistically unique commit hash that allows that commit to be referenced for future checkouts, change analysis, merging, and log analysis. To make the typing easier, you can use a *short hash* that is the first seven characters of a hash. In other words, you can reference the hash `17472f40e9cd64c588e3d73d2e9d956f7fef7595` with `17472f4`. The diff you did in the example could execute with short hashes with the command `git diff 17472f4...92e8f6d`.

- *Head revision*: The most current revision of a file or files. When you update a folder to the *head revision*, you're updating all of the files to the most current versions that exist in the Git repository.

Some people find the command line most comfortable to use, but many Joomla users prefer graphical environments. Fortunately, Git is easiest to grasp in a GUI environment, so we'll use Git Gui to demonstrate the most common features.

■ **Tip** If you want to learn more than the basics of GIT, I highly recommend you download and read the free book offered online at http://Gitbook.red-bean.com/. It is available for download in HTML and PDF formats and is highly readable. I can't recommend it enough.

Using Git Gui

Git Gui provides a GUI interface for the system and is installed with the standard Git setup on Windows, Mac OS, and Linux desktop systems. In this demonstration, you'll use Git Gui to access the local repository you created, check in some files, look at file modifications, and commit changes to the repository. By going through a process similar to the one you performed using the command line, you can decide which style suits you best.

If you execute the Git Gui application for the first time, you'll see the basic command screen as shown in Figure 10-1 that allows you to create a new repository, clone a repo from a remote source, or open an existing repo.

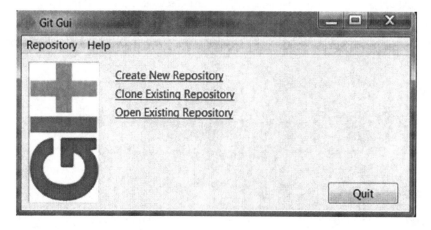

Figure 10-1. *The Git Gui home screen allows you to create a repository, or clone or open an existing one*

To begin using Git Gui, let's access the repo you created from the command line so you can examine a repository that already has a couple of commits.

Opening the Local Repository

Begin by clicking on the *Open Existing Repository* link and navigating to the mod_demo/ directory where you created the repo. When the repository opens, the Git Gui window will show four nearly empty panes. The default Git Gui window is devoted to examining, staging, and committing changes. Because we haven't made any modifications since our last commit, these panes are empty. Before we make some fresh changes, let's take a look at the history of the repository.

From the Repository menu, select the Visualize Master's History option and the history of commits will be shown, as in Figure 10-2. The repo commits appear in the pane in the top-left corner of the window. Clicking on an individual commit will display the log information about the commit and the diff of the file in the bottom-left pane. In the middle of the window is a Find pane that lets you search the commits for particular text, paths, or strings.

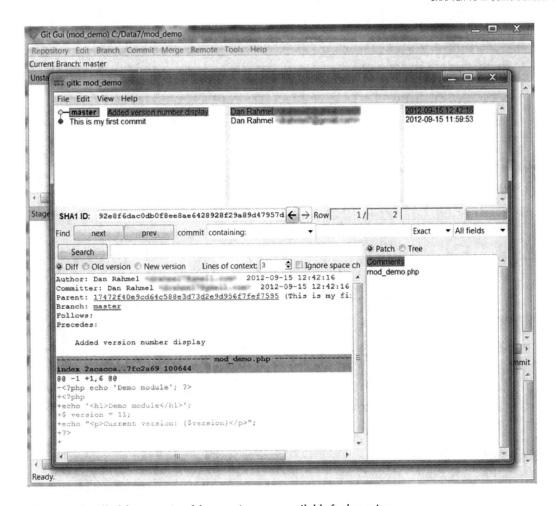

Figure 10-2. *All of the commits of the repository are available for browsing*

Close this window for the moment so we can return to the main window. Let's see what the interface looks like if it has a change to handle. Open the mod_demo.php file in your editor, make a few changes, and save the changes.

When you return to the Git Gui interface, you won't see any changes. Git Gui does not automatically detect changes to the repository. If you click the Rescan button (the top button in the button set near the bottom of the window), you should see your most recent changes appear in the window. In the top-left pane ("Unstaged Changes") you should now see the file you changed and in the top-right pane ("Modified, not staged") you should see the changes.

Git has a two-phase commit process: stage and commit. In the command-line example, you used the -a switch when performing your commit, which actually stages the commit and then executes the commit. Describing the usefulness of the two-phase commit process is beyond the scope of this book (see http://programmers. stackexchange.com/questions/69178/what-is-the-benefit-of-gits-two-stage-commit-process-staging for more information). If you understand that you first need to stage changes before you commit them, that will be good enough for now.

Therefore, to stage your new changes, select the *Stage to Commit* option from the Commit menu to move your altered files from phase #1 to phase #2. Enter a commit message in the text box in the bottom-right corner of the screen and then select the *Commit* option from the Commit menu. Your changes should disappear from the window, as they have now been committed to the repository.

■ **Note** One of the benefits of using the Git Gui interface over the command line is the diffs that are displayed at each stage. Although you can perform a diff at each phase of the command-line commit process, the interface makes them always visible, so you naturally examine changes before you actually commit. This process is very useful to prevent committing unwanted echoes, console.log() calls, or temporary code overrides.

Let's use the Git Gui for something that is more complicated at the command line: comparing any two revisions.

1. Open the Visualize Master's History window again and you should see three commits now.

2. In the top-left pane, click on the most recent or HEAD revision to select it.

3. Right click on the first commit (should have the commit message "This is my first commit") and select the *Diff this* ➤ *selected* option.

In the bottom-right pane, you will see all of the changes between these two commits. This type of comparison can be tremendously useful when you're trying to recover old code or debug a current problem that was not a problem in earlier revisions.

Cloning a Remote Repository

With your own development projects, you will often create a new repository and get to work. Even if you have an existing project that isn't under SCC, you can simply navigate to that folder, create a repository in the folder, and add the existing files. However, there are often times when you want to work with other remote developers or modify the code of an existing project. This is generally accomplished by cloning a Git repository that has been posted to Github (www.github.com).

■ **Note** Github is a popular central repository for most popular open source projects. Projects as diverse as Joomla, Node.js, and Twitter Bootstrap are all hosted there. Github, after a simple registration, will host public projects in their repository for free. To have them host your private projects, you pay a reasonable monthly fee. If you or your company wants to use a Git access control server and don't want to set up your own Gitorius (http://gitorious.org/) or Gitosis (https://github.com/res0nat0r/gitosis) server, you should take a close look at Github.

The Joomla source code is held in a Git repository on Github, so why don't we clone the code and take a look?

1. Close Git Gui and open it again.

2. This time, select the Clone Existing Repository link.

3. In the Source Location text box, enter the following address:

    https://github.com/joomla/joomla-cms.git

4. For the Target Directory, select (or create) a local directory where you want to store the code.

5. Click the Clone button to begin the clone process. Joomla has a lot of files, so this process may take a few minutes.

If you open the Visualize Master's History window, you'll see thousands of commit messages (see Figure 10-3) and a great many committers (developers who have committed changes to the repository).

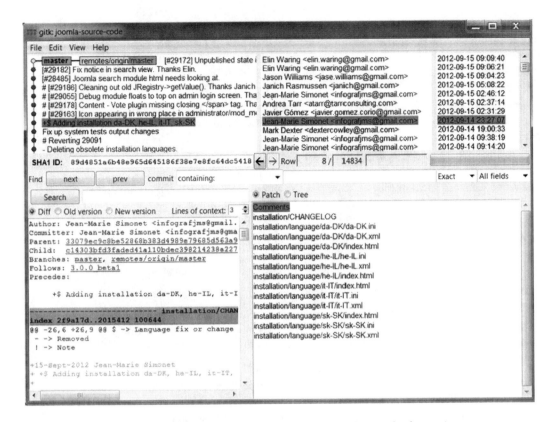

Figure 10-3. *The Joomla repository has dozens of committers and thousands of commits*

If you look through the commits, you can see some of the working process that the Joomla teams uses. You can also see how the team of developers who are located around the world can effectively collaborate by using the Git tool.

Creating a Branch and Performing a Custom Modification to a Core Joomla File

One of the great features of Git is its distributed architecture. That means that the repository of Joomla that you just cloned to your local drive is a complete, self-contained repository. You could begin working on the Joomla platform right now in that repository as if it originated on your local machine.

You can make modifications, commits, rollbacks, and use any feature of Git except the operation to push your changes to the master or trunk on the Github server (unless you're a member of the Joomla team). Even that is possible if you fork the current Joomla master (a little more on that later). So you can use the repository on your current machine with almost no constraints.

There is a better way than modifying the main Joomla files in the master branch, however. Git (as with most other SCC systems) has a feature called branching. Imagine that a repository is a tree and the central and most important source code in the repository is the trunk of the tree. Now imagine that this source code tree needs custom modifications. Following the tree metaphor, these changes from the trunk are *branches* from the main tree. Here are some examples of branches that often are created in a repository:

- *Release version branches*: If a product or web site releases v1.0, you don't want developers to stop work on v2.0. However, you still need to keep a copy of v1.0 so if a bug is discovered and needs to be corrected, you don't have to rush v2.0 to release to make the change. If you have a release v1.0 branch (or v2.0 is a branch), you can make the change without affecting either project.

- *Development branch*: With a team of developers, individual work is typically performed on individual branches. So Developer A has a branch and Developer B has a separate branch. The developers will never collide with their changes and won't corrupt the trunk with features that aren't complete. When the work is ready for inclusion into the trunk, each developer merges their branch into the trunk and resolves any conflict with existing code.

- *Feature branches*: Often, development features are given separate branches. For example, one feature branch might be called feature/new_login_module and another might be feature/custom_header.

- *Multiple site branches*: If you have three Joomla sites (for example, www.example1.com, www.example2.com, and www.example3.com), the trunk may be a clone of the main Joomla platform code. Then each site may be a branch off the trunk. That way, when there are updates to Joomla, you can pull down the changes from the main repo on Github. Then you can merge the changes to the trunk into the various branches as desired.

In Git, the *trunk* is called the master branch (in another SCC system called SVN it is called the trunk). So developers can branch from the master or even branch from a branch.

For our example, let's create a branch from the Joomla trunk and change the name of one of the standard menus.

1. At the command line, change to the directory that holds the clone of the Joomla master.

2. Type git checkout -b custom_joomla. The -b switch on the checkout command will create a new branch from the master (or branch from whichever branch you currently have checked out). Now any changes that are committed will be made to the branch, leaving the master intact.

3. Type git status. The output will tell you the current branch (in this case, custom_joomla) that is selected.

4. Open the administrator/language/en-GB/en-GB.mod_menu.ini file in your favorite editor

5. Search for the variable MOD_MENU_SYSTEM_INFORMATION and change the text "System Information" to "Sys Info"

6. Type git commit -a -m "Changed the text of the Administrator menu"

7. Go to the Administrator interface, click the Site menu, and you should see the System Information menu is now named Sys Info.

8. At the command line, type git checkout master

9. Refresh the Administrator interface and you should see your change is gone.

10. At the command line, type git checkout custom_joomla. If you refresh the Administrator interface again, you'll find that your change has returned.

This example should demonstrate how a developer can work on many different features and keep them isolated. Additionally, there are no changes to the master, so you can retrieve changes that the Joomla team has made to the central master without affecting the current work. Let's update the Joomla master (or trunk) in our local repository and merge any changes into our current branch.

11. At the command line, type git checkout master. This will return your checkout to the current master.

12. Type git pull origin master. This command will look in the repository for the origin (more about that shortly), download any changes to the Joomla master, and merge them into the master branch in your local repo.

13. Type `git checkout custom_joomla`

14. Type `git merge master`. This command will merge any changes from the current master into the branch. You could merge changes from one branch to another simply by entering the name of that branch instead of master. For example, `git merge developer_joe` would merge Joe's branch (if he named it that) into your branch. This type of branch merging is very common when two or more remote developers are working on the same feature or module.

In most working environments, the master is not used for active development. Development occurs on one or more Git branches and when each piece is ready for production, the branch is merged into the master. For a member of the Joomla team, for example, after they finished work on a new feature, they would check out the master branch and then type:

```
git merge feature/mybranch
```

Once it was merged, they would push the changes to the origin master.

Pushing a Repository to a Remote SSH Server

Most people think that in order to have a remote Git repository, you need some type of Git server like Github, Gitosis, or Gitorious. Fortunately, that's not the case! In fact, any server that can accept SSH connections can act as a remote repository. This includes nearly any Linux box (by default, most versions accept SSH connections), Mac OS (enable System Preferences ➤ Sharing ➤ Remote Login), and even GoDaddy (`http://support.godaddy.com/help/article/4942/enabling-ssh-on-your-linux-shared-hosting-account`) if you have a Linux hosting account. On a Windows machine, you can install and run freeSSHd (`http://www.freesshd.com/`).

The one small catch is you need to be able to create a Git "bare" repository as a directory on the target machine. In the case of a host like GoDaddy, you'll have to create the repository on your local machine and then transfer it to the host, which is not too difficult.

Let's imagine that you have a local Linux box with a static IP address of 192.168.1.50. Follow these steps:

1. From the command line, SSH to the box with a command such as `ssh myusername@192.168.1.50` and log in with your password.

2. Create the directory where you'll have your git repository, such as typing `mkdir -p /home/gitrepos/custom_joomla` at the command line.

3. Change to the directory by typing `cd /home/gitrepos/custom_joomla`

4. Initialize a bare repository using `git init --bare`. A bare repository is not an active working directory like a normal Git repo. Bare repositories are only the repo itself that is used for receiving remote pushes.

5. Make sure it has the proper permissions so any SSH user can push to it by typing `chmod -R 777 /home/gitrepos/custom_joomla`. Using 777 privileges is just an example because it allows everyone with login access to read and write to the repo. Check your Linux manual for instructions on restricting the repo to only specific users or groups.

6. Log off the server. That's all you need to set up on the server.

Now that the remote repo is created and configured, let's point our current copy of Joomla at it.

7. Look at the currently available remotes by typing `git remote -v`. This command will list all of the remote servers where you can push your current repo. You should see the default Github origin address listed like this:

```
origin  https://github.com/joomla/joomla-cms.git (fetch)
origin  https://github.com/joomla/joomla-cms.git (push)
```

8. Add a new remote to point at your Linux server by typing `git remote add mine ssh://myusername@192.168.1.50/home/gitrepos/custom_joomla`. This will create a new remote target called *mine* where you can push your changes.

9. Push your current repo to the remote repo by typing `git push mine`. This will upload any files or changed files to the remote repository.

That's it. Any time you have commits to your local copy that you want shared with the remote repo, simply type `git push mine` or, if you want to push a particular branch (more common), then specify the branch by typing `git push mine custom_joomla`. The great thing about this method—aside from the ease of adding new repos—is that you don't need to maintain separate user security. Through traditional Linux security, you can limit user access to specific repository directories and the server itself.

Forking the Joomla Master

Projects stored in Github can be easily forked. Think of a fork as simply a formalized version of branching. One great thing about forking is the ability to contribute to a major project like Joomla.

For example, imagine that you wanted to improve the Joomla caching system. This isn't something that could be effectively developed as an extension. The changes would need to be made to the core Joomla framework for the caching to be effective. To improve this feature, you could go to the repository on Github and simply click the Fork button as shown in Figure 10-4. This operation will create a branch of Joomla in your Github account.

Figure 10-4. *The Fork button will branch the repo, and Pull requests shows how many people have developed features they want merged into the master*

If you complete the modifications to the caching system, you would then make a Pull Request to the Joomla team. If they decide that your feature is worthwhile and the code is clean, they will merge your changes into the master branch. If they don't like your feature and decline to include it, but you think others would find it useful, you can publicize it on your blog or elsewhere and people can come directly to your fork and clone it themselves.

Using Git to Develop Joomla Extensions

Development of Joomla Extensions including templates, components, modules, and plug-ins can benefit from adopting version control. There are several primary reasons including:

- *Centralization*: Often a single extension may be comprised of a component and one or more modules. Keeping development synchronized can be difficult. Perhaps a revision to the component may break compatibility with one of the modules. This might be difficult to notice or remember because each part of the extension is located in a different folder. A typical extension may have files in `/administrator/components`, `/components`, and `/modules`. Creating a folder in the GIT repository and having all of the pieces of the extension be checkouts from the same repositories can aid you in managing the extension.

- *Deployment*: If you have several Joomla sites, they may all draw from the folders on the repository. Updating each one becomes much simpler.

- *Update logs*: Because Git uses unique hashes to manage the revisions of the files in a repository, you can use these hashes or even the commit date to track the status of files. If you upload a version of an extension to your web site and make a simple note of the current hash (or tag it in the repo), it is an easy process later to have Git report what files changed between then and the current revision. You need only update the files that have changed.

Because most development of Joomla extensions occurs after the extension is installed in the system, I would recommend modifying the foundation of an existing extension such as one of those introduced in Chapter 12 and installing that extension into the Joomla system. Then add the extension to the GIT repository after it is in-place in the Joomla installation file structure.

Unlike other version control systems such as SVN or CVS, which maintain a central repository, Git uses a distributed version control topology, so each working copy maintains its own complete repository. Repositories are cloned from other repositories and can easily be merged later.

▓ **Tip** Many users run Git from the command line, but on the Windows platform, TortoiseGit (`http://code.google.com/p/tortoisegit/`) is available that provides an excellent graphical user interface and integration with Windows Explorer. Nearly identical to TortoiseSVN, TortoiseGit provides a right-click menu for files and folders that lets you easily manage your Git repositories. It can co-exist with TortoiseSVN, so you can use both tools on the same computer.

Using Eclipse IDE and XDebug for Joomla Development

One of the top development systems in the world is Eclipse (`www.eclipse.org`). It is a free, open source, Integrated Development Environment (IDE) written in Java (see Figure 10-5), but usable for development in almost any available computer language. Its plug-in architecture makes it an ideal platform for expansion and thousands of developers offer both free and commercial plug-ins.

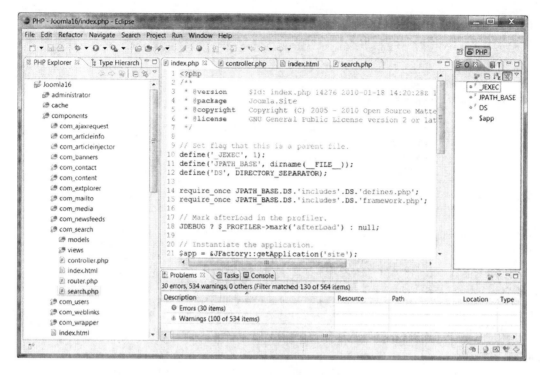

Figure 10-5. *The Eclipse IDE is excellent for Joomla development*

In fact, the reason it is probably the single most popular IDE for PHP development is the PDT (PHP Development Tools) framework that is included with the Eclipse for PHP Development download (www.eclipse.org/pdt). It provides syntax highlighting of code, code assist, code folding, PHP project explorer view, PHP debugging, and many other features.

Although Eclipse doesn't ship with a debugger, it supports debugging using the Zend debugger (http://static.zend.com/topics/Zend-Debugger-Installation-Guide.pdf) or XDebug (http://xdebug.org/). Installing a debugger can be one of the most important steps in truly learning how Joomla functions. It is extremely educational to follow the execution process of a Joomla page load to see exactly how Joomla handles the process of dynamically generating the HTML for transmission to the web browser.

Since debugging Joomla itself can be very informative and setting up the debugger (particularly on the Windows platform) can be a challenge, this section will lead you through the steps of configuring Eclipse to use XDebug on a localhost version of Joomla.

Start by downloading the Eclipse for PHP Developers (http://www.eclipse.org/downloads/packages/eclipse-php-developers/heliosr) package. You will need a fast connection because the archive is nearly 150MB. Once you have the archive saved on your local machine, you don't need to perform any installation. Simply expand the files of the archive into a folder (I usually create a folder c:\eclipse). Eclipse doesn't need any installation to run (except Java, of course), so you can have multiple copies/versions on a single machine if you want.

To run Eclipse, open the main folder and run the executable. On the Windows platform, you need only double-click the EXE file. The environment will load and display an opening navigation screen or *perspective*. In Eclipse, the organization of the windows and the presentation of items is determined by the currently selected perspective. The Workbench perspective is the main coding perspective that displays the editor windows, a project explorer, and other items relevant to coding. The Debugger perspective shows debugging information and the Subversion perspective has windows or panels that are useful for managing source code control.

To import a copy of Joomla into Eclipse, select File ➤ New ➤ PHP Project. The new project window will be displayed and let you enter a project name. Select the *Create project from existing source* option and navigate to the folder containing Joomla. Click the Next button and follow the subsequent screens to select the rest of the options you want (all can be left to the defaults).

The Joomla project will be imported and you should see all of the files displayed in the PHP Explorer panel on the left side of the screen. Double-clicking on one of the file entries should display that file in the editor. To run Joomla in your web browser through Eclipse, you need to set up a run configuration.

From the Run menu, select the Run configurations option. You should see a list of configuration types and one entry should be "PHP Web page." Right-click on that entry and select the New option. The panel at the right displays the default settings for the run configuration. For the Server Debugger option, select the XDebug option. You can leave the Default PHP Server option (if you're using localhost) or click the Configure button to the right of the entry to set the server options.

You also need to set the default file for the run configuration. Figure 10-6 shows that I have Joomla not at the root of my web server, but located in the joomla folder. Set this to match the configuration of your Joomla server.

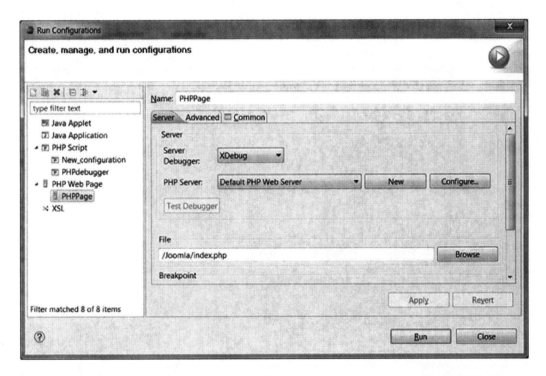

Figure 10-6. *Set up a run configuration that matches the settings of your server and your PHP information page should show these settings*

You can leave all of the other settings to their defaults. Click the Advanced tab to select browser launch settings and the Common tab to specify how the Eclipse environment will handle the process launch. Click the Apply button to save these settings. Now let's configure the XDebug extension on the Apache server before we start a debugging session running on Eclipse.

Install XDebug on Your Web Server

Generally, the most difficult part of using XDebug is activating it on your web server. Go to the XDebug home page (http://xdebug.org/) and download the version that is appropriate for your system configuration. If you are running Linux and have a package installer such as yum, there is probably an existing package that you can install with a single command.

On the Windows platform, usually the most confusing selection is the "thread safe" versus "non thread safe" extension. If you are running a standard Apache/PHP installation, you are most likely running thread safe and that is the version of the XDebug extension you should select. If you want more information, go to your favorite search engine and search for "PHP thread safe" and you will find a number of articles discussing the subject.

Once you have downloaded the plug-in, place it in the proper PHP extensions folder. On Windows, the path to the folder is generally a subfolder called ext/ in the path of the PHP installer. You can also find the path by looking at the phpinfo() data. In Linux, you can find the location using a single line at the command prompt:

```
php -i | grep extension_dir
```

Place the extension in this folder. Now you have to configure the php.ini file in order to find and load the extension.

For Windows, the following configuration settings may be helpful. The configuration shown in Listing 10-1 actually works on several machines I have tested these running Windows 7 with PHP 5.2 (as well as more recent versions of PHP). You will need to update the path and the file name to match the module that you have installed on your server. Note that many of the XDebug configuration examples on the Web simply don't work at all—and some of them would never work because of errors in implementation—so use the parameters here exactly as specified.

Listing 10-1. A sample Windows XDebug configuration to be inserted into the php.ini file

```
[PHP_XDEBUG]
zend_extension_ts="C:/Apache22/PHP5/ext/php_xdebug-2.0.5-5.2.dll"
xdebug.remote_enable=1
xdebug.remote_handler=dbgp
xdebug.remote_host=localhost
xdebug.remote_port=9000
; Port number must match debugger port number in NetBeans IDE Tools > Options > PHP
xdebug.profiler_enable=1
xdebug.profiler_output_dir="C:/Apache22/PHP5/"
```

Be sure to specify the path to the extension as an absolute path and not a relative path. Also, even though it is on the Windows platform, forward slashes are used for the directory separators. Finally, the enable parameters (remote_enable and profiler_enable) are specified as the number "1" instead of "true". I have had problems enabling XDebug on some configurations with the "true" value, even though it should work properly.

This configuration enables profiling, which saves the execution timing of all individual PHP script executions. This can slow down execution if you don't have a fast processor and will create execution profile files in your PHP directory. Most of the time you will want this disabled, but I have left it enabled in this example so you know all of the features of XDebug are working properly.

After you have added the necessary configuration to your php.ini file and installed the proper XDebug extension in the extensions folder, you will need to restart your Apache server for the extension to load.

Once your web server is restarted, create a page that calls the phpinfo() function (it can be a page as simple as <?php phpinfo(); ?> in a .php file) or navigate to the Joomla Administrator interface and select the PHP Information panel under Site ➤ System Information. You should see the various XDebug settings as shown in Figure 10-7. If this panel of settings is not available, XDebug didn't load properly. Check the Apache access log file (which records PHP errors) and the Apache error.log to see if you can find details of the failure.

xdebug

xdebug support	enabled
Version	2.0.5

Supported protocols	Revision
DBGp - Common DeBuGger Protocol	$Revision: 1.125.2.6 $
GDB - GNU Debugger protocol	$Revision: 1.87 $
PHP3 - PHP 3 Debugger protocol	$Revision: 1.22 $

Directive	Local Value	Master Value
xdebug.auto_trace	Off	Off
xdebug.collect_includes	On	On
xdebug.collect_params	0	0
xdebug.collect_return	Off	Off
xdebug.collect_vars	Off	Off
xdebug.default_enable	On	On
xdebug.dump.COOKIE	no value	no value
xdebug.dump.ENV	no value	no value
xdebug.dump.FILES	no value	no value
xdebug.dump.GET	no value	no value
xdebug.dump.POST	no value	no value
xdebug.dump.REQUEST	no value	no value
xdebug.dump.SERVER	no value	no value
xdebug.dump.SESSION	no value	no value
xdebug.dump_globals	On	On
xdebug.dump_once	On	On
xdebug.dump_undefined	Off	Off
xdebug.extended_info	On	On

Figure 10-7. *The settings for the XDebug extension should now appear in the phpinfo() function output*

Once the XDebug panel is listed by phpinfo(), refresh the home page of your localhost Joomla installation and then open the PHP directory. You should find a file with a name like cachegrind.out.15348. If you see the file there, you know that XDebug is running properly and outputting the execution profile information.

■ **Tip**   To examine the execution profile output by XDebug, you will need another program that can read the files and parse the information. On Linux, KCacheGrind (http://kcachegrind.sourceforge.net/html/Home.html) is an excellent free program, while the Windows version is called WinCacheGrind (http://sourceforge.net/projects/wincachegrind/). These will show you where the individual timing cycles of a page execution occur. This information isn't especially useful for Joomla developers because the Joomla system will occupy most of the long execution time positions, but provides a wealth of information for normal PHP development.

Configure Eclipse to Communicate with XDebug

With XDebug available, you need to configure your development environment to talk to the debugger. The configuration settings that you added to the php.ini specified the port number and the name of the debugging process. Eclipse needs to have these information settings so that for the duration of the PHP execution, a communication channel can be opened between the program and the extension.

When you begin a debugging execution, the Eclipse perspective will automatically change to the Debugger perspective (as shown in Figure 10-8). Unlike the Project perspective, the Debugger perspective shows all of the relevant information to the current execution. The code panel will highlight the current execution line and allow you to set breakpoints. The Debug panel shows the current execution stack and the Variables panel allows you to select individual variables and examine their contents.

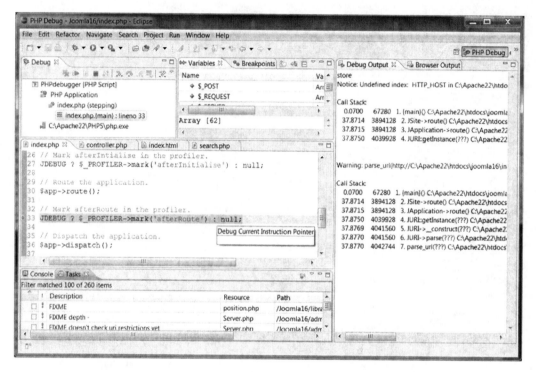

Figure 10-8. *The Debugger perspective will show the current breakpoint line, the content of variables, and other information*

The Console panel at the bottom displays any errors or warnings sent to the debugger, while the Debug Output panel on the right shows the actual execution output.

Eclipse Tips and Tricks

When you first begin using Eclipse, it can be a little overwhelming. There are so many features and menus that it can seem like it is impossible to master. In fact, most professional developers only use a small fraction of the available features. Once you learn the key items that you need to use Eclipse effectively, you can learn the rest of the IDE at your leisure.

For Joomla development, here are a few useful tips that can decrease your learning curve:

- *Top-right corner Perspective drop-down*: You can change perspectives by going to the drop-down menu in the top-right corner of the Eclipse window. This is particularly useful after you've run in debugging mode, which switches the perspective to Debugger when running, but does not return to the Workbench perspective when debugging is complete.

- *Team menu when right-clicking on a file*: In the PHP Explorer, right-clicking on a file shows a long menu of options, but the Team menu is one of the most important. The Show Local History option displays the Local History panel below the editor and contains all the changes that you've made on your local system for that file. You can compare change versions or revert to an earlier version. If you have the Subclipse (Subversion/SVN plugin) installed (http://subclipse.tigris.org/), the Team menu also contains the SVN options.

- *Back up before installing plug-ins*: One problem that has always plagued Eclipse is the common problem of the installation or removal of a plug-in that makes Eclipse inoperable. While this problem has declined in recent years, at the time of this writing it just happened to me again recently. If this happens to you and you're in the middle of a project, it can be very frustrating and consume many hours as you try to restore or reinstall Eclipse. The only real remedy is to be sure to back up Eclipse before you perform any installation or removal. If the change breaks Eclipse, simply restore from your backup.

- *Use the F3 key to open class definitions*: If you are looking at a file that contains a reference to the JFactory class, for example, selecting that word and then pressing the F3 key will open the file that contains its definition (in this case, factory.php). This feature is very useful for navigating the Joomla library structure.

Eclipse also has excellent help resources available on the Web. You can look at the Eclipse documentation (www.eclipse.org/documentation) or ask a question in the community forum (www.eclipse.org/forums), where other Eclipse users are very helpful.

Using the NetBeans IDE

An alternative to Eclipse is the NetBeans IDE (http://netbeans.org). Also written in Java, I find NetBeans a bit more responsive and less cluttered than the Eclipse IDE. It contains most of the central features of Eclipse, although it lacks the tremendous library of plug-ins for PHP that are available to the Eclipse system.

Like Eclipse, NetBeans is free and open source. It is owned by Sun Microsystems, so it is well-supported and development is well-funded. New versions are released frequently and the opening screen bulletin system that announces new developments and tutorials is an excellent feature to keep you up-to-date.

NetBeans really shines when debugging Joomla applications. The single-step debugger with breakpoints, variable watches, and in-code debug reporting allows you to monitor the execution of the Joomla platform more easily and more quickly than the same functionality in Eclipse. Before you settle on Eclipse, give NetBeans a try.

Using the jEdit for Joomla Development

The cross-platform, open source, Java-based editor jEdit (http://www.jedit.org) provides an excellent tool to remotely edit your Joomla site files. There are many features of jEdit that aid in Joomla development, including a file project manager, an in-editor database browser, source code control, macro recording, XML processing, tag matching, a CSS editor, and an enormous number of plugins and extensions.

One extremely useful feature is jEdit's ability to do regular expression searches across an entire file directory tree. With the jEdit search box shown in Figure 10-9, you can search all of the files in a directory. Although there are programs on Linux such as grep that will perform this type of search, none are so user friendly.

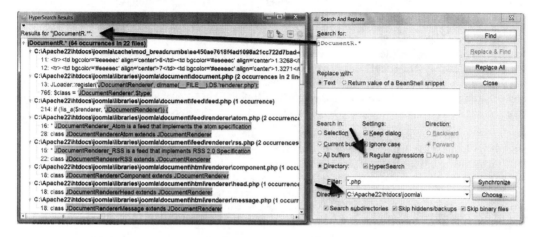

Figure 10-9. *The jEdit text editor allows for regular expression searches even to remote servers*

Additionally, the results window allows you to see the context of the found expression. With a single click, jEdit will open the file to the exact line where the search string was located. When looking for code in the core Joomla platform files, this type of expedience is fantastic.

Joomla Developer Site Overview

The Joomla Developer site (http://developer.joomla.org) is a very under-utilized resource for information. It contains numerous useful resources including:

- *Code repository information*: All of the Joomla code (including alpha releases) is stored in various Git repositories. The repository location and login information is available in the source code section (http://developer.joomla.org/code.html) of the developer site.

- *Bug tracker*: The bug tracker (http://joomlacode.org/gf/project/joomla/tracker/) has all of the resolved and unresolved bugs for each Joomla release.

- *API Reference*: Tremendously useful, the API Reference (http://api.joomla.org/li_Joomla-Framework.html) has all of the packages, classes, methods, and properties for the entire Joomla framework. Most have explanations of the functionality of the particular programming construct in plain language so it's understandable to a developer. For example, the description of the JController class reads "Controller (controllers are where you put all the actual code) Provides basic functionality, such as rendering views (aka displaying templates)."

- *Security Center*: The security center (http://developer.joomla.org/security.html) has all of the security bulletins and information relating to Joomla and site vulnerabilities.

There are also developer documentation, tutorials, reviews, and task list roadmaps for the future releases of Joomla. Be sure to add the Developer site to your bookmarks.

Conclusion

In this chapter, you were introduced to tools that can make your Joomla development much more effective. You learned to use Git for source code control for both custom extensions and making modifications to core Joomla files. You covered the general concepts of version control and the specific functionality of Git. Adopting version control in your development and design efforts can provide dramatic benefits when you need to retrieve a backup or historical version of a file. It also lets you see the differences between any number of versions of a file for debugging or code retrieval.

You learned to configure Eclipse and Netbeans to allow you to develop on Joomla and its individual extensions. You also saw how to configure these IDEs to access XDebug for single-step debugging of the Joomla platform. If you want to work on the Joomla core, there is no better way of learning it than tracing the execution of page renders on Joomla line-by-line.

In the next chapter, you will learn how to use code to manage the Joomla system. This is a place where you can use source code management to great effect.

CHAPTER 11

■ ■ ■

Creating Joomla Menus, Articles, and Categories with PHP

Once you've been using Joomla for any length of time, you will probably want a more effective method of bulk creating objects such as menus and articles than directly through the user interface. While the user interface is effective when you need to create a small number of items or you need to make minor improvements to an existing site, large changes or bulk site configurations require something more powerful.

There are literally hundreds of reasons for programmatic or batch creation of Joomla items; here are a few sample cases:

- The creation of a dozen menus, one for each month of the year. For an archive, perhaps you need to create multiple years with one for each month.

- An existing static web site needs to be converted to Joomla and you would like to take all of the individual HTML pages and generate a Joomla article from each one of them. Copying and pasting each page by hand with the additional overhead of working through the Joomla article interface makes this task impossible with the resources you have available.

- A list of ten items is copied from another document and you need to create menus from that clipboard list. Creating each menu by hand would be literally about a 30-step process and you need to create 10 new menus every week.

- Importing all of your recipes from an existing database and creating individual Joomla articles for each recipe so they can be shared easily and managed online.

- There is a common article template that is to be used for 100 articles that will be farmed out to individual writers, so the blank articles need to be created that have all the boilerplate formatting and text.

- Now that Joomla can handle more than two levels of category depth, you want to convert the entire site to match the tree structure of the products that are organized in your company's product catalog. Manually creating all of these tree branches and nodes would be a long process—but you have the tree in a text file that an automated script could use to create the nodes.

- For best SEO, you want to control the exact names of the menus where you would normally let the Joomla system handle things automatically. For this batch of prominent items, you need to create custom alias menus that will have an exact URL that occurs at the root of the system (for example, `http://www.example.com/my-cobrand-a`).

For any of these tasks, it would quickly become tedious to create each item individually. Beyond a half-dozen or so items, it becomes a time-consuming process to create items manually. And even worse, the greater the number of similar items you create, the more likely a mistake will be made when repetitiously creating all of them.

This chapter will teach you how you can use code to create the key Joomla objects including articles, menus, and categories. By directly programming the item creation system, you can quickly and easily create macro type functions to perform batch processes or a complete extension to provide custom item creation that matches your workflow process.

With this type of code-based item creation, you could augment your Joomla site to provide capabilities that allows external interfacing to the system such as building an extension that allows menu editing through a custom iPhone application. Once you understand the basics of the Joomla object system, you can create any type of automated functionality that you might need.

Creating an Article Through Code

To access the Joomla system through code, we'll begin with the cornerstone of every Joomla site: the article. In this section, you'll create a basic article template that you can use for fast and simple formatted article creation. Let's face it—creating individual article templates and formatting each one can take a great deal of time that could be better spent writing. What if we made a simple form with the necessary fields so the article could be written in plain text and then our macro could perform the layout for us?

Articles produced through such a system would gain several benefits:

- Authoring speed would be greatly increased because the writer could simply fill in the fields for the various content without having to manually select and format parts of the article.

- The writing environment can be adjusted to the individual writer preferences, such as font size, so editing can be performed with any desired display without affecting the final presentation of the article.

- All articles would use the same stylesheet formatting selections so the presentation of such articles could be changed site-wide easily.

- If you have contributors to your Joomla site, this provides a useful way that those authors can write their articles without having to worry about formatting conventions. At the same time, your article creator component can take this text and properly format the HTML or xHTML that conforms to the rest of the site.

- Each article could have an image field that requires choosing appropriate clip art to represent the article. This image could be automatically resized into a thumbnail to represent the article and could be explicitly included in Facebook OpenGraph tags.

- The editor could inject appropriate JavaScript such as Expand/Collapse or Tooltips that apply to particular fields for each article.

You will create a simple component that uses a preset number of fields and creates and edits articles in this style. You can expand and extend the extension to add any functionality required for your application.

This extension will use the Model-View-Controller architecture adopted by the rest of the Joomla system. Using this structure helps you leverage a great deal of functionality that has been built into the Joomla infrastructure. While not all extensions in this book use this structure, that is primarily dictated by the difficulty in communicating basic program ideas across the many-file structure of this MVC system. This article creation extension will provide a basic model that you can use for your other projects.

Creating the Main Component File

Start by creating an `articlestencil/` folder that will hold the code and subfolders. You can create this folder anywhere on your system—generally outside the Joomla directory. We'll need to create the basic extension and then install it into the Joomla system where we can work on it.

When complete, the file and folder structure of the extension should appear like this:

- com_articlestencil/
  - articlestencil.php
  - controller.php
    - views/
      - form/
        - view.html.php
        - tmpl/
          - default.php
  - models/
    - stencil.php

First, create the XML descriptor file `articlestencil.xml` and add the following code:

```xml
<?xml version="1.0" encoding="utf-8"?>
<extension type="component" version="2.5.0">
    <name>Article Stencil</name>
    <creationDate>March 2013</creationDate>
    272103_1_EnDan Rahmel</author>
    <authorUrl>http://www.joomlajumpstart.com</authorUrl>
    <version>0.1.0</version>
    <description>Component that allows fast article creation
    for blog entries and article placeholders.
    </description>

    <files>
        <filename>articlestencil.php</filename>
        <filename>articlestencil.xml</filename>
        <filename>index.html</filename>
        <folder>models</folder>
        <folder>views</folder>
    </files>
    <administration>
    <!-- Administration Menu Section -->
        <menu>Article Injector</menu>
        <files>
            <filename>index.html</filename>
        </files>
    </administration>
    <media destination="com_articleinjector" folder="media">
        <filename>index.html</filename>
    </media>
</extension>
```

Save this file at the root of the component folder. The `<folder>` tags will include all of the subfiles within the folders.

You will need to create an extension with a main file named `articlestencil.php`. The Joomla system enforces particular naming standards on files and the classes they contain so the system can effectively find the appropriate class without a custom method registration system. Be sure to carefully name your extension at the beginning or you will need to change a number of class names to allow for a new component name.

In this case, our file must be named `articlestencil.php` where the file name is identical to the component name aside from the removal of the `com_` prefix. Our main component file will be small because it need only perform the framework setup and then execute the requested function on the component controller.

Enter the code shown in Listing 11-1 and save it with the file name `articlestencil.php` at the root of the component directory.

Listing 11-1. The `articlestencil.php` file will be the only file called by the Joomla system—all other files are support files

```php
<?php
defined('_JEXEC') or die;

// Execute the task.
$controller     = JController::getInstance('ArticleStencil');
// Set default controller task to "display"
$app = JFactory::getApplication();
$controller->execute($app->input->get('task','display'));
$controller->redirect();
```

The code of this file is very simple. Once the code establishes that it is executing within the Joomla context (by checking the _JEXEC constant), the JController static class is executed to load the controller for this component. By default, it will execute the *display* task to present the proper view, but it will also execute a different task action if the request contains it.

The final call to the `redirect()` method will perform a redirect if it is needed. Many component developers favor an execution process where a form submission activates a save or update of the necessary form data and then performs a redirect back to the display task to handle the presentation of the record after the save.

In the interest of brevity, our component will save the record and then simply internally call the view display function to present the form with the saved data. For this controller, that save or update of the data will be handled by the *insert* task that allows a record to be saved to the database.

Building the Controller

The controller contains all of the core logic for the component. It receives tasks such as *display* or *insert* and handles them. The controller is the main switchboard of the extension in that it controls what is actually executed. All of the core logic is held in the controller, making it easier to debug because the internal logic of a component (such as calculating an amortization schedule in a finance application) should only reside here; it should never appear in the model or view code.

Executing a controller typically proceeds in the following sequence:

1. The system determines the name of the requested task and executes the identically named method in the controller class. To add additional tasks, simply add appropriately named methods to the class and they will automatically be available for request execution.

2. The method performs any necessary calculations or processing. This may include set up of a Model object that can access the database or other data source and pass information to the necessary view.

3. Selects the appropriate view for display of a particular request. The view provides the actual display HTML and presentation logic. A different view may even be selected for the same task. For example, the request of display may include formatting parameters (such as HTML vs. xHTML) that allows the controller to select the appropriate view.

4. Makes a call to the method to actually display the specified view. Views are objects managed by the Joomla system, so the method call will request the render of the view.

Seldom does the controller deviate from this execution model. For some controller methods, they may call other controller methods when logic is shared between one or more of the tasks. Otherwise, most of the controller code you will find in the Joomla system will follow this pattern.

DATA DOES NOT PASS DIRECTLY FROM THE CONTROLLER TO THE VIEW

One important thing to understand about the separation of controller logic and the view: **they are not made to pass data directly between them**. For example, if the controller included logic to display an article, it would not simply pass the text of the article to the view for display in a variable. Instead, the controller must request the data be populated into a *model* that is an abstract of data access. The controller can then assign this model to a view and the view can read data from the model.

This may seem overly complex, but it allows even small components to be built with an eye toward a broader reach in the future. For example, in our component, the model will access an article through the Joomla framework and store the article there. But what if the implementation details of the Joomla article access were to change? Or what if you wanted the component to also write articles into a different format such as saving articles to a WordPress site?

By using a model, the application would not need to be rewritten to accommodate a different or altered data source. Simply modifying the model portion of the component or adding another model would allow the extensions to seamlessly accommodate the change. That means that the component can interface with new or modified data access types by changing only one of the three parts of the component.

For many components, this functionality will likely be used to expand the data source possibilities to interface to Microsoft SQL Server, Oracle, or other backend server systems.

For the Article Stencil component, the controller uses a simple model to pass the basic article data to the view. Data is supplied both from the Joomla objects for the particular type of objects used by the component (in this case, the article object) and from the form data submitted by the user during an article posting.

One of the great things about the Joomla object storage system is that by simply leaving the id property empty or setting it to a null value, Joomla will automatically create a new table row entry. If it finds an id, it will presume this operation is an update and handle the data accordingly. Therefore, to create any type of script that copies items, you can simply load an existing record into a Joomla object, clear the id property, and execute the store() method, which will save a new record.

As shown in Listing 11-2, the controller class file begins the same way as the main component file, assuring the run context. The class name of the controller must match the name of the component and add the suffix of Controller so the controller library can find it properly.

Listing 11-2. *The controller logic is stored in the* controller.php *file with the* display() *method as the default execution task*

```php
<?php
defined('_JEXEC') or die;

class ArticleStencilController extends JControllerLegacy
{
    protected $_modelSet = false;

    public function display($cachable = false, $urlparams = array()) {
        $app = JFactory::getApplication();

        // Get the view name from the request or use the default "form"
        $viewType = $app->input->getWord('view', 'form');
        $app->input->set('view', $viewType);

        $document = JFactory::getDocument();
        $vFormat     = $document->getType();
        $view = $this->getView($viewType, $vFormat);
        $model = $this->getModel('Stencil');
        $model->storeFormVars();
        $view->setModel($model);

        $user = JFactory::getUser();

        if($user->get('id') ||
            ($app->input->getMethod() == 'POST' && $viewType = 'category' )) {
            $cachable = false;
        }

        $safeurlparams = array('id'=>'INT','limit'=>'INT','limitstart'=>'INT',
            'filter_order'=>'CMD','filter_order_Dir'=>'CMD');

        parent::display($cachable,$safeurlparams);
    }

    function insert() {
        $app = JFactory::getApplication();
        $viewType = $app->input->getWord('view', 'form');
        $app->input->set('view', $viewType);
        $model = $this->getModel('Stencil');
        $model->storeFormVars();

        $this->_modelSet = true;
        $this->display();
        $db = JFactory::getDbo();
        $user = JFactory::getUser();
        $app = JFactory::getApplication();
        // Check if the user access object for the user
        $canPublish = $user->authorise('core.create','com_content');
```

```php
// load the category
$catID = 1;
$cat = JTable::getInstance('category');
$cat->load($catID);

// Include the content plugins for the onSave events.
JPluginHelper::importPlugin('content');

$title = $app->input->get('title');
$text = $app->input->get('text');
$category = $app->input->get('category');

// Get an empty article object
$article = JTable::getInstance('content');
$value = 0;
if ($value) {
    $article->load($value);
}
$article->title = $title;
$article->alias = strtolower(str_replace(' ','-',$title));
$article->introtext = $text;
$article->fulltext = '';

$article->catid = $catID;
// At the time of this writing, these had no default values,
// so needed to be sent through
$article->images = '';
$article->urls = '';
$article->attribs = '';
$article->metakey = '';
$article->metadesc = '';
$article->metadata = '';
$article->language = '';
$article->xreference = '';

$date = JFactory::getDate();

$article->created = $date->toSql();
$article->created_by = $user->get('id');

$article->publish_up = $date->toSql();
$article->publish_down = $db->getNullDate();
$article->state = ($canPublish) ? 1 : 0;

if (!$article->check()) {
    echo JText::_('Post check failed');
    return false;
}
```

```
        $article->version++;
        $result = $article->store();

        // At the time of this writing, JRoute isn't working properly
        //$articleURL = JRoute::_('index.php?option=com_content&id='.$article->id);
        $articleURL = '/joomla16/index.php?option=com_content&view=article&Itemid=1&id='
            .$article->id;
        // create a new content item
        echo json_encode(array('id'=>$article->id,'title'=>$title,'text'=>$text,
            'category'=>$category,'url'=>$articleURL));
    }
}
```

The controller only has two methods: display() and insert(). The display() method is the default call of the controller and the insert() method is called from the form that is rendered by the display method. Many of the basic components that you create will only need these two methods, while some may add a third method—delete()—to remove a previous entry. This controller doesn't include a delete method to keep the controller simple.

The display() method populates the model of the component with either existing data or it retrieves the necessary information from the database. The execution begins by using the getWord() method on the input object to determine the type of form that will be displayed. The method uses the getModel() call to load the variable data about the current stencil through the database model. The storeFormVars() method is used to populate the form variables that will be used to show the form.

The $safeurlparams are used to specify the names of the various acceptable parameters and select their type for safe processing. This step is important in the security of many applications. By selecting exactly the parameters expected by the extension, you minimize the possibility that extraneous parameters may somehow be sent into the system by a hacker. By forcing type selection, the hacking techniques such as buffer overflow and SQL injection attacks are all but eliminated. These safe parameters are then processed by the controller when the view display is invoked.

The insert() method handles any write requests necessary to store the posted form data to the article database. You can see that the setup of the method mirrors the parameter input and model creation of the display() method. After the setup, the specific inputs for the stencil are read (from posted fields such as title, text, and category). An empty article is then instantiated to hold the input data. If the article already exists, the Joomla article library routines load the data of the article.

Whether it is a new article or an existing article, the input parameters are written into the article object. The check() method is invoked to make sure that the data input is valid. If the data is valid, the store() method is called, which will check the id property and, if populated, it will handle the store as an update, while an article object missing an article ID is inserted as a new article. Once the store is complete, the information (including the URL reference to the article) is returned as JSON data for the Ajax call to process and display in the view.

To make all of this possible, we need to construct a model for the database table so the Joomla system can properly load and manage the stencil data.

Creating a Model for Data Access

For most components, the model layer handles the necessary database access for the extension. Because all database access is already handled by the Joomla article library, a model is unnecessary for that function. In our component, the model is used simply to handle processing of the information posted by the form and act as a go-between to pass data from the controller to the view.

The model class shown in Listing 11-3 will accept data from the form submission, clean the various passed data, and make it available to the view.

Listing 11-3. The model code for the Article Stencil compononent is used mostly as a go-between for the controller to the view

```php
<?php
// No direct access
defined('_JEXEC') or die;

<?php
// No direct access
defined('_JEXEC') or die;

class ArticleStencilModelStencil extends JModelItem {
    protected $_context = 'com_articlestencil.stencil';
    protected $_cleanVars = array();
    protected $_previewStr = '';

    public function _populateState() {
        $app = JFactory::getApplication();
        $params = $app->getParams();
        return;
        // Load the object state.
        $id = JRequest::getInt('id');
        $this->setState('weblink.id', $id);

        // Load the parameters.
        $this->setState('params', $params);
    }

    public function storeFormVars() {
        $previewStr = '';
        $cleanVars = array();
        // These are the fields that may come through the form POST
        $fields = array('title','htmlintrotext', 'htmlbodytext','keyword1', 'keyword2','keyword3',
            'resource1_title','resource1_url',
            'resource2_title','resource2_url',
            'resource3_title','resource3_url'
            );
        // For the intro and body text, we'll allow these tags to be used
        $allowableTags = '<b><i><p><a><br><br/><hr><hr/><ul><li><img>';
        // Loop through the fields and see if any of the post variables match the expected fields
        foreach($fields as $field) {
            $temp = '';
            if(isset($_POST[$field])) {
                if(substr($field,0,4)=='html') {
                    $temp = trim(strip_tags($_POST[$field],$allowableTags));
                } else {
                    $temp = trim(strip_tags($_POST[$field]));
                }
            }
            $cleanVars[$field] = $temp;
        }
```

```php
        // Create a preview of the article that will be posted
        if(isset($_POST['stencil_submit']) && $_POST['stencil_submit']=='1') {
            foreach($cleanVars as $key => $data) {
                $tempStyle = empty($data) ? ' style="display:none" ' : '';
                $previewStr .= "<div class='$key' $tempStyle>";
                $previewStr .= $data;
                $previewStr .= "</div>\n";
            }
        }
        $this->_previewStr = $previewStr;
        $this->_cleanVars = $cleanVars;
    }
    public function getCleanVars() {
        return $this->_cleanVars;
    }
    public function getPreviewStr() {
        return $this->_previewStr;
    }

}
```

A majority of the code in this model handles the form data. The private method _populateState() loads the default state of the model object and stores the requested id of the particular model in the object. The storeFormVars() method does most of the work because it specifies what data fields can be used that come through the post variables. The model class is subclassed from the JModelItem class included in the Joomla system and inherits all of the functionality that has been added to that class.

The fields are each examined and sanitized individually. If the stencil accepts HTML, a list of acceptable tags (such as bold, italic, and other formatting tags) are ignored, while all other tags are stripped. If there is no acceptable HTML, then all tags are preemptively stripped from the text. Once the fields are cleaned, the HTML preview for the stencil is returned by the method.

Most models include the necessary file, cache, or database access logic. Because we're using existing Joomla structures, that type of code is not needed in our model. Our model is kept very simple and uses most of the existing logic provided by the parent class.

■ **Note** Generally, you want to use a model to abstract the data access from the extension. This example provides an example of that functionality only in terms of the form posting data. For a complete example of these concepts, take a look at the models used by the core Joomla newsfeed extension in the /components/com_newsfeeds/models directory. The category.php file is particularly instructive because it even includes methods that build a data structure used especially by the presentation layer of the component.

Creating the view.html.php File

The view of a component displays the HTML for user interaction. The view is made up of several parts—most notably the view logic contained in the view.html.php file that performs any necessary model access and makes a selection of the final presentation template.

```php
<?php
// No direct access
defined('_JEXEC') or die;
```

```php
class ArticleStencilViewForm extends JViewLegacy {
    protected $previewStr = null;
    protected $cleanTags = null;

    function display($tpl = null) {
        // Check for errors.
        if (count($errors = $this->get('Errors'))) {
            JError::raiseWarning(500, implode("\n", $errors));
            return false;
        }
        $model = $this->getModel('Stencil');
        $model->storeFormVars();
        // Clean the variables for HTML display
        $cleanVars = $model->getCleanVars();
        $this->assignRef('cleanVars',$cleanVars);
        $this->assign('previewStr',$model->getPreviewStr());
        // Assign variables to the view for use in the template
        $this->_prepareDocument();

        parent::display($tpl);
    }

    protected function _prepareDocument()
    {
        $app = JFactory::getApplication();
        $menus = $app->getMenu();
        $title = null;

        // Because the application sets a default page title,
        // we need to get it from the menu item itself
        $menu = $menus->getActive();
        if($menu) {
            $this->params->def('page_heading',
                $this->params->get('page_title', $menu->title));
        }
        $title = $this->params->get('page_title');
        if (empty($title)) {
            $title = htmlspecialchars_decode($app->getCfg('sitename'));
        }
        $this->document->setTitle($title);
    }
}
```

The view code should hold all of the logic needed to display the information held in the model. Even on the view level, separating the processing logic from the display logic will assist in later maintainability. The display() method instantiates the model to obtain the data. The model methods that we created in the last section are used to clean the variables and prepare the preview. Note that the assignRef() method will assign a reference to the selected data structure to the current view, while the assign() method makes a copy of the specified data or constant. The assignRef() method is useful because the data structure is large so that multiple copies are not created in memory (the passed reference allows the template to operate on the same data object that was created in this method).

The _prepareDocument() method creates the necessary aspects of the view such as the page title so the user's browser will display it correctly. Generally, this method is also used to add any special metadata to the head section. For example, many widgets (such as the Facebook Like button) use meta tags that are injected to send information to a third party API. In this case, we only set the title of the document so the browser tab (and history) will display correctly.

You can see that there isn't any actual HTML in view.html.php because the final display occurs in the view template.

Creating the View Template

The view template is the file that contains the HTML that is actually sent to the browser as well as any display-time logic (such as a PHP loop to output the rows of a table). As you've seen in Chapter 4, you can override this view with a custom template override. Joomla uses PHP in template files for maximum performance.

■ **Note**   Some other CMS systems use templating engines such as Smarty (www.smarty.net) or Template Lite (http://templatelite.sourceforge.net) instead of raw PHP because the template systems can slightly simplify the logic that must go into the final presentation execution. However, the trade-off of rendering speed and learning a "template language" is generally not worth the slight simplification that a templating system can bring. There is no question that optimized PHP code (especially when a system such as APC is active on the server) is substantially faster than even the best templating system.

Listing 11-4 shows the template, which consists almost entirely of HTML with small snippets of PHP code to echo variables into the output. Create the file default.php and save it in the path views/form/tmpl:

Listing 11-4. The view template holds the presentation HTML code of the form

```php
<?php
// no direct access
defined('_JEXEC') or die;

JHtml::addIncludePath(JPATH_COMPONENT.'/helpers');
// If the page class is defined, wrap the whole output in a div.
$pageClass = ''; //$this->params->get('pageclass_sfx');
?>
<h1>Article Template</h1>
<form id="inputArea" method="post"
    action="/index.php?option=com_articlestencil&task=insert&view=form">
    <input type="hidden" name="stencil_submit" id="stencil_submit" value="1" />
    <input type="submit"/>
    <div class="title">
        <h2>Task</h2>
        <input name="title" type="text" style="width:100%"
            value="<?php echo $this->cleanVars['title']; ?>"/>
    </div>
    <div>
        <div class="section">
            <h2>Description</h2>
```

```
        <textarea name="htmlintrotext" id="htmlintrotext"
            cols="80" rows="3">
                <?php echo $this->cleanVars['htmlintrotext']; ?></textarea>
</div>
<div class="section">
    <h2>Deliverables</h2>
    <p>1. <input type="text" name="deliverable1" id="deliverable1"
        style="width:90%"
        value="<?php echo $this->cleanVars['keyword1']; ?>" /></p>
    <p>2. <input type="text" name="deliverable2" id="deliverable2"
        style="width:90%"
        value="<?php echo $this->cleanVars['keyword1']; ?>" /></p>
    <p>3. <input type="text" name="deliverable3" id="deliverable3"
        style="width:90%"
        value="<?php echo $this->cleanVars['keyword1']; ?>" /></p>
</div>
<div class="section">
    <h2>Subtasks</h2>
    <p>1. <input type="text" name="subtask1" id="subtask1"
        style="width:90%"
        value="<?php echo $this->cleanVars['keyword1']; ?>" /></p>
    <p>2. <input type="text" name="subtask2" id="subtask2"
        style="width:90%"
        value="<?php echo $this->cleanVars['keyword1']; ?>" /></p>
    <p>3. <input type="text" name="subtask3" id="subtask3"
        style="width:90%"
        value="<?php echo $this->cleanVars['keyword1']; ?>" /></p>
</div>
<div class="section">
    <h2>Relevant files</h2>
    <input type="text" name="relevant1" id="relevant1"
        value="<?php echo $this->cleanVars['keyword1']; ?>" />
    <input type="text" name="relevant2" id="relevant2"
        value="<?php echo $this->cleanVars['keyword2']; ?>" />
    <input type="text" name="relevant3" id="relevant3"
        value="<?php echo $this->cleanVars['keyword3']; ?>" />
</div>
<div class="section">
    <h2>Details</h2>
    <div>
        <label for="resource1_title">Level of Effort</label>
        <input type="text" name="resource1_loe" id="resource1_loe"
            size="8"
            value="<?php echo $this->cleanVars['resource1_loe']; ?>" />
        <label for="resource1_url">Points</label>
        <input type="text" name="resource1_points" id="resource1_points"
            size="8"
            value="<?php echo $this->cleanVars['resource1_points']; ?>" />
        <label for="resource1_url">Estimated Time</label>
        <input type="text" name="resource1_esttime" id="resource1_esttime"
            size="8"
```

```
                    value="<?php echo $this->cleanVars['resource1_esttime']; ?>" />
                <label for="resource1_url">Priority</label>
                <input type="text" name="resource1_pri" id="resource1_pri"
                    size="4"
                    value="<?php echo $this->cleanVars['resource1_pri']; ?>" />
                <div>
                <label for="resource1_url">Possible Problems</label>
                <input type="text" name="resource1_probs" id="resource1_probs"
                    size="40"
                    value="<?php echo $this->cleanVars['resource1_probs']; ?>" />
                </div>
                <div>
                <label for="resource1_url">Comments</label>
                <input type="text" name="resource1_comments" id="resource1_comments"
                    size="40"
                    value="<?php echo $this->cleanVars['resource1_comments']; ?>" />
                </div>
            </div>
        </div>
    </div>

</form>
<hr/>
<?php echo $this->previewStr; ?>
```

The view code contains the actual HTML of the stencil. In this case, you'll notice all of the fields that we specified in the allowable fields of the controller. Each field is provided to allow input values to be entered by the user of the form. The form itself is simply a number of input fields that will include any values that have already been entered (where the echo commands output the various cleaned variables). Below the form, you can see the previewStr that was composed by the main view code is output to display how the stencil will actually appear.

When you have all of the pieces saved, use the install from directory option to install the component. If you're not running your Joomla development system on a local machine, zip and upload the component into the Joomla system.

In your browser, access this URL, substituting the local.joomapples.com with the domain entry of your Joomla installation:

```
http://local.joomapples.com/index.php?option=com_articlestencil&
    task=display&view=form
```

Once you are logged in to Joomla, the component will display the input form, as shown in Figure 11-1. You can quickly enter a new article or, if you know the ID of an existing article created by the stencil component, you can load that one.

Article Template

Submit

Task

Description

Deliverables

1.

2.

3.

Subtasks

1.

Figure 11-1. *The article input form allows fast entry of standardized article content*

After you use the component stencil a few times, you will understand how much more quickly you can author formatted content than using the traditional Article Manager. That helps you focus on the information you want to convey instead of the formatting that is tedious to do properly for every article.

■ **Note** Keep in mind that the different object types vary primarily in the types of parameters that are required for initial creation. That means that you can readily adapt this code for almost any other object type. All of the standard objects that write to the database use the load() and store() methods for retrieving and saving object information, respectively. You can find the definitions of the various objects in the subdirectories contained in the /libraries/joomla directory. For example, in the /libraries/joomla/database/table/content.php file, you'll find the class that is used to interface with the jos_content table that is used to store documents. In that same folder, you'll find classes to interface to the menu, category, language, session, user, and other table types. Examining the code for these classes is very useful to learn of the minimum requirements and restrictions of the object types.

Creating a Menu Through Code

Although creating articles through code is the most common need of a site administrator, having the power to create other Joomla entities such as menus through code can be nearly as useful. Because the entire visible structure of a Joomla site is determined by the organization of menus and many features of site configuration (such as module display and CSS class suffix) are determined at the menu level, having the ability to make batch changes through code takes Joomla to an entirely new level of site management sophistication.

Some Examples of Automated Menu Creation

You may need an automated way to create menus for:

- *Mass-create alias-based menus from a master menu*: If your site adopts the flexible organization of creating a master-menu backbone for the site, this can substantially increase the site organization. Creating the individual menu alias's that reference the identical branches of the master-menu can be very tedious. Writing a script to create the alias branches for you is a valuable time saver.

- *Organize archived articles for easy access*: When a site reaches a certain volume of articles, the web master may want to organize the archived articles by month and year. You could create a script to generate the menus for any number of from-to menus and organize the articles under the proper branch.

- *Generate a menu hierarchy from an existing tree*: You may have an existing custom web site that you are moving to the Joomla system. Creating an automated method of duplicating the existing site structure and moving content to the proper area can perhaps best be handled using a custom menu creation routine.

- *Reorganize a taxonomy for improved SEO*: Large sites tend to reorganize content occasionally to optimize the site for best search performance. If one category has hundreds of articles while another only contains a handful, this can hide valuable content within the mass of less useful content. With a custom menu creation routine, you can create new nodes easily to alleviate node congestion for better search performance.

- *Add or remove a single module from a majority of pages*: With pages that have custom module display settings (not the simple All or None settings), enabling or disabling a module across numerous menus can not only be difficult, but potentially dangerous to site functioning. Often, modules are selected for display out-of-order so one menu will have 60% of the modules selected while another may have a different assortment of 70% of the modules selected. A single click followed by a Save can destroy that entire custom selection for a menu. Having a macro that performs laser-like changes across many menus can be a life saver.

These are a few of the common reasons a Joomla site administrator may need to create an extension to generate or modify menus in bulk. Just as often, there are one-off reasons specific to a particular site where creating menus with code may come in handy. Implementation of a particular script may take under an hour and immediately save a half-dozen hours of manual, error-prone drudgery.

The extension capabilities presented in this section will be only a primitive implementation that demonstrates the basics of creating menus. Because the features of such an application will often be very specific to the specific purpose for which it is needed, this code is provided primarily to build upon. Similarly, such applications generally don't require a substantial user interface as they will be used only occasionally, so this example accepts the creation request through request string parameters much like an API.

Adding the insertMenu() Method to a Controller

Begin by creating a class that will contain the core functions for inserting menus. For these examples, we'll merely add an additional method to the Article Stencil class so you can quickly see how such functionality can work. If you need a more permanent implementation, simply create a new extension that contains this and other methods.

Open the articlestencil.php file of the Article Stencil extension and add the method shown in Listing 11-5. This simple code accepts parameters such as the title, alias, path, and link for a menu and dynamically creates that item. The code uses the input->get() method with defined default values, so all or none of the request parameters may be explicitly specified. The defaults will simply be used in each case where an explicit value has not been included.

Listing 11-5. This method, when added to a controller class, will accept request string parameters to create a new menu item

```
function insertMenu() {
        // Get an empty menu object
        $menu = &JTable::getInstance('menu');
        $menuID = $app->input->get('id','');
        if(!empty($menuID)) {
                $cat->load($menuID);
        }
        $menu->title = $app->input->get('title','');
        if($app->input->get('alias')) {
                $menu->alias = $app->input->get('alias');
        } else {
                $menu->alias = str_replace(' ','-',strtolower($cat->title));
        }
        $menu->menutype = $app->input->get('title','');
        $menu->path = $app->input->get('path','');
        $menu->link = $app->input->get('link', 'index.php?option=com_content&view=article&id=82');
        $menu->type = $app->input->get('type','component');

        $menu->published = $app->input->get('published',0);
        $menu->parent_id = $app->input->get('parent_id',1);
        $menu->level = $app->input->get('level',1);
        $menu->checked_out = 0;
        $menu->checked_out_time = '0000-00-00';
        $menu->params = $app->input->get('params','');
        $menu->img = $app->input->get('img','');
        $menu->component_id = $app->input->get('component_id',99);
        $result = $menu->store();
}
```

The code contains dummy values for settings such as the checked_out_time and link so that the item will insert properly. You will want to replace these with data specific to your application.

You can access the component with this URL:

```
http://local.joomapples.com/index.php?option=com_articlestencil&task=insertmenu
```

Inserting a menu is as easy as specifying a menu title. You can easily adapt this code to most menu creation needs. Note that this implementation is more of a proof-of-concept than real menu creation utility. Even an admin tool is likely to use a form to send these various parameters as a POST command. Alternately, you could add the menu creation capability as a separate class and place it in a library so one or more components could call it. By keeping the code here simple, you should be able to see how to use this effectively in the context where you might need it.

The third type of automated Joomla object creation, categories, will be the final type that you'll add to the Article Stencil extension. Batch category access and modification using the category objects can be particularly compelling when you need to read or write the entire category tree hierarchy.

Creating a Category Through Code

Since version 1.5, the Joomla team has added the ability to have more than two levels of organization for content (previously only sections and categories were available) so your site hierarchy can go much deeper than was possible before. Now categories are hierarchical, so you can nest them in a tree that has as much depth as desired. This presents the problem of reorganizing content to take advantage of the new tree possibilities.

Creating a category in code is very easy and can be an even more effective organizational method than creating specific menu entries. By combining all three item creation functions (article, menu, and category), you can script the system to create an article, place it in an appropriate category, and create a menu entry to this category. This sort of end-to-end possibility will likely be used a great deal as the web becomes more integrated through information sharing interfaces such as Facebook's implementation of the Open Graph protocol.

Navigating a tree structure can be difficult unless you use an advanced programming method known as *recursion*. Recursion is the process where a function or method can call itself in order to solve problems such as navigating a free-form tree hierarchy like the Joomla categories. You do not need to understand this difficult concept to use Joomla category creation, but it is important to mention it because most programs navigate trees using this method.

Before we can insert a new category, we need to know the parent of the category where we will be adding the new category. The parent defines where the category will appear on the taxonomy tree and therefore, the depth of the node. If the category node has no parent, that category is said to be a *root node*.

■ **Note** If you want to see how the category tree is organized, take a look at the jos_categories table in the Joomla database. You will see all of the categories listed there individually. You may have noticed the lft and rgt columns (that are abbreviations for "left" and "right"—which are reserved MySQL keywords) and the numbers they hold. To optimize category navigation, Joomla uses the Nested Set Model to organize the data for the category tree. This demonstrates one of the great advantages of using existing Joomla methods to create new items—the Joomla category object automatically handles the definition of these columns for you, so you don't even need to understand the tree traversal algorithm. If you're interested in learning more about the use of the Nested Set Model to organize hierarchical data in a MySQL database, check out the excellent tutorial at http://dev.mysql.com/tech-resources/articles/hierarchical-data.html, where you can read about this and other types of hierarchical data storage.

Like the previous tool, this one will be created as a barebones Joomla Administrator method. Add the method shown in Listing 11-6 to a Controller class so it can easily be called for example execution. Like the earlier insertMenu() method, you could easily convert this method to a method in a library class for calling by other batch functions.

Listing 11-6. You can add the insertCat() method to a Joomla controller for easy URL-based execution

```php
function insertCat() {
        $app = JFactory::getApplication();
        $cat = JTable::getInstance('category');
        // These are the minimum parameters you need
        $catID = $app->input->get('id','');
        if(!empty($catID)) {
                $cat->load($catID);
        }
        $cat->title = $app->input->get('title','');
        if($app->input->get('alias')) {
                $cat->alias = $app->input->get('alias');
        } else {
                $cat->alias = str_replace(' ','-',strtolower($cat->title));
        }
        $cat->metadesc = $app->input->get('metadesc','');
        $cat->metakey = $app->input->get('metakey','');
        $cat->metadata = $app->input->get('metadata','');
        $cat->language = $app->input->get('language','en_GB');
        $cat->extension = $app->input->get('extension','com_content');
        $cat->created_time = $app->input->get('created_time','0000-00-00');
        $cat->published = $app->input->get('published',0);
        $cat->parent_id = $app->input->get('parent_id',1);

        $result = $cat->store();
}
```

The Joomla framework class that holds the logic to create the Joomla category handles all of the details for creating the categories including inserting the necessary related rows into other tables. You can see that the code uses the getInstance() method of the JTable object to create an object instance of a category object. If an id value has come through the request, the load() method is used to retrieve the existing information about the category. The various fields are retrieved (and sanitized) through the get() method of the input object. You can see that a proper alias is created from the text of the category name.

By default, the category published field is set to unpublished, unless the user of the form has specified the contrary. If this component was being published to the Joomla extension directory, the defaults for most of the fields would be included as extension parameters so the site administrator could determine exactly the desired values without having to reset them all after initial insertion.

Conclusion

Inserting Joomla items through code can make a big difference in the set up and maintenance of a large-scale Joomla site. The ability to automate key processes that are traditionally done through the Administrator interface can mean the difference between launching a site on time and not. You can implement tasks that would be laborious and error-prone to complete to execute with a simple method call.

In this chapter, you learned how to create the three main items that make up a Joomla site: articles, menus, and categories. You can adapt the core projects that you created in this chapter to almost any administrative need from batch insertion of existing HTML pages to automatic menu organization restructuring via scripts or macros. In the next chapter, you'll create a variety of components (including the Article Librarian) that will further aid you in streamlining your administrative processes.

## CHAPTER 12

Creating Core Extensions

A tremendous advantage of programming in the robust language of PHP is access to the rich number of libraries that are included with the PHP system. Many of these can be harnessed to add functionality to Joomla. In this chapter, you'll construct several components that will significantly augment the capabilities of Joomla for both user-facing improvements and backend/administrator features.

In this chapter, you'll do the following:

- Create the Article Historian component that will store revisions of articles with each article update. The component will allow you to restore any previous version.

- Make the Form Builder component, which lets you quickly and easily create forms for input of user information. Whether you want to do a survey or accept newsletter user registration information, this component will help you to create these forms without any programming.

- Build a charts component that will enable you to create server-side charts for display to users. This component is most useful as a base for your own image applications, whether you need server-side image scaling or CAPTCHA generation.

Each of these components adds to the core functionality of a Joomla site. By creating reusable components such as these, you can expand the base of your site's capabilities. The Article Historian component, for example, could be repurposed for storing revisions of menus, site URL redirects, and any other information stored in the database. The extendable nature of each of these components provides a good model for how you might think about other custom Joomla development.

Creating the Article Historian component

Because Joomla lacks a version control system for content, updates to articles, menus, menu items, or any other Joomla data simply write over the previous version in the database. There is no way to examine an older version or revert the current item. This can be a bitter pill when an article is erroneously saved or an editor deletes pieces of content that can't be recovered.

The most common method of preventing loss of Joomla data has been to use an automated backup system that takes frequent snapshots of the production database. If content is lost, the database can be imported into a holding database and the lost content recovered. This process is tedious and unwieldy, and requires a fair amount of technical expertise. It is also overkill if you need to restore a single article and there were changes made to other data since the change.

If your Joomla site uses the MySQL 5 database for storing content, however, you can take advantage of a feature of MySQL technology called a *database trigger* to back up key information items for later recovery. A trigger is a small SQL routine that will run when a particular event such as an update or delete occurs. By adding a trigger to each content table that needs to record previous versions, you can create a simple version control system that prevents data from being lost.

The Article Historian component (see Figure 12-1) relies on a trigger to store a copy of each article before an update is made to the record. The component displays all the previous revisions of the article and allows you to restore an older version of the article. The key to the system is the setup of the trigger and the historical table that will store a copy of the article before the update occurs.

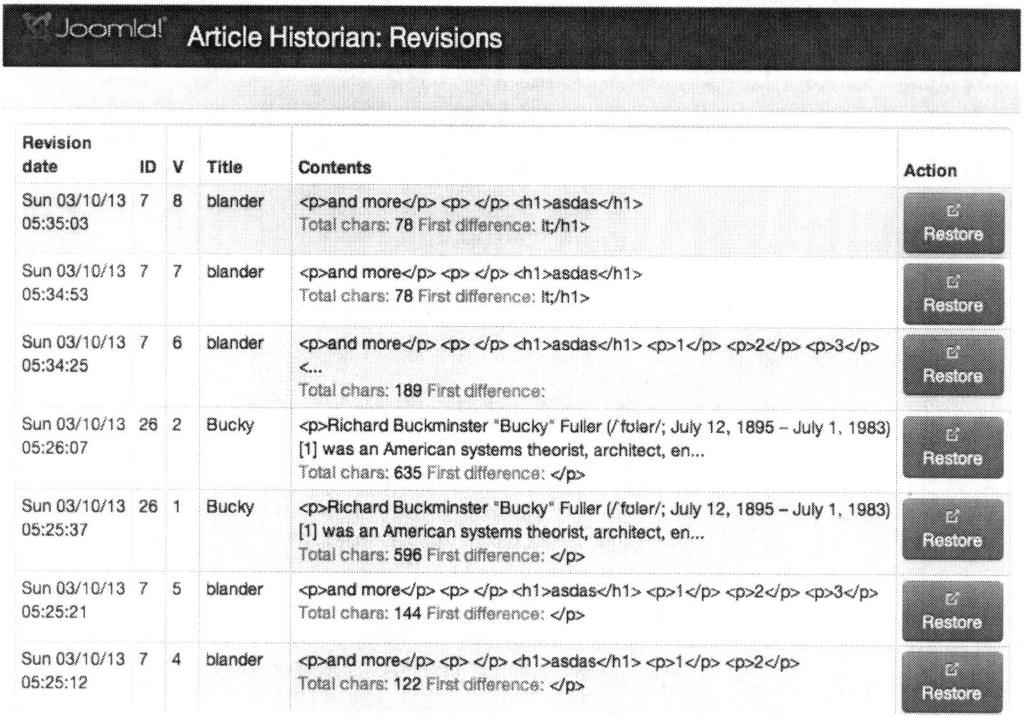

Revision date	ID	V	Title	Contents	Action
Sun 03/10/13 05:35:03	7	8	blander	\<p\>and more\</p\> \<p\> \</p\> \<h1\>asdas\</h1\> Total chars: 78 First difference: lt;/h1\>	Restore
Sun 03/10/13 05:34:53	7	7	blander	\<p\>and more\</p\> \<p\> \</p\> \<h1\>asdas\</h1\> Total chars: 78 First difference: lt;/h1\>	Restore
Sun 03/10/13 05:34:25	7	6	blander	\<p\>and more\</p\> \<p\> \</p\> \<h1\>asdas\</h1\> \<p\>1\</p\> \<p\>2\</p\> \<p\>3\</p\> \<... Total chars: 189 First difference:	Restore
Sun 03/10/13 05:26:07	26	2	Bucky	\<p\>Richard Buckminster "Bucky" Fuller (/ foler/; July 12, 1895 – July 1, 1983) [1] was an American systems theorist, architect, en... Total chars: 635 First difference: \</p\>	Restore
Sun 03/10/13 05:25:37	26	1	Bucky	\<p\>Richard Buckminster "Bucky" Fuller (/ foler/; July 12, 1895 – July 1, 1983) [1] was an American systems theorist, architect, en... Total chars: 596 First difference: \</p\>	Restore
Sun 03/10/13 05:25:21	7	5	blander	\<p\>and more\</p\> \<p\> \</p\> \<h1\>asdas\</h1\> \<p\>1\</p\> \<p\>2\</p\> \<p\>3\</p\> Total chars: 144 First difference: \</p\>	Restore
Sun 03/10/13 05:25:12	7	4	blander	\<p\>and more\</p\> \<p\> \</p\> \<h1\>asdas\</h1\> \<p\>1\</p\> \<p\>2\</p\> Total chars: 122 First difference: \</p\>	Restore

Figure 12-1. *The Article Historian displays previous versions of articles and allows you to restore one*

Duplicate the Joomla Article Table

To store past edits of your articles, you need to create a duplicate table of the article table (`jos_content`) and add an additional field (or column). Each row in the table will store all the standard article columns, but the table needs an additional `revision_date` column; otherwise, the identical key fields (in this case, the article id) of various revisions of the same article would conflict.

▪ **Note** This process will make a copy of the entire article when any update to the article occurs. If you have a large site with many revisions taking place, this could mean a large amount of extra storage will be used. In that case, you will need to manually prune the revision database often or set up an automatic job to do it for you. For most Joomla users, however, the extra space used will be trivial.

First use the LIKE statement of the CREATE TABLE command to duplicate that schema of the jos_content table like this (executing the SQL using either the command line or the phpMyAdmin web interface):

```
CREATE TABLE jos_content_history LIKE jos_content;
```
Once you execute this command, you'll have a table that has a database structure (or schema) that mirrors the current content table. We need to add a revision_date field to the table and alter the primary index to include the new column.

■ **Note** In the SQL statements, I have used the old jos_ prefix standard for the table names to simplify the text and increase readability. You will need to substitute your table prefix throughout the chapter for the jos_ prefix. You can find your current table prefix in the configuration.php set as the variable $dbprefix.

This table will be storing multiple versions of the same article (and therefore the same primary key id field). If you tried to insert the second version of the article row with an identical key into the table, it would create a conflict. By modifying the primary key to include both the id and the revision_date, every row written will be unique. Run this ALTER statement on the table:

```
ALTER TABLE 'jos_content_history'
  ADD COLUMN 'revision_date' DATETIME
  NOT NULL DEFAULT '0000-00-00 00:00:00' FIRST,
  MODIFY COLUMN 'id' INT(10) UNSIGNED NOT NULL,
  DROP PRIMARY KEY, ADD PRIMARY KEY (revision_date,id);
```

You now have a slightly modified copy of the jos_content table in the database. In the next step, you'll create a routine that automatically executes every time there is an update to the main content table.

Adding the Trigger to Store the Old Revision

Triggers in MySQL can be set to execute under three main conditions: INSERT, UPDATE, and DELETE. For each of these events, a trigger can be constructed to execute before or after the event. For the Article Historian, we need to create a trigger that will execute before the data in the jos_content table is changed so the old data can be saved before the new data writes over it.

Through the phpMyAdmin interface, execute the following SQL code to create the trigger:

```
DELIMITER $$

DROP TRIGGER IF EXISTS articlehistorian $$

CREATE TRIGGER articlehistorian
  BEFORE UPDATE ON jos_content
  FOR EACH ROW
    BEGIN
      IF NEW.version <> OLD.version THEN
        INSERT INTO jos_content_history
        (revision_date,'id','asset_id','title','alias','introtext',
        'fulltext', 'state','catid', 'created', 'created_by',
        'created_by_alias','modified','modified_by', 'checked_out',
        'checked_out_time', 'publish_up', 'publish_down', 'images',
```

```
      'urls','attribs','version','ordering','metakey', 'metadesc',
    'access','hits','metadata','featured','language', 'xreference')
     VALUES
    (now(),OLD.'id', OLD.'asset_id', OLD.'title', OLD.'alias',
    OLD.'introtext', OLD.'fulltext', OLD.'state', OLD.'catid',
    OLD.'created', OLD.'created_by', OLD.'created_by_alias',
    OLD.'modified', OLD.'modified_by', OLD.'checked_out',
    OLD.'checked_out_time', OLD.'publish_up', OLD.'publish_down',
    OLD.'images', OLD.'urls', OLD.'attribs', OLD.'version',
    OLD.'ordering', OLD.'metakey', OLD.'metadesc', OLD.'access',
    OLD.'hits', OLD.'metadata', OLD.'featured', OLD.'language',
    OLD.'xreference');
    END IF;
  END $$

DELIMITER ;
```

This trigger performs a simple check to make sure the Joomla version number has changed (which the Joomla system automatically increments with an article change) and, if so, copies the old values (before the update request) into the jos_content_history table. The version is checked so that other updates to the article row (such as recording the number of hits) are ignored. The trigger will duplicate all the existing values into the history table before the update occurs.

■ **Note** You must include all the column names individually in the trigger because the OLD. reference is required to access the older row. If, since the time of this book writing, the column names have changed (or additional columns have been added), execute the SHOW CREATE TABLE jos_content command against the MySQL server and it will display all the columns in the table. If there are any missing columns, just add them to the content history table and the previous trigger.

With the trigger in place, all older versions of the article will now be stored in the new jos_content_history table. I would suggest you make a change to an article in the Joomla Administrator interface and then query the jos_content_history table from phpMyAdmin. You should see a row containing the original version of the article from before it changed. By making changes and looking at the table, you can verify that the trigger is working properly.

Even without a nice user interface, the trigger is useful because you can use phpMyAdmin or other MySQL tools to recover past data and restore past articles. Even if you aren't going to immediately create and install the Article Historian component, I recommend setting up the trigger so all revisions of the article will be saved by the system.

■ **Note** You may wonder why the trigger presented here is not simply included in the installation script for automatic creation on the MySQL server during the extension install process. Creating triggers on a database requires root or super user access. You should not have Joomla accessing the database through the root account; it should have a separate limited MySQL account that doesn't have super user permissions. That way, if hackers ever obtain access to the Joomla configuration.php file, they don't have the root password with full control of the database.

Now that we have the trigger in place to save past revisions, let's create a component that can manage the revisions directly from the Joomla Administrator interface. The Article Historian component will allow an administrator to see all past article versions and selectively restore versions on a remote server at the click of a button.

Creating the Article Historian component

The Article Historian will list all the changes made to articles including their modification date, the ID of the article, the title, and an abbreviated excerpt of the beginning of the article. Through the interface, any revision of the article can be selected to replace the current version.

Because the trigger is in place to record any update, clicking the Restore button will replace the current version with an older revision, which automatically triggers a copy of the current version. Therefore, after a restore, even the current version that was replaced will become part of the revision history and can be restored at a later date if need be.

The Article Historian component will be an administrator component because only administrators need access to this functionality. To begin making the component, create a folder called com_article_historian/, in which all the files will reside. Within that folder, create a file called article_historian.php that will hold the standard controller functionality and start the file by entering the following:

```php
<?php
// no direct access
defined( '_JEXEC' ) or die( 'Restricted access' );

// Get request ID from query string variable
$task = JFactory::getApplication()->input->get('task','display');
switch($task) {
    case 'restore':
        JToolBarHelper::title(JText::_
            ('Article Historian: Restoring Version'));
        restoreRevision();
        break;
    default:
    case 'display':
        JToolBarHelper::title(JText::_
                    ('Article Historian: Revisions'));
        showRevisions();
        break;
}
```

This controller simply looks for two tasks: restore and display. The restore task calls the function that will restore a particular revision of an article. The display task renders a table that shows all the available revisions and their related information. The call to JToolBarHelper::title() will set the title of the window that is displayed automatically by the Joomla Administrator interface.

To the end of the article_historian.php file (after the switch() statement), add the function to read the current version for comparison:

```php
function getCurrentArticleVersion($id) {
        static $articles = array();
        if(isset($articles[$id])) {
                return $articles[$id];
        }
        $conf = JFactory::getConfig();
        $dbprefix = $conf->get('dbprefix');
        $db = JFactory::getDBO();
        $query = "SELECT introtext FROM {$dbprefix}content WHERE id = $id";
        $db->setQuery( $query, 0);
```

```
        if ($rows = $db->loadAssocList()) {
                $articles[$id] = $rows[0]['introtext'];
                return $articles[$id];
        }
        return '';
}
```

This function uses a static array to cache the text of the current version. That way, even if there are 20 revisions of the article, the current version is read only once from the database. If it is not in the static cache, then the introtext for the article is read into the array and returned to the calling function.

■ **Tip** In the sample code, the database prefix is retrieved from the configuration settings with the get() method. You can retrieve any configuration setting with this method. For MySQL statements, you could have alternately used the #_ operator in the query, which Joomla will automatically replace with the proper prefix. That would make the FROM statement appear like FROM #_content in the code.

Next, add the find_first_diff() function that is used to locate the first different between two versions for display in the interface:

```
function findFirstDiff($str1,$str2) {
        $len1 = strlen($str1);
        $len2 = strlen($str2);
        $max_len = max($len1,$len2);
        $found_diff = false;
        $diff = '';
        $pre_pos = 10;
        for($i=0;$i<$max_len;$i++) {
                $char1 = $i<$len1      ?      substr($str1,$i,1)      :      '';
                $char2 = $i<$len2      ?      substr($str2,$i,1)      :      '';
                if($char1!=$char2) {
                        if(!$found_diff) {
                                $found_diff = true;
                                $start_pos = max(0,$i-$pre_pos);
                                $diff = substr($str1,$start_pos,$pre_pos)
                                        ."<span  class='text-info'>";
                        }
                        $diff .= $char1;
                }
        }
        if($found_diff) {
                $diff .= "</span>";
        }
        return $diff;
}
```

This function performs a simple character-by-character search for the difference and then returns some of the changes in a highlighted span. This small function can help the user see exactly what differences exist between the revisions. A more robust version of the component might include a complete diff of the two articles (with a library such as PHP Diff at https://github.com/chrisboulton/php-diff), but full diffing is a complicated process and beyond the scope of this extension.

Next, add the cleanString() function that is used to create the display of the excerpt of the article in the interface:

```
function cleanString($in,$strip_string=false) {
        if($strip_string) {
                // Strip all the HTML from the article text
                $in = strip_tags($in);
                // Strip all non-alpha, numeric, or punctuation
                $in = preg_replace(
                        "/[^a-zA-Z0-9 .?!$()\'\"]/", "", $in);
        } else {
                $in = htmlspecialchars($in,ENT_QUOTES);
        }
        return $in;
}
```

This function can either be used to strip everything away so only the alphanumeric text is displayed or it can HTML encode the characters so the HTML tags such as <p> and <li> will be displayed as text by the system. The HTML encoding is the default used by the function.

To simplify the code, we won't create a Model-View-Controller (MVC) structure for this component. We'll let the code output a simple table. To the article_historian.php file, add the display function:

```
function showRevisions() {
    $max_intro = 150;
    $conf = JFactory::getConfig();
    $dbprefix = $conf->get('dbprefix');
    $componentURL = "/administrator/index.php?option=com_articlehistorian&";
    // Get instance of database object
    $db = JFactory::getDBO();
    // Create query to return id, title, and text of article
    $query = "SELECT UNIX_TIMESTAMP(revision_date)
        ts,id,version,title,introtext
        FROM {$dbprefix}content_history
        ORDER BY revision_date DESC, id
        LIMIT 100";
    $db->setQuery( $query, 0);
    // Execute query
    if ($rows = $db->loadAssocList()) {
        echo "<table class='table table-striped table-bordered table-hover table-condensed'>";
        echo "<tbody>";
        echo "<thead><tr>
            <th>Revision date</th>
            <th>ID</th>
            <th>V</th>
            <th>Title</th>
            <th>Contents</th>
            <th>Action</th>
            </tr></thead>";
```

```php
            $lastID = -1;
            $btn_style = '';
            foreach($rows as $row) {
                $id = $row['id'];
                if($id!=$lastID) {
                    $btn_style = ($btn_style=='btn-info') ? 'btn-success'
                        : 'btn-info';
                    $lastID = $id;
                }
                $current = getCurrentArticleVersion($id);
                $current = cleanString($current);
                // Load article title and text into variables
                $articleTitle = $row['title'];
                $articleBody = cleanString($row['introtext']);
                $articleVersion = $row['version'];
                $total_chars = strlen($articleBody);
                $diff = findFirstDiff($articleBody,$current);
                // If length is > $max_intro, truncate length
                if(strlen($articleBody) > $max_intro) {
                    $articleBody = substr($articleBody, 0,
                    $max_intro).'...';
                }
                echo "<tr>";
                //$ts = strtotime($row->revision_date);
                $ts = $row['ts'];
                $dateStr = date('D m/d/y h:i:s',$ts);
                echo "<td>{$dateStr}</td>";
                echo "<td>{$row['id']}</td>";
                echo "<td>{$articleVersion}</td>";
                echo "<td>$articleTitle</td>";
                echo "<td><div>$articleBody</div>"
                    . "<div><span class='muted'>Total chars:</span>"
                    . " {$total_chars} <span class='muted'>"
                    . "First difference:</span> {$diff}</div></td>";

                echo "<td><a class='btn {$btn_style}' href='{$componentURL}"
                    . "&task=restore&id={$row['id']}&ts={$ts}'>"
                    . "<i class='icon-out-2 small icon-white'></i>"
                    . " Restore</a></td>";
                echo "</tr>";
            }
            echo "</tbody></table>";
    }
}
```

The showRevisions() function will perform a SELECT query to retrieve the most recent 100 revision entries to articles in the system. Note the MySQL function UNIX_TIMESTAMP(), which will return an integer value such as *1292394342* for the date and time of the revision. Having a single number to represent this data and time makes it easy to select this entry later and also allows PHP to effectively format the output into any character string that we might need for display.

After the function performs the SELECT, it uses the loadAssocList() method to read all the rows into an array. A foreach() statement then loops through every row, outputting a table display row for each revision. A variable called $lastID is used to track the article id that was last displayed. If it is different from the one currently being output, the color of the restore button changes. That allows an administrator to quickly see whether a number of revisions are all related to the same article.

Finally, add the restoreRevision() function, which performs the actual restoration of a selected revision:

```php
function restoreRevision() {

    $conf = JFactory::getConfig();
    $dbprefix = $conf->get('dbprefix');
    $componentURL = "/administrator/index.php?option=com_articlehistorian&";
    $id = JFactory::getApplication()->input->getInt('id');
    $ts = JFactory::getApplication()->input->getInt('ts');
    $verbose = JFactory::getApplication()->input->getInt('verbose');
    if($id>0 && $ts>0) {
        $db = JFactory::getDBO();
        echo "<div class='lead'>Restoring ID#$id to revision dated ".
            date(DATE_COOKIE,$ts). "</div>";
        $sql = "SELECT * FROM {$dbprefix}content_history
            WHERE UNIX_TIMESTAMP(revision_date)='$ts'
            AND id='$id' ";
        $db->setQuery( $sql, 0);
        // Execute query
        if ($row = $db->loadAssoc()) {
            $sqlCurrent = "SELECT * FROM {$dbprefix}content
                WHERE id='{$id}' ";
            $db->setQuery( $sqlCurrent, 0);
            $updateArray = array();
            $currentVersion = $db->loadAssoc();
            foreach($currentVersion as $key => &$val) {
                // Skip version key -- we'll increment it
                if($key=='version') {
                    $updateArray[$key] = $val+1;
                    if($verbose) {
                        echo "<strong>"
                        .JText::_("UPDATING").":</strong> "
                        ."$key = {$updateArray[$key]}<br/>";
                    }
                    continue;
                } elseif($key == 'hits') {
                    if($verbose) {
                        echo "<div class='muted'>"
                        ."NO CHANGE: Keep current hits: $val</div>";
                    }
                    continue;
                } elseif($key == 'modified') {
                    $updateArray[$key] = date('Y-m-d h:i:s');
                    if($verbose) {
                        echo "<strong>UPDATING:</strong> "
                            ."$key = {$updateArray[$key]}<br/>";
                    }
```

```
                continue;
            }
            $shortCurrent = substr($val,0,50);
            $shortRevision = substr($row[$key],0,20);
            if(isset($row[$key]) && $row[$key]!=$val) {
                if($verbose) {
                    echo "<strong>Reverting</strong>: "
                        ."$key from {$shortCurrent}
                        <strong>to</strong> {$shortRevision}<br/>";
                }
                $updateArray[$key] = $row[$key];
            } else {
                if($verbose) {
                    echo "<div class='muted'>NO CHANGE:"
                    ." $key from {$shortCurrent}
                        <b>to</b> {$shortRevision}</div>";
                }
            }
        }
        if(!empty($updateArray)) {
            $sqlUpdate = "UPDATE {$dbprefix}content SET ";
            $count = 0;
            foreach($updateArray as $field => $val) {
                if($count > 0) {
                    $sqlUpdate .= " , ";
                }
                $data = $db->escape($val);
                $sqlUpdate .= " $field = '{$data}' ";
                $count++;
            }
            $sqlUpdate .= " WHERE id = '$id' ";
            $db->setQuery( $sqlUpdate, 0);
            $db->execute();
            $updatedRows = $db->getAffectedRows();
            echo "<h2>Updated ".count($updateArray)." fields ("
                .implode(',',array_keys($updateArray))
                .") of $updatedRows row.</h2>";
        } else {
            echo "<div>Nothing to update.</div>";
        }
        if($verbose) {
            echo $sqlUpdate;
        }
    }
    echo "<div><a class='btn btn-success' "
        ."href='{$componentURL}'>Return to revision list</a></div>";
}

}
```

This function will load the old row and compare it field-by-field (or column-by-column in database terminology) to the current row. We want to make sure that there are updates to be made and report on the number and type of updates. There is no point in executing an update when nothing will be changed.

The function begins by checking the request parameters for the id and timestamp of the version to be restored. It also detects the verbose parameter if verbose reporting is desired. Once it establishes that it has a valid id and timestamp, a reference to the database object is created. A SQL SELECT statement is generated to retrieve the specified version if the loadAssoc() method is executed to load the older version into an array. If a valid row is loaded, the database is queried again to obtain the current version.

With the current version in memory, the routine loops through each available field with special handling for a few fields. The version field is incremented from the current version. The hits field value is kept intact. The modified date is set to the current moment. If no special handling of the field is required, it is restored to the value held in the older revision.

Once completed, the update array is used to construct a SQL UPDATE statement that is executed against the server. Remember that this update will cause the MySQL server to execute the trigger again, so the current version (before the revert) will be added to the revision history.

I have included a "verbose" mode that you can activate by adding the verbose parameter to the end of the restore URL like this:

```
/index.php?option=com_article_historian&task=restore&id=66&ts=1
    &verbose=1
```

The verbose mode outputs every step of the update which can be useful in seeing how the component executes and also allows you to debug problems in the code that might occur. It even outputs a summary of what the fields will be changing from and to.

You will need the XML descriptor file to install the component to the administrator interface, so create the following file in your favorite text editor and save it as articlehistorian.xml in the root of the component folder:

```
<?xml version="1.0" encoding="utf-8"?>
<extension type="component" version="2.5" method="upgrade">
    <name>Article Historian</name>
    <author>Dan Rahmel</author>
    <creationDate>May 2010</creationDate>
    <version>1.0.0</version>
    <description>Article Historian will allow past versions of articles to
        be examined and restored.</description>

    <files>
        <filename>articlehistorian.php</filename>
        <filename>articlehistorian.xml</filename>
    </files>
    <administration>
        <menu>Article Historian</menu>
    </administration>
</extension>
```

When you access the component after installation, you will see a list of all the article revisions made since you installed the trigger as shown in Figure 12-2.

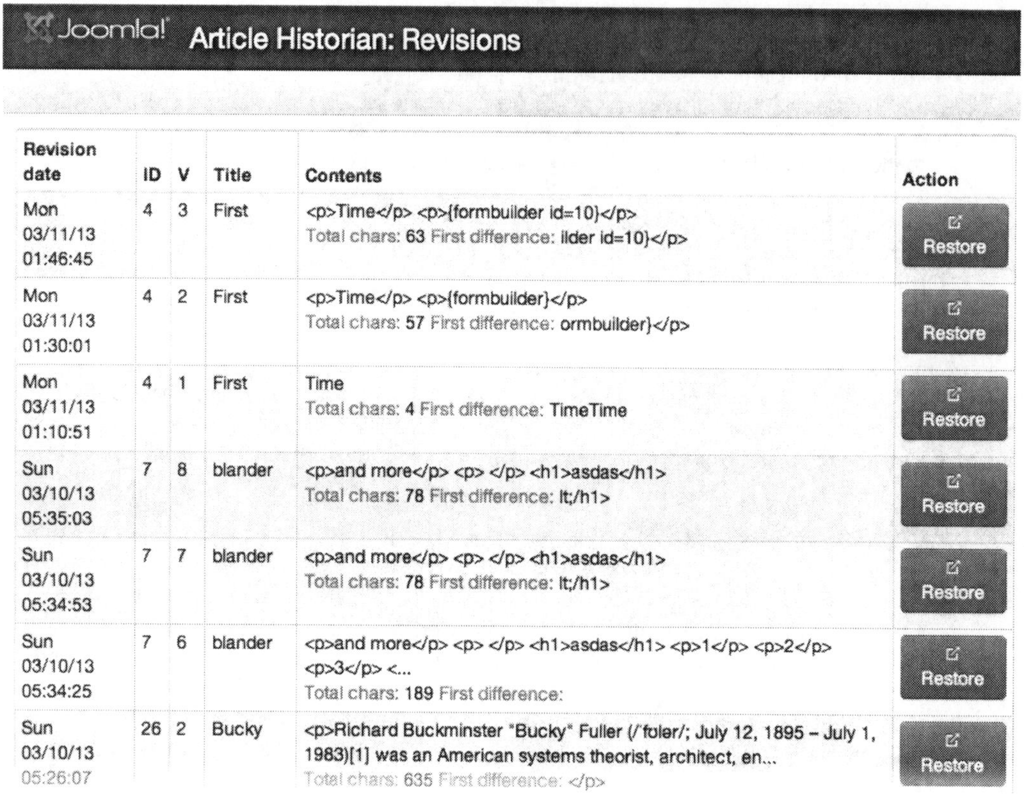

Figure 12-2. *Article revisions that were made since installation of the MySQL trigger will be shown in the Article Historian interface*

If you click the Restore link in the far-right column, you will be presented with the restore screen, as shown in Figure 12-3.

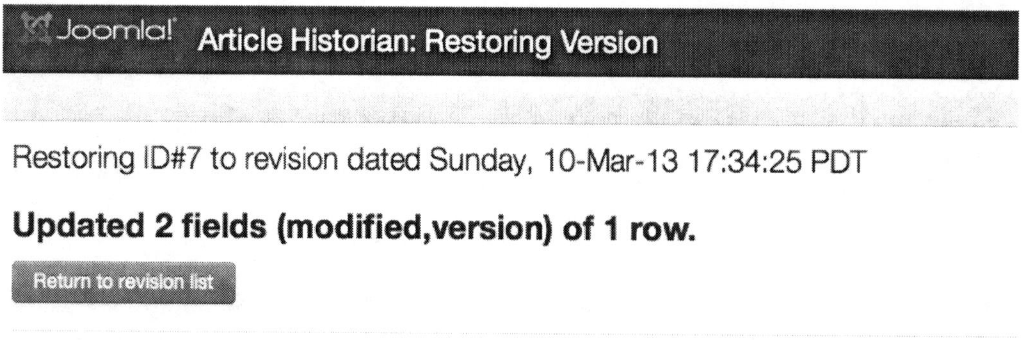

Figure 12-3. *Clicking the restore link in the far-right column will restore the selected version and create a revision of the current version*

I've found the Article Historian to be one of the most useful components on a production site because it provides a safety net for rushed changes. It is impossible to count the number of times that I've made what seems like a trivial change in TinyMCE, which the editor considers a major change in formatting, becomes confused, and messes up the entire article. Often when the editor has problems, these issues appear late in the article so you might not even notice them before clicking the Save button.

The Article Historian lets you recover from such Save clicks. It is equally useful if you have contributors and moderators/editors that make changes to each other's documents and may have accidentally deleted something important.

Creating the Form Builder

Most developers dread the addition of new forms to a web site. Each new form, while appearing simple on the surface, means implementing a large number of tedious programming items such as client-side form validation, server-side form validation, the creation of a new table to store form data, and many other details. Tracking whether a form is operating properly is a further challenge because each form has its own codebase and peculiarities. For example, one form needs to store a valid email while another needs to check for a username with only alpha-numeric characters (see Figure 12-4).

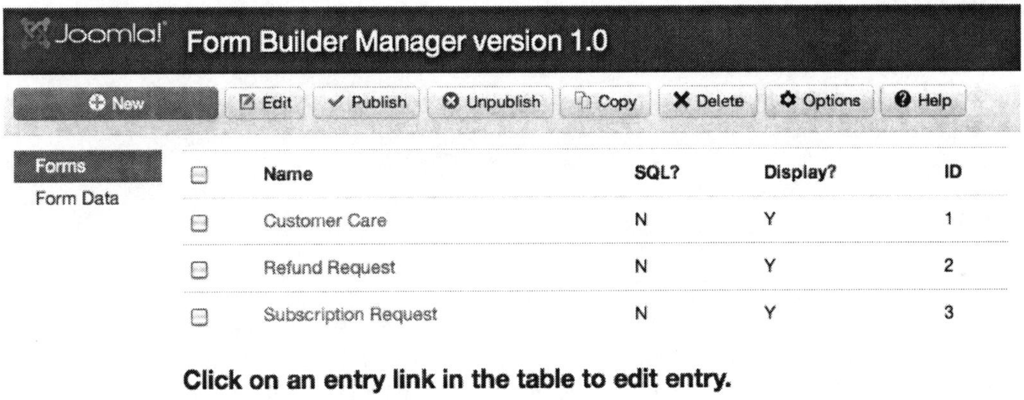

Figure 12-4. *The Form Builder lets you create many different forms without programming*

Creating a core component to streamline form building and eliminate the need for custom development with each form can be a powerful new feature for a developer. Form Builder will fill that role. Most form-creation components focus on an extended user interface that allows form construction through some type of GUI or other visual interface. That makes things inherently complex and not very extensible.

Form Builder relies on a developer having basic abilities to create the form definition using simplified code, and the component takes care of the rest of the details. That keeps the component simple yet far more powerful because an intermediate developer can easily extend the capabilities of the component and this extension can then be used by any forms constructed in the future.

Examining the Form Builder architecture

A brief description of the Form Builder architecture will make the code easy to understand and modify. Although Article Historian had a very simple structure (a single file) that held all the controller and function logic, Form Builder will be constructed as a complete Joomla MVC application.

You'll note that all the components that ship with Joomla use this same structure. It enforces the best coding practices for development and allows a developer to effectively leverage much of the Joomla framework that exists to minimize reinventing the wheel.

A foundation of the MVC structure is the folder hierarchy. It is through standardized layout of directories that the Joomla application framework knows where to locate the individual pieces of the application.

The Form Builder extension actually consists of three separate pieces (only the Administrator component uses MVC) that are installed as two separate extensions:

- Administrator component – Within this component, you define the form including any necessary fields.

- Ajax component – Accepts input that is posted from the user form and writes it into the database.

- Plugin – Allows a form to be added to any article by simply adding a tag such as {formbuilder id=1}

We'll start by creating an installer for the Administrator and Ajax components. Begin by creating folders for the Form Builder component with this hierarchy somewhere on your development system, in which you can install from a folder or zip all the files for remote installation:

- com_formbuilder/

  - ajax/

  - controllers/

  - helpers/

  - models/

  - sql/

  - tables/

  - views/

Once you create these directories, you can begin populating the code files. Let's start with the descriptor file. At the root level of the directories you created (inside the com_formbuilder/ directory), use your favorite text editor to make the XML descriptor file called form_builder.xml and enter the following text:

```
<?xml version="1.0" encoding="utf-8"?>
<extension type="component" version="2.5.0">
    <name>Form Builder</name>
    <author>Dan Rahmel</author>
    <version>1.0.0</version>
    <description>Setup and configuration for display of Form Builder component.</description>

    <update>
        <schemas>
            <schemapath type="mysql">sql/updates/mysql</schemapath>
        </schemas>
    </update>

    <files folder="site">
        <filename>index.html</filename>
        <filename>formbuilder.php</filename>
    </files>
```

```
    <administration>
        <menu>Form_Builder</menu>
        <files folder="admin">
            <filename
                component="formbuilder">formbuilder.php</filename>
            <filename>formbuilder.xml</filename>
            <folder>controllers</folder>
            <folder>tables</folder>
            <folder>views</folder>
        </files>
    </administration>
</extension>
```

This descriptor file will install both the Administrator and Ajax components. It will also provide the necessary SQL to create the tables that are needed to store both the form definitions and the form data storage. First we'll create the Administrator component so you can see how the form creation operates.

Creating the Form Builder administrator component

The Administrator component is the most complicated part of the system because it follows the full Joomla MVC structure. Let's begin by defining the main controller files and then we'll create the SQL needed for the database setup.

Create a file called form_builder.php (inside the com_formbuilder/ directory) and enter the following code:

```php
<?php
// no direct access
defined( '_JEXEC' ) or die( 'Restricted access' );
define('DS','/');
// Make sure the user is authorized to view this page
$user = & JFactory::getUser();
if (!$user->authorize( 'com_formbuilder', 'manage' )) {
        $mainframe->redirect( 'index.php', JText::_('ALERTNOTAUTH') );
}

// Set the table directory
JTable::addIncludePath(JPATH_ADMINISTRATOR
        .'/components/com_formbuilder/tables');

JToolBarHelper::title(JText::_('Form Builder Manager'));

$controllerName = JRequest::getCmd( 'c', 'formbuilder' );

addSubmenu($controllerName);
switch ($controllerName)
{
        default:
                $controllerName = 'formbuilder';
                // allow fall through

        case 'formdata':
                // Temporary interceptor
                $task = JRequest::getCmd('task');
```

```
        if ($task == 'listclients') {
                $controllerName = 'client';
        }

        require_once( JPATH_COMPONENT.DS
                .'controllers'.DS.$controllerName.'.php' );
        $controllerName = 'FormBuilderController'
                .$controllerName;

        // Create the controller
        $controller = new $controllerName();

        // Perform the Request task
        $controller->execute( JRequest::getCmd('task') );

        // Redirect if set by the controller
        $controller->redirect();
        break;
}
```

This controller performs the basic administrator setup. After it ensures that the user has permission to access the component, it adds the necessary reference to the tables that are used by the model. Once those references are established, it loads the proper controller and executes it based on the passed controller name.

With the basic controller defined, add the addSubmenu() function to the end of the file that creates the necessary menu items:

```
function addSubmenu($vName = 'formbuilder',$original=true)
{
        if($original) {
                JSubMenuHelper::addEntry(
                        JText::_('Forms'),
                        'index.php?option=com_formbuilder',
                        $vName=='formbuilder');
                JSubMenuHelper::addEntry(
                        JText::_('Form Data'),
                        'index.php?option=com_formbuilder&c=formdata',
                        $vName=='client' );
        } else {
                JHtmlSidebar::addEntry(
                        JText::_('Forms'),
                        'index.php?option=com_formbuilder',
                        $vName=='formbuilder');
                JHtmlSidebar::addEntry(
                        JText::_('Form Data'),
                        'index.php?option=com_formbuilder&c=client',
                        $vName=='client' );
                echo JHtmlSidebar::render();
        }
}
```

This function adds the menus that appear in the left column. You can see the $vName variable holds the name of the currently selected menu. The function uses this name to pass the boolean true or false to the addEntry() method to specify if the menu has been selected.

Now, let's define one of the controllers for Form Builder. Inside the controllers/ folder, use your text editor to create the formbuilder.php file:

```php
<?php
// no direct access
defined( '_JEXEC' ) or die( 'Restricted access' );

class FormBuilderControllerFormBuilder extends JControllerAdmin {
        function __construct( $config = array() ) {
                parent::__construct( $config );
                // Register Extra tasks
                $this->registerTask( 'add','edit' );
                $this->registerTask( 'apply', 'save' );
                $this->registerTask( 'resethits',        'save' );
                $this->registerTask( 'unpublish',       'publish' );
        }
}
?>
```

This code sets up the basic interface. We want to add methods to handle the display, edit, and save functionality of the interface. Let's start with the display by adding this code to the end of the file:

```php
public function display($cachable = false, $urlparams = array()) {
    $db = JFactory::getDBO();

    // Set title in Administrator interface
    $version = '1.0';
    JToolBarHelper::title( JText::_( 'Form Builder Manager' )
        .' ' . JText::_( 'version ' ).$version , 'addedit.png' );
    JToolBarHelper::addNew('formbuilder.new');
    JToolBarHelper::editList();
    JToolBarHelper::publishList();
    JToolBarHelper::unpublishList();
    JToolBarHelper::custom( 'copy', 'copy.png', 'copy_f2.png', 'Copy' );
    JToolBarHelper::deleteList();

    $query = "SELECT * FROM formbuilder_forms ORDER BY id; ";
    $db->setQuery( $query );
    $rows = $db->loadObjectList();
?>

<form action='/administrator/index.php?option=com_formbuilder'
    name='adminForm'  id='adminForm'>
<table class="table adminlist">
<tr>
    <td class="title">
        <input type="checkbox" />
    </td>
```

```
        <td class="title">
            <strong><?php echo JText::_( Status ); ?></strong>
        </td>
        <td class="title">
            <strong><?php echo JText::_( 'Name' ); ?></strong>
        </td>
        <td class="title">
            <strong><?php echo JText::_( 'JSON' ); ?></strong>
        </td>
        <td class="title">
            <strong><?php echo JText::_( 'ID' ); ?></strong>
        </td>
</tr>

<?php
    foreach ($rows as $row) {
        // Create url to allow user to click & jump to edit article
        $url = "index.php?option=com_formbuilder&task=edit&" .
            "&id=" . $row->id;
        $link = 'index.php?option=com_formbuilder&task=edit&id='. $row->id;
        if(strlen($row->sql)>0) { $hasSQL = "Y"; } else { $hasSQL = "N"; }
        if(strlen($row->json)>0) { $hasJSON = "Y"; } else { $hasJSON = "N"; }
        $target = "";
        echo "<tr>"
        . "<td><input type='checkbox' /></td>"
        . '<td><div class="btn-group">
            <a class="btn btn-micro active" rel="tooltip"
                href="javascript:void(0);"
                onclick="return listItemTask(\'cb0\',\'articles.unpublish\')"
                data-original-title=
                "Published">
            <i class="icon-publish"></i></a>
        <a href="#" onclick="return listItemTask(\'cb0\',\'articles.featured\')"
            class="btn btn-micro hasTooltip" data-original-title=
            "Toggle to change article state to Featured">
            <i class="icon-star-empty"></i></a>
            </div></td>
            '
        . "<td><a href='" . $url . "' $target >" . $row->name . "</a></td>" .
        "<td>" . $hasJSON . "</td>" .
        "<td>" . $row->id . "</td>" .
            "</tr>";
    }
    echo "</table></form>";
}
```

This controller handles the display of the list of available forms. From this interface, new forms can be added, or existing forms can be edited or deleted. The code adds a title to the Administrator window so the location appears properly in the browser tab. Then the various stock buttons are added to the interface.

A query is created to retrieve all the forms in the database. In contrast with the earlier database that used the loadAssoc() method to retrieve the data as an array, this code uses the loadObjectList() method to obtain the results as a set of nested objects. Which method you use is strictly a matter of personal preference. This code uses the alternate method to provide an example of using objects instead of arrays for data retrieval.

From the data returned from the database, the table showing each available form is displayed with all the necessary publish/unpublish and other functionality. From this interface, the Administrator can manage the forms that are available on the site.

Add the edit() function to the end of the file to allow the editing of the new or existing fields of a form:

```php
function edit() {
    JToolBarHelper::title( JText::_( 'Form Builder Editor' ), 'addedit.png' );
    JToolBarHelper::apply('apply');
    JToolBarHelper::save( 'save' );
    JToolBarHelper::cancel( 'cancel' );

    $db = JFactory::getDBO();
    $query = "SELECT a.id, a.name,a.sql,a.json,a.html" .
        " FROM formbuilder_forms AS a" .
        " WHERE a.id = " . $app->input->get( 'id' );
    $db->setQuery( $query, 0, 10 );
    if($rows = $db->loadObjectList()) {
    ?>

    <form id="form_update" name="form_update" method="post"
        action="index.php?option=com_formbuilder&task=update">
      <p>SQL:<br />
        <textarea name="sql" class="span12" rows="4" id="sql"><?php
        echo $rows[0]->sql;
        ?></textarea>
      </p>
      <p>JSON:<br />
        <textarea name="json" class="span12" rows="8" id="json"><?php
        echo $rows[0]->json;
        ?></textarea>
      </p>
      <p>HTML:<br />
        <textarea name="html" class="span12" rows="12" id="html">
            <?php echo $rows[0]->html; ?>
        </textarea>
      </p>
      <p>
        <input name="id" type="hidden" id="id"
        value='<?php echo $rows[0]->id; ?>'
        />
      </p>
      <p>
        <input type="submit" name="Submit" value="Record Changes" />
      </p>
    </form>

    <?php }
}
```

This function allows the Administrator to edit the form that will be displayed by the plugin. The code first adds the necessary toolbar editing buttons. Note that for compatibility reasons, Joomla still uses the apply button name, even though the button itself will display the button as Save. Likewise, the Save button will appear as Save & Close. Keeping the titles of the older Joomla functionality prevents breaking the numerous components that have used these conventions.

A query is generated to get the form specified by the id sent in the request. The remainder of the code simply populates the form with the data retrieved for the selected form. Earlier examples used the echo command to output various HTML items. This code instead closes the PHP block with the ?> operator so the actual HTML can be used within the function. If you have more than a tiny bit of HTML, using echo commands can quickly become cumbersome and error-prone, so this method can be more useful.

When the user clicks the Record Changes button of the form, the information about the form is stored into the database by the save() method (please add this method to the end of the code file):

```php
function save()  {
    JToolBarHelper::title( JText::_( 'Update Form Entry' ), 'addedit.png' );

    $db = JFactory::getDBO();
    $app = JFactory::getApplication();
    // Retrieve data from form
    $fldMessage = "'" . $db->getEscaped($app->input->get('message')) . "'";
    $fldLocation = "'" . $db->getEscaped($app->input->get( 'location' )) . "'";
    $fldID = "'" . $db->getEscaped($app->input->getInt( 'id' )) . "'";

    // Record updates to jos_guestbook table
    $insertFields = "UPDATE formbuilder_forms " .
      " SET message=" . $fldMessage . ", " .
      " location=" . $fldLocation .
      " WHERE id = " . $fldID ;
    $db->setQuery( $insertFields, 0);
    $db->query();
    echo "<h3>Field updated!</h3>";
    $url = "/administrator/index.php?option=com_formbuilder";
    echo "<a href='{$url}'>Return to Form Builder</a>";
}
```

This final function of the formbuilder.php file writes the various fields into the database. Once the form is written into the database, it can be accessed by both the Ajax component and the plugin. However, we haven't yet added the files to the installer to create the tables within the Joomla database.

To perform this operation, we'll simply add the necessary file containing the SQL table definitions to the installer. Create a file createTables.sql in the sql/ folder of the component. Add the following SQL statement:

```sql
CREATE TABLE 'formbuilder_forms' (
  'id' int(10) unsigned NOT NULL AUTO_INCREMENT,
  'json' text,
  'name' varchar(255) DEFAULT NULL,
  'type' varchar(2) DEFAULT NULL,
  'enabled' int(11) NOT NULL DEFAULT '1',
  'alias' varchar(255) DEFAULT NULL,
  PRIMARY KEY ('id')
) ENGINE=InnoDB
```

This statement creates the forms table that holds the JSON definition of the form (which stores all the fields and field types used by the form) as well as the standard metadata for data items in the Joomla interface such as the `alias` and `enabled` fields.

Also, add the table definition for the data table:

```
CREATE TABLE 'formbuilder_data' (
  'id' int(11) NOT NULL AUTO_INCREMENT,
  'form_id' int(11) DEFAULT NULL,
  'json' text,
  'user_ip' varchar(45) DEFAULT NULL,
  'date_modified' timestamp NULL DEFAULT CURRENT_TIMESTAMP,
  PRIMARY KEY ('id')
) ENGINE=InnoDB
```

This table holds the data entered by the user when the form is displayed on the front end. You can see that once again, the `json` field is used to store data that may contain many different fields and data types. We also record the `user_ip` field so if spam becomes a problem, you can block an IP address with the technique shown in Chapter 7.

Try running the component and creating a new form. If you access the Form Builder in the Administrator interface, you can click the New button to create a new form or click on an existing form to edit it.

In Figure 12-5, you can see the Form Editor defining a form with standard JSON. You can define new fields by simply adding items to the `fields` dictionary entry. Each field can take the standard user interface settings for form fields including `label`, type, CSS `class`, `placeholder` text, and whether the field is `single` or multiple lines.

Figure 12-5. *You can use the Form Builder Editor to create and edit new forms*

You can define the fields of the form in simple JSON. Clicking the Save button will store the form to the database. Before we create the plugin that will show the form to the world, let's create the Ajax component that will record the input from the form and will be installed at the same time as the Administrator component.

Creating the Form Builder Ajax component

The recording of the form data is handled by a component that has no user interface, but merely provides an endpoint where data can be posted. This component will perform only that single operation.

Create a formbuilder.php file in the ajax/ folder and add the following code:

```php
<?php
// no direct access
defined( '_JEXEC' ) or die( 'Restricted access' );

$controllerName = JRequest::getCmd( 'c', 'formbuilder' );

switch ($controllerName)
{
    default:
        $out = array('success'=>0);
        $task = JRequest::getCmd('task');

        if($task=='update') {
            $jinput = JFactory::getApplication()->input;
            $formID = $jinput->get('formbuilder_id',-1,'int');
            if($formID>0) {
                $db = JFactory::getDBO();

                // Confirm form exists
            $query = "SELECT * FROM formbuilder_forms WHERE id=$formID";
                $db->setQuery($query);
                $rows = $db->loadAssocList();
                if($rows) {
                    $form = $rows[0];
                    $data = json_decode($form['json'],true);

                    $field_data = array();
                    foreach($data['fields'] as
                        $field_name => $field) {
                        $val = $jinput->get($field_name,'','string');
                        $field_data[$field_name] = $val;
                    }
                    $user_ip =
                        (isset($_SERVER["HTTP_X_FORWARDED_FOR"]))
                        ? $_SERVER["HTTP_X_FORWARDED_FOR"] :
                            $_SERVER["REMOTE_ADDR"];

                    $store_data = array('form_id'=>$formID,
                        'json'=>json_encode($field_data),
                        'user_ip'=>$user_ip);
                    $sql = "INSERT INTO formbuilder_data SET ";
                    $count = 0;
                    foreach($store_data as $field => $val) {
                        if($count > 0) {
                            $sql .= " , ";
                        }
                        $data_item = $db->escape($val);
                        $sql .= " $field = '{$data_item}' ";
                        $count++;
                    }
```

```
                    $db->setQuery( $sql, 0);
                    $db->execute();
                    $out['store'] = $store_data;
                    $out['success'] = 1;
                }

            }

        }
        echo json_encode($out);

        break;
}
```

This controller accepts only the update command. It checks for a valid form id (passed in the values) and reads it if available. From the form itself, only the fields specified in the form declaration are read from the input variables (so even if a hacker would inject a rogue field it would be ignored), the user's IP address is determined, and then all the form data is written into the database.

Now that we have the storage layer, let's create the plugin that will display the form.

Creating the Form Builder plugin

You may be wondering why the form display is built as a plugin. One method of displaying the form is to provide it as a component, so essentially a separate menu (and associated URL) would display the form. The problem with a component implementation is that the component would then need to include a lot of display logic.

For example, if you wanted a customer care form that allowed for feedback, wouldn't it be useful to include a FAQ on the same page so the user could see whether their question is already answered there? Or perhaps to feature the same form on two different pages with a different graphics theme? Or include a number of images to explain the task flow of the form?

To accommodate any of these options, a lot of extra logic would need to be incorporated into the form display component. By adding the form as a plugin, a form (or multiple forms) can be easily added to any Joomla article. All the available formatting, layout, pagination, and other features can be leveraged and used to create the form page. And adding a form to an article requires only adding a very simple Form Builder tag, as shown in Figure 12-6.

Figure 12-6. *Adding a form to an article is as simple as adding the Form Builder tag*

In a new folder (separate from the components you built earlier) called `plugin_formbuilder/`, create the `formbuilder.php` file and enter the following:

```php
<?php
// no direct access
defined( '_JEXEC' ) or die( 'Restricted access' );

class plgContentFormBuilder extends JPlugin {
    var $dbConnect;
    var $myTinkerForm;

    // Name function same as event so it will be called.
    public function onContentPrepare($context, &$article, &$params, $page=0) {
        // Get the parameters in case we need them in a later plug-in
        $plugin = JPluginHelper::getPlugin('content', 'formbuilder');
        $tag = "formbuilder";
        $startTag = "{".$tag;
        $i = 0;
        $startPos = 0;
        $newArticle = "";
        // Set maximum number of forms on a page
        while($i<10) {
            $i++;
            $curPos = JString::strpos($article->text, $startTag,$startPos);
            if($curPos!==false) {
                $endPos = JString::strpos($article->text, "}",$curPos);
```

```
                    // If there isn't a close bracket,
                    // use the tag length to designate the end
                    if($endPos==0) {
                        $endPos = $curPos + strlen($startTag);
                    }
                    $fbRequest=substr($article->text,$curPos+1,$endPos-$curPos-1);
                    $fbRequest=trim(str_replace($tag,'',$fbRequest));

                    $newArticle.=substr($article->text,$startPos,$curPos-$startPos)
                        . $this->renderForm($fbRequest) ."\n\n";
                    $startPos = $endPos+1;
                } else {
                    break;
                }
            }
        }
        if(strlen($newArticle)>0) {
            $newArticle .=substr($article->text,$startPos);
            $article->text = $newArticle;
        }
        return true;
    }

    function renderForm($inReqStr) {
        require_once("cFormBuilder.php");
        $output = cFormBuilder::renderForm($inReqStr);
        return $output;
    }
}
?>
```

This plugin binds to the onContentPrepare event. The code starts by setting up a reference to the plugin object created by the system. The reference can be used to obtain parameters if you add any settings that can be configured in the Plug-in Manager interface. A plugin receives all the text from an entire article and must process that text and return modified content if necessary. In our case, we set up the variables to find the {formbuilder} tags and replace them with the actual form content. The loop will search for up to 10 form tags in one article.

If a form tag is found in the text of the article content, it is replaced by the form rendered from the data stored in the form table. You can see that once the text is modified, the $article->text property is set with the modified content that is then used by the Joomla system.

The renderForm() method performs a call in the cFormBuilder class, which can be used by other extensions on the system. Create another file called cFormBuilder.php at the same directory level and enter the following code:

```
<?php

class cFormBuilder {
    static $configArray;
    static $formid = 1;

    public static function renderForm($inReqStr) {
        $output = "";
        // Use the functions for parsing INI strings to get settings
        parse_str(html_entity_decode($inReqStr),self::$configArray);
        $db = JFactory::getDBO();
```

```php
        // Make sure there is a form id included
        if(!isset(self::$configArray["id"])) {
            return "No form id is set";
        }
        // Confirm form exists
        $formID = intval(self::$configArray["id"]);
        $query = "SELECT * FROM formbuilder_forms WHERE id=$formID; ";
        $db->setQuery( $query );
        $rows = $db->loadAssocList();
        if(!$rows) {
            return "Form #{$formID} not found.";
        }
        $form = $rows[0];
        // Render the form
        return self::renderHTMLForm($form);
    }

    static function renderHTMLForm($form) {
        if(!$form['enabled']) {
            return '';
        }
        $data = json_decode($form['json'],true);
        if(true) {
            $data = array(
                'submit'=>'Send comment',
                'submit_class'=>'btn btn-info',
                'submit_msg'=>'Thanks for your feedback!',
                'fields'=> array(
                    'name'=>array('label'=>'Name',
                        'type'=>'text','class'=>'span6',
                        'placeholder'=>'(or nickname)',
                        'single'=>1),
                    'email'=>array('label'=>'Email',
                        'type'=>'text','class'=>'span6',
                        'placeholder'=>'(optional)','single'=>1),
                    'comment'=>array('label'=>'Comment',
                        'type'=>'textarea','class'=>'span6',
                        'placeholder'=>'Please tell us what you think',
                        'single'=>1),
                )
            );
        }
        // Create a form alias so the JavaScript can find the form
        $form_alias = $form['alias']."-".self::$formid;
        // Setup the form
        $output = "<form id='{$form_alias}' method='POST'>";
        foreach($data['fields'] as $field_name => $field) {
            $field_str = "<label>{$field['label']}";
            if($field['type']=='textarea') {
                $field_str .= "<textarea name='{$field_name}' "
                    ." placeholder='{$field['placeholder']}' "
                    ." class='{$field['class']}'></textarea>";
```

```
        } else {
            $field_str .= "<input type='{$field['type']}'
                    ." name='{$field_name}' "
                    ." placeholder='{$field['placeholder']}'
                    ." class='{$field['class']}' />";
        }
        $field_str .= "</label>";
        if($field['single']) {
            $output .= "<div>".$field_str."</div>";
        } else {
            $output .= "<span>".$field_str."</div>";
        }
    }
    $output .= "<button onclick='submitForm(\"{$form_alias}\");"
        ." return false;' "
        . " class='{$data['submit_class']}' >{$data['submit']}</button>";
    $output .= "<input type='hidden' name='formbuilder_id' "
        ." value='{$form['id']}'>";
    $output .= "</form>";
    $output .= "<div id='thanks{$form_alias}'
        ." style='display:none;'>"
        . "<h3>{$data['submit_msg']}</h3></div>";
    // Add the function to submit the form to the head of the document
    $js = "function submitForm(alias) {
            jQuery.post('/index.php?option=com_formbuilder'
                +'&task=update&format=raw',
                jQuery('form#'+alias).serialize()
            )
            .done(function(data) {
                jQuery('form#'+alias).hide();
                jQuery('#thanks'+alias).show();
            });
        }";

    JFactory::getDocument()->addScriptDeclaration($js);
    // Increment formid to handle more than one form on the page
    self::$formid++;
    return $output;
    }
}

?>
```

This class accepts the form definition and renders a proper form. It starts by using the parse_str() function
to process the parameters from the tag. This function is really useful because it handles parameters such as quoted
strings for you. The first parameter it checks for is the form id, and it aborts the rendering if there is no passed id. It
then checks the database and also aborts if the form specified is not found. Once the form is loaded, the method calls
the renderHTMLForm() to generate the actual HTML of the form.

The renderHTMLForm() method decodes the JSON and processes each field. It also renders the JavaScript form
submission code. When the user clicks the form submission button, the jQuery post() method is called and it sends
the update to the component that you created earlier.

When the form is returned by the class to the plugin, it injects a JavaScript tag to allow for the saving of form data, which it posts to the component you created earlier. When the form is displayed in the article, the Customer Care form we defined earlier is displayed as shown in Figure 12-7.

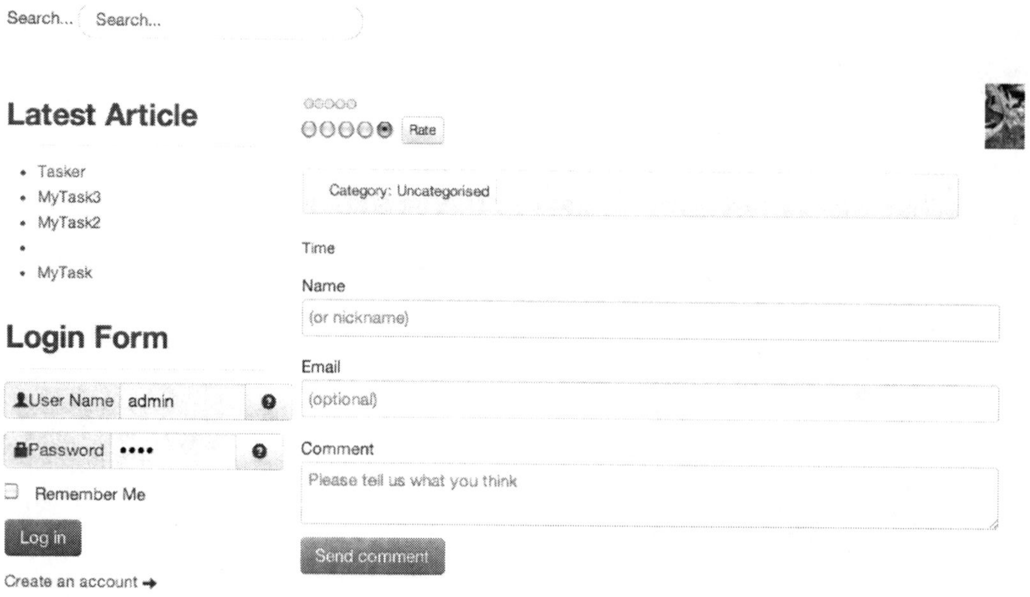

Figure 12-7. *The form will render within the article where you've used a Form Builder tag*

If you install and access the components and plugins, you can create a new form as easily as you create a banner or use any other component in the Administrator interface! Because you can add the form by inserting a small tag into the content of an article, you can use any presentation for the form that you want, including surrounding banners or custom CSS.

You have now created an end-to-end extension that uses an Administration component, a site component, and a plugin to get the job done. Next, you'll get a little more sophisticated by using the image-rendering capabilities of the GD PHP extension to generate server-side images on-the-fly.

On-the-fly image generation with GD

PHP comes with everything from encryption to postscript output to XML handling to image creation libraries. Since version 4.3, PHP has come bundled with the GD library of image generation functions that can be used for dynamic on-the-fly image creation. With a small amount of programming, the GD library can be harnessed to create everything from dynamic image backgrounds to bar charts.

In this section, you'll learn how to create a Joomla component that generates an on-demand **bar chart** based on data that is either directly passed to the component in a request string or obtained via a MySQL query.

■ **Tip**   Using a server to create dynamic images consumes a fair amount of server resources and processing power. Before you implement a solution that uses dynamic images in high-traffic areas of your site, make sure there isn't another method that can be used that is less resource-intensive.

The bar chart is actually a fairly advanced rendering. It uses color gradients for both the bars and the background. Figure 12-8 shows a black and gray representation of the color chart, but your Joomla site visitors will be treated to the polished rich colors that show off the power of server-side image rendering.

Figure 12-8. *The bar chart component will render the bar chart image in colorful gradients*

What are the Advantages of Server-Side Chart Generation?

If you need to generate bar charts, you have many options. For simple bar charts, the grid layout available from an HTML table makes certain kinds of charts possible. There is a large amount of demonstration code on the web that shows some pretty impressive table-based charting. However, the chart types are limited to the bar and column types, restrictive in their display limitations, and tend to be pretty fragile depending on the browser and other display requirements.

More-advanced charting is possible with CSS and JavaScript. Some of the client-side chart rendering is very impressive, flexible, and often open-source so they are free for download, use, and modification. Best of all, it places very little burden on your server because the client machine performs the actual rendering.

However, your visitors will need a robust browser and computer that can handle the client-side processing requirements. Further, if you want to give your users the ability to save a chart and use it elsewhere (such as included in a report), this can be very difficult – often requiring the use of a screenshot to make it possible.

■ **Tip** If you want to do simple JavaScript charts or diagramming, check out the JavaScript Diagram Builder (www.lutanho.net/diagram). It provides the JavaScript-based drawing of bar charts, pie charts, arrows, and other basic graphics. For very advanced charting including area, line, bar, and pie charts with an excellent variety of presentation options, check out the Dojox Charting widgets that are available for the open-source Dojo JavaScript framework. You can see them in action at DojoCampus.org (http://dojocampus.org/explorer) or access them through the main Dojo web site (http://dojotoolkit.org).

The server-side image rendering method gives both the greatest flexibility and the greatest compatibility. Using the server to render the image gives the following advantages:

- Complete compatibility – If the visitor's browser can view web pages with images, it will display the chart image. With HTML- or JavaScript-based charting, you have no idea whether the browser is displaying the chart at all or whether the visitor browser has some incompatibility that prevents proper display. For example, people are increasingly using cell phone–based browsers that may not include the more advanced features of JavaScript compatibility.

- Image integrity – One of the frustrations of web developers and web designers is the inability to accurately predict how content sent to a browser will be rendered on the user's screen. In addition to platform differences, each browser seems to have its own take on baseline JavaScript execution and CSS implementation. As you saw earlier in the book even the default margins and font sizes are different in different browsers! For charts and other diagrams, the same display may appear completely different from visitor to visitor, browser to browser. Not so with server-generated images that, aside from slight monitor calibration differences, will appear identical wherever they are viewed.

- Drawing flexibility – A client-based chart is limited to mostly basic color schemes and an even more limited selection of fonts. Server-side image generation allows you to use everything from gradients to transparencies without having to make browser exceptions and multiple implementations. Additionally, the image may use any font available to the server system, which is particularly important if an organization has standardized on a particular font for official documents.

- Image storage and caching – On the client side, the image rendered by the server can be easily saved for later referral or inclusion in a report. On the server side, commonly requested images can be cached on a CDN, allowing fast transmission and effective resource balancing.

To give Joomla all this powerful image generation and charting abilities, it is possible to design a component that can render the image which can then be embedded in any article. While this is not meant to be a complete charting solution, it will provide you with an excellent basic application that demonstrates the fundamentals of image generation and the use of PHP library functions inside a deployable component.

Creating a PHP Color Name List

Before you begin constructing the chart component, it is helpful to create a library of color names that can be used to define items such as the chart background and bar colors. CSS took a large step toward readability of code when it included a list of standard color names that could be used in a style definition. That means a style definition can specify color: dark green instead of color: #FE199A, which makes easier to read the code later. Even more important is the communication that color names allow.

I have found that communicating with people (particularly clients and graphic artists) using color names such as Orange, Lime Green, Magenta, etc. is a radically better method of exchanging color information than any other that I've happened upon. This is particularly true if you have a color page that displays samples with the name of each color underneath.

Let me give you an example of the type of conversation I've witnessed many times:

> *Client: I want something that's darker.*
>
> *Graphic Artist: So you want me to reduce the Brightness?*
>
> *Client: I don't want the site less bright! Just use a better color.*
>
> *Graphic Artist: Better color?*
>
> *Client: Yes, something like Joe's web site has, but in green.*

Now imagine that conversation with using a color palette as a shared touchstone:

> *Graphic artist: So you can see that I've used Lime Green as the background color.*
>
> *Client: I would like something darker – like Olive Green. And the same thing with the other colors.*
>
> *Graphic artist: You want desaturated colors like Sea Green is to Lime Green?*
>
> *Client: Yes.*

Although this conversation is between a client and a graphic artist, it's just as likely to occur between a graphic artist and a developer, a manager and a programmer, or a father and his more-technical daughter. Having colors explicitly named makes communication something that can occur in English and that generally sets a better tone for the conversation. Even people who aren't educated in color models feel comfortable speaking of slate-gray and maroon.

■ **Note**   Some graphic artists don't like the CSS color names because there are some variations when the color is displayed in different browsers. This obviously won't be a problem with our Joomla application because we'll be hard-coding the values in the PHP. However, even when there are slight variations in the CSS colors from browser to browser, the communication and understanding enabled by using the names, at least in my experience, far outweighs the problems of these small deviations.

You can use one of the popular browsers to generate the list of color names for you. Enter the following code in an HTML file called `coloroutput.html`:

```html
<html>
<body>
<script type="text/javascript">
function changeBgColor() {
    var tempArray = new Array(
    'aliceblue', 'antiquewhite', 'aqua', 'aquamarine', 'azure', 'beige',
   'bisque', 'black', 'blanchedalmond', 'blue', 'blueviolet', 'brown',
   'burlywood', 'cadetblue', 'chartreuse', 'chocolate', 'coral',
   'cornflowerblue', 'cornsilk', 'crimson', 'cyan', 'darkblue', 'darkcyan',
   'darkgoldenrod', 'darkgray', 'darkgrey', 'darkgreen', 'darkkhaki',
   'darkmagenta', 'darkolivegreen', 'darkorange', 'darkorchid', 'darkred',
   'darksalmon', 'darkseagreen', 'darkslateblue', 'darkslategray',
```

```
'darkslategrey', 'darkturquoise', 'darkviolet', 'deeppink', 'deepskyblue',
'dimgray', 'dimgrey', 'dodgerblue', 'firebrick', 'floralwhite',
'forestgreen', 'fuchsia', 'gainsboro', 'ghostwhite', 'gold', 'goldenrod',
'gray', 'grey', 'green', 'greenyellow', 'honeydew', 'hotpink', 'indianred',
'indigo', 'ivory', 'khaki', 'lavender', 'lavenderblush', 'lawngreen',
'lemonchiffon', 'lightblue', 'lightcoral', 'lightcyan',
'lightgoldenrodyellow', 'lightgray', 'lightgrey', 'lightgreen', 'lightpink',
'lightsalmon', 'lightseagreen', 'lightskyblue', 'lightslategray',
'lightslategrey', 'lightsteelblue', 'lightyellow', 'lime', 'limegreen',
'linen', 'magenta', 'maroon', 'mediumaquamarine', 'mediumblue',
'mediumorchid', 'mediumpurple', 'mediumseagreen', 'mediumslateblue',
'mediumspringgreen', 'mediumturquoise', 'mediumvioletred', 'midnightblue',
'mintcream', 'mistyrose', 'moccasin', 'navajowhite', 'navy', 'oldlace',
'olive', 'olivedrab', 'orange', 'orangered', 'orchid', 'palegoldenrod',
'palegreen', 'paleturquoise', 'palevioletred', 'papayawhip', 'peachpuff',
'peru', 'pink', 'plum', 'powderblue', 'purple', 'red', 'rosybrown',
'royalblue', 'saddlebrown', 'salmon', 'sandybrown', 'seagreen', 'seashell',
'sienna', 'silver', 'skyblue', 'slateblue', 'slategray', 'slategrey',
'snow', 'springgreen', 'steelblue', 'tan', 'teal', 'thistle', 'tomato',
'turquoise', 'violet', 'wheat', 'white', 'whitesmoke', 'yellow',
'yellowgreen');

    var outStr = '';      for(var i=0;i<tempArray.length;i++) {
        document.body.bgColor=tempArray[i];
        if(i>0) {
            outStr += ', ';
        }
        outStr += "'"+tempArray[i]+"'=>'"+document.body.bgColor+"'";
    }
    document.write(outStr);
    document.body.bgColor='white';
}
changeBgColor();
</script>
</head>
<body>
</body>
</html>
```

When you load this code into a browser, it will generate a list of all the available CSS color names and their specific color values. Later, you will copy and paste this list into the PHP class so it can be used by the chart-rendering software.

Checking for GD

In order to use the bar chart class presented in this chapter, you'll need to confirm that your server installation has the GD library compiled and activated. The easiest way to make this check is to use the phpinfo() function. Create a PHP file that has the following line:

```
<?php phpinfo(); ?>
```

When you access the page through your web browser, you need to find the GD info. Look for the GD section; if GD is available, you should see the Enabled flag set to True and the version of the GD library. You can additionally (or instead) try and call the GD library directly. You can use the following line to output the exact specifications of the library:

```
<?php print_r(gd_info()); ?>
```

This code will generate output like this:

```
Array ( [GD Version] => bundled (2.0.28 compatible)
[FreeType Support] => 1
[FreeType Linkage] => with freetype
[T1Lib Support] => 1
[GIF Read Support] => 1
[GIF Create Support] => 1
[JPG Support] => 1
[PNG Support] => 1
[WBMP Support] => 1
[XBM Support] => 1
[JIS-mapped Japanese Font Support] => )
```

If you don't have GD installed, you will get an error that says the gd_info() function doesn't exist. If it doesn't exist, you will need to modify your php.ini to activate the extension. On Windows, you might find an entry like this:

```
;extension=php_gd2.dll
```

On Linux, it's more likely to appear like this:

```
;extension=php_gd2.so
```

Remove the semi-colon at the front of the line and reboot the server and try executing the script again. If your php.ini doesn't have an inactive line referencing GD, your system probably loads all the extensions from a particular folder, and the proper extension is not there. Check the GD installation instructions on the main PHP site (www.php.net/manual/en/image.setup.php) for more information.

Once you've established that the GD library is active and available for use, you're ready to get started.

Create the cChart class

Most of the power of the chart component draws from the cChart class that you'll construct in this section. It's a straightforward drawing class that can be used to render a variety of bar charts. This class will be called by the component to actually render the chart for display. It will be "included" by your main Joomla component file and passed the information from either the database query or the data sent into the program from the outside.

■ **Note**   If you're not that familiar with PHP classes (object-oriented PHP), you should still have no problem constructing this component. Classes are an excellent way to organize code (among other advantages), and this is especially true when you want to re-use the code or the code structure in the future. For more information regarding PHP's object-oriented capabilities, see Jason Gilmore's excellent *Beginning PHP and MySQL: From Novice to Professional* (9781430260431).

Overall Design of the Class

The cChart class holds the code that does the actual rendering of the bar chart image. It is broken up into several different routines:

- getColorVals() – Returns red, green, and blue decimal color values when passed a color name.

- getColor() – Returns an image color allocation (required by GD for each color to be used in the image) when passed a color name.

- renderText() – Renders text onto a passed image. Accepts X and Y coordinates as well as a font number and color of the text.

- renderGrid() – Renders the horizontal and vertical lines of a grid onto the passed image.

- renderBars() – Routine that performs the actual bar drawing when passed an associative array of data.

- drawGradRect() – Renders a bar of specified width and height in the start and end colors passed to the routine.

- renderBarChart() – Central function that performs the creation of the chart and calls the subroutines to render the various pieces.

- sampleData() – Outputs random sample data that can be used for testing and demonstration of the cChart class.

The class will be broken down into these separate parts so each can be explained individually. When you're finished, the construction of the class should look like this:

```php
<?php
class cChart {
    var $black,$gray,$yellow,$red,$blue;
    static function getColorVals($colorName) {
    ...
    }
    static function getColor($image,$colorName) {
    ...
    }
    static function renderText($image,$inStr='',$tx=10,$ty=10,
        $fontNum = 3,$fontColor='black') {
    ...
    }
    static function renderGrid($image,$maxval,$l,$t,
        $chartWidth,$chartHeight,$base,
        $labelFontNum=2,$numLines=4) {
    ...
    }
    static function renderBars($image,$data,$l,$t,
        $chartWidth,$chartHeight,$base,$labelFontNum=2,$numLines=4) {
    ...
    }
    static function drawGradRect($image, $l, $t, $r, $b,
        $startColorName, $endColorName) {
    ...
    }
```

```
    static function renderBarChart($titleText,$inData,
        $imageType='png',$width=480,$height=250,
        $ox=38,$oy=20,$titleFontNum = 3,$titleColor = 'darkblue') {
    ...
    }
    static function sampleData($maxVal=400) {
    ...
    }
}

cChart::renderBarChart("Widget A - Units",cChart::sampleData());
?>
```

Each of the various routines is detailed in its individual section that follows. Insert the code for each section where the placeholder indicates.

■ **Tip** Building this bar chart routine is very useful in helping you understand how to use the GD library and how it can be integrated into the Joomla system. If you actually need a robust plotting solution, you can download phpPlot (www.phplot.com) or PHPGraphLib (www.ebrueggeman.com/phpgraphlib/index.php). These open-source libraries can draw bar, line, area, pie, and other charts and use the GD library for server-side chart rendering.

Creating the Color Routines

Add the following methods to the cChart class in the place specified by the placeholder in the class code presented earlier. We'll start with the color methods that generate color values and allocate the requested color on the GD image. GD requires each individual color to be created in the image using the imagecolorallocate() function. Note that for the $colors array, you should copy and paste the list of colors generated earlier by the HTML-based JavaScript.

```
static function getColorVals($colorName) {
        static $colors;
        if(!is_array($colors)) {
                $colors = array('aliceblue'=>'#f0f8ff','antiquewhite'=>'#faebd7'
...
'yellow'=>'#FFF799');
        }
        if(!isset($colors[$colorName])) {
                $colorName = 'black';
        }
        return array(hexdec(substr($colors[$colorName],1,2)),hexdec(substr($colors[$colorName],3,2)),
hexdec(substr($colors[$colorName],5,2)));
}
static function getColor($image,$colorName) {
        $colorArray = cChart::getColorVals($colorName);
        return imagecolorallocate($image, $colorArray[0],$colorArray[1],$colorArray[2]);
}
```

These methods can be used in your own code for easy adoption of color names. Note that the getColorVals() method can be used alone to retrieve HTML-based color values when passed a name string. This can be very useful in all types of PHP image generation.

Creating the Text Renderer

The text renderer function is very simple: it just outputs text and specified coordinates. It can later be extended to handle various alignments, drop shadows, and other advanced display settings.

```
static function renderText($image,$inStr='',$tx=10,$ty=10,$fontNum = 3,$fontColor='black') {
        $fontColor = cChart::getColor($image,$fontColor);
        imagestring($image, $fontNum, $tx, $ty, $inStr , $fontColor);
}
```

Creating the Grid Renderer

The gridlines that form the background of the chart are drawn by the renderGrid() method. This function also draws the text legends on the x and y axes. The method sets up variables with the basic distances needed to draw the gridlines and obtains hex values for the black and gray colors that will be used by the function. The loop executes to add the various labels with center text alignment at the proper intervals.

```
static function renderGrid($image, $maxval,$l,$t,$chartWidth,
    $chartHeight, $base,$labelFontNum=2,$numLines=4) {
    $colDistance = $maxval / $numLines;
    $lineDistance = $chartHeight / ($numLines + 1);

    // Setup basic colors
    $black = cChart::getColor($image,'black');
    $gray = cChart::getColor($image,'gray');

    imagerectangle($image, $l, $t, $l + $chartWidth, $t+$chartHeight,$black);

    for($i=0;$i<=($numLines+1);$i++) {
        $ydat = intval(($i * $colDistance));
        $labelWidth = imagefontwidth($labelFontNum) * strlen($ydat);
        $labelHeight = imagefontheight($labelFontNum);

        $xpos = intval((($l - $labelWidth) / 2));
        $xpos = max(1, $xpos);
        $ypos = $t + $chartHeight - intval(($i*$lineDistance));

        imagestring($image, $labelFontNum,
            $xpos, $ypos - intval(($labelHeight/2)),
            $ydat, $black);

        if (!($i == 0) && !($i > $numLines)) {
            imageline($image, $l - 3, $ypos, $l + $chartWidth, $ypos, $gray);
        }
    }
}
```

The `imagefontwidth()` and `imagefontheight()` functions return pixel values for the rendered text. These functions can be very useful for dynamically arranging text. Because server-side code can specify exact fonts that are available on the server, the layout and rendering of text can be a lot more precise and consistent than performing these types of operations within a browser.

Creating the Bar Gradient

To make the bars look more visually appealing, each bar is drawn with a gradient which makes the chart look far more polished. It is also an effect that is very difficult to do properly with client-side chart rendering.

■ **Tip** Instead of using a gradient, with a little modification you can substitute an actual illustration. For example, if the chart you need visualized monetary figures, the image of the dollar sign or the Euro might be substituted for a unique custom bar chart. If you do choose an image, try to select one that is normally tall and thin. Also, make sure it has a visually obvious top (generally something that ends in a flat surface) so the bars will be useful when compared against their figures.

The `drawGradRect()` function accepts coordinates for left, top, right, and bottom, as well as the color names for the beginning and end of the gradients. The code to create a gradient is actually very simple: after the start and end color values are input, a step amount is determined, and the loop increments the color values to reach between the two main values.

```
static function drawGradRect($image, $l, $t, $r, $b, $startColorName,
        $endColorName) {
    $startColorVals = cChart::getColorVals($startColorName);
    $endColorVals = cChart::getColorVals($endColorName);
    $colorStep = array();

    $inc = 5;
    $height = $b-$t;
    if($height==0) {
        $height=1;
    }
    for($i=0;$i<3;$i++) {
        if($startColorVals[$i]==$endColorVals[$i]) {
            $endColorVals[$i] -= 1;
        }
        $colorStep[$i] = ($endColorVals[$i]-$startColorVals[$i]) / $height;
    }
    for($i=$inc;$i<$height;$i+=$inc) {
        $color1 = ($i*$colorStep[0])+$startColorVals[0];
        $color2 = ($i*$colorStep[1])+$startColorVals[1];
        $color3 = ($i*$colorStep[2])+$startColorVals[2];
        $col=imagecolorallocate($image,$color1,$color2,$color3);
        imagefilledrectangle($image,$l,$b-$i,$r,$b-$i+$inc,$col);
    }

}
```

Creating the Bar Renderer

The renderBars() function calculates the coordinates of the bars and calls the gradient rectangle drawing function. Each bar is rendered for the values passed to it. The code sets up basic color values and loops through the available data bars, automatically sizing the bars and leaving the proper margins between them.

```
static function renderBars($image, $data,$l,$t, $chartWidth, $chartHeight,
        $base,$labelFontNum=2,$numLines=4) {
    // Setup basic colors
    $black = cChart::getColor($image,'black');
    $indigo = cChart::getColor($image,'indigo');

    $maxval = max($data);
    $colDistance = $maxval / $numLines;
    $padding = 3;
    $yscale = $chartHeight / (($numLines+1) * $colDistance);
    for ($i = 0; list($xval, $yval) = each($data); $i++) {
        $ymax = $t + $chartHeight;
        $ymin = $ymax - intval(($yval*$yscale));
        $xmax = $l + ($i+1)*$base - $padding;
        $xmin = $l + $i*$base + $padding;

        cChart::drawGradRect($image,$xmin, $ymin, $xmax, $ymax,
            'black','indigo');
        $labelWidth = imagefontwidth($labelFontNum) * strlen($xval);

        $xpos = $xmin + intval((($base - $labelWidth) / 2));
        $xpos = max($xmin, $xpos);
        $ypos = $ymax + 4;

        imagestring($image, $labelFontNum, $xpos, $ypos, $xval, $black);
    }
}
```

Creating the Core Chart routine

The chart-rendering routine does most of the setup for the image foundation where the graphics will be drawn. It accepts all the basic input parameter data such as the width and the height of the image. With these parameters, it uses the imagecreate() function provided by GD to create an empty drawing canvas. The function then sizes and centers the title and uses the renderText() method you created earlier to draw the text onto the image canvas.

```
static function renderBarChart($titleText, $inData, $imageType='png',
        $width=480, $height=250, $ox=38,$oy=20,$titleFontNum = 3,
        $titleColor = 'darkblue') {
    $numRows = count($inData);

    $base = floor(($width - $ox) / $numRows);
    $chartHeight = $height - (2 * $oy);
    $chartWidth = $numRows * $base;
    $maxval = max($inData);
```

```
$image = imagecreate($width, $height);
// With GD, the first color allocated becomes the background color
$white = cChart::getColor($image,'lightyellow');

$textWidth = imagefontwidth($titleFontNum) * strlen($titleText);
// Calculate x & y of title
$tx = intval(($ox + ($chartWidth - $textWidth)/2));
$ty = 5;
cChart::renderText($image,$titleText,$tx,$ty,$titleFontNum,$titleColor);

cChart::renderGrid($image,$maxval,$ox,$oy,$chartWidth,
    $chartHeight,$base);
cChart::renderBars($image,$inData,$ox,$oy,$chartWidth,
    $chartHeight,$base);

// Send header with MIME-type and render image in proper format
switch($imageType) {
    case 'jpg':
        header("Content-type: image/jpeg");
        imagejpeg($image);
        break;
    case 'png':
        header("Content-type: image/png");
        imagepng($image);
        break;
    case 'gif':
        header("Content-type: image/gif");
        imagegif($image);
        break;
}
imagedestroy($image);
}
```

The renderGrid() and renderBars() methods are called to draw the grid and then the data bars. The routine checks the type of image desired and then sends the appropriate HTTP header so the browser will recognize the image type properly. The specific image output function is used – imagejpeg(), imagepng(), or imagegif() – to render the image into the output stream.

Note that the imagedestroy() function is called after the image is output to the HTTP stream. It is called to unallocate the memory used by the image canvas. This is important to make sure that the memory allocation on the server is kept to a minimum.

■ **Note** Because this example uses gradients, the cChart class needs to allocate a large number of colors on the image. For this reason, you may want to use the imagecreatetruecolor() instead of the more common imagecreate() function. The truecolor() function gives 24-bit color palette (16,777,216 colors) instead of the more standard 8-bit color palette (256 colors), so the gradients look proper but also uses a large amount of server resources. If your application is routinely generating a large number of images, use the imagecreate() function to conserve resources. If you need more than the 256 colors that imagecreate() allows, you'll start seeing the fills use black instead of the specified color. To observe this effect, change the creation function in cChart to the lower color number one and render a chart with a dozen bars.

Generating Sample Data

Although you want to pass in data for display on the bar chart, it is useful to have some automatically generated dummy data available for testing. It will allow you to get the plugin up and running without dealing with the complications and feeding the proper data to the charting routine.

Add the following function to the cChart class:

```
static function sampleData($maxVal=400) {
    return array('Jan'=>rand(0,$maxVal), 'Feb'=>rand(0,$maxVal),
        'Mar'=>rand(0,$maxVal), 'Apr'=>rand(0,$maxVal),
        'May'=>rand(0,$maxVal), 'Jun'=>rand(0,$maxVal,
        'Jul'=>rand(0,$maxVal),'Aug'=>rand(0,$maxVal),
        'Sept'=>rand(0,$maxVal), 'Oct'=>rand(0,$maxVal),
        'Nov'=>rand(0,$maxVal), 'Dec'=>rand(0,$maxVal));
}
```

When the routine is called, it creates random data for 12 months to provide a common bar chart display.

Creating the Joomla Component Wrapper

With the cChart class complete, you now need to wrap it into a component so it can be properly used on the Joomla system. Enter the following code and save it as barchart.php in the root of the component folder:

```
<?php
// Check to ensure this file is included in Joomla!
defined('_JEXEC') or die( 'Restricted access' );
$app = JFactory::getApplication();
$outFormat = $app->input->get('format');
if($outFormat!='raw') {
        echo "<h1>Only output in Raw format is available.</h1>";
        exit;
}

require_once('cChart.php');

// Get request parameters if they're available
$chartType = $app->input->get('type');
$xStr = $app->input->get('xdata');
$yStr = $app->input->get('ydata');
$titleStr = $app->input->get('title');
$imageType = $app->input->get('imgtype');
$chartWidth = $app->input->get('width');
$chartHeight = $app->input->get('height');

// If chart is a DB query, then query the database for the data
if($chartType=='db') {
        // Get a copy of the Joomla database object
        $db = &JFactory::getDBO();
        $datenow =& JFactory::getDate();
```

```
                // Setup query to return the 5 most popular articles --
                //     ordered from most popular to least popular
                $titleStr = 'Most Popular Articles -- '.$datenow->toFormat( '%m/%d/%Y' );
                $sql = "SELECT title as x,hits as y FROM #__content "
                        ." ORDER BY y DESC LIMIT 5;";
                $db->setQuery($sql,0);
                if(!$db->query()) {
                        JError::raiseError( 500, $db->stderror());
                        exit;
                } else {
                        $rows = $db->loadObjectList();
                        $xData = array();
                        $yData = array();
                        for($i=0;$i<count($rows);$i++) {
                                //print_r($rows[$i]);
                                $xData[] = $rows[$i]->x;
                                $yData[] = $rows[$i]->y;
                        }
                        $xStr = implode(',',$xData);
                        $yStr = implode(',',$yData);
                }
} else {
        // If not a database query, use the REQUEST string data
}
// Render the chart with the current parameters
cChart::renderBarChart($titleStr,$xStr,$yStr,$imageType,$chartWidth,
        $chartHeight);
?>
```

The component first checks to see whether the raw format is selected (which doesn't display the standard Joomla HTML rendering) and aborts if it isn't. Then it loads the chart class and obtains all the parameters from the request variables. It can query the database for the data or use data from the request string (if that is included). Finally, it calls the renderBarChart() method to actually output the chart.

You need to create the XML descriptor file to make it an installable component. In your favorite text editor, create a file called barchart.xml and enter the following text:

```
<?xml version="1.0" encoding="utf-8"?>
<extension type="component" version="2.5.0">
    <name>Bar Chart</name>
    <author>Dan Rahmel</author>
    <version>1.0.0</version>
    <description>Demo of server-side image generation.</description>

<files folder="site">
        <filename>barchart.php</filename>
        <filename>barchart.xml</filename>
        <filename>cChart.php</filename>
        <filename>coloroutput.html</filename>
    </files>
    <administration>
        <menu>Barchart</menu>
        <files>
```

```
            <filename
                component="barchart">barchart.php</filename>
            <filename>barchart.xml</filename>
        </files>
    </administration>
</extension>
```

Compress all four files (`barchart.xml`, `barchart.php`, `cChart.php`, and `coloroutput.html`) into a ZIP archive and install it to the Joomla system. It should install properly and be ready for use. You may be wondering how to use it now that it's all set up as a Joomla component. You won't be addressing it the way you usually load a component – as an article in the center column of a page. Instead, you'll be addressing it through the component RAW output format.

Embedding the Image

A component normally outputs a page that is displayed in the center column of the Joomla output screen. However, you can request that the raw data be sent by the component – and that's exactly what you'll do when you embed the image reference to it.

You can test the component by itself by referencing it directly through a URL like this:

```
http://localhost/index.php?option=com_barchart&format=raw
```

The chart should appear as shown in Figure 12-9.

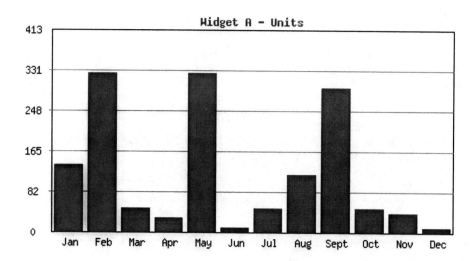

Figure 12-9. *The bar chart display when addressed directly by its URL*

You can test other parameters for the chart by adding them directly to the URL request string. For example, to increase the width of the chart to 1000 pixels, you can use a URL such as this:

```
index.php?option=com_barchart&format=raw&width=1000
```

Or set the title with this:

```
index.php?option=com_barchart&format=raw&title=MyChart
```

You can even pass data directly to the component with this:

```
index.php?option=com_barchart&format=raw&xdata=A,B&ydata=5,10
```

To perform the actual query, set the type to 'db' like this:

```
index.php?option=com_barchart&format=raw&type=db
```

From Joomla, it is nearly as easy to set up this type of chart inclusion. Use the Article Manager to create a new article. Enter some dummy text and, at the place where you want the chart to appear, click the Insert/Edit Image button on the TinyMCE button bar. When the image dialog appears, enter the following into the Image URL box:

```
index.php?option=com_barchart&format=raw&xdata=A,B&ydata=5,10
```

As soon as you tab to the Image Description field in the text box, you should see the chart appear in the Preview box. Add a brief image description and click the Insert button. The chart in all its glory should appear in the article, as shown in Figure 12-10.

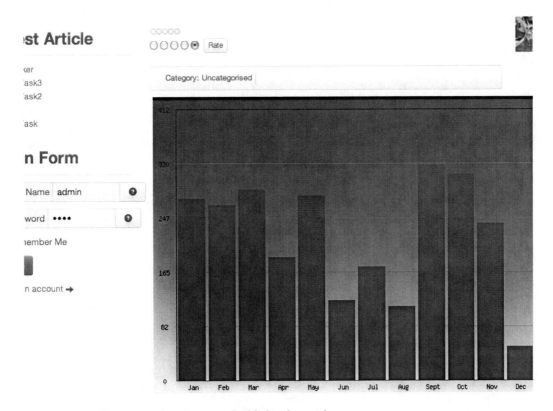

Figure 12-10. *The current chart image embedded in the article*

335

That's it! You can add any of the other parameters to customize the chart to the current page. This sample bar chart is a launching point rather than a destination. Now that you know how to encapsulate GD functionality into a Joomla component, you can perform any number of graphically related tasks. You could easily create other components to do things such as these:

- Add more robust querying capabilities to the bar chart so one or more SQL queries can be selected using the request string.

- Allow the gradient colors to be passed to the chart for page-custom displays.

- Make the robust features of PHP Plot available to the Joomla system.

- Create a CAPTCHA image-rendering component.

- Generate graphical custom tickers such as the number of days remaining in the year or a countdown to the birthday celebration of your web site.

These are just some of the possibilities that are not difficult to implement with a basic understanding of PHP programming and a desire to enhance your Joomla site.

Conclusion

The extensions you created in this chapter provide an excellent demonstration of PHP and MySQL technologies (such as triggers, GD, jQuery, and so on) that can be leveraged to produce more robust Joomla web applications. The bar chart component demonstrated here can be an excellent foundation on which to create other image-generating components. Because it works through the Joomla database system, it takes advantage of the standardized database access and it is portable to any Joomla site.

In the next chapter, we'll extend the creation of extensions to allow the integration of Joomla with social media. By building on the knowledge you gained in this chapter, you'll be able to create extensions that take advantage of Facebook and make your site an important node in the social graph universe.

■ ■ ■

## CHAPTER 13

Connecting Joomla and Facebook

Facebook has taken the world by storm in recent years. With hundreds of millions of users around the globe, Facebook is becoming as pervasive to the web community as Google has become for web searching. Like the rise of Google, Facebook brings with it many opportunities for web sites of all sizes. Joomla provides the ideal platform to incorporate Facebook capabilities into a web site. As a robust CMS, simple upgrades to the Joomla template or extension infrastructure can instantly turn the entire web site into an integrated social media provider.

The Joomla system is also particularly well-suited for using the various Facebook widgets such as the Like button, Recommendations box, Facepile, Timeline, Activity feed, or many others. In this chapter, we'll create some module wrappers that will let you quickly and easily add the key Facebook features so you can leverage the popularity of Facebook technology. With this functionality, your site will be an important node in the social network!

■ **Note**   At the time of this writing, changes by Facebook to their API (`https://developers.facebook.com/docs/opengraph/`), Likes system, and general web policy are beginning to slow. A short time earlier, though, things were changing on an almost daily basis. Code conflicted with documentation and one Facebook release would revise what had been "set in stone" only days earlier. Key strategic partners would implement features in direct opposition to the stated documentation leaving each developer in the unenviable position of guessing which implementation to adopt—the Facebook-sponsored documentation or the "live" implementation of the Facebook strategic partner. Although things have settled down a great deal, it is important to note that Facebook policy is fluid. Therefore, it is always a good idea to consult the current Facebook API and documentation to make sure the individual items described in this chapter comply with current implementation guidelines.

Create a Facebook Fan Page

In 2009, Facebook introduced the technology that allowed corporations, organizations, and web sites to create custom Fan pages that contained information relevant to a particular topic. These Fan pages became the touch point of an organization's presentation on Facebook. Information could be published to a Fan page that would automatically propagate to the activity feeds of users who became Fans of the page. Companies such as Starbucks, Nike, and Coca-Cola focused a great deal of attention and resources on their Fan pages to make them popular and cutting edge.

Your Facebook account and a Facebook Fan page are the bridges that will join your Joomla site to the Facebook world. All Facebook Fan pages must be linked to an actual user account—you can't have a Fan page without linking it to at least one valid and confirmed user Facebook account. The user account is used to associate your Facebook account login, Fan page, analytics, and applications. So if you don't already have a Facebook account, sign up for one now.

■ **Note**   Facebook originally called all pages created on its site Fan pages. However, since the introduction of the Like button, the terminology has been changing. In the past, a page might have 50 Fans, but now it has 50 Likes—although the effect is the same. There is also the alternative to Like, which is Recommend, that can be used on pages where Like does not provide the proper connotations (for example, users might not want to Like a page called Cancer). All three of these terms, however, mean the same thing in the Facebook system.

Once you have an account, you can create a Facebook page. This page will be your location on Facebook where you can post information that publishes to the pages of Fans or Likes of your page. It will also provide links into the Facebook analytics system so you can track the popularity of your site on the Facebook infrastructure.

To create a Fan page, log in to your Facebook account and then access this URL:

```
http://www.facebook.com/pages/create.php
```

Select the option to create an Official Page for a "Brand or Product" and then select the Website option from the drop-down list. Enter a page name that should match the name of your Joomla web site. When you click the Create button, you will be taken to a setup page such as the one shown in Figure 13-1. Fill in the appropriate information about your web site.

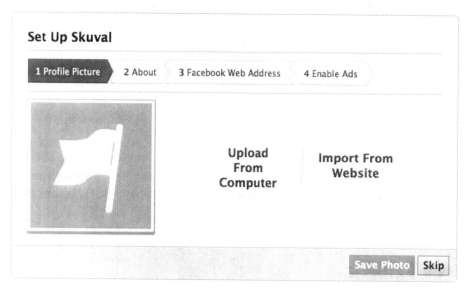

Figure 13-1. *Use the setup screen to complete the information about the Fan page for your Joomla site*

Once you've completed the setup process, your Fan page should have a URL like this:

```
http://www.facebook.com/pages/Joomla-Jumpstart/117743991584876
```

Make sure to immediately post some of the existing content from your web site on the Fan page. An empty Fan page is a sure way to indicate to people that you aren't serious about your Facebook presence. Also, when people comment on any of your posted entries, be sure to respond in a reasonable amount of time. The more activity you can encourage, the more connections and associations in the social graph will be made—increasing your Facebook presence.

The URL of your Fan page contains an ID number of the page itself. For example, the Joomla Jumpstart page ID is 117743991584876 and that number appears in the URL of the page. Write down the page ID number (or Copy it to somewhere convenient). You will need it later to set up the page tags on your Joomla site to link the Like button to the page and track the access traffic through the Facebook analytics system called *Insights*.

■ **Tip** When your page becomes popular, be sure to note when you have over 100 Fans of your page. When you reach this threshold, you can get a root URL on Facebook so that instead of a long URL with the /pages/ reference and ID number, a user can type in a short URL such as www.facebook.com/starbucks and reach your page. Monitor the number of Fans that you have for your page and apply for a root URL as soon as you can.

Create a Facebook App

To take advantage of all of the Facebook features, you will need to create a Facebook "app" on the Developer page (developers.facebook.com). This may seem a little confusing since you may have no desire to create an application on Facebook. Nonetheless, if you create a Facebook app with basic configuration parameters, you can use it for everything from connecting to the Facebook analytics to implementing a Facebook Connect login to your site. So let's get started!

Go to the Facebook Developer Apps page (developers.facebook.com/apps) and click on the Create New App button in the top-right corner of the screen. You will see a popup dialog that requests App Name, App Namespace, and hosting selection. Enter a name that specifies what site the application will be used on such as "JoomlaJumpstart App" or similar name. The name isn't very important for our needs. For the namespace, you probably won't be addressing this app through the Open Graph (OG) API directly, so you can leave that blank. You won't need hosting for the app so you can leave the hosting option unchecked. Click the Continue button to create the app.

Once the app is completed, you should see a screen like the one shown in Figure 13-2. The page will display the App ID and a secret key. You will need the App ID for the OG tags. If later you want to modify your site to accept Facebook Login, you will use the secret key to confirm to the Facebook system that you are authorized to administer this app. For now, just copy down the App ID somewhere as you will use it later to configure the OG extension.

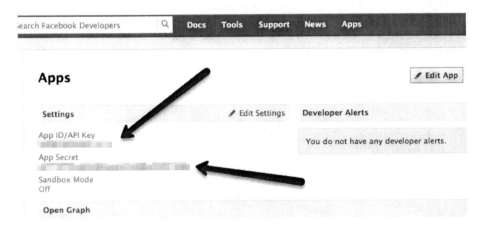

Figure 13-2. *Once the Facebook app is created, the App ID and the Secret Key will be displayed*

Adding Facebook OG Tags

Many people jump into social networking by adding a Facebook Like button to their pages. However, it is better that your site adds the appropriate Meta tags first so you can take advantage of the user interaction analytics and the growing Facebook search presence. By adding proper Meta tags, clicks on the Like button will add the page to both the Like social graph and into the social search graph.

These special Meta tags provide information about the page and promote better integration of your site pages into the system that sits behind the social network. Look at almost any popular web site and you will see the Facebook tags integrated into the header of the HTML document. For example, here are the tags that appear on the home page of the Answerbag site (`www.answerbag.com`):

```
<meta property='og:type' content='website' />
<meta property='og:title' content='Answerbag.com' />
<meta property='og:url' content='http://www.answerbag.com' />

<meta property='og:image' content='http://i.abimg.net/ui/images/logos/answerbag_footer.jpg' />
<meta property='og:description'
    content='Ask questions on any topic, get real answers from real people. Have a question?' />
<meta property='fb:admins'
    content='100000747480 ' />
<meta property='og:site_name' content='Answerbag' />
```

The properties contained within these tags add a great deal of information about the page to the social graph. When Facebook decided to push for wide adoption of its Like button, the company made the tag specification a public standard by empowering the Open Web Foundation (`www.openwebfoundation.org`) to determine the details of the standard. The specification is available on the Open Graph web site (`http://ogp.me/`), hence the name "Open Graph" tags.

By placing the specification with a non-profit organization, other companies can freely adopt the standard and it can grow and evolve to meet the needs of many voices (somewhat like the Open Source Matters organization that stands behind Joomla). If it's easier for you to think of OG tags as Facebook tags, that's fine. At the time of this writing, that is pretty much the reality of the moment.

OG tags provide metadata (or information about information) about the page where they're located. This data is not visible to the visitor of the web page, but provides additional specific information that spiders, bots, and other machine-driven readers of the site can use. You can see some examples of effective use of OG tags on the Internet Movie Database web site (`www.imdb.com`), which includes tags for specific page types such as actor, director, writer, and so forth.

On a web page about an actor, the page includes information specific to that actor. For example, the IMDB page about the actor Marlon Brando includes these tags:

```
<meta property="og:url" content=" http://www.imdb.com/name/nm0000008/" />
<meta property='og:image' content='http://ia.imdb.com/images/M.jpg'>
<meta property='og:type' content='actor' />
<meta property='fb:app_id' content='115109575169727' />
<meta property='og:title' content='Marlon Brando' />
<meta property='og:site_name' content='IMDb' />
```

When the user clicks a Like button on such a page, the social graph system reads the OG tags on the page where the button is located in order to understand the context of this page and categorize it accurately. In this case, it will load the specified image of Brando and store a connecting link to the actor's page. Once the information about this Liked page is stored in Facebook, the page will be categorized. In searches for movies or Hollywood, this page will rank higher in the search results than other less-relevant page types.

Rather than using a massive spidering engine that retrieves page information and tries to make sense of it (such as those used by search engines), the OG tags provide a shortcut for the Like parsing software. The Facebook software can simply record the meta tag information since it is in a format the system can understand. Facebook can then easily relate this page data to other information about actors, directors, movies, and additional cinema-related material.

To learn to use OG tags effectively on your page, let's start by examining which tags are required to get the page into the social graph and which tags are optional that you can add later if they are relevant to the page content.

■ **Note** Publishing proper content into the Facebook system will be very important to your web site as the social networking aspects of the web increase in importance. Because the Facebook engine "believes" what you tell it much more than the Google spider, providing inaccurate information to Facebook will likely cause your pages to be mis-filed in the social graph index. If your page is classified in the wrong area, it will minimize the chances that users interested in your content will actually find it. Therefore, try to make sure the meta information is accurate at the beginning and you will have much more success getting the page information recognized by the Facebook system. Also, unlike the general web, Facebook keeps an iron grip on the information it hosts on its web site. Therefore, trying to game the system or somehow misrepresent your content will likely have severe ramifications so it's a good idea to populate these tags as accurately as possible.

Examining the Basic OG Tags

A standard format applies to all the OG tags and defines how the tags should be formatted. For example, every tag begins with the prefix og: that indicates it belongs to the OG system. There are four primary tags that every page should include: og:title, og:image, og:url, and og:type. The og:title, og:image, and og:url tags are pretty self-explanatory. It is the og:type tag that requires some explicit definition.

■ **Note** The URL supplied in the og:url tag should be the "canonical" URL of a web page. This means that the url should not have unnecessary extra code or request string parameters, For example, the URL www.example.com/mypage/adcampaign1?adrun=1290&refer=mymag should be rendered as simply as www.example.com/mypage. This doesn't apply to Joomla sites that do not have Search Engine Friendly URL options activated since the request string parameters are used to determine the page that will be displayed.

The most basic og:type is the article tag, which should be the default type for all pages that don't have an appropriate alternative. The og:type tag designates how the page should be categorized. In the Brando example earlier, the type was set to actor.

Here are some other popular tags:

- Websites—article, blog, web site
- Activities—activity, sport
- Businesses—bar, company, cafe, hotel, restaurant
- Groups—cause, sports_league, sports_team
- Organizations—band, government, non_profit, school, university

- People—actor, athlete, author, director, musician, politician, public_figure

- Places—city, country, landmark, state_province

- Products and Entertainment—album, book, drink, food, game, movie, product, song, tv_show

Take care in choosing the proper type. After a page that has a Like button has been Liked over 10 times, the type will be frozen in the Facebook system. Until that threshold is reached, changes to the type will be reflected in the Facebook categorization.

On most Joomla sites, the `article` and `website` tag types will be the most popular choices, since the other page types are very specific to types of content. The `article` tag should appear on all of the individual article pages of the Joomla site. This will make up the majority of pages on most Joomla sites.

■ **Note**   Not all tags are created equal. If a tag represents a real-world object (such as a city or an actor), then the admin of that page can publish to the feed of the user that Liked the page. These tags also appear in the interests section of the user's profile. There is an unpublished "ranking" of these types within Facebook, so product and brand pages will have less visibility than the page of a musician or author. The tags that don't represent real-world objects (such as website and blog) do not have the ability to publish to the stream of the Liker. Article pages are special in that they don't (generally) represent a real-life object and although they won't appear in the interests area of the profile page, they will generate a feed entry.

Use the `website` type for the site home page as well as other landing pages such as category pages. Since the category pages are essentially miniature web sites where users would go to find a variety of articles on the same topic, the website type will tell Facebook that these might be landing pages of interest. For the OG tags module you'll learn how to construct in the next section, these rules are followed—category pages and the home page have the `website` type and the `article` is used for others.

Create an OG Tags Module

While you could add OG tags to your Joomla site by manually editing the site template, in most cases you will want to have the tags automatically include information about the pages where they are being displayed. With a small amount of effort, you can create a simple module that reads information about the page and injects the appropriate tags into the Joomla header.

For example, the standard `<title>` meta tag and the `og:title` tag can be almost identical—although the OG specification places a few more restrictions on what can be used within the tag. Likewise, you can use the `<description>` meta tag, already available for entry through the Joomla interface, in the `og:description` tag as well.

Some of the tags, such as `og:type`, do not have a similar entry in the normal meta tags available through the Joomla interface. However, we can "repurpose" other items—such as meta keywords that are ignored by Google, Bing, and other big search engines anyway—to be able to create and edit tags through the standard Joomla interface.

The code executing in any module can obtain a wealth of information about the current display context including the article title and current URL. If the page displayed isn't an article page, the module can test for the type of page and change the OG type to match the page type. Most often you want to do this at the category page level, which should be given the type designation of "website" so they can have top-level Landing pages (described in a later section).

Let's begin by creating the necessary module. Create a new folder called mod_ogtags/ and start a new file called mod_ogtags.php in that directory with your favorite text editor. Here is the code for mod_ogtags.php:

```php
<?php

// no direct access
defined( '_JEXEC' ) or die( 'Restricted access' );

// Get a reference to the current document object
$document = JFactory::getDocument();
// Get meta information set through the Joomla admin interface
$desc = $document->getMetaData('description');
$title = $document->getMetaData('title');
$ogType = $document->getMetaData('keywords');

// Get sitename and environment (dev or prod) from config
$sitename = JFactory::getApplication()->getCfg('sitename');
$environment = JFactory::getApplication()->getCfg('env');


// Get the OG information from the module parameters
$appID = trim($params->get('app_id'));
$adminIDs = trim($params->get('admin_ids'));
$pageID = trim($params->get('page_id'));

// Add Facebook metatags
$fbTags = array(
        'og:title'=>$title,
        'og:type'=>'article',
        'og:url'=>JURI::current(),
        'og:description'=>$desc,
        'og:site_name'=>$sitename,
        "fb:admins"=>$adminIDs,
        "fb:app_id"=>$appID,
        "fb:page_id"=>$pageID
);

// Test if we're showing the home page or category menu
// -- then set the OG type to website
$app = JFactory::getApplication();
$menu = $app->getMenu();
$item = $menu->getActive();

$id = JRequest::getInt('id');
$vName = JRequest::getWord('view', 'categories');

// Check if this is the home page
if($item && intval($item->home)=='1') {
        $fbTags['og:type'] = 'website';
        $fbTags['og:title'] = $sitename." home page";
```

```
// Check if this is a category page
} elseif ($vName=='category') {
        $fbTags['og:type'] = 'website';
        // If this category has an associated Joomla menu,
        // use the title of the menu
        if($item) {
                $fbTags['og:title'] = $item->title." articles";
        } else {
                $fbTags['og:title'] = $sitename." category page";
        }
}

// Setup the standard OG types
$basicOGTypes = array(
        'article', 'blog', 'website',
        'activity', 'sport',
        'bar', 'company', 'cafe', 'hotel', 'restaurant',
        'cause', 'sports_league', 'sports_team',
        'band', 'government', 'non_profit', 'school',
        'university',
        'actor', 'athlete', 'author', 'director', 'musician',
        'politician', 'public_figure',
        'city', 'country', 'landmark', 'state_province',
        'album', 'book', 'drink', 'food', 'game', 'movie',
        'product', 'song', 'tv_show'
);
// If an OG type has been specified using the Meta keywords field,
// use it
if(in_array($ogType,$basicOGTypes)!==false) {
        $fbTags['og:type'] = $ogType;
}

// Add the tags to the header
foreach($fbTags as $fbTag => $fbContent) {
        $document->addCustomTag('<meta property="'.$fbTag.'" content="'.$fbContent.'" />');
}

return;
```

Create the mod_ogtags.xml XML descriptor file in the same directory:

```
<?xml version="1.0" encoding="utf-8"?>
<extension type="module" version="2.5.0">
    <name>Open Graph tags</name>
    272103_1_EnDan Rahmel</author>
    <creationDate>January 2013</creationDate>
    <copyright>(C) 2013 Dan Rahmel. All rights reserved.</copyright>
    <authorEmail>admin@joomlajumpstart.com</authorEmail>
    <authorUrl>www.joomlajumpstart.com</authorUrl>
    <version>1.0.0</version>
    <description>Facebook Open Graph tags module</description>
```

```
    <files>
        <filename module="mod_ogtags">mod_ogtags.php</filename>
    </files>
    <config>
        <fields name="params">
            <fieldset name="basic">
                <field name="app_id" type="text" />
                <field name="admin_id" type="text" />
                <field name="page_id" type="text" />
            </fieldset>
        </fields>
    </config>
</extension>
```

After you have created these files in the usual manner, zip them, and install them onto the desired Joomla site. Once you've installed the module, you will need to set a few parameters in the Joomla admin interface for the module. Set these three parameters using the Module Manager:

- page ID—The ID of the Facebook Fan page that represents your site. In a section earlier in the chapter, you learned how to set up this page if you didn't already have one. This page is the key to linking web analytics data (such as the demographics of people that Like your page) with the individual pages on your site.

- appID—The ID of your Facebook application (setup was also shown earlier in the chapter) that you can use to later set up Facebook integrated login.

- fbadmins—The Facebook user IDs of the administrators of the Facebook pages. Only users with IDs listed in the `fb:admins` tag will be allowed access to the analytics for those pages in the Facebook system. An administrator has full access to the analytics of every page that has been Liked where he or she is an admin. This provides visit statistics, demographic information, and a wealth of other analytics that help you to see how well your page is performing in the social ecology.

The `fbadmins` parameter is one of the most important parameters because it provides analytics access, but it is also one of the most neglected—so be sure to add your Facebook ID in this parameter. You can find your Facebook ID easily by clicking on a link to your own profile. The URL of the page will be something like this:

```
http://www.facebook.com/profile.php?id=100000227392052
```

The Facebook ID in the URL is the one you should set for the `fbadmins` parameter in the module's extension page. When Facebook has recognized you as an administrator of the page, even the Like button on your site will show you an admin link as shown in Figure 13-3. When you click on the admin link, it will take you to the landing page of that Liked item, which will be explained in more detail later in the chapter.

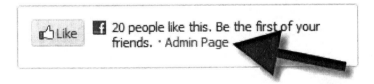

Figure 13-3. *The Like button will display an admin link to the Facebook landing page for a liked item if your user ID is listed in fb:admins*

When you set the `pageid` parameter for the module, it should match the ID parameter that you've included in your Like button code. This specifies the Facebook landing page that will be associated with this page for the overall analytics summaries.

Once the module is installed and activated on all of the pages on the site, you should be able to see the OG tags when you select the View Page Source option in your web browser. For example, here are the `meta` tags output by the module on the Joomla Jumpstart home page:

```
<meta property='og:title' content='Joomla Jumpstart home page' />
<meta property='og:type' content='website' />
<meta property='og:url' content='http://www.joomlajumpstart.com/' />
<meta property='og:description' content='The latest in Joomla technology' />
<meta property='og:site_name' content='Joomla Jumpstart' />
<meta property='fb:admins' content='100000227392052' />
<meta property='fb:app_id' content='130425443647406' />
<meta property='fb:page_id' content='117743991584876' />
```

With these tags in place, you're ready to add the Facebook Like button. When people Like your pages, they will now be properly published into the social graph and you can examine related analytics using the Facebook Insights system.

Using and Customizing the Facebook Like Button

There was no more visual sign of Facebook's significance to the web as the widespread appearance of the Facebook Like button across tens of thousands of web sites. Only days after the release, Facebook Like buttons appeared on small and large sites, spreading like wildfire. In a very short span of time, there were literally millions of web pages feeding user Likes into the Facebook system.

One of the reasons these Like buttons spread so quickly was the ease of implementation. With only about three lines of HTML code, a site creator could add a Like button to the page and become part of the Facebook web ecosystem. You can auto-generate these three lines using the Facebook provided graphical wizard to create the precise parameters.

■ **Caution** Many people that didn't like writing JavaScript or using the provided iFrame implementations for the various Facebook widgets had an alternative called Facebook Markup Language (FBML). Unfortunately, Facebook has announced that FBML has been discontinued (`http://developers.facebook.com/docs/reference/fbml/`). If you're considering using FBML, it would be a good idea to reconsider using the iFrame or JavaScript implementations instead to ensure future support.

Add the Facebook Like Button

To connect your Joomla site to Facebook, go to the Like box wizard on the developer page at:

`http://developers.facebook.com/docs/reference/plugins/like-box`

The wizard allows you to enter various parameters about the implementation you want, including: Facebook Page URL, Width, Color Scheme, and Connections. Select the parameters you need that you will use on your Joomla site.

To add a Like button to your Joomla site, simply follow these step-by-step instructions and you should have it on your site in less than 10 minutes:

1. Go to the Facebook developer page here:
    `http://developers.facebook.com/docs/reference/plugins/like-box`

2. Enter the page number (found in your Facebook page URL) of your Facebook page.

3. Enter the height (typically 400 pixels) that you want for the Like widget.

4. Click the Get Code button to generate the Facebook Code.

5. Open the Joomla Administrator on your site. Make sure you have the No Editor option specified as your editor (as described in Chapter 2) to make sure Joomla doesn't truncate or eliminate the Facebook code you'll be adding.

6. Navigate to the Module Manager.

7. Click the New button.

8. Select Custom HTML.

9. Paste the code into the HTML box (make sure the editor is turned off).

10. Give the module a name.

11. Click the Hide Title radio button.

12. Select the Module Position where you want the widget to appear.

13. Click Save.

For the simplest implementation of the Like button, that's all you need! If you have an advanced web site, you probably want this code packaged into a module so you can leverage all of the Joomla technology to control when, where, and how it appears on your site.

Creating Multiple Like Buttons on the Same Page

There are many times when multiple pieces of content are displayed on the same page, such as the Joomla category blog layout. In these circumstances, a Like button that reads the URL where the button was located would attach the Like to the category page (probably not especially useful) instead of the piece of content that the user is attempting to Like.

If you need multiple Like buttons on a single page, you can add a URL parameter to the link code that specifies a particular article. You can then place Like buttons on summary pages that contain more than one content item and allow visitors to Like one particular piece of content.

When you used the Like button wizard, you may have noticed that the second piece of code it generated looked something like this:

```
<div class="fb-like-box"
data-href="http://www.joomlajumpstart.com"
data-width="292" data-show-faces="true" data-stream="true"
data-header="true"></div>
```

The `data-href` parameter is the one you want to modify. Set that attribute to the URL of the individual item on the page that you want the user to Like. When the user clicks the Like button, Facebook will actually pull the OG tags from the specified page instead of the summary page that is currently being displayed.

■ **Note**   There are several strategies relating to the optimization of Facebook Like and Share annotations. For a smaller site, many experts suggest that you use a single Like button across the entire site rather than allowing individual Likes for individual articles. The strategy is based around the idea that it is better to have a Like button showing 100 Likes than 100 Like buttons each showing a single Like per article. It's up to you what Facebook strategy you choose for your web site.

Adding Facebook Comments

You can add Facebook Comments to your Joomla site with the same process you used to add the Facebook Like. Create a new Custom HTML module, but instead of using the Like button Wizard, you can access the Comments wizard here:

```
https://developers.facebook.com/docs/reference/plugins/comments/
```

Once you enter the URL, width, number of displayed posts, and so on, the wizard will provide you with two pieces of HTML code. You can put them in one module like this:

```
<div id="fb-root"></div>
<script>(function(d, s, id) {
  var js, fjs = d.getElementsByTagName(s)[0];
  if (d.getElementById(id)) return;
  js = d.createElement(s); js.id = id;
  js.src = "//connect.facebook.net/en_US/all.js#xfbml=1&appId=130425443647416";
  fjs.parentNode.insertBefore(js, fjs);
}(document, 'script', 'facebook-jssdk'));</script>
<div class="fb-comments" data-href="http://www.joomlajumpstart.com"
    data-width="470" data-num-posts="2">
</div>
```

Then place the module at the position you want it to appear on the template. Comments will automatically be displayed correctly for the page where visitors entered them.

Understanding Facebook Insights

Like Google Analytics, Facebook has its own analytics package that allows you to track such activities as Like clicks, demographics of site friends, and other relevant information called Facebook Insights. You can analyze trends in growth, demographics, and consumption of content. Insights is activated once your site has over 30 Likes in the social graph. Analysis of the Insights data will allow you to plan content that most accurately reflects what your Facebook users want. Hopefully, you can create a piece of content that "goes viral" so people recommend it to other people. If a piece of content achieves enough connections in the social graph, that content can dominate Facebook searches for its topic.

The Insights Dashboard (see Figure 13-4) shows a variety of trends for your site content. Only page administrators (the Facebook IDs you included in the fb:admins meta tag) have the ability to review these statistics.

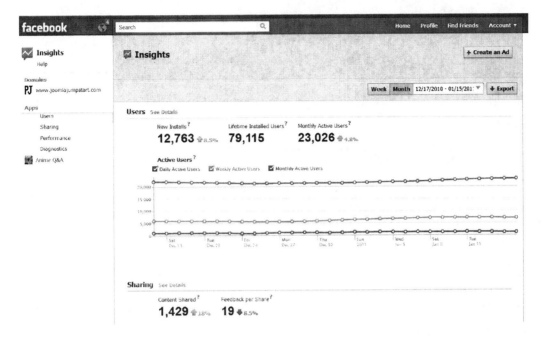

Figure 13-4. *The main Insights Dashboard will allow you to see the top-level statistics about your Facebook page*

You will see an admin link on pages for which you are an administrator (as described earlier). You can also obtain diagnostic information (as shown in Figure 13-5) that will show you the effectiveness of your API calls and their success rate. All of the data that is available through the Insights Dashboard (and a great amount of data not shown in the dashboard) is available directly through the OG API, so you can create your own administrative interface if that is useful.

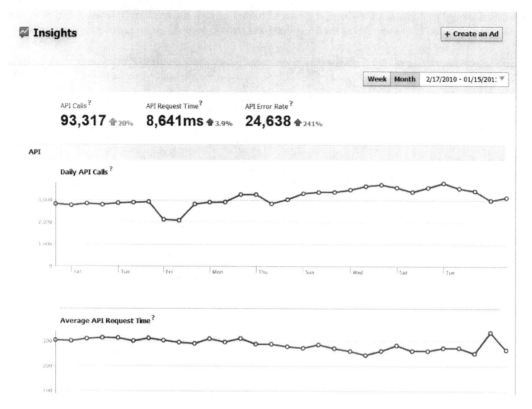

Figure 13-5. *The diagnostics portion of the Insights Dashboard lets you see API calls and possible problems*

To directly query the Insights data, you can also use Facebook Query Language (FQL) to find and process specific information through a query. For more information about the powerful FQL, visit the FQL developer page (http://developers.facebook.com/docs/reference/fql/) and look in the Insights section.

Programming to Facebook Topic Pages

When someone Likes a page that has OG tags on it, a "topic" page is created on the Facebook system. I'm calling them *topic* pages because, at the time of this writing, Facebook hasn't announced a name for these pages. Like a traditional Fan page, they allow posting content that publishes into the feeds of Fans or Likers of the topic.

If you have a page with OG tags (other than an og:type of article) with even a single Like, it is probably already in the Social Graph. You can look at the entry by using the Graph API from any browser like this:

```
https://graph.facebook.com/FULLURL
```

Replace the FULLURL parameter with any page you want to check. For example:

```
https://graph.facebook.com/http://www.joomlajumpstart.com/
```

This will display the JSON-formatted information about the page. Information returned from the API will contain a variety of different information depending on the entry of the URL in the Graph. For example, articles don't create topic pages in the Social Graph, so the information returned for an article will likely be short and simple, like this:

```
{
    "id": "http://www.joomlajumpstart.com/general-joomla/13-joomla-resources/43-add-facebook-like-to-your-joomla-site",
    "shares": 10
}
```

Fields will be included if they are available. In the case of an article, you can see that the id is actually the URL of the page instead of the unique Facebook ID assigned to all objects. In contrast to that short entry, here is the JSON returned by the API for the Joomla Jumpstart homepage object in the Graph:

```
{
    "id": "133596576697644",
    "name": "Joomla Jumpstart home page",
    "picture": "http://profile.ak.fbcdn.net/hps.jpg",
    "link": "http://www.facebook.com/pages/Joomla-Jumpstart-home-page/133596576697644",
    "category": "Website",
    "website": "http://www.joomlajumpstart.com/",
    "description": "The latest in Joomla technology",
    "fan_count": 81
}
```

Missing from these parameters, for example, is the number of Shares for this URL. While this page hasn't been Shared, it does have a few Fans that have clicked the Like button. It also has a proper Facebook ID and a link to the topic page that was automatically created for it when the first Facebook user Liked it. If you know the ID, you can access this information page with it like this:

```
https://graph.facebook.com/133596576697644
```

If you would go to the topic page listed in the link when it was first created, you would see an empty page like the one shown in Figure 13-6.

Figure 13-6. *Use the setup screen to complete the information about the Fan page for your Joomla site*

Publishing entries on the Wall of the topic page (see Figure 13-7) is just like posting to any other Facebook Fan page.

Joomla Jumpstart home page Joomla and Facebook are perfect partners in the s

Wall   Info   **+**

What's on your mind?

Attach: ▼   **Share**

Joomla Jumpstart home page + Others   **Just Joomla Jumpstart home page**   Just Others

Spam   ⚙ Settings

WWC
PLEASE!

Joomla Jumpstart home page Joomla and Facebook are perfect partners in the social web.

Post Insights not yet available, please check back later.

a few seconds ago · Like · Comment · Promote

Figure 13-7. *Posting to a topic page works just like posting to a normal Facebook wall*

And just like posting to a Fan page, any posts appear in the feed of anyone who Liked the page. I believe you can see how powerful these topic pages can be for your site. The more pages that get published into the Graph, the more opportunities become available to syndicate your content directly into Facebook.

Facebook Like Button vs. Share Button

The Share button was the original way to put code on your page and have individual pages published into the Facebook graph. The Like button came along and offers much of the same functionality. So which should you use or should both appear on your Joomla pages?

Like buttons do this:

- Publish the Liked page into the social graph

- Create a Fan page for each Liked page that isn't `og:type` of `article`

- Become accessible to the analytics tool Insights

- In the timeline, a Like produces a link with text (such as "John Doe likes `My Super Joomla article`")

Share buttons can do the following:

- Publish the Shared page into the social graph

- Display an excerpt of the page (and image if available) in your Newsfeed that is displayed on other friends pages

- In the timeline, a Share produces a simple link (such as "John Doe shared a `link`")

Progressively, it appears that Facebook will augment the functionality of the Like until it has all the features of the Share button—but that seems as though it will take a while. If you already have Share buttons on your Joomla site, you should probably keep them for now. If not, optimizing your site for the Like buttons is probably a wise choice. Although the Share button is more powerful in that the content item is distributed to the newsfeeds of all your friends, it is more difficult to get people to Share content than Like it.

Conclusion

Facebook has become the new golden child of the Web. It is increasingly becoming a key part of millions of people's online lives. Joomla sites are perfectly suited for integration into the "social graph"—the social connections that are increasingly becoming standard infrastructure on the Web.

In this chapter, you learned about Facebook's OG API and how it could be linked to Joomla. Since the Facebook environment is essentially a "walled garden" that is shielded from search engines such as Google and the general web environment, connecting your web site to a page inside that wall can have great benefits. With the modules and know-how presented in this chapter, you can take advantage of the social connectivity that seems to form the backbone of the new social web. In the final chapter, you'll be learning how to optimize your site deployment and streamline future development.

CHAPTER 14

Development and Deployment

When you're actively developing your Joomla site, it can be easy to overlook the adjustments you'll need to make when you launch the site to the real world. There are numerous considerations and configurations to be made in order to get the site ready for a production environment. Planning ahead for these options can make the launch of a new site (or optimization of an existing one) a significantly smoother process.

Likewise, there are many ways you can set up your development environment to maximize flexibility to accelerate development. Too often, little time and energy is given to the proper selection of the development tools and setup of the environment where a developer spends a substantial amount of time working.

A small up-front investment of time for configuration at the server and the code level can result in great rewards in productivity in the development cycle. Simply taking control of the execution profile during a code run can make debugging a complicated problem simpler by orders of magnitude.

This chapter will describe some of the most useful configuration and tuning that you can use to optimize both production and development environments (often referred to as Prod and Dev, respectively). Different Joomla sites will have different needs, so not all of the techniques described here will fit all sites. I suggest that you skim this chapter and choose the items that will be important to your deployment.

Let's begin with the development environment where all settings and configuration can be tested without risk to the live web site. You should always try new settings that are destined for the production environment on the development system first. Testing in the development environment can be critical to understanding the effects of the various configurations on execution and security.

Optimizing the Development Environment

A Joomla development environment should be as flexible as possible. The very nature of development means that you can try and test and innovate before you push to production. And that means you should have a capable environment where you can quickly and effectively experiment. Since PHP-based development tools are nearly all open source, and a low-end laptop has the power to run all but the most advanced web-based technologies, even a single developer has no excuse not to have a world-class development system in place.

Tip Many Joomla developers perform development on their production environment—which is almost always a bad idea. No matter how small the Joomla site, this is simply a bad practice to adopt. By developing in production, it is very simple to make a mistake and expose items that pose a security risk to potential hackers. Who wants their site to be penetrated and erased or defaced? If any time has been invested in the site, developing on the production site poses too great a risk to site stability and security for something that is a bad idea to begin with. Further, creating a development environment means that you always have a backup of your main web site in case anything happens to it.

All advanced Joomla development should occur at a minimum on a server that is setup with the necessary configuration for debugging and code profiling. A development server serves two purposes: it provides the best environment for fast development and it emulates the production server as closely as possible. While these two objectives may seem to conflict, they seldom do in actuality.

While a development environment will include settings that a production environment would never include, such as those to display errors, there is no point in having a development server so different from production that code can't easily be moved from one to another. If the development build always breaks when moved to production, the development environment should be altered to more closely resemble the final destination. Common reasons for a development build breaking on production include:

- *Hard-coded paths*: Most commonly, developers will hard-code included link paths as well as paths to source code used by include() and require() statements.

- *PHP or Apache is configured differently*: PHP has a myriad of configuration settings and many of them can fundamentally affect how an application executes. Executing a phpinfo() function call and comparing the differences between the two servers can help to spot problem differences. If you can access the command line on each environment, you can dump the configuration for each into a text file using a command such as php -i > dev_config.txt and then diff the two files.

- *MySQL is configured differently*: Something as simple as default character encoding or insert settings for missing field values can have a dramatic impact on whether two servers operate similarly. Use the MySQL show variables; command on each server and compare the settings.

- *Version differences*: Many beginning developers run different versions of key technologies such as PHP and MySQL between the two servers. Tracking down a problem on MySQL can be nearly impossible if production is running MySQL 5.1 and the development server is running MySQL 5.6. Synchronizing versions (even if that means running an older version on your Dev server) can substantially improve your debugging abilities.

- *Permissions issues*: These are some of the most difficult to debug and, just as often, prevent. Many Joomla users develop on a Windows machine and deploy to a Linux production machine. Because each OS has a completely different security setup, this problem is only solvable by trial-and-error.

- *Local vs. remote servers*: A development environment generally runs all servers locally on a single machine (such as Apache, MySQL, Memcache, etc.) while most production environments will run each server on a separate machine (for example, Apache on one machine and MySQL on another). This setup can cause problems especially if the development environment uses a host name of localhost instead of an actually qualified domain name.

From this list of problems, you can see that the closer to parity the two servers become, the more likely production pushes will go smoothly. This similarity between Dev and Prod should include execution speed considerations. If the production server is substantially faster (from a user standpoint) than the development environment, it will be difficult to optimize a Joomla site for an acceptable experience.

Making them speed-similar also opens the door to the possibility of load testing on the Dev box to simulate the production environment. This testing can yield very useful information if performance can be approximated on a particular extension or subsystem before it is put live in production. Use the Apache AB test tool (see Chapter 9) to determine if the servers are comparable.

Initial setup of a Joomla server can be found in the Joomla documentation (http://docs.joomla.org/ Installing_Joomla!) or, for a more thorough explanation, in Chapter 3 of *Beginning Joomla!*. After the initial setup, you should implement virtual hosts to allow you to have multiple Joomla sites running on a single machine.

Using Apache Virtual Hosts to Host Multiple Sites on One Server

Very often, you will need your development server to host more than one Joomla site at the same time. By setting up the multi-hosting environment, you can create different Joomla sites including development, staging, and production for a single site or create completely different Joomla sites—all on the same machine. Potentially even more useful, you can host independent open source web applications such as MediaWiki (www.mediawiki.org) or SugarCRM (www.sugarcrm.com) on the same machine for Joomla integration.

Joomla lets you have multiple sites on the same web server by allowing a functioning Joomla site to execute in a sub-directory. For example, you could have one Joomla site at this address:

```
http://localhost/joomapples
```

And another at this address:

```
http://localhost/joomoranges
```

And a third one here:

```
http://localhost/joombananas
```

While a Joomla site lives happily anywhere in the directory path, using subdirectories in this way can cause problems for Joomla extensions, third-party APIs, secure keys, plug-ins, url() references in CSS files, and other difficulties.

For example, in a CSS file, a reference like this will go back to the root of the localhost:

```
background-image: url(/images/background.png)
```

Hard-coded subdirectories like this make it usable only on the subdirectory specified:

```
background-image: url(/joomapples/images/background.png)
```

Using relative paths in your CSS creates other problems such as confusion with mod_rewrite rules causing broken images. Instead of dealing with all of these problems, there is a much better choice: use Apache virtual hosts with your web server.

■ **Tip** You can overcome some problems with the paths to static files using the <base> tag in your template file. This tag sets a new "root" for static file loading including JavaScript, CSS, images, and so forth. For example, putting the <base href="http:// localhost/joombananas/static" /> tag in the head section of a document will make all relative references look in the static/ folder. Within Joomla, this can create other problems including the need to include this reference in all your templates.

You can easily define multiple virtual hosts that map to individual directories. If multiple copies of Joomla had specific URLs mapped to individual directories, the URLs might look like this:

```
http://local.joomapples.com
http://local.joomoranges.com
http://local.joombananas.com
```

These directories can be located at any path on your drive. These three directories, each containing a separately configured version of Joomla (even different versions such as 1.5 and 3.0), may have paths like this:

```
C:\Apache22\htdocs\joomapples\docs\
C:\Apache22\htdocs\joomoranges\docs\
C:\Apache22\htdocs\joombananas\docs\
```

With this setup, an absolute CSS reference (`/images/background.png`, for example) would go to the proper location because the root of the web directory is set up in Apache rather than the path containing a subdirectory of the root. Further, you can host other PHP applications at such URLs as:

```
http://local.mediawiki.com
http://local.sugarcrm.com
http://local.tomcat.com
```

Setting up such virtual hosts is easy with a few changes to your Apache configuration. Unlike many remote hosted environments where the Apache configuration is limited if not entirely inaccessible, most development environments are run locally and can be easily modified and restarted.

■ **Tip** In the examples, all of the domains had the format of `http://local.DOMAINNAME.com` so they have a standard naming convention. You don't have to follow this convention—you can literally use any convention you want. A domain such as `http://jokes.mysillydomain.thisisdifferent` could be a valid vhost route. I would recommend, however, that you standardize on a convention so you always know from the URL that the route is a local machine-specific one. Host routing is so flexible that you can even re-route existing domains (for example, `http://www.google.com`) to a directory on your local machine, but this tends to cause confusion so it's a practice that's best to avoid.

Let's set up a sample route. First, locate your configuration file (usually `httpd.conf` or `apache2.conf`) and make a backup copy. This file is generally located in the `conf/` path that sits at the same level in the Apache server path hierarchy as the `htdocs/` folder in a default installation.

Open the configuration file in your favorite text editor and look for an existing vhosts include file. Most often, this include will look like this:

```
Include conf/vhosts.d/*
```

If this line exists, you have a `vhosts/` folder where you can simply add additional Apache vhosts configuration files and they will automatically be included by the loaded configuration when the server is restarted. If a wildcard include like this doesn't exist, create a reference to a new file to hold the vhost configurations. If you don't have a `vhosts.d` include, add this line after the last line of your configuration file:

```
Include conf/httpd-vhosts.conf
```

Although you could place vhost definitions in your main `httpd.conf` file, it is a good idea to place them in a separate file both for organization and stability. Using a vhost file or files that are separate from the main configuration file allows you to edit a file easily without risk of accidentally making a modification error to the main file and corrupting it.

Let's start adding some individual routes so that it is easier to understand.

Adding Individual Virtual Host Routes

Create the new `httpd-vhosts.conf` file in the `/vhosts.d/` directory (if your Apache config already uses that folder) or create the file in same folder as your `httpd.conf` file. Add the following two entries:

```
<VirtualHost *:80>
    ServerName localhost
    DocumentRoot "C:/Apache22/htdocs/"
</VirtualHost>

<VirtualHost *:80>
    ServerName  local.joomapples.com
    DocumentRoot "C:/Apache22/htdocs/local.joomapples.com/"
</VirtualHost>
```

The first one simply establishes the default localhost location (which you may want to change) and the second establishes the routing for the new "joomapples" site. Modify the directory paths to ones appropriate to your system.

Restart (or stop and start) your Apache web service to load the new configuration. Now you need your system to route the URL request to Apache for it to load the proper web site. For this example, you need to edit your `hosts` file.

The `hosts` file on a machine allows you to set up custom URL routes to specific IP addresses. On Windows, you'll find your hosts file here:

```
C:\Windows\System32\drivers\etc\hosts
```

On Macintosh and Linux, you'll find it here:

```
/etc/hosts
```

Open the file in your favorite text editor and add the following entry:

```
127.0.0.1       local.joomapples.com
```

Save the file and the system generally recognizes the change instantly. Go to your web browser and enter the following URL:

```
http://local.joomapples.com
```

If you have a copy of Joomla in the specified path (in the case of this example, `C:/Apache22/htdocs/local.joomapples.com/`), the home page of the routed Joomla site should now appear! You can set up any number of these virtual hosts and route them to the appropriate directory.

If you want to use a little more advanced vhosts setup, you can automatically route any site with the `local.` prefix and the `.com` suffix to the proper folder. I keep all of my vhost sites in a data directory so they are easy to backup. On Windows, my vhosts configuration looks like this:

```
<VirtualHost *:80>
    VirtualDocumentRoot "C:/data/vhosts/%0/docs"
    ServerName local.*.com
    ServerAlias local.*.com

    <Directory "C:/data/vhosts/">
        Order allow,deny
        Allow from all
```

```
        AllowOverride All
    </Directory>
</VirtualHost>
```

This configuration means that I can create any folder such as `local.joomkiwi.com` and add an entry for it to my `hosts` file (you still have to do that) and the web site will be available in Apache. No rebooting of the web server required. That makes creating as many development instances as I require on a single machine simple and fast. I have the same setup on my Linux machines (except the root directory is `/var/www`) and my MacOS machines (where the root is `/Users/MYUSERNAME/Sites`).

The configuration also places the web accessible directory in the `docs/` folder inside the site root folder. That makes the Joomla `index.php` located at this path:

```
C:/data/vhosts/local.joomapples.com/docs/index.php
```

This structure allows me to put other files outside the web accessible path. For example, I often have the following other folders that are associated with the web site (such as the `bin/` folder for command line executables) at this root. And by creating the `docs/` folder one level below the root, I can keep all of the files related to the web site in one source code repository (in Git or SVN).

▓ **Note** To use virtual document root directories (which are required for this wildcard method), you need to have the `mod_vhost_alias` Apache module activated. Open your main Apache `httpd.conf` file and make sure that module is active. If not, add or activate the line that reads `LoadModule vhost_alias_module modules/mod_vhost_alias.so`.

Using virtual hosts is an excellent method of setting up a development environment for multiple sites on the same machine or multiple versions of the same site on the same machine. That's one of the first configurations you can make to a development environment. The second step is usually setting the error reporting levels.

Error Display Settings and Overrides

For a development environment, you should display all of the errors that occur during execution (even the small ones) so you can detect and correct them. In a production environment, the opposite is true because you don't want hackers to have a window into your system—something that error reporting will do.

PHP makes it easy and convenient to set the error level and the error display with directives in the `php.ini` file such as this:

```
LogLevel warn
display_errors = On
```

With this set to display errors, even the warning errors are shown on the page as they occur. If turned off, the errors are written to the error logs. On Linux, the error log file is generally located at either `/var/log/httpd/error_log` or `/var/log/apache2/error_log`. On Windows, there is a `logs/` folder at the root of the Apache installation and the errors are stored in `error.log` file. You can specify where you want the log to be stored with this command in your Apache configuration:

```
ErrorLog "logs/error.log"
```

You can also set the error display in code. For most Joomla installations that I create, I add a configuration parameter to set the error reporting based on the deployment scenario. I add a small piece of code to see if the URL begins with the prefix local. and, if so, turn on the display errors. To add this functionality to Joomla, follow these steps:

1. Create a backup copy of the Joomla index.php file.

2. Open the index.php file if your favorite text editor.

3. Add the following code on the line after the <?php tag:

```
if(isset($_SERVER['HTTP_HOST']) &&
    substr($_SERVER['HTTP_HOST'],0,6)== 'local.') {
        ini_set('displayerrors',true)
}
```

4. Save the file.

If you've used the same URL mapping suggested previously for your Apache virtual hosts, these few lines will make any URL that starts with the local. path display all PHP errors. You can also use this type of Dev-only setting for increasing memory used by each execution or eliminating the execution time limit by adding these lines:

```
ini_set('memory_limit', '1990M');
set_time_limit(0);
```

Increasing the memory limit or changing the time limit are very useful on Dev when you're code is just being tested or you have a routine performing batch operations. For example, I've built a component that harvests remote content and creates Joomla articles from that content. By expanding the memory, the system can process the content faster, and eliminating the time limit prevents timeout failures.

You now have a development environment that supports multiple sites on a single machine and automatically displays errors when run from a local URL, but your development server can make life even easier if you can incorporate execution profiling to determine bottlenecks in your site extensions. You can add profiling to each page execution with the XHProf utility.

Using XHProf for Execution Profiling

Simple PHP code runs very quickly, but once the code achieves a certain level of sophistication, delivering the page to the user's browser can be delayed long enough that visitors feel that your site is slow. This can be especially problematic when installing third-party extensions or building code on top of a complete code platform like Joomla that already uses a lot of processing cycles to ready the foundation of a page.

By performing execution profiling on a page, you can learn exactly where in the code most of the execution time is being spent. If it's your own code, you can optimize it. If it is someone else's code, perhaps you can find an alternate extension that provides the same functionality but executes more quickly.

Execution profiling is a practice that even intermediate developers often don't practice because of the lack of knowledge about it in the development community. Because activating a profiler requires alterations to the web server, it may seem difficult or even mysterious to someone who hasn't done it before. In reality, the setup process is fairly quick and straightforward and the optimization benefits can be substantial. In this section, I'll walk you through setting up XHProf, an execution profiling tool created and open-sourced by Facebook.

First check if XHProf is already installed. Open a command prompt or console window and type the following command:

```
php -m
```

This lists the available modules in alphabetical order. If it is installed, you should see xhprof in the output. On Linux or MacOS, you can use grep to find it for you by typing this on a single line:

```
php -m | grep xhprof
```

Alternately, you can create a page with the phpinfo(); function call and search the output to find if it is installed. If it isn't installed, the following instructions will help you install it.

Installing XHProf

If XHProf isn't installed, you can use the PECL installer at the command line like this:

```
pecl install xhprof
```

If that doesn't work, you can download and install it by hand. If you are an Ubuntu user, you can check out the excellent installation tutorial at http://techportal.inviqa.com/2009/12/01/profiling-with-xhprof/.
On Linux or MacOS, you can use these commands to download and install it:

```
wget http://pecl.php.net/get/xhprof-0.9.2.tgz
tar xvf xhprof-0.9.2.tgz
cd ./xhprof-0.9.2/extension/
phpize
./configure --with-php-config=/usr/local/bin/php-config
make
make install
make test
```

If the installation works properly, you should receive a message like this:

```
----------------------------------------------------------------------
Libraries have been installed in:
   /Users/USERNAME/xhprof-0.9.2/extension/modules

If you ever happen to want to link against installed libraries
in a given directory, LIBDIR, you must either use libtool, and
specify the full pathname of the library, or use the '-LLIBDIR'
flag during linking and do at least one of the following:
   - add LIBDIR to the 'DYLD_LIBRARY_PATH' environment variable
     during execution

See any operating system documentation about shared libraries for
more information, such as the ld(1) and ld.so(8) manual pages.
----------------------------------------------------------------------
Installing shared extensions:     /usr/lib/php/extensions/no-debug-non-zts-20090626/
```

After installation is complete, reboot the Apache server and check if the module is active by typing this on one line:

```
php -i | grep xhprof
```

The module should be available now. If it still isn't, make sure it's located in the PHP extensions folder. You can find the extensions folder by executing the php -i command and looking for the extension_dir parameter. It will tell you the folder that is being searched for the extension. Look in that folder and make sure the xhprof.so (on Linux or MacOS) or xhprof.dll (Windows) is located there.

If it is, you probably only need to add an entry to your php.ini file to have it load properly. On Linux:

```
[xhprof]
extension=xhprof.so
xhprof.output_dir="/var/tmp/xhprof"
```

On Windows:

```
[xhprof]
extension=xhprof.dll
xhprof.output_dir="c:/xhprof"
```

Reboot the Apache server again and you should see it listed in the modules section now. If not, look at the Apache error log to help you determine the problem.

Profiling a Joomla Page Execution

Let's modify Joomla a little bit so we can profile a page execution. We need to change the core Joomla index.php file so that before Joomla execution begins, the profiler can record execution steps and the profiler can close recording once the page render is complete. You can also place the profiling code around the code that executes a particular extension if you want a more specific profile.

At the top of the core Joomla index.php file, place the following code just inside the <?php tag:

```
<?php
define('XHPROF_ENABLED',true);
if(XHPROF_ENABLED) {
    xhprof_enable(XHPROF_FLAGS_CPU + XHPROF_FLAGS_MEMORY);
}
```

The first line that defines the constant XHPROF_ENABLED acts as a switch. When you're not profiling code, change this constant to false and all of the profiling routines will be deactivated. If profiling is enabled, the remaining lines of code activate XHProf to begin profiling. The act of profiling itself slows down page execution and uses a lot of extra memory, so you shouldn't have profiling activated on your production server.

At the very end of the index.php file, add the following PHP code that will stop the profile and create a link to the profile report:

```
if(XHPROF_ENABLED) {
    $id='general';
    $type='none';
        $xhprof_data = xhprof_disable();

        $XHPROF_ROOT = realpath(dirname(__FILE__) .'/../');
        include_once $XHPROF_ROOT . "/admin/xhprof_html/xhprof_lib/utils/xhprof_lib.php";
        include_once $XHPROF_ROOT . "/admin/xhprof_html/xhprof_lib/utils/xhprof_runs.php";
```

```
    // save raw data for this profiler run using default
    // implementation of iXHProfRuns.
    $xhprof_runs = new XHProfRuns_Default();

    $ns = "xhprof_$type";
    // save the run under a namespace "xhprof_foo"
    $run_id = $xhprof_runs->save_run($xhprof_data,$ns);

    $url = "/administrator/xhprof_html/index.php?run=$run_id&source=$ns";
    echo "<a href='$url' target='_xhprof_$id'>Profile available here: $url</a><br/>\n";
    echo "$run_id<br/>\n";
}
```

Now, every time you access any page on your Joomla system from your browser, at the very bottom of the rendered page is a link that you can click on to access the profile report. The report will appear as shown in Figure 14-1.

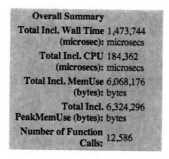

[View Full Callgraph]

Displaying top 100 functions: Sorted by Incl. Wall Time (microsec) [display all]

Function Name	Calls	Calls%	Incl. Wall Time (microsec)	IWall%	Excl. Wall Time (microsec)	EWall%	Incl. CPU (microsecs)
main()	1	0.0%	1,473,744	100.0%	1,202	0.1%	184,362
JSite::render	1	0.0%	1,344,682	91.2%	147	0.0%	68,950
JDocumentHTML::render	1	0.0%	1,331,699	90.4%	19	0.0%	57,276
JDocumentHTML::_renderTemplate	1	0.0%	1,331,645	90.4%	106	0.0%	57,222
JDocumentHTML::getBuffer	11	0.1%	1,331,307	90.3%	259	0.0%	56,891
JDocumentRendererModules::render	8	0.1%	1,328,284	90.1%	180	0.0%	53,899
JDocumentRendererModule::render	6	0.0%	1,326,761	90.0%	522	0.0%	52,409

Figure 14-1. *Clicking on the link at the bottom of your Joomla page will display an XHProf profile report like this*

If you want a graph of the execution and its problems (often much easier to read), you can select the View Full Callgraph link. That will show a graph as shown in Figure 14-2.

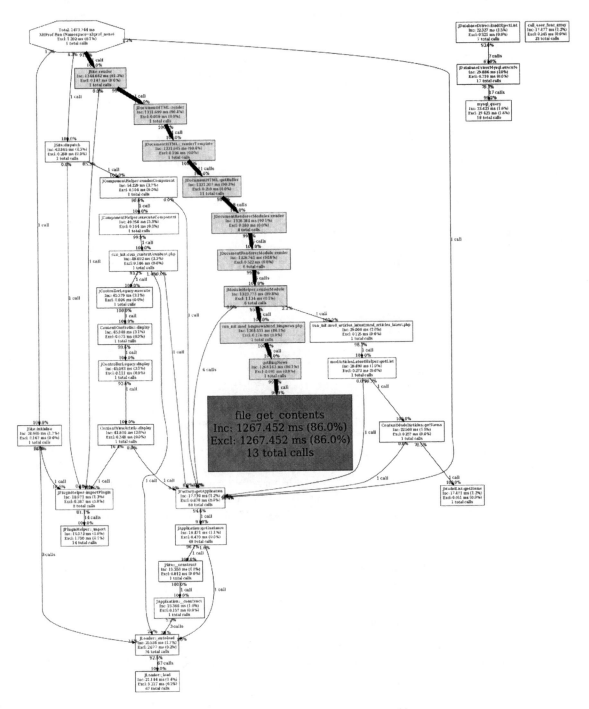

Figure 14-2. *The XHProf Callgraph report often makes it very easy to spot problem areas*

XHProf allows you to drill down into the execution report by clicking on the report links for each summary area. You can see exactly where the page render is using execution cycles. This profile can show not only problem areas in your code, but in the main Joomla code or third-party extension code as well. While Joomla code is always fairly well optimized, code for third-party extensions runs the gamut from very well executing to terribly inefficient. If an extension is slowing down your site, the profile can help you spot it and either find an alternative extension or refactor the code for better performance.

Setting up your development environment properly will increase the speed that you can develop new templates or debug existing code. Equally as important is tuning the Prod server because the more effectively your production site serves web pages, the more likely you'll have return visitors.

Optimizing the Production Environment

Optimizing the production environment can be quite a bit more challenging than setting up a development environment. Whether your production environment uses paid ISP sharing hosting, a virtualized setup, or your organization has netadmins who control the setup and maintenance of the servers, you will often not have direct access to key parts of the production environment. At the same time you have less control of the environment, the conditions can change rapidly with waxing and waning visitor loads and seasonal load changes. All of these challenges can make configuring your Joomla site very difficult.

Understanding how to work around some of the roadblocks of production deployment can be very important to the proper setup and configuration of your Joomla site. Some of these factors include:

- Moving the Joomla Configuration File

- Analyzing the server setup

- Setting the resource expirations

- Optimizing the resources to maximize the use of caches

- Using a Content Delivery Network (CDN)

- Using a cookies-less domain

By making sure these are implemented, your Joomla site can run much more quickly.

Moving the Joomla Configuration File

By default, the `configuration.php` file is located at the root directory of a Joomla installation. This location is not ideal from a security standpoint. If the security of the web site can be breached, this file is in a web-accessible directory, which means a hacker may be able to download it. Because it contains the database information, including the database password and other sensitive information, it is a good idea to place it at another location.

■ **Note** Moving the configuration file out of a web-accessible path has been a long-standing security best practice. Recently, some security experts have argued convincingly that this practice provides no extra protection and is not worth the bother. I will leave it to you to read the pro and con arguments. You will find an excellent piece on leaving the configuration file where it is on Nicholas Dionysopoulos' blog (`http://www.dionysopoulos.me/blog/134-keep-your-files-where-i-can-see-them.html`). For the counter argument, see Aaron Adams explanation on moving the `wp-config.php` file (Word Press' configuration file) on the Word Press Answers blog (`http://wordpress.stackexchange.com/questions/58391/is-moving-wp-config-outside-the-web-root-really-beneficial`).

Moving it to a non-web-accessible location is fairly easy. You only need to copy it to the new directory and then use the PHP require() command to load it from there. You might recall the earlier directory structure I recommended for a Joomla site. In that case, the path to your Joomla site configuration file might look like this:

```
/var/www/local.joomapples.com/docs/configuration.php
```

If you move the file up one level in the structure, the path to the configuration file would look like this:

```
/var/www/local.joomapples.com/configuration.php
```

Once moved, you can create a new configuration file where the original was located (/var/www/local.joomapples.com/docs/configuration.php) and it contains only these few lines:

```
<?php
require('../configuration.php');
?>
```

When the new configuration file is loaded by Joomla, it simply reads the real file from a non-web-accessible directory one level up in the folder hierarchy. This simple change can add a small but important extra level of security to your Joomla site.

■ **Note**   Joomla has been subject to automated hacking attacks in the past where a security hole is found in Joomla itself and then a hacker sets up a script that exploits the hole and hacks literally tens of thousands of sites. I have lived through two such attacks. In both cases, the sites that had this configuration were much better protected. In the first case, database information from the standard configuration was stolen. In the second, the site offline message was changed to a hacker tag and then the site was put offline. In both cases, for the sites I had configured in this manner, the script didn't know how to interpret the non-standard configuration and although the sites were penetrated, no change or information loss occurred.

Analyzing the Server Setup

When performing the initial setup on a production server, you need to analyze the settings and resources that are available to you. The basic Joomla installation screen (see Figure 14-3) informs you of the most important settings that are relevant to Joomla execution. This list is a good starting point but will not tell you what PHP extensions are installed, what the various memory settings are, or the level of permission settings.

Pre-Installation Check

PHP Version >= 5.3.1	Yes
Magic Quotes GPC Off	Yes
Register Globals Off	Yes
Zlib Compression Support	Yes
XML Support	Yes
Database Support: (mysql, mysqli, pdo, sqlite)	Yes
MB Language is Default	Yes
MB String Overload Off	Yes
INI Parser Support	Yes
JSON Support	Yes
configuration.php Writeable	Yes

Recommended settings:

These settings are recommended for PHP in order to ensure full compatibility with Joomla.
However, Joomla! will still operate if your settings do not quite match the recommended configuration.

Directive	Recommended	Actual
Safe Mode	Off	Off
Display Errors	Off	On
File Uploads	On	On
Magic Quotes Runtime	Off	Off
Output Buffering	Off	On
Session Auto Start	Off	Off
Native ZIP support	On	On

Figure 14-3. *The Joomla installation screen provides a basic feature overview of the PHP settings*

A much more robust list of server features is available in the Administrator interface through the System ➤ System Information menu. There are five tabs on this screen that provide the following information:

- System Information: Displays key system information including the PHP build, database version, PHP version, web server version, current Joomla build number, and other information. If you have problems deploying Joomla to a production environment, check these versions for compatibility. Performing a Google search on Joomla and the particular server versions will often reveal postings or technotes about Joomla issues with a particular version.

- PHP Settings: These are mostly cited in the Joomla installation page. It is likely the Display Errors setting will be different for Production than your Development environment. Other than this setting, it is best to take the advice of the Joomla installer and adjust settings to fit the recommendation made there.

- Configuration File: These are the settings for Joomla itself. Most of these settings are available to customize through the Global Configuration interface.

- Directory Permissions: You should examine these after your initial installation. A number of these are required to be writable and still others (such as the components/ directory) may be writable in a production environment depending on the security level required for the site. Some production sites require a full code push to bring new extensions to a production server and when the push occurs, the permissions of the various installation directories are reset and may be disabled from writing (causing later problems for extensions). If you check the PHP logs and you see permission write problems, you can usually use an FTP client to set the permissions properly.

The last tab, PHP Information, displays a filtered version of the phpinfo() function call, which contains the most important information relating to the production server and needs to be examined in detail. The details on this screen will provide the most information of the power available on your Production server.

Here are a few highlights in the PHP Information settings that are worthy of close examination:

- Loaded Configuration File: Shows you where the PHP configuration file is located. This is useful because many netadmins will select a non-standard location to locate the file on Unix-based platforms. On Windows, the php.ini may be located in several places (including the \Windows directory) and it is important to know which one is being used.

- Thread Safety: Tells you if this is a thread-safe build and thread-safe execute is enabled. Many extensions are available in thread-safe and non–thread-safe versions, so this setting will tell you which one is needed for your installation. Thread safety is a complicated technical subject. I recommend doing a web search on the topic for many different perspectives. This IIS article by Dominic Ryan (http://www.iis-aid.com/articles/my_word/difference_between_php_thread_safe_and_non_thread_safe_binaries) provides a pretty good summary of some of the issues.

- extension_dir: Contains the location of the PHP extensions. If you need to add a PHP extension, it will need to be located in the specified directory.

- max_execution_time: Amount of time in seconds a PHP script is allowed to execute before the system automatically aborts execution. This is generally set much higher on the development environment than production. The Apache default of 30 seconds is generally good for production.

- memory_limit: The maximum amount of memory that a single script can use. The executing program can override this setting, which is useful for memory-intensive batch processes such as cron jobs.

- HTTP_ACCEPT_ENCODING: Specifies the type of acceptable encoding. For best performance, this value should contain "gzip, deflate" to show the server can perform gzip compression for compact transfer to a browser that supports the compression (IE, Firefox, Safari, and Chrome all support it).

These settings are all located in the PHP Core Configuration and the Apache settings sections. Following the server configuration settings are the sections for the various activated PHP extensions. In the PHP Information, you should see some of the sections listed as follows. I've put the list in general order of usefulness rather than alphabetical order, although on the config screen, they will be listed alphabetically.

Some of the most important extensions include:

- mysql/mysqli: These extensions provide the core connectivity to the MySQL server. Although considered standard, they are not activated in a default PHP installation, although both your development and production servers should have them active.

- session: The extension that handles sessions, including storing sessions on external caches such as Memcache. This extension is enabled in a default PHP installation.

- dom/simplexml/xml: If your server does any interfacing with an XML-based system or loads any XML-based configuration files, these extensions should be active.

- gd: The server-side graphics library that was described in detail in *Beginning Joomla!* is very useful if you provide the ability to upload images into a photo gallery (for automatic thumbnail creation) or want to generate dynamic charts or graphs for display to the user.

- curl: If your Joomla site needs to interface with any external sites via API such as the Facebook API, Twitter API, or the Flickr API, you will need the curl library for the server to emulate a browser session and make external HTTP calls to other sites. This extension is very important for many server-based applications and most ISPs provide the optional ability to enable this extension.

- APC: The Alternate PHP Cache (APC) is one of the most useful and powerful extensions because it compiles PHP code, making execution much faster and provides a server-side cache where data can be stored between processes. For example, if there was a compact zip code directory array that is used with every page load, that directory could be cached in memory once and then all pages on that server could access it. The apc.localcache.size property will report the total amount of RAM in kilobytes/K that is reserved for the cache. If you're seeing slower performance on Prod than Dev, it could be that you're running out of cache space. In that case, you can try increasing the allocation size.

- mbstring: If your Joomla site makes extensive use of international extensions, the mbstring extension will likely be required as it allows PHP to handle strings with multi-byte characters.

- json: The JavaScript Object Notation (JSON) format is a powerful, compact, and effective data storage and transmission format. With a simple call to the `json_encode()` function, any PHP variable can be serialized and encoded for transmission. Likewise, `json_decode()` will decode a JSON-formatted string into a PHP variable. JSON is quickly becoming the de-facto standard for inter-machine data transmission because it is so widely available. JSON is supported by all major operating systems and most programming languages, including .NET languages, PHP, Python, Ruby, and so forth.

- openssl: If you need to include an SSL certificate on your site for secure transmission of information, make sure the openssl library is enabled so the Apache server can communicate with the SSL protocol so your site can include `https://` addressed pages.

- mcrypt: A secure encryption library that supports both symmetrical and asymmetrical key systems. If encryption is needed by your Joomla application, you will need to activate this extension.

- xmlrpc: Joomla supports XML-RPC for remote system calls. For example, if you have a desktop program that can post to the Joomla system, you will need to enable XML-RPC to allow Joomla to accept the remote posting call.

- memcache (optional): For memcache access, you will need to install the memcache extension on the PHP server. If your site is a high-volume, high-traffic site, memcache is an essential technology—and it's free. Additionally, Joomla has built-in capabilities to use memcache servers to cache its data.

- mongo (optional): MongoDB is quickly becoming one of the most popular heterogeneous data stores. PHP fully supports access to Mongo through the mongo extension.

- phpdoc: For automated system documentation, the phpdoc extension will generate a whole host of documents using PHP reflection.

- soap: For extensions that need to interface to a system that uses the SOAP protocol, you must enable the SOAP extension. Numerous systems (including many .NET implementations) have standardized on the SOAP protocol and you will need to use it for inter-process communication with these systems. One PHP-based example, SugarCRM, is a popular open source Customer Relationship Management application that uses SOAP for all its external API access.

- xdebug: On your development platform, you will want to install and activate XDebug (XDebug provides a more granular alternative to XHProf for profiling). XDebug enables the ability to perform line-by-line execution debugging as well as do complete execution profiling.

- zip/zlib: Required for gzip and zip compression from PHP. The zlib library is required to allow for deflation between the browser and the server.

While there are a great number of extensions available with the default PHP installation as well as available through third parties, these are the ones you will generally need to install or have activated for a majority of Joomla-based applications.

Setting a Server Expire for Images

When users visit your Joomla site more than once, you don't want to force them to download the same images and other files repeatedly—especially if those files haven't changed since their last visit. If you're using Apache as your web server, a simple configuration file change can automatically add expiration headers to all of your images.

You can add this simple server directive to the main Apache configuration file your system uses (whether it is `httpd.conf` or `apache2.conf`):

```
<FilesMatch "\.(css|flv|gif|ico|jpg|jpeg|js|pdf|png|swf)$">
  Header set Cache-Control "max-age=290000000, public"
</FilesMatch>
```

Reboot your Apache server and the web server will send a long expire to browsers so images, icons, flash files, and other static files will remain cached on the user's browser and not require reload.

■ **Note**   Use this in combination with the cache control information in the "Planning for Caches, Proxies, and CDNs" section in Chapter 3 so you can control how long your static files are cached.

Performing Custom Redirects

There are a large number of extensions that can perform redirects for Joomla content. However, some problems can benefit from a custom redirect solution. For example, if you wanted to create a custom CSS minifier, you might have to use a PHP file the readings in the various CSS files, executes a minifying algorhythm, and outputs the minified result. However, the file name may need to be something like "minify.css." If you name a PHP file with that name, it won't execute the PHP code. However, if you name it with the .php extension, it may not be properly recognized by proxy servers as an authentic PHP file.

You could solve this problem through a special .htaccess instruction. However, it is often easier to handle these types of rules in code (with a single redirect in the .htaccess file). It is simply a matter of using a custom 404 page that receives the failed requests and handles them as a custom request.

The .htaccess redirect for the 404 would look like this:

```
htaccess 404 redirect
```

Then in the 404.php code, you can simply check the server redirect variable and redirect appropriately. For the minify.css file, the code in the 404 file would look like this:

```php
if($_SERVER['REDIRECT_URL']=='/minify.css') {
        header("HTTP/1.0 200 OK");
        require_once "minify.php";
        exit;
}
```

This code checks for the URL that generated the 404 error. It then sets the header to send the HTTP code of 200 (the OK code instead of the 404—file not found), includes the desired PHP file (in this case, `minify.php`), and exits. To the user's browser, the file `minify.css` loaded just like a static CSS file.

Setting Up a Memcache Server

One of the secrets of high-volume web sites that most small- to medium-range web sites haven't even heard of is *Memcache*. Memcache is the secret weapon of scaling large volume traffic while keeping server costs low. Memcache is a very fast RAM-based caching server that allows a site to store pre-accessed database information, pre-rendered HTML, or nearly any type of data. Once you understand how memcache is used, you can understand how a site can handle high-volume traffic without requiring a dedicated server farm.

Ask web site professionals what is the number one bottleneck for serving fast pages, and they will always tell you it's the database. Whether it is MySQL, PostgreSQL, Mongo, or any other data source, heavy volume nearly always becomes blocked at the database level. If ten users simultaneously request an article, a MySQL database server can easily be queried and return that article text. If 1,000 users request that article, all users will experience a slowdown as the database attempts to serve this batch of connections. And if it's ten thousand simultaneous requests, the whole database server could be blocked. How best to solve this problem?

If you were a big company, you could buy a very fast and very expensive database server to handle that type of burst load. That would require a large investment in hardware and administrative costs. What if there was a better way?

Imagine if, on the first request, the database was read for the article and that data was stored or cached in a memory cache. Then the subsequent 9,999 requests were filled by simply reading this piece of cached data and sending it directly to the users? Even if the database could easily handle the 1,000 requests, it would be slower than the same reads directly from memory. Relatively speaking, adding RAM is much, much cheaper than adding more processing power for a database server. Even better, caches can be spread across multiple cheap servers which means it is almost infinitely scalable.

Memcache is just such a caching server. It allows information to be quickly stored or cached to serve subsequent requests. By default, Joomla can perform file caching where database information is stored in cached files on the server. Reading the files, while faster than reading from the database, is still much slower than retrieving the data from memory. Fortunately, Joomla has built-in support for memcache.

Memcache (`http://memcached.org/`) is a free, open source, memory-based caching server. It is used by many professional high-volume sites including LiveJournal, Wikipedia, Flickr, Twitter, Typepad, eHow, Yellowbot, YouTube, Digg, WordPress, Craigslist, and Mixi. Often referred to as Memcached (for Memcache-D or Memcache-Daemon), Memcache can run on a server independently in the background. On a Linux server, Memcache runs as a daemon while on Windows, it runs as a Windows service.

On Linux, you can generally install Memcache through the standard operating system installer (such as yum or apt-get). On Windows, you can get a port of Memcache here:

```
http://code.jellycan.com/memcached/
```

Alternately, you can run the cross-platform Java version of memcache called jmemcache-daemon, available here:

```
http://code.google.com/p/jmemcache-daemon/
```

Often, it is handy to run Memcache simply as an application for testing. You can do this easily from the command line on Windows with a single command:

```
memcached.exe
```

Much more useful for testing, you can execute it in the Very Verbose mode with this command:

```
memcached.exe -vv
```

Executing Memcache with this command will show an output like this:

```
slab class   1: chunk size     80 perslab 13107
slab class   2: chunk size    100 perslab 10485
.
.
.
slab class  38: chunk size 323000 per slab    3
slab class  39: chunk size 403752 per slab    2
slab class  40: chunk size 504692 per slab    2
```

Memcache begins with a default memory allocation of 64 MB, dividing that memory area into chunks, or "slabs." You will not need to know how to custom configure slab settings until you become a very advanced Memcache user. When Joomla executes with Memcache activated, if you're running Memcache in Very Verbose mode, you will see the output showing items stored in the cache that will be reported like this:

```
<1952 server listening
<1916 new client connection
<1916 get cache__system-1b6c477049031dedde86d77c021f96ae
>1916 END
<1916 set cache__system-1b6c477049031dedde86d77c021f96ae 1 900 34128
>1916 STORED
<1916 get cache_com_content-ea6dae327045ee6764473abe2a032cbd
>1916 END
```

Caching can substantially increase the positive user experience of your site and can allow you to scale a site very effectively for many users. While your Joomla site might not have the traffic volume now to justify running Memcache for scaling, if you have your Joomla site running on a virtual machine, adding Memcache can greatly increase the speed that your Joomla pages are served – and visitors always like fast server response. If your site does dramatically increase in traffic, you can often add Memcache and increase your serving capacity by many multiples without adding any new hardware.

When you develop your own extensions, if they do a lot of database access, add support for the built-in Joomla caching mechanism and it can automatically use Memcache if configured for it. The caching library is one of the many shared libraries available on the Joomla platform. With the autoloader, you can add your own libraries that can be used by any extension or custom loading in the framework.

Using the Joomla Autoloader

When PHP was in its infancy, one problem that plagued developers was the errors thrown when redefining an existing function. If a function already exists and code tries to define a function with the same name, the PHP engine throws an error and stops executing. This problem occurred more and more often as PHP applications grew and matured.

For example, if you had a function cleanString() that stripped foreign characters from a string, you would probably want to use this function many places in your application. Generally, this function is then located in a utility function file that is loaded once at the start of page execution. Unfortunately, as PHP applications became more sophisticated, files containing these utility functions grew and grew until page load speed was suffering as numerous functions—most never used on all pages—were loaded and defined. For this reason, the autoloader was born.

As object-oriented PHP became more common, PHP added an autoloader for classes. Early in the code, one or more directories are defined where classes reside. When the execution process hits code that calls a class that hasn't been loaded, PHP pauses execution, loads the class automatically, and then allows the code to call it—all transparently. The autoloader made it possible to build large applications that dynamically loaded only the classes that were needed for execution of the currently loading page.

Joomla has built a more advanced loader on top of the standard PHP autoloader. It allows you to pre-register classes that might be needed in the code itself. So if your module *may* need classA, classB, and classC that are in three different folders, it can register them regardless of their location. When one of them is requested, it automatically loads from the correct place.

So if you had a directory called customclasses/ and a class stored in the file called testcustom.php, you could register the class with a call like this:

```
JLoader::register('testcustom', JPATH_LIBRARIES.
    '/var/www/customclasses/testcustom.php');
```

Or if your class was located in the libraries/ directory in the Joomla root, you could register it like this:

```
JLoader::register('testcustom',
   JPATH_LIBRARIES.'/ customclasses/testcustom.php');
```

This registration does not actually load the classes—it only registers them with the autoloader. So you can register as many classes at as many locations as you want without any real performance penalty. When the classes are needed, they will automatically be loaded by the autoloader.

For classes you know you'll need, however, you should load them at the beginning of the execution cycle, so the autoloader doesn't have to pause execution and look through the autoloader folders to find the unloaded class. To preload classes, Joomla includes the jimport() function, which will import classes stored in the libraries/ folder with a simplified path. The jimport() function is smart and doesn't reload classes that already exist in memory.

The function also uses class-like dot notation to reference the class files. To import the same class we registered previously, you would use the jimport() function like this:

```
jimport('customclasses.testcustom');
```

The function will automatically look for libraries/customclasses/testcustom.php, load the class it finds there, and register it with the importer system. If it is called again, it won't be reloaded.

Some modules use both routines to load the classes that they know will be needed and register those they may not need. For example, in the fields model, the following references are at the top of the file:

```
jimport('joomla.html.html');
jimport('joomla.language.helper');
jimport('joomla.form.formfield');
JLoader::register('JFormFieldList', JPATH_LIBRARIES.'/joomla/form/fields/list.php');
```

In this case, it's clear that the JFormFieldList class may not be needed, so it is only registered. The Joomla development team is probably more conscientious of this type of minimal loading than a traditional programmer because their application must work in a broad spectrum of environments where resources (processing or memory) may be more limited than would be the ideal.

This autoloading functionality is one of the features that make Joomla such an excellent development platform. Many of the core functions that make the programmers reinvent the wheel for every new system they develop are already included, the problems already solved in an effective way.

Conclusion

Setting up environments for development and production require special handling. Development settings allow you to quickly locate bugs, resolve problems, and optimize execution. You learned how to use virtual hosts, override various configuration settings in code, and profile page execution. Production settings assure security and optimize performance. You learned how to perform redirect mapping, set server expire times, and adopt best-practices to allow for various forms of caching. The better optimized your Production server environment can be, the greater the load it can handle while maintaining responsiveness and keeping server costs low.

Proper setup of your Joomla environments can make development much easier. It can also make the Production environment reliable and manageable. It doesn't take a great deal of time to properly set up servers and configure PHP and Apache settings and the time spent on these procedures are a good investment.

Thank You

We've reached the end of the book, but I'm sure you'll have a long adventure ahead with Joomla. Joomla is one of the most amazing pieces of software I've had the privilege of using. In many ways, I became the developer I am today by studying the Joomla code and learning from some of the best software engineers in the world. I hope you are fortunate enough to do the same.

Over the years I have had many, many clients that have used Joomla for their web sites and it has been phenomenal to see these sites expand and flourish. The number of templates and extensions that are becoming available every day means that a Joomla site never needs to be static. For minimal work, your site can easily adopt the newest technologies.

Thank you for purchasing this book and allowing me to show you some of the more advanced features of Joomla and the broader web world. I will continue to add my own material and extensions to my web site Joomla Jumpstart (`www.joomlajumpstart.com`) and I hope you get a chance to visit and share some of your Joomla successes!

Index

CPSIA information can be obtained at www.ICGtesting.com
Printed in the USA
LVOW11s1829040913

350980LV00008B/551/P